ahimsa
non- violence / non-injury

Thou shalt: recycle
cure / heal
Thou shalt not: injure
pollute wound
destroy

# Gandhi's Truth
## On the Origins of Militant Nonviolence

life — reality
not
law ideas

# ERIK H. ERIKSON

# Gandhi's Truth

## On the Origins of Militant Nonviolence

W · W · NORTON & COMPANY

*New York · London*

W. W. Norton & Company, Inc., 500 Fifth Avenue,
New York, N.Y. 10110
W. W. Norton & Company Ltd. 37 Great Russell Street,
London WC1B 3NU

W. W. Norton & Company, Inc. is also the publisher of the
works of Erik H. Erikson, Otto Fenichel, Karen Horney, Harry Stack
Sullivan, and The Standard Edition of the Complete Psychological
Works of Sigmund Freud.


ISBN 0-393-00741-3

Published simultaneously in Canada by
Penguin Books Canada Ltd,
2801 John Street, Markham, Ontario L3R 1B4.

Library of Congress Catalog Card No. 68-54964.
Printed in the United States of America.

2 3 4 5 6 7 8 9 0

*This was to be Joan's book.*
*We are now dedicating it together to the*
*memory of Martin Luther King.*

# Contents

# Contents

# Preface and Acknowledgments

THIS BOOK describes a Westerner's and a psychoanalyst's search for the historical presence of Mahatma Gandhi and for the meaning of what he called Truth.

My first trip to India in 1962 led me to the city of Ahmedabad, where I had been invited to lead a seminar on the human life cycle. Ahmedabad, largely bypassed by the tourist, has a unique history among Indian cities. It has been altogether dominated by the manufacture and export of textiles from antiquity to modern times. Today's industrialized and highly unionized city is often slandered as Pittsburgh is (or was) in America. And yet the city is of unique interest precisely because of the unbroken manner of its development from a municipality built on a medieval guild structure to a modern industrial city, financed primarily by local investments, and managed by some great families.

Living on the estate of one of these families, I soon became newly aware of the role which Gandhi had played in the labor relations of this city and of the significance of that role for his rise to national leadership. I say "newly aware" because I experienced that sense of *déjà vu* which can come to a visitor in a foreign city that he has been able neither to visualize nor to pronounce properly before. When I was young, I had known that Gandhi lived in or near the city of Ahmedabad or, at any rate, by the Sabarmati River. My generation of alienated youth in Europe had, in fact, read of Gandhi's first trial between the World Wars and had compared it with that of Socrates: this trial had taken place in the "Circuit House" which in Ahmedabad we passed daily on our early morning walks. And I had read in Gandhi's autobiography of a strike in 1918 which he had led in Ahmedabad, his main opponent at the time having been, as I finally realized, the very mill owner on whose estate we were living. Gandhi's main supporter and helper, in turn, had been the mill owner's sister. As I met others who had known Gandhi in those days as either devoted followers or puzzled opponents, I began to suspect that what was described by him and by some biographers as a mere episode in his life—and in Indian history—was, in fact, an event of vital importance in his advent as a national leader and as the originator of militant nonviolence.

For mark the year: it was on the Ides of March of 1918, the year of massive mechanized slaughter on the front in France, the year when empires collapsed and new world alliances were formed, the year of Wilson and above all of Lenin. And here in Ahmedabad one of the great charismatic figures of the postwar world was concentrating on a strictly local labor dispute, putting his very life on the line by fasting—an event scarcely noticed even in India at the time. That Mr. M. K. Gandhi chose to fast as part of a new method of civic and political leadership meant as yet nothing to anyone but a few friends, and the immediate consequence did not call for national or world attention. In fact, a certain embarrassment seems to govern later accounts —as though the Event itself had not proved quite worthy of the Mahatma's subsequent career. But this kind of denial does not exactly serve to divert a psychoanalyst's curiosity; and so—whether because it all happened in a city which had given me the first "feel" of India, or because I sensed that there was more to the story than the books allowed—I became fascinated with those months in Gandhi's middle years. I decided to reconstruct what in this book we will call the Event as a focus for some extensive reflections on the origins, in Gandhi's early life and work, of the method he came to call "truth force."

I am not a historian and not an expert on India. What "discipline" there is to my enterprise is best revealed in the telling of its story. The order of the chapters themselves reflects the problems encountered.

The first chapter will convey, as subjectively as seems proper, the way in which the Event came to capture my attention. Since any *reviewer* of a bit of history makes it his own by the mere circumstance of his selective attention, a reviewer trained in clinical observation must account—at least to himself—for his own initial involvement much more systematically than has been the rule in most writing of history. A man's personal involvement, however, includes his friends, some of whom, in this instance, are well-known men and women; and some are also members of the family of the very man who was "pitted against" Gandhi in the Event and is respectfully mentioned throughout his autobiography. Not knowing what they had bargained for when they invited me to India, they now find themselves among the cast of a story which I did not know then I was going to write.

The *witnesses* to and the *recorders* of an event also make it "their own," whether they are the first ones to render it historical by recording it or, indeed, the last ones to remember it when prompted by the reviewer. The second chapter, therefore, will discuss the autobiographer Gandhi as his own witness and my encounters with the living witnesses after I had decided to become a reviewer of the history in which they had participated.

Gandhi's existential experiments, as he makes abundantly clear, began in his youth. In the third chapter, then, we will go back to Gandhi's beginnings and see with a mixture of clinical and historical hindsight why what led up to the Event had to happen the way it did. This hindsight also helps to clarify why and how Gandhi came to choose or to get involved with the witnesses, and what it was in *their* past lives that now seems to make it so plausible that they were there and took a chance with their lives by involving them with his.

When in Chapter III the Event, as well as its immediate causes and consequences, can finally be retold in day-by-day detail, I trust that the real happenings will not come as an anticlimax. The fact is that without a knowledge of its place in Gandhi's life and in India's history, the Event could, indeed, be considered a rather minor affair, hardly contributive to the fact that Gandhi was to emerge exactly a year later as the leader of the first nationwide act of civil disobedience.

In the final chapter we will at last be able to take for granted what we now know to have occurred after Gandhi's rise to the Mahatmaship of India. Only then can we ask in retrospect how the man, his method, and some of his first followers converged in Ahmedabad in 1918 in such a way that his philosophy of militant nonviolence became a *political instrument* ready to be used on a large scale and reaching far beyond the issue of industrial peace in the city of Ahmedabad. Only then can we see the place of such events in man's psychosocial evolution and recognize the singular importance of Gandhi's Truth in a future which will pit man's naked humanity against the cold power of super machineries. But this will also call for detailed attention to the rigorous *discipline* which, for Gandhi, was an intrinsic part of the instrument of activism which he created.

I hope that these remarks will suffice to reassure the more systematic reader with a promise of hidden method. This very method, however, decrees that I should begin by letting subjectivity and even circumstantiality reign. I will, therefore, start with a brief travelogue. This consists of excerpts from letters such as those I like to send to family and friends when traveling, perhaps because I like to address my diary to those I wish were with me to share my impressions. And impressionistic it will be, this beginning, for I am the kind of worker who must find his way from personal observation to what seems relevant enough to be recorded; and this means also that I must find my way from strong esthetic impressions to what survives as ethically urgent. Eventually, most of these early impressions will re-emerge as major themes in later chapters.

\*     \*     \*

I can only attempt to acknowledge the support I received from those who were or became my friends in the course of this inquiry. That they are still my friends bespeaks their generosity, for I have not only attempted to surmount cultural obstacles of great tenacity, but in doing so, I have employed psychoanalytic methods which add some hazard to any communication anywhere. Where I seem to have betrayed some trust, may my friends forgive me, my métier, and my Westernness. Otherwise, may they accept my thanks for being what they are and for sharing this so freely with us.

I do not remember when it first occurred to us that my wife and I should visit Ahmedabad. Gardner and Lois Murphy had been there and had told us about the Sarabhais' remarkable civic, scientific, and clinical work; and the Murphys had told them about us. At any rate, when we first met Gautam and Vikram Sarabhai in this country, they made it seem natural that we should come. The person who finally took a tender and determined hand in the matter and provided both rationale and facilities for a seminar in Ahmedabad was Kamla Chowdhry of the Indian Institute of Management and Harvard University.

There would not be enough space to enumerate what each member of the Sarabhai family has done for us in daily detail and in over-all solicitude. As with others, I must let the text record their contributions to the enterprise that became this book. I was still able to interview Ambalal Sarabhai, the patriarch of the family and the city, who has since died. There were many hours of joyful conversation with his sister, Anasuya Sarabhai. To them, and above all to Shankerlal Banker, I owe the details which permitted me to retell the story of the Event as already known in the literature. As to the existing documents, Professor K. Swaminathan helped immeasurably by letting me see the galleys of the *Collected Works of Mahatma Gandhi* which contain the existing documents concerning the Event. The varied applicability of this monumental collection will be demonstrated even in my unorthodox uses of the texts.

Many Indians have received and attempted to help me, among them the former and the present president of India as well as members of the Cabinet and of Parliament; mill owners, mill workers, and labor union officials; Gandhi's principal biographers and some directors of public libraries. Where they contributed from personal experience to the clarification of the Gandhian period here under consideration, they will appear in the text and thus in the index. Otherwise, a mere listing of names could not convey the light which came through in many conversations or the deliberate twilight maintained in others. In interviewing, I jot down only an occasional word. Quotations, then, must be taken as approximations of what I remembered my informants to have said, in word and in tone. Thanks are due to Dr. Anand Paranjpe for excerpting the Poona Journals of 1918 for me, and to Nandini Joshi for orally translating for me certain Gujarati passages in Gandhi's writings. Where a literal translation seems to clarify a passage, it appears as a bracketed insert in the quotation in question.

Research trips cost air fare and local maintenance. Regular contributions of the Shelter Rock Foundation for my research at the Austen Riggs Center paid for my first trip to India, while the Karmakshetra Educational Foundation of Ahmedabad took care of our needs in that city. The Center for Advanced Study in Stanford permitted me to make another trip as part of a fellowship, while the American Institute of Indian Studies provided travel and portal-to-portal expenses in India. Finally, I completed the manuscript in my capacity as FFFF—the First Field Foundation Fellow. My thanks for the sympathetic support received from these foundations.

As always, Joan Erikson was with me and "with it," soul and body. Her specific contribution, too, will be named in the text; her contemporaneous work on St. Francis helped greatly to clarify the gay kind of sainthood also found in Gandhi. The completed manuscript was, of course, edited by her. Some chapters would have been more unduly long but for the gentle severity of Kai T. Erikson. The manuscript was also read by Sudhir Kakar, friend and assistant at Harvard. It received a final check, both textually and bibliographically, from Pamela Daniels, my enthusiastic and painstaking associate at Harvard.

Chapters of this book were discussed in my seminars at Harvard and at Riggs, and above all in the meetings of the psycho-historical study group, hosted by Robert Lifton during several summers at Wellfleet, and supported by the American Academy of Arts and Sciences. What I learned in these discussions is summarized in "On the Nature of Psycho-Historical Evidence: In Search of Gandhi," *Daedalus*, Summer 1968.

Finally, I would like to linger over a few names, the mere sound of which has come to mean a world to us: Vikram and Mrinalini, Gautam and Kamalini, Gira, Mani. There were quiet evenings by the Sabarmati with Kamla, visits to the Gandhi shrines with Romila Thapar, and vigorous walks in Delhi with Prem Kirpal. NAMASTE.

E. H. E.

*Stockbridge, Massachusetts*

# PROLOGUE

## Echoes of an Event

# CHAPTER
# I

# India: First Encounters

As THE PLANE SETS DOWN at the Delhi airport before dawn, the newcomer is enveloped in a new world of sights, sounds, and smells which darkly command him to reset all his senses before asking any questions. The faces of Indian friends glow with that special dawn responsiveness which is born of the ability to sleep any time and to awake any time. Kamla and Prem, two strong and warm Punjabis, firmly took Joan and me out of the travel circuit; they and their circle of friends would shelter us against and yet guide us slowly toward unknown depths and heights of experience.

We drove through the still, dark avenues of the imperial capital to the International Center, a modern hospice for scholars. Of modern Mogul style, it overlooks the ancient Lodi Gardens and their huge, sinister domes. Stepping out on the balcony, before trying to catch a bit of sleep—and then to awake in India—we had the almost guilty feeling of seeing India as one dreams it to be. For months we had strenuously read about the "realities" of this subcontinent in order not to be fooled either by ancient images or modern pretenses. But now, only the senses continued to register. Jackals were yapping in the distance and down in the caves of their day-time existence, and some early morning walkers appeared, gliding through the trees like white shadows. There was time, we had to tell ourselves.

And this would remain: feeling almost lethargically at home with our senses and our affects as we never had anywhere else and yet a sense, too, of incomprehensible dread.

We stayed in Delhi two days, beginning each day by joining the early walkers in the Lodi Gardens.

But to be in the India of today, one has to escape Imperial New Delhi. In Old Delhi, traffic has Asian style. It overflows and contracts with the yielding and the ruthlessness of fast-flowing water. In an hour's walk one sees men, women, and children who call to mind every step in the history of the human species and every physical state of grace and crookedness, vigor and infirmity. The mere sight of the anonymous mass grips one with an apprehension matched only by the prevailing sense of unknown hazards to health. Stray off the tourist beat, and one is in a different, almost hostile ecology of mores and microbes. To survive and to begin to understand, one must mobilize some unlived portions of individual and racial existence. One thinks of the riots (or the "furors," as somebody called them) which erupted in the vacuum left by Gandhi's dying influence and by the departing British. But breathing is ever again restored by the handsome motion and the gay and warm expression of many of these people; and even the public urination and defecation (which at first the stranger cannot ignore) bespeaks a naive dignity. Only a day or so before, we had swum in the Lake of Galilee and had walked at night on the shores where, even among militant and pragmatic Israelis, one can never forget Him who had the gift to speak to fishermen in a manner remembered through the ages. Now I sensed again what I had known as a youth, namely, the affinity of that Galilean and the skinny Indian leader enshrined in Delhi. There is a word for what they seem to have had in common: presence—as pervasive a presence as only silence has when you listen.

On our first evening in Delhi I had experienced what would happen often: a trusting Indian could be quietly transfigured if he perceived that I knew of that presence; while others who were doubtful of me (after all, was I not a psychoanalyst?)

would mildly slander the Mahatma in order to show that they were not easily fooled (did I know that as an old man "he used to sleep with his niece"?).

In Washington, we seldom stay overnight without visiting the Lincoln Memorial. In Delhi, we went to Birla House and the place where Gandhi was assassinated. If shrines must be, I find the garden of Birla House peculiarly impressive, not because of its formality, but for a low building in the very background which contains nothing but a mural extending over three walls. None of our friends had seen it, we found later, partially because they avoid the whole location, and partially because the painting appeals more to the common people. It is not "great." Naive, like Haitian folk art but decidedly more austere, it simply depicts scenes from Gandhi's life, mostly as reported by him in his Autobiography. On the left, his life is traced to his spiritual and historical ancestors: an old seer, author of an epic; the prince of the Bhagavad Gita, turning his face away from the drawn-up battle lines which shine, on both sides, with the armed splendor of his brothers and cousins; hermits, poets, and monks; Buddha himself—and the great emperor Ashoka. So far, so traditional. However, moving to the right, the mural reveals a strange concept of a leader's emergence. It shows Gandhi's self-confessed temptations, errors, and procrastinations on his way to becoming the man in the loincloth and the voice of the people. He is shown sinfully eating meat as a youth; leaving in utter panic the house of a yelling prostitute; waltzing in cutaway and high white collar with an English redhead; and, as a barrister, paralyzed with stage fright before a contemptuous judge. One scene stopped me: it shows Gandhi in front of his ashram, receiving a packet of money from a wealthy man who has stepped out of a Model T Ford. Was that ashram not Gandhi's settlement in Ahmedabad? And was not the wealthy man the very mill owner who was to be our host there? His identity has become known, although Gandhi reports in his Autobiography only that this man who wished to remain anonymous had continued to support the ashram when all other contributors deserted it because a family of Untouchables had been admitted into the colony.

In contrast to this intimate memorial, the place of Gandhi's cremation is being turned into a monument which, in the Mogul grandeur of its outlay, bespeaks the ambiguity of all greatness. To this place, the remains of the man of peace who never held public office were transported on a gun-carrier drawn by soldiers and sailors. In contrast, again (and contrasts tell you of a nation's dimensions), the nearby Gandhi Museum offers an exceedingly sober review of his life in enlarged photographs, capped with stark quotations. Over the entrance door: "I am told that religion and politics are different spheres of life. But I would say without a moment's hesitation and yet in all modesty that those who claim this do not know what religion is." We saw only Indians (and, to all appearances, mostly of the lower classes) visiting any of these shrines. No tourists.

THE Sarabhai family is like a grove of tall trees, tightly linked in a family resemblance, yet all strong and striving individuals, in their strength and their inner conflicts true products of the individualistic upbringing they received from their father. The oldest daughter is a calmly, almost mournfully, controversial woman, a friend and follower of Gandhi's in his lifetime. She met us for lunch in a hotel dining room. In the midst of all the loud and ostentatious informality of modern Indians and American tourists, she appeared in homespun khadi, with a dark face as "lived in" as any you will ever see. Like her brothers and sisters she has an outspoken profile—and an overweening cause: hers is the demand for a solution of the Kashmir dispute which would be equally acceptable to Pakistan and to the people of Kashmir—one of those inescapabilities of modern politics vigorously represented by her friend Sheikh Abdullah, and equally stubbornly ignored by another, Jawaharlal Nehru. He let her go to jail, in fact, for two years, and she is sadly angry with him.

Our friend, the physicist Vikram Sarabhai, the mill owner's youngest son, came to fetch us in Delhi for a quick trip to

Kashmir before the snows would cover the approach to the Himalayan site of his Cosmic Ray Laboratory. On our flight over the formidable mountain ranges into the bucolic valley of Kashmir, we exchanged notes on the International Pugwash Conference from which he had just returned, and on the American Academy's conference on "alternatives to armed conflict," which I had recently attended on Cape Cod.

Our hearts were heavy. Up there along the snow-capped horizon of our flight view, the Chinese were streaming through the passes. "Border incidents?" Nobody professed to know. But I was only too aware of the fact that our destination, the airport of Srinagar, was the single potential landing place for Chinese jets. And indeed, the airport was an armed camp. But on landing, rather than being delayed by security measures, we found ourselves suddenly engulfed in a pageant. The Vice President of India, Zakir Husain, a Muslim highly welcome to the Kashmiris, had landed at about the same time for an official visit. Our driver could not avoid attaching himself to the slow cavalcade into the city. So we drove through lanes and lanes of waving children and youngsters, who beamed into our car with that intense and gay curiosity with which Indians "take in" strangers.

We stayed in a wing of the Maharaja's palace, which is now a hotel. Before daybreak we heard the rolling thunder of transport planes overhead conveying soldiers and equipment to the distant front.

In the morning we met Gautam Sarabhai, bearded and princely, who took us across the lake to that great mosque which houses a strand of Mohammed's hair. Kashmiris from all over the valley converged on this sacred spot in hundreds of small boats, debarked at long pools in order to wash their private parts discreetly, and went to the grounds of the Mosque, to kneel and bow to the ground in endless straight files, fusing in a ceremonial identity what was a moment earlier a scrambling mass.

THE next morning, on the way to the Cosmic Ray Laboratory, we hiked the last three miles up to about 9,000 feet, although most travelers rode horseback or jeeps. This was the last week in the year before the snows close in; the air was crisp, and yet the sun strong. Now and again one could step out on the edge of a rock and look for a timeless instant into those pensive valleys; but not even here was one ever alone for long. Indian tourists would pass on horseback and ask whether we *enjoyed* the climb? And were we *Canadian* perchance?

RAILROAD stations afford a singular view of the Indian people, to whom each station is a center of intense sociability and scrambling argument. The arrival at night in Ahmedabad proved to be an infernal experience. The station was jammed with overcrowded trains and filled with gratuitous whistle noises; and we made our first acquaintance with that Indian phenomenon of hundreds of people sleeping in isolated spots or in dense rows inside and outside the station building, a few on mats, some on newspapers, many on the naked asphalt. Westerners sometimes seem perversely eager to believe that all these people are homeless and starving to death right in front of their eyes. The trouble is, it is hard to know. A few are apt to die like this in any night, and many during famines, but the general phenomenon of sleeping outdoors is a more normal and more complex one. Most of these people, while looking terribly thin, are not in worse condition than tens of millions sleeping "at home." Many have never known a "bed," and some have come to prefer sleeping on streets to sleeping in overcrowded rooms. And, at any rate, there are no hotels in India for ordinary Indians. But in view of such masses of indistinct and emaciated bodies I could recover only very gradually a sense known to me when I was young, namely, how at home one can feel in a sleeping crowd of strangers.

The upper class, however, sleeps with friends; and a car was expecting us to take us to the mill owner's "Retreat." Here we were lodged in a small house in a corner of the estate where, I was told, C. F. Andrews, the friend of the greatest of all friends, had stayed in the past. In the morning we were awakened by what sounded like a rattling earthquake overhead. It turned out to be only the gleeful bounces of holy monkeys from a nearby temple demolishing the tiles of the roof. The servants were helpless; they could only try to scare the rascals with rocks but had to avoid hitting them, as the monkeys well knew.

THE immediate deep attachment to India is shaken first by two experiences: the poverty, abysmal and as wide as the horizon—and the near-inevitability of dysentery.

We had felt it coming on during the railroad trip, and it hit Joan on arrival. She was soon too dehydrated for the best of home care. At this point the mill owner's family showed us how in this civilization the joint family takes over in a way comparable to that of dolphins lifting a sinking member of their school to the surface. Having waited out the matter for about four days, they went into action within hours. Five or six family members converged on our house, as did the medical school's chief of internal medicine, the head doctor of the mills, and the Chief Secretary of the State of Gujarat. They all discussed the matter in an urgent and ominous way—in Gujarati, of course—and then asked me, as the head of my family, what my decision was: to wit, did I agree to the hospitalization they had agreed on? The mill owner's regal wife—diminutive mother of that strong-willed clan of sons and daughters—drove off with three of her servants to clean a hospital room doubly clean for a foreign lady. Others went off with bed sheets and flowers, and eventually the mother reappeared in her limousine to pack Joan off. But by this time the patient let herself be carried away by the wave of familial sympathy, much too entertained to worry about her hopelessly leaking condition. A graceful "nurse matron," at the head of a small army of young nurses, all Syrian Christians from South India, took over. In the next room one sick child was attended by father, mother, and two healthy little brothers who all slept on mats on the floor. Thus, the all-pervasive spirit of the "joint family" transformed this frightening experience. And in the back of my mind, I remembered having read somewhere that the mill owner and his wife, decades ago, had come to the rescue of Gandhi when he was prostrate somewhere near Ahmedabad, exceedingly weak in body and low in mood.

All the Sarabhais have overweening causes. They have money

and do not deny it, but they also have a passion for spending it relevantly: one is tempted to call them (with some sharp corrections of detail) the Medicis of Ahmedabad. Unnecessary to say, this generosity is widely met with ambivalence, and their patronage will make us, too, suspect in the eyes of some. However, I had a barter agreement with them: they would provide room, board, and local transportation (and that means, in India, a servant, a cook, and a driver) for us, as wealthy Indians have always done for their traveling friends and the friends of their friends, and as they are now wont to do for foreigners with intellectual or artistic offerings. In return, I would offer my seminar on the human life cycle, in order to give me and a number of interested citizens of Ahmedabad a chance to compare our clinical ideas of the stages of life with those of Hindu tradition.

ALL well again, we had Divali morning breakfast at the palatial house of Ambalal Sarabhai, with all the shiny young of the family present. Divali is the New Year Festival of Lights, and the city was alive with firecrackers exploding every half-second on the half-second, even though Nehru had tried to suggest over the radio that at this moment in India's history shooting had all too painful connotations. On the spacious terrace feudal scenes were repeated when servants and gardeners, colorfully clad, lined up with their families to bring New Year's greetings, some by touching their master's feet, and some by receiving good wishes and sweets.

Then we went next door to offer New Year's regards to Ambalal's sister, the venerable Anasuya Sarabhai. As we entered her simple villa, the firecrackers suddenly sounded far away. One of Gandhi's earliest supporters, the saintly yet simple old woman was holding court of a different order. In her cool and modestly appointed living room sat the labor minister of Gujarat State and some of the city's labor leaders in white khadi and Gandhi caps, wishing a good new year to this staunch old "Mother of Labor," now so frail and detached. There was a photo of Tolstoy on the wall, inscribed to Gandhi by Tolstoy and willed to Anasuya by the Mahatma; and next to it hung a photo of the Mahatma himself, deep in thought, in the corner of a train-bench—third class, as we were pointedly advised. The labor leaders looked prosperous and hardy.

AFTERWARDS Ambalal Sarabhai led me to one of his terraces, which overlook a sea of trees, and offered it to me as a study, not without telling me—more reverently than ostentatiously—that Tagore had worked here.

To be guests in such a compound permitted us to gather our thoughts while making forays into Ahmedabad as mood and necessity dictated. At dawn men and boys hurry all over the countryside with little pitchers of water for their morning toilet; the women, apparently, precede them when it is still dark. At dusk the air is permeated by the odor of burning (dried) cow dung, which is the only fuel available to the poor. At all times one is conscious of one's own heavy-footed tramping while those about one move with the gliding agility of the barefooted.

Between the residential surroundings of the Sarabhais' Retreat and the broad riverbed of the Sabarmati is the old city. To walk through the city streets is (or once must have been) like swimming in a friendly but turbulent element. But to drive into the city is a hair-raising experience, like boating through rapids. Everybody and everything spills out into the middle of the street, people on foot and on bicycles, on oxcarts and occasionally on camels—and erratic goats, trotting donkeys, ambling cows, and bulky buffaloes. All of this seems to approach one's car like a solid phalanx not yielding an inch until the very last moment and only at the shrieking insistence of the driver's horn. But then it yields easily, almost elegantly. Accidents are rare, which is lucky since drivers and passengers are apt to be roughly handled, especially if a cow gets hurt. And, indeed, in the middle of all of this one may suddenly look into the big round eye of a sacred cow. These creatures have never learned to anticipate danger or malice and walk through it all with dull majesty. And all roads eventually lead to the wide bed of the river Sabarmati.

Joan soon began to visit the craftsmen by the river, and she described how nowadays, as in the past, the weaving, printing, and dyeing of textiles takes place in the streets and on the sands of the Sabarmati, whose water is said to contain special properties for the setting of dyes, while the river flats are ideal for drying and bleaching the cloth. As great factories belch out smoke and blow sirens to call their workers, the life on the river retains the ancient patterns of hand work.

Hand work is family work, and the river bed is alive with men and women, boys and girls—and babies. But all the sounds of the river are topped by the constant rhythmic banging of cloths on large stones. The washermen stand holding the cloth by one end and beat it firmly and noisily, letting out a great gasp of breath with each stroke. Sometimes this gusty accompaniment emerges as the fragment of a song, or as a breathy "Sita" or "Rama." How any cloth survives is a wonder, but it seems to be woven to meet this test. The river bed sings with colors—blue, yellow, purple, and green—as hand-printed and hand-dyed fabrics are spread out under the burning, blinding glare of the sun.

This is the craftsman's view of the unchanging life of the river bed.[1] The old walled city, however, is a merchant's city, or better, a mercantile fortress, subdivided into caste fortresses, each with its secret life. I had as a guide an erudite socialist born into this city and yet critical in his analysis; and he helped me to begin to weigh, as one must, the rigidities and cruelties of the caste world-view against the security and identity it once provided to some people in some ways—and, mind you, it provided an identity which lasted through a whole series of rebirths.

The old city and the adjoining river are surrounded by fast-growing greater Ahmedabad, a city of avenues and bridges, and above all, of mills—85 mills, 125,000 workers in a population of a million and a quarter. As Pittsburgh has, or once had, its rich mixture of unreconstructed immigrants, Ahmedabad attracts a variety of rural tribes who live under the poorest conditions before being absorbed into the labor population, finding a function in city life, or joining the slum dwellers. Among the most impressive are the red-turbaned Tachartas, very lean, masculine "cowboys," and their beautiful fast-moving women. These cowboys now cut a kind of mammal centaur figure, by riding on bicycles with enormous milk cans dangling on either side. Each of these urbanized tribes has its dances and ceremonies, and often we heard the drums all night (interrupted only by the shrieking factory sirens) from one or another torch-lit dead-end street.

An acquaintance with Pittsburgh somehow helps one in Ahmedabad. For one thing, Indians everywhere, when informed that one is going to or coming from this city ask, "Why Ahmedabad?!" the way Americans once wondered what could lure one to Pittsburgh. But here, too, belching smoke means prosperity. Whatever wealth, culture, and public welfare exists was first a feudal gift from a few wealthy families and was only subsequently secured as a right by the bargaining unions. And the Ahmedabad industrialists, like the early ones in Pittsburgh, are widely spoken of as robber-barons with cultural pretensions. The repugnance is reinforced by the fact that this is a city dominated by the "Banias," some of them members of an ancient merchant caste, adhering to what they insist is a religion in its own right, Jainism. Only the combination "Pittsburgh Yankee" might be a vague American analogue to the national image of the Ahmedabad Bania. The more respectable traits attributed to them are enterprise, caution, realism, compromise, and shrewdness. Gandhi, incidentally, was from a small-town Bania caste—his very name means "grocer"—and on return from South Africa, he settled here in his ashram across the river for the very reason that he felt he should approach his vast homeland from the region and with the language of his origin. But few of the educated young want to live here; the trend is to Bombay—or beyond.

In mere numbers and in national importance, Ahmedabad is, of course, overshadowed by Calcutta, Bombay, Delhi, and Madras. But it is and always has been the most unified and the most unionized city in India, and certainly the one with the most modern welfare institutions. One must see labor relations at work (in the mills, at the teeming Association building, or in the "integrated" maternity hospital) in what is otherwise still a poverty-stricken and caste-ridden population, to realize what the continued "presence" of one such man as Gandhi was able to accomplish at one time—with the help of such rebels from the Bania élite as Anasuyaben.

Across the river, there is still Gandhi's old ashram, now part memorial, part orphanage for formerly "Untouchable" children. We spent Christmas morning there, having been invited to attend the prayer meeting of the children. The solemnity of the occasion was lightened only by the children's subdued giggles when they saw my Western efforts to sit Indian fashion next to the slim and saintly man who presided.

Not far from the Retreat on a boulevard leading to the governor's mansion is Gujarat's official "Guest House." One day we stopped there on our morning walk and were accosted by a friendly and dignified old man named Shankerlal Banker, whom we had met that Divali morning at Anasuyaben's house. We had passed him often on our morning walks, but he had always modestly avoided any conversation. He is a man of seemingly unmanly traits: wrapped in khadi and countless shawls, completely toothless, and shy in an almost coy manner. In this he is not entirely un-typical; but it contrasted with what I had heard of the man, namely, that in the days of Gandhi's ascent he was a superb organizer. He later became the secretary of the national khadi (home spinning) movement.

"You know what happened here?" he asked that morning, calling the "Guest House" a court house. This had been the place of Gandhi's trial in 1922! In my youth we had read with awe the dialogue of the encounter between Gandhi and his British judge. The judge had said:

Mr. Gandhi, you have made my task easy in one way by pleading guilty to the charges: nevertheless, what remains, namely, the determination of a just sentence is perhaps as difficult a proposition as a judge in this country could have to face. . . . It would be impossible to ignore the fact that in the eyes of millions of your countrymen you are a great patriot and a great leader. Even those who differ from you in politics, look upon you as a man of high ideals and of noble and even saintly life. . . . But it is my duty to judge you as a man subject to the law.

The judge then consulted the accused as to the sentence which should be imposed: "You will not consider it unreasonable, I think, that you should be classed with Mr. Tilak [before his death in 1920, the most powerful of India's militant nationalists who had once been sentenced to six years' imprisonment in exile.] If the course of events in India should make it possible for the Government to reduce the period and release you, no one will be better pleased than I." Gandhi affirmed that it was "his proudest privilege and honour" to receive the same sentence as Tilak—a sentence he considered as light as any judge could impose on him.[2]

I then realized that nearly all of the people whom I could now consider my friends had been present at that trial, if only as children; and had not Shankerlal Banker been, in fact, Gandhi's lone co-defendant? I asked our friend whether he had ever written up the memories of the year which he had subsequently spent in jail with Gandhi. But he shook his head in a kind of mock-horror.[3] It also appeared that he had been energetically involved in the strike which was, through many conversations, gradually emerging for me as a memorable event, in the context of which I might visualize Gandhi's presence in this city in all the humor, candor, and forcefulness of his personality. I told Shankerlal how much Romain Rolland's book had meant to me when I was young, and the next day he brought me a copy. Here is Romain Rolland's description of Gandhi:

Soft dark eyes, a small frail man, with a thin face and rather large protruding eyes, his head covered with a white cap, his body clothed in coarse white cloth, bare-footed. He lives on rice and fruit, and drinks only water. He sleeps on the floor—sleeps very little, and works incessantly. His body does not seem to count at all. There is nothing striking about him—except his whole expression of "infinite patience and infinite love." W. W. Pearson, who met him in South Africa, instinctively thought of St. Francis of Assisi. There is an almost child-like simplicity about him. His manner is gentle and courteous even when dealing with adversaries, and he is of immaculate sincerity. He is modest and unassuming, to the point of sometimes seeming almost timid, hesitant, in making an assertion. Yet you feel his indomitable spirit. He makes no compromises to admit having been in the wrong. . . . Literally "ill with the multitude that adores him" he distrusts majorities and fears "mobocracy" and the unbridled passions of the populace. He feels at ease only in a minority, and is happiest when, in meditative solitude, he can listen to the "still small voice" within.

This is the man who has stirred three hundred million people to revolt, who has shaken the foundations of the British Empire, and who has introduced into human politics the strongest religious impetus of the last two hundred years.[4]

# CHAPTER
# II

# A Seminar in Ahmedabad

BUT I HAD WORK TO DO; and work is a welcome counterbalance when impressions become too varied and too crowded. It was good to meet a small group of sincere men and women of all ages at appointed times, to close the doors (in India, always a figure of speech) and to engage in a familiar procedure: a seminar. And in trying to join what craftsmanship one brings along with some vital concerns of one's hosts, there is always a better chance to become aware of the universally human in the fleeting phenomena. The participants in the seminar included physicists and industrialists, physicians and educators. Saraladevi alone, in her khadi sari, represented the Gandhian past.

I, of course, presented my life stages, not without arousing some mirth as well as an incredulity tempered only by an accustomed deference to authority. Each of the other members contributed in *his* "currency"—from the poet Uma Shankar Joshi,[5] who reconstructed the life cycle as depicted in Sanskrit scriptures, to Vikram's dancer-wife, Mrinalini, who gave a recital in her open-air theater by the river, illuminating the Hindu stages of life with her partner and her troupe. Others reported on particular crises of life: Tagore's childhood; identity problems of a youth from one of the formerly "criminal" tribes or castes; the relationship of women students to their mothers. The concepts discussed ranged from caste to indeterminacy. I wrote memoranda, distributed between the sessions, in an attempt to tie the wealth of material together and to relate it—where this could be done without violence—to "my" stages.[6] The Vedas and I, of course, are both constrained to follow closely what is given in phylogeny and ontogeny. But exactly what image of human life appears in a given age and culture, an image so conscious and obvious that no explanation seems necessary, or what image is (as the physicist Ramanathan discussed in the seminar) so much "in a man's bones" that he need not be conscious of it—*that* must be put into words in each age, if a mutual understanding is desired. It becomes clear, then, that the changing images provided by modern psychology, scientific as they may be in the verification of some details, nevertheless harbor what Freud himself called a "mythological" trend. And even in the most rational world, the continued presence of traditional (and maybe consciously repudiated images) is, to the clinician, an inescapable fact. For such images and ideas are absorbed early in life as a kind of space-time which gives coherent reassurance against the abysmal estrangements emerging in each successive stage and plaguing man throughout life: against early mistrust as well as against shame and doubt, against a sense of guilt as well as against a sense of futility of effort, and, finally, against a confusion of identity as well as against a sense of isolation, stagnation, or senile despair. And even where such explicit world-images are dispensed with in the expectation—or under actual conditions—of "happiness" or "success," they reappear implicitly in the way man reassures himself when feeling adrift.

But I can report here only on my first comparative encounter with Hindu stages of life, as described and lived by men and women who (depending on their ages) have grown up with them more or less explicitly. Here I must be schematic.

The Hindu scriptures are "platonic" in the sense that they outline the eternal meaning of the pre-ordained stages which pervade the variety of mortal lives and local customs. "Eternal meaning" can, of course, become righteous tyranny at the height of priestly power, and something of a hoax in an era of cultural disintegration; but since today we know so much more systematically and attend so much more passionately to the distortion and perversion of all meaning than to the values always to be restored or regained, it may be well to try to recognize, even in glaring deviations, the order suggested by the way in which human beings strive to grow. From clinical and developmental observations, we have gained much insight into the strategic stages of infancy and childhood; and in my own attempt to give these stages a place in the whole course of life, I have postulated that the first year of life establishes the fundamental "virtue" of hope, while childhood forms the rudiments of will and of purpose, of initiative and of skill, before adolescence grounds adult life in some system of fidelity.

First, it must be noted that traditional Hindu images of life, in contrast to our clinical emphasis on infantile vulnerabilities, do not conceptualize stages before the "sense" age is reached, that is, before a child can listen attentively to things told and read and sung and shown to him, and when he is eager to attach himself to people who will teach him: until a boy is eight years old, he is like one newly born, marked only by the caste in which he is born.[7] Up to then ceremonies are held "over" him, as it were, but without his comprehension and participation. Nevertheless, the ceremonies do emphasize the critical stages known to us—only that, where we would view hope as the fundamental human strength emerging from the first year of life, the Hindu view would (fairly enough) allocate it to the beginning of all time:

"Whence, however, does Hope arise? . . . Hope is the sheet-anchor of every man. When Hope is destroyed, great grief follows which, forsooth, is almost equal to death itself. . . . I think that Hope is bigger than a mountain with all its trees. Or, perhaps, it is bigger than the sky itself. Or, perhaps, O King, it is really immeasurable. Hope, O Chief of *kurus*, is highly difficult of being understood and equally difficult of being conquered. Seeing this last attribute of Hope, I ask, what else is so unconquerable as this?"[8]

What we would ascribe to the beginnings of the life cycle the Hindu view projects into previous lives which determine the coordinates of a person's rebirth in this one: not only *where* a child was to be reborn (*desha*) and *when* (*kala*), but also his *innate* trends (*gunas*) and therefore the efforts (*shrama*) which can be expected of one thus endowed and growing up in his caste at his period of history. He may emerge, then, in the caste of the Brahmans and learn to be literate, or in that of Kshatrias and learn how to fight and to rule, among the Vaisyas and handle goods or hold land, or among the Sudras to toil in the sweat of his brow. Or, indeed, he may miss all of these honored occupations and go through this life doomed to touch what others will avoid and, therefore, be untouchable himself. But the Untouchable, too, has unlimited chances ahead of him.

We in the West are proudly overcoming all ideas of predestination. But we would still insist that child training can do no more than underscore what is given—that is, in an epigenetic development fixed by evolution. And we can certainly sense in any seminar—clinical or historical—how we continue to project ideas of doom and predetermination either on hereditary or constitutional givens, on early experience and irreversible trauma, or on cultural and economic deprivation—that is, on a past, as dim as it is fateful. And let us face it: "deep down" nobody in his right mind *can* visualize his own existence without assuming that he has always lived and will live hereafter; and the religious world-views of old only endowed this psychological given with images and ideas which could be shared, transmitted, and ritualized.

The first well-defined stage in the Hindu life cycle is *Antevasin*, the stage of apprenticeship, of youthful orientation. It knits together the basic skills allocated to one's caste and transfers to a certified teacher (guru) the blind attachment to parental figures in order to anchor one's fate and personality in concrete techniques and in significant persons. This corresponds closely to the way in which we would have school age develop a rudimentary sense of competency, and would consider adolescence the source of a sense of fidelity basic to the stage of youth, and essential for a sense of identity. Yet, again, what we treat as a matter of maturational stages for the Hindu is *dharma*—a life task determined by previous lives as well as by acquisition and choice. And *dharma* is both highly personal and as determining as what we call identity: "Better one's own *dharma*, [though] imperfect, than another's well performed; Better death in [doing] one's own *dharma*; Another's *dharma* brings danger."[9]

Yet only the linkage of individual *dharmas* holds the world together. "Neither the state nor the king, neither the mace nor the mace-bearer, govern the people; it is only by *dharma* that people secure mutual protection," says the *Mahabharata*.[10] There is much in *dharma*, then, which we have conceptualized as Ego, if understood as that which integrates the individual experience and yet is also always communal in nature.[11] If individuals depend on each other for a maximum and optimum of *mutual activation*, *dharma* is a consolidation of the world through the self-realization of each individual within a joint order.

In young adulthood the stage of *Antevasin* is replaced by that of the householder (*Grhastha*). I find it very congenial that this whole scheme allows for a succession of pointedly different life styles. Instead of the almost vindictive monotony of Judean-Christian strictures by which we gain or forfeit salvation by the formation of one consistently virtuous character almost from the cradle to the very grave, the Hindu system first decrees that the *Antevasin* delay and sublimate his sexuality in order to be a devoted student of eternal values, but then assigns to him as the first duty of young adulthood the experience of all those varied sexual and sensual pleasures which are so comprehensively depicted on temples devoted to this aspect of life.

But he must not get lost in these, either; as he settles down to marry, he is encouraged to devote himself to *Artha*, the "reality" of family relations, of communal power, and of productivity. The *Manusmriti* declares, "He only is a perfect man who consists of three persons united, his wife, himself, and his offspring."[12] Much of this corresponds to our assumption that the varied intimacies of young adulthood will ripen to a capacity for true Intimacy which is a fusion of identities. This, in turn, is the basis for that sense of Care which crowns what we call Gen-

erativity and becomes a source of strength for all who are united
in procreation and productivity.

This successive involvement in the orders of learning, of sexual
mutuality, of family-building, and of communal consolidation is
gradually replaced by the third stage, *Vanaprastha*, or the inner
separation from all ties of selfhood, body-boundness, and communality and their replacement by a striving which will eventually lead to *Moksha*: renunciation, disappearance.

This traditional scheme shows correspondences to what I have
come to emphasize as a *sequence* of stages and an *aggregate* of
the strengths developed in each. Manu says: "Some declare that
the chief good [of man] consists in the acquisition of *dharma*
and *Artha*, others place it in the gratification of *kama* [sensual
enjoyment] and the acquisition of *dharma* alone and others say
that the acquisition of *Artha* alone is the chief good here below:
but the correct decision is that it consists of the aggregate of
those three."[13]

It would be fruitless as well as impossible to compare these
schemes point for point. What is more important is the principle
which makes them comparable at all—that is, the epigenetic
principle[14] according to which in each stage of life a given
strength is added to a widening ensemble and reintegrated at
each later stage in order to play its part in a full cycle—if and
where fate and society permit.

Such correspondence as outlined here, however, makes both
schemes suspect in the eyes of the modern sceptic; and it did so
in our seminar. A group of otherwise well-trained individuals
when confronted with religious world-images never quite
knows whether to consider the existence of such remnants of
magic thinking the result of meaningless habituation or an irrational systematization. And yet, a pragmatic world-view which
shuns all concepts of the cycle of generations can cause widespread disorientation. In such a dilemma, one cannot help admir-
ing the ideational and ceremonial consistency of the older world-
images.

For what an ingenious scheme this is: all caste, subcaste, and
not-yet-caste having been predetermined, one comes into life

with a curse that can be lived down if one lives up to minutely prescribed ways; and by living and dying well, one becomes deserving of ever better lives until, having exhausted the available life cycles, one is ready for release from the whole big cycle.

All world-images are apt to become corrupt when left to ecclesiastic bureaucracies. But this does not make the formation of world-images expendable. And I can only repeat that we deny the remnants of old-world images at our own risk, because we do not overcome them by declaring them—with all the righteousness of scepticism—something of a secret sin. They are not less powerful for being denied. In India, I found, outside the seminar at any rate, that anyone who trusts a stranger not to smile will soon confide to him the magic reaffirmations he receives from sources other than those the West calls rational— from astrology to mysticism. But it is true for us, too, that the imagery of our traditional inner resources must be transcended, rather than denied, by what we are learning to learn.

So MUCH FOR my encounter with the wise. But in Ahmedabad there is also a combined school and clinic under the patronage of the Sarabhais, and there Kamalini Sarabhai, Gautam's wife, arranged for me not only to attend the discussion of case-histories, but also to "listen" to Indian school children by seeing them repeat a play performance, which has taught me much about our children. As described in *Childhood and Society*, one method of play study consists simply of confronting one child at a time with an empty table (the "stage") and a series of toys (the "cast") and of asking him to build a "scene." I tried to induce my friends to treat this matter methodically and to provide each child brought in to construct a play scene with exactly the same instructions and the same general setting. But, since I was sitting behind a one-way screen in order not to be seen, I could not interfere when some children appeared in the playroom accompanied by members of their families or by some additional staff member, while others were led in by only one adult; or when one child was given an instruction five times as long as the others. In either case the explanation later given was that the child *needed it* in order to do his *best*. In the end I learned to forget about the scientific imperatives of psychologists at home and to enjoy the social habits which, at least in a preliminary experiment, provide the only true context for such a study in India.

In America we had asked the children to invent scenes from an imaginary moving picture; here we suggested a *folk play*. If I should say what difference first appeared forcefully in the few constructions I saw emerging, it was this: American children select a few toys carefully and then build and rebuild a circumscribed scene of increasingly clear configuration. Indian children, in contrast, attempt to use all the toys at their disposal, creating a play universe filled to the periphery with blocks, people, and animals but with little differentiation between outdoors and indoors, jungle and city, or, indeed, one scene from another. If one finally asks what (and, indeed, *where*) is *the* "exciting scene," one finds it embedded somewhere where nobody could have discerned it as an individual event and certainly not as a central one. Once it is located, however, a Gestalt emerges and suggests some relation to the child's history and background—as do the scenes at home. And since, with all my wordiness, I am a "seeing" type, what the children did before my eyes merged with configurations that had impressed me in case-histories and, indeed, in Indian fiction.

Significant moments embedded in a moving sea of unfathomable multiformity: does not life on the street or at home anywhere offer such an over-all configurational impression? In fact, this is the way I have come to feel about India, often not without a trace of sensory and emotional seasickness. For one moves in a space-time so filled with visual and auditory occurrences that it is very difficult to lift an episode out of the flux of events, a fact out of the stream of feelings, a circumscribed relationship out of a fusion of multiple encounters. If, in all this, I should endow one word with a meaning which unites it all, the word is *fusion*. And I am inclined to indulge in the generalization that Indians want to give and to get by fusing—actively and passively. This may come as a shocking observation to those who, on the basis of one-sided reading, emphasize the *isolation* of the Indian individual and a lifelong nostalgia for solitude and meditation. But fusion and isolation are polar themes. I have suggested in *Childhood and Society* that one may begin rather than end with the proposition that a nation's identity is derived from the ways in which history has, as it were, counterpointed certain opposite potentialities; the ways in which it lifts this counterpoint to a unique style of civilization, or lets it disintegrate into mere contradiction. In this sense, the fusion enforced and, no doubt, often enjoyed in the joint family and in crowded life in general results in a polarity. There is, no doubt, a deep recurring need to escape the multitude, and there is a remarkable capacity for being alone in the middle of a crowd. I have, in fact, never seen so many individuals in a catatonic-like isolation in the middle of a chattering crowd. But aloneness, too, is often dominated by a deep nostalgia for fusing with another, and this in an exclusive and lasting fashion, be that "Other" a mentor or a god, the Universe—or the innermost Self.

To change the subject, but only seemingly so: Westerners have "principles." Truth, for us, is the sum of what can be isolated and counted. It is what can be logically accounted for, what can be proved to have happened, or what you really mean at the moment when you say it, while keeping it somehow consistent with what you meant earlier or expect to say later. Deviation from such truth makes you a liar; and I have heard it said often enough that Indians, because truth means something different to them, are habitual liars. Now Gandhi himself tried to infuse into Indian life an almost Christian or, at any rate, Socratic "Yes, yes" and "No, no," sometimes insisting on factualness of content, sometimes on honesty of confession, and sometimes on unequivocal cooperation. To him all this was enveloped in a Truth which would reveal itself only in intuitive fusion with the innermost self or (or *and*) the will of the masses. But of course he too has been called, in the East and in the West, a hypocritical politician and a saint of uneasy honesty. It is, therefore, important to note the baseline of truthfulness in India and to realize that such "principles" as *dharma, Artha, kama* and *Moksha* cannot be compared with Western principles in the sense that they provide categorical permissions or prohibitions. Rather, they are forms of *immersion* in different *orders* of *self-abandonment*. That these orders, because of their very lack of guidelines, become expressed in minutely detailed handbooks of ways to abandon oneself with utmost conscientiousness—that is another matter. Westerners on first acquaintance are apt to admire the self-abandonment of the Kama Sutra or the affluent eroticism of the temple statuary, as expressing a freedom denied for too long to our artistic and erotic imagination: yet the Kama Sutra is really a most bureaucratic inventory of coital variations, and the author is said to have been ascetic himself. Even the steaming eroticism of temple sculptures suggests, after the first shock of stimulation or revulsion, a gigantic endeavor not to leave out anything, while not emphasizing any one possible (or impossible) form of erotic gymnastics more than any other.

One must learn, then, to see a dynamic polarity rather than an inner contradiction in what at first looks like a basic inconsistency, such as that between fusion-in-the-mass and utter solitude, between sensual license and compulsive order, or between an utterly a-historical sense of living and inventories of assembled facts.

And this is my first impression of some basic quality of family life: something a man of my training always tries to sense in order to orient himself. The deep nostalgia for fusion is reborn, it seems, from generation to generation out of the diffusion of the mother in the joint family, in which she must respond to each and, at the same time, to all, and thus can belong to the individual child only in fleeting moments and to nobody for good or for long. A tentative interpretation would suggest that the child feels guilty in a way largely unknown in the West (except to those on the border of schizophrenia). For the child wants his mother to himself, while she must spread her love. He cannot blame her for a single and consistent betrayal as the oedipal boy in the West can, who therefore also has a clear rival enemy *and* hero, his father. Furthermore, there is the often unbelievably intense importance in Indian life of aunts and uncles and of brothers and sisters, which attests to the difficulty of applying to the Indian scene any interpretations derived from the Western family: for there is always the passionate "transfer" of filial, incestuous, and jealous affects onto close relatives who provide parental affection and circumspection but escape the oedipal rivalry. The wider family, therefore, permits a closeness, often expressed physically and affectively in a true "togetherness," deeply touching and yet somewhat disturbing to the Western observer. To hurt or to abandon the uncle or the aunt or the older brother or older sister, therefore, can provoke a peculiar and lifelong guilt; and to be hurt by them, forever gnawing resentment. Thus many live always dependent, expectant, demanding, sulking, despairing, and yet always seeking the fusion which affirms, confirms, fulfills. Such expectance of reunification by fate *can*, in turn, lead to an utterly passive sense of non-responsibility as an individual, and to a waiting for salvation by some form of re-immersion.

For "Father Time" in India is a Mother. The World is an Inner Space; and if Freud gently chided Romain Rolland for his "oceanic feeling," a sense of being enveloped, embedded, and carried by the world—that feeling is what made Rolland (and also Hermann Hesse) a Western spokesman for at least the more self-conscious Indian's sense of time and space. Now every man's inner life is a composite of the modern and the archaic, the logical and the nonrational, the proper and the passionate. But Indians, I believe, live in more centuries at the same time than most other peoples; and every Indian, be he ever so well educated and pragmatic, lives also in a feminine space time that is deep inside a HERE and in the very center of a NOW, not so much an observer of a continuum of means and ends but a participant in a flux marked by the intensity of confluence. "Purpose" is to move on augmented, rather than to complete and leave behind. Where else in the world is the promise that something will soon be "finalized" used with such magic evasion? But it often expresses only the grim determination to pretend to be striving toward a definite goal—and to postpone the reaching of that goal at all cost. (The word "hopefully" may well be an equally defeatist counterpart in America today: it often means that one continues to go through the motions, although one strongly suspects the enterprise to be hopeless.) Indians know all this, and cartoons in the press are the best in the world in making fun of a nation's efforts to confound its inconsistencies while pretending to rise above them. All of this makes the truly pragmatic and scientific Indian of today only that much more outstanding —and often tragic.

Historically all this *may* be related to an ancient and stubborn trend to preserve the India of the mother goddesses against all the conquerors, their father gods, and their historical logic. The power of the mother goddesses probably has also given India that basic bisexuality which, at least to her British conquerors, appeared contemptible and yet also uncanny and irresistible in every sense of the word. Gandhi, so it seems, tried to make himself the representative of that bisexuality in a combination of autocratic malehood and enveloping maternalism. He may thus have succeeded in gathering in what was at loose ends in the lives of his followers and, indeed, of the masses. Against all this (I began to realize), Gandhi had tried to erect a bulwark based on radical factualness, obsessive punctuality, and absolute responsibility—all within a meaningful flux which he called Truth. In doing so, he wrought such changes in people that meeting him remained *the* irreversible encounter of their lives. He seemed to be the One who could be the counterplayer of all. Thus fusion led to an immersion which he could transform into lifelong commitment and a competence of service beyond the powers previously suspected in the individuals so selected. This, at any rate, seemed to be true (and worth following up) for those who joined him in Ahmedabad, in the decisive year of 1918.

# CHAPTER
# III

# The Elusive Event

NOW THAT I KNEW THE SCENE, the strike of 1918 seemed to me to have not only a certain dramatic and psychoanalytic interest but also a crucial importance in history, a feeling which was growing stubbornly against what little evidence had come my way. True, there is only one little paperbound pamphlet on the strike; it is less than a hundred pages long and costs 35 cents.[15] And what the witnesses of that Event could tell me was highly fragmentary. In Gandhi's biographies and even in his Autobiography, this first fast is even described as somewhat of a mistake, a failure of nerve if also obviously the first use of a mighty weapon. Such a failure by no means diminishes a clinician's interest: for how did Gandhi get into this situation in the first place? And if, indeed, he failed, why did he, or why did he think so? He was "drawn into it," his followers say; but I began to doubt that this wily little man ever was drawn into a decision which he did not choose for long- (very long-) range reasons.

This is how Gandhi reports the Event in his Autobiography.[16] In a chapter called "In Touch with Labour"[17] he gives more than half the space to a previous campaign in which "my co-workers and I had built many castles in the air, but they all vanished for the time being." Then he reports on the "delicate situation" in Ahmedabad, where "Shrimati Anasuyabai had to battle against her own brother, Shri Ambalal Sarabhai." His relations with both, he reports, were friendly, and "that made fighting with them the more difficult." But he considered the case of the mill hands strong, and he therefore "had to advise the labourers to go on strike." There follows a summary, less than one page long, of twenty-one days which will, of course, be retold in great detail once we have prepared our case for claiming a central position for the Event in Gandhi's life history, in the history of Indian Labor, and in that of militant nonviolence. On the one page devoted to the strike, however, there are two mismemories, as I will show later.

The Mahatma then drops the whole matter (without any concluding moral or, indeed, conclusion to the story), only to offer as his next installment "A Peep into the Ashram."[18] Recounting that because of the plague the ashram had been removed from the suburb of Kochrab to its present site by the Sabarmati, then far removed from the city, he takes time out to be lyrical in the description of the landscape and humorous in regard to its exact location:

> . . . Its vicinity to the Sabarmati Central Jail was for me a special attraction. As jail-going was understood to be the normal lot of Satyagrahis, I liked this position.[19]

There they lived at first under canvas with a tin shed for a kitchen. Half of this installment, however, is devoted to the daily encounter of his ashramites with the snakes which infested the ashram grounds. And the Mahatma concludes:

> The rule of not killing venomous reptiles has been practiced for the most part at Phoenix, Tolstoy Farm and Sabarmati. At each of these places we had to settle on waste lands. We have had, however, no loss of life occasioned by snake bite. . . . if it be a superstition to believe that complete immunity from harm for twenty-five years in spite of a fairly regular practice of nonkilling is not a fortuitous accident but a grace of God, I should still hug that superstition.[20]

Today we have naturalistic grounds for believing that this was no superstition; and we will discuss in a later chapter other instances of pacific propensities on the part of beasts. Here the point is that only after this "peep into the ashram" does the

Mahatma return to the strike and report on his first fast and on its ambiguous outcome. He seems to have felt that by fasting he had blackmailed the employers as much as he had kept the weakening workers in line, so that the relative success of the strike was marred by a failure of moral nerve. But what could the nonkilling of snakes have to do with the Ahmedabad strike and with Gandhi's relation to the mill owner?

I came to suspect, then, that that strike and that fast represented a demonstrable crisis in the middle age of a great man and was worthy of study as such. I had been asked often, of course, how and where Gandhi "solved his identity crisis." But that—if any one event ever symbolizes it—had happened way back in the railroad station of Maritzburg in South Africa when he, the ineffectual and yet stubborn young barrister-made-in-England, was ejected from a train because he insisted on traveling first-class although he was a "coolie," that is, "coloured." There, instead of effecting his plans to go home to the hated practice of law, he abandoned his shy self literally overnight and committed himself to his political and religious destiny as a leader. In 1918, however, Gandhi was already nearly fifty years old. But the surviving witnesses were in their middle and late twenties and could be suspected to have joined him while still in *their* identity crises. So here was a crisis in a middle-aged leader which I could study by studying those who, when they met him, had been struggling for their identity.

My growing interest in this confrontation of Gandhi and Ahmedabad seemed to be leading me into an "in-between" period of Gandhi's life: the South African Gandhi already had become historical and had earned himself the renown due to *a* mahatma, while the history of Gandhiji, *the* Mahatma of all India, had not yet begun.

Saying good-bye to Ambalal, to Anasuya, and to Shankerlal, I knew that in order to see whether there *was* a story here, I would have to come back with the sole purpose of talking to them and to some other people of their age group and experience. Shankerlal agreed strongly, and he asked me to speak on my last day in Ahmedabad to the daily prayer meeting at the

Textile Association. In hearing myself talk to them about 1918, I knew I had some kind of story to tell.

Before I left India, I took a quick glance at old newspapers and documents. Nothing could have been more discouraging. The London *Times* had only noted sarcastically:

Passive resistance is an obsession with Mr. Gandhi, and he applies it to every issue. Recently he sought to coerce Ahmedabad mill owners into granting their employees a 37 per cent increase in wages by vowing abstention from food until the increase was granted. The dispute was settled by a childish compromise. Mr. Gandhi's honesty is recognized, but some of those associated with him want to embarrass the Government.[21]

And even this was more than the Indian papers had to say about the event. The *Bombay Chronicle*—the English-language paper in the Bombay Presidency (which then included Gujarat and Ahmedabad)—only wondered why Mr. M. K. Gandhi had staked so much on this local matter from which he had "little to gain and everything to lose."[22] This attitude could be classified as a "pre-historic" view conducive to retrospective correction after Mr. M. K. Gandhi's entry into national and international history. But there was also a decidedly ahistoric undertone in some of the news of the day which did not augur well for any inquiry. Of the group of mill owners headed by Ambalal, the same correspondent from Ahmedabad reported to the *Chronicle:*

. . . When its labours are over and the task it has put its hand to is accomplished, it will again melt away and no one will care to know what it was and how it came into being.[23]

And things did not improve when I looked for other documents. It soon seemed as if there had been no fire or flood, no lonely bookworm or busy tribe of ants, no fire-setting rebel or neglectful bureaucrat who had not set out to destroy the bits of fresh evidence which I felt I needed. The British Commissioner of Ahmedabad had at one time ordered all the records of the Navajivan Trust (Gandhi's literary heirs) destroyed, while his own records went up in flames in 1946–47.

I visited the Ahmedabad Millowners' Association. Climbing up the ramp to that fortress built by Le Corbusier with all the wastefulness of concrete which characterizes the post-Mogul grandeur of modern India, I found the halls grand, cool, and airy, but the offices empty. Only chattering sweepers were to be seen and heard. Finally peeking into an open door, I saw handsome old Professor Acharya, erstwhile teacher of Sanskrit and new secretary of the association, sitting at his desk like the statue of a Roman senator. 1918? No, there was no use looking. There was "not a scrap of paper" from the time before the middle twenties, and even after that much material had been lost in transit from inner Ahmedabad to this colossal new home by the river.

The Library of the State of Maharashtra in Bombay, heir to many files of the State of Gujarat, refused outright to let me see them. But the Library of the Government of India in Delhi (who are not planning, as is the Government of Maharashtra, to use these documents in a major publication of their own) did not hesitate to let me see some of what I had been refused in Bombay. So there, at last, the Index of the Home Department registered: "1918, Part B, Regarding a dispute by the mill owners and their employees at Ahmedabad." But a parenthesis added "destroyed."

Assuming that the Commissioner and others must have reported to their home offices in London, I subsequently inquired at the library of the old India Office in London, only to be told that the documents of 1918 would not be released until 1969. I was notified that

. . . any official comments by the governments, Local Commissioner, etc., on the strike would be most likely to be found in the series of Official Records, such as the Proceedings of the Judicial and Public Department, and such series, under the law by which official documents less than fifty years old may not be made available to the public, are only available for consultation up to the year 1914.

An influential Indian who graciously offered his help received this notification from the India Office records:

I have examined the Judicial and Public and Revenue and Statistics Departments' Registers and Indexes, but we appear to hold no documents relating to the Ahmedabad Mill Strike of 1918 and Gandhi's first fast. I have also tried Parliamentary Papers and the *Bombay Native Newspaper Reports* without success. An official of the Library's European Manuscripts section has consulted the Montagu and Chelmsford Collections but also without result.

At the end my best friends were the British spies of the Criminal Intelligence Division of the old Home Department, who dutifully reported what they had observed, in documents which had been marked "to be burned" but, of course, had escaped this fate. Those men had observed well. Sitting at my desk in the National Archives in Delhi, I found myself saluting smartly (to the wonderment of the studious readers around me) the memory of a secret operative who had left this bit of prophecy in the intelligence file for February, 1918:

Whilst I am not disposed to attach any importance to Muhamidan ebullition at the Calcutta meeting, I fear that Mr. Gandhi's advice may not fall on altogether deaf ears. Combining as he does with the earnestness of a fanatic, the unselfishness and simplicity of living of a Sanyasi, his advice is more likely to be followed than that of any other agitator in the Presidency.[24]

A month later there was another weekly report which had escaped the fate of burning with equal insubordination: "In reality, the mill owners are afraid of Gandhi and hope to break his power."

But I could find no reference to Gandhi's first fast in any public document or in the news sections of any major Indian newspaper of 1918. What a historical distance, then, from that first fast to the later ones when the world held its breath and when Indians would speak in whispers and many would refuse to light their candles and lanterns in the evening while the Mahatma fasted!

The later grandeur of his public fasting as a political act was in 1918 simply not part of anybody's expectation—except, so I have come to believe strongly, his own. And, indeed, at the time, Gandhi told Mahadev Desai, the fast had been "the most valuable lesson of my life" and his "best deed so far."[25] And finally, in leafing gingerly but determinedly through a crumbling number of the *Bombay Chronicle* of March 1918, I found back among the letters to the editor a long epistle signed M. K. Gandhi and coolly captioned "Mr. Gandhi's Opinion."[26]

The letter commenced with the sentence:

Perhaps I owe an explanation to the public with regard to my recent fast. Some friends consider the action to have been silly, others cowardly and some others still worse. In my opinion, I would have been untrue to my Maker and to the cause I was espousing if I had acted otherwise.[27]

And it ended thus:

. . . I felt that it was a sacred moment for me, my faith was on the anvil, and I had no hesitation to rising and declaring to the men that a breach of their vow so solemnly taken was unendurable by me and that I would not take any food until they had the 35 per cent increase given or until they had fallen. A meeting that was up to now unlike the former meetings, totally unresponsive, woke up as if by magic.[28]

Gandhi, then, had himself attempted to bring the fast to the immediate attention of the major papers of India! But, alas, it was not "newsworthy."

I left India with the determination to study this matter, and to return in order to interview those who had witnessed the Event. My curiosity was increased by two factors:

When I came to Ahmedabad, it had become clear to me (for I had just come from the disarmament conference of the American Academy of Arts and Sciences) that man as a species can no longer afford any more to cultivate illusions either about his own "nature" or about that of other species, or about those "pseudo-species" he calls enemies—not while inventing and manufacturing arsenals capable of global destruction and while relying for inner and outer peace solely on the superbrakes built into the superweaponry. And Gandhi seems to have been the only man who has visualized *and* demonstrated an over-all alternative.

Less nobly, I should admit that I must have been looking for a historical figure to write about. What could be more fitting than (as my students put it) letting "Young Man Luther" be followed by "Middle-Aged Mahatma"? And here I had witnesses: the survivors of a generation of then-young men and women who had joined or met Gandhi in 1918, and whose lives had not been the same since, as if one knew what they might have been. They included, besides the mill owner and his sister, individuals now retired or still in the forefront of national activity in industry, in the Union Cabinet, or in Parliament. These I set out to meet and to interview on my subsequent visits to India.

# PART ONE

## The Inquiry

IF HISTORY is a collection of events which come to life for us because of what some actors did, some recorders recorded, and some reviewers decided to retell, a clinician attempting to interpret an historical event must first of all get the facts straight. But he must apply to this task what he has learned, namely, to see in all factuality some relativities which arise from the actors', the recorders', and the reviewers' motivations. Having been altogether impressionistic in describing some of my experiences at the time when the plan for this review emerged, let me now be didactic and say that the psycho-historian will want to inquire in some detail after the *stage of life* in which the actor acted, the recorder recorded, and the reviewer reviewed. He will want to learn about the place of that stage in the *life cycles* of each of these individuals; and he will want to relate their life cycles to the *history* of their communities.

In all this, the clinician wants to remain as analytical and, in fact, self-analytical as the data permit, that is, he would like to fathom as much of the unconscious motivation involved as is feasible and useful. Where this concerns the reviewer's self-analysis, the reader, I am sure, will thank him for being altogether candid only with himself, workably candid with his coworkers and discussants, and candid with his readers only within the limits of readability. With this, I have made a beginning which will permit me to account, as necessity arises, for my personal involvement in the data to be gathered. So far, I hope to have said enough to indicate that the psycho-historian's choice of subject often originates in early ideals or identifications and that it may be important for him to accept as well as he can some deeper bias than can be argued out on the level of verifiable fact or faultless methodology.

But enough of me. What is fair for the reviewer is fair also for the recorders of the Event, whether they now retell it for me at my request, or have recorded it in writing in the past. In Gandhi's case, however, the recorder is the actor turned autobiographer a decade after the Event.

# CHAPTER

# I

# The Witnesses

## 1. THE AUTOBIOGRAPHY

IN ASKING why Gandhi may have understated the Event in his Autobiography, disregarding or having forgotten the fact that he had himself announced it to the six main newspapers in India as newsworthy and as deeply representative of his impending leadership, we face the general questions as to when in Gandhi's life the Autobiography was written; why it was written at that time; what sense it made in the context of Gandhi's previous life; what community it was written for; and what sense such communication made in the history of that community. The general dearth of data, as we have seen, does not necessarily bespeak the historical negligibility of the Event, but is explainable by the very nature of the historical moment, namely, a lull just before the Mahatma's sudden ascendance. But why would Gandhi himself treat the Event as he did? If this is the first question to be asked, it will also be the last to be answered in this book. It is the first because, in attempting to understand any part of Gandhi's life, one almost reflexively turns to the Autobiography, to see what it meant to him. It is the last to be answered because Gandhi wrote the Autobiography at the very end of the period to be reviewed here. Nevertheless, the Autobiography is the work to be quoted most often throughout this book and undoubtedly is the only work written by and about Gandhi which most readers have read—or tried to read.

Gandhi commenced what is alternately called *An Autobiography* or *The Story of My Experiments with Truth* in 1925. By
then he had risen high, far above the leadership of the Indians in
South Africa, not to speak of some local peasantry or workmen
in India. By then, he had, in fact, led the first national civil disobedience in history. But he was now at a certain standstill. His
first period of leadership had been cut short by the trial in
Ahmedabad in 1922. He had spent a period in jail much shorter
than the six years decreed by his sentence, because he was
removed to a hospital when he developed an acute appendicitis
and then was released. Yet, there is reason to assume that
Gandhi, who never wanted to get away with anything, had
accepted the sentence of six years (on which, after all, he had
proudly insisted) as somehow binding, so that to himself he was,
as it were, an extramural prisoner of the British until the period
of the sentence expired. At any rate, during those six years he
showed a remarkable restraint in attacking the British, while
concentrating entirely on a reform of the festering dangers of
India's inner conditions. For at the time he was jailed, he had
come to the conviction that India had not proven ready for civil
disobedience; he had, in fact, countermanded that great undertaking right in the middle of it, facing the double accusation that
he had led his people into a revolt for which they had not been
ready and that he had abandoned them before success or failure
could be proven. No wonder that both the Mahatma's health and
his mood were highly vulnerable during this period. After the
Bombay riots in November 1921, C. F. Andrews had already described him as "haggard and emaciated, as one who had just
passed through the valley of the shadow of death."[1]

After his release in 1924, furthermore, he had found the
political climate changed. What unity he had been able to create
between Hindus and Muslims and between loyalists and non-
cooperators had been decisively weakened. His followers in
nonviolence and noncooperation who had tried to maintain his
program until he could take over again had widely acquired the
nickname *no-changers*. Gandhi himself withdrew from politics

and devoted himself to his own purification and to that of India, both to be achieved by spinning, praying, and ascetic living according to the faith which never left him, namely, that purity is (and brings) freedom, even as truth is (and results in) non-violence. He said he wanted again to work his way into the people's hearts "silently so far as possible, even as I did between 1915 and 1919." But he had now tasted the danger of violence ensuing from ill-applied nonviolence. He was often depressed, and he fasted to fight depression. Concluding a twenty-one-day fast in 1924 (that is, when he was contemplating his Autobiography), he said a prayer which can only impress us with his conflict between power and spirit:

Presently from the world of peace I shall enter the world of strife. . . . O! God, make me Thy instrument and use me as Thou wilt. Man is nothing. Napoleon planned much and found himself a prisoner in St. Helena. The mighty Kaiser aimed at the crown of Europe and is reduced to the status of a private gentleman. God has so willed it. Let us contemplate such examples and be humble.[2]

During this period he instituted his "silent days," and even as he started the Autobiography, he entered into a year of "political silence." In the speaking and writing of these years, he consolidated the Mahatmaship exactly midway between the life of a culturally influential saint and potential creator of a new secular religion—and that of a resurgent politician, this time on the solid basis of a wide popular appeal and a disciplined following. And although at that point he had already reached the end of the plateau and saw that a sudden new upsurge of power was ahead of him, he concluded the Autobiography as he had started it years earlier:

. . . I must reduce myself to zero. So long as a man does not of his own free will put himself last among his fellow creatures, there is no salvation for him. Ahimsa is the farthest limit of humility.

In bidding farewell to the reader, for the time being, at any rate, I ask him to join with me in prayer to the God of Truth that He may grant me the boon of Ahimsa in mind, word, and deed.[3]

Certainly these three little words—mind, word, and deed—insist on a rank order of concerns not typical for politicians.

Yet, none of the foregoing is meant to obliterate the public and private image of Gandhi as a ceaseless reformer and a pilgrim with spurts of enormous energy. It is only to indicate the philosophical and, on occasion, emotional mood with which the autobiographer looked back on the little boy and the youth he had been, on the man he had become, and on the time when he had settled in Ahmedabad, had been supported by Ambalal and other mill owners, and yet in 1918 had led the strike against them.

What has been said, then, about the Autobiography is essential for an understanding of Gandhi's references to all the preceding stages of his life and thus is a necessary background also for his account of the events in Ahmedabad. But before I come to that, I must point to certain hindrances to a truer recognition of Gandhi's style of living and speaking, at least for those who read only his Autobiography or interpretations based on it. The first is the fact that it was written in Gandhi's native Gujarati, a language spoken by only less than one tenth of his countrymen. For the rest of them it was translated into at least a dozen other Indian languages, while for his English-speaking countrymen, as for us, it was translated by that same Mahadev Desai to whom we owe the story of the strike. He translated it, no doubt, faithfully, with a pedantic devotion such as Gandhi cultivated in his secretaries, although some later transcended it in their own literary work. I should make it quite clear that I do not doubt the *factuality* of either the Autobiography or the translation; yet I believe that, together, they manage to submerge the subdued passion, the significant poignancy, and the gentle humor which often characterize Gandhi's Gujarati, as well as his use of English.

Another difficulty is the later appearance of Gandhi's autobiographic accounts in book form: they were in no way written as a book. Here is Gandhi's honest and much-ignored statement of method—the method of writing columns or homilies:

. . . as I have finished the history of Satyagraha in South Africa, I am tempted to undertake the autobiography for *Navajivan*. The Swami [Anand] wanted me to write it separately for publication as a book. But

I have no spare time [I do not have that much time]. I could only write a
chapter week by week. [If I write it, it could be for *Navajivan* only.]
Something has to be written for *Navajivan* every week. Why should it
not be the autobiography? The Swami agreed to the proposal [accepted
the decision], and here I am hard at work.[4]

It took the Mahatma years to write the installments which, at
the end, became a book that was no book, and which yet, maybe
for that very reason, impressed millions of readers who could
"take" a chapter at a time, as one takes a sermon and a lesson at
a time. The historical researcher, however, must know that the
very soul of the Autobiography—and even the soul of its propaganda—is a striving for *Moksha*.

## 2. THE SURVIVORS

MY WITNESSES, men and women now in their middle seventies,
had met Gandhi in their twenties, the age on which I focused in
my book on young Luther. Whatever their identity conflicts
were when they met Gandhi—and I will describe later how he
selected and seduced them—their pasts have now become part of
his life and his death. The history they made together has left
them in varying degrees the heirs of both a political and a
spiritual revolution—heirs charged with the practical and even
opportunistic maintenance of a new nation; or men and women
forever living in a glorious past when historical actuality had
been quickened to a rare intensity and pace; or—as in the case of
the mill owner—occupied with the continuance of their lives
and businesses under vastly changed conditions.

There were, then, first of all Ambalal and Anasuyaben
Sarabhai, who had been twenty-five and twenty-seven years old,
respectively, at the time of the strike. I returned to the Sarabhais'
Retreat in 1964, a year after the Seminar, in order to interview
them—none too early, for later that year Ambalal suffered a
severe stroke. But it so happened that by far the most energetic
and consistent helper in my work turned out to be Shankerlal
Banker, the man I had met on the morning walks of our initial
stay in Ahmedabad; he had been twenty-eight when he first met
Gandhi. I also interviewed Ambalal's neighbor, the powerful

industrialist, Kasturbhai Lalbhai, a mere twenty-four in 1918. Very briefly, I spoke to Home Minister Gulzarilal Nanda, who as a young student put his services at Gandhi's disposal and was chosen by him to be the first secretary of the Textile Labor Association in Ahmedabad at the age of twenty-two; and to the M. P. Indulal Yagnik, who in his early twenties had assisted Gandhi and now was the most vociferous, if not violent, opponent to this labor organization—a representative of everything the Event had failed to accomplish for labor. I have, of course, talked to many more individuals, but a somewhat more detailed account of my first meeting with some of them will prepare an account of the Event and at the same time convey the flavor of a biographic inquiry in India.

But first, again, a few general remarks. It would seem that psychoanalytic experience, applied to a formulated task and equipped with a firm conception of the life cycle, should have made it easy to grasp the dynamics of such interviewing. But it would be foolish to assume or, indeed, to wish that the element of initial noncomprehension and of subsequent surprise which characterizes any worthwhile encounter with patients should be absent here. And since this kind of work is relatively new, I will not hesitate to put before the reader some of the newness and much of the methodological and personal immaturity which plagues a new worker (of any age) when he comes up against the "resistances" offered by those who are asked to remember and re-record events of their pasts.

The central and aged figures in my account look back on Gandhiji with a certain detachment—as they must, for it is in the logic of the life cycle that they should try to end their lives with *their* integrity and not only with a reflection of the Mahatma's. It may be for this reason that I have learned most from individuals who, when he was alive, could meet Gandhi man to man or woman to man and who could differ with him openly just because they would not think of either submitting to or competing with him. With them he could laugh, and they now have a better conscience in being without him; they do, in fact, laugh with him as they pensively smile at his memory.

But all these men and women are in a permanent state of mild mourning as, indeed, India is. They, as did all India (at least for some periods of unity), felt augmented in his presence beyond personal desert and native capacity, and now they have to overcome a certain reluctance to be drawn back into an all-too-concrete memory of that presence. I will not forget the consternation which I caused in some of Gandhi's old friends when I asked them to stand up and show me how tall he was as compared with them. It became clear that, while in fact small, he seemed immeasurable. The passing of such a pervasive light leaves the dark even darker and the once-enlightened suddenly forlorn. For the numinous person has the strange power to make the participant feel part of him and yet also feel augmented in himself; and both of these augmentations are apt to wane when the great moment is over. Then defensiveness may set in: each tries to hold on to his own version of the uniqueness of what has passed, and each mistrusts the other for trying to appropriate and to "sell" (sometimes without quotation marks) one version of what was a collective and yet also a deeply individual experience.

Those men and women who *had* been in Ahmedabad in 1918 or had come there immediately afterward as a consequence of the founding of the labor movement—those I asked, of course, to tell me what they knew of the strike. But not all my informants had been "in" on the Ahmedabad Event itself. Some I met only by way of courtesy visits; and yet I asked them all these questions: where and when did you first meet Gandhiji? And what would you say was to you the essence of his presence?

Mostly, the answers would be preceded by a quick smile which was like a dawn breaking through fog, while each reply was highly personal. "Gandhiji?" Ambalal, sitting behind his big desk, said without a moment's hesitation. "Oh, he was like a good night's sleep." "Gandhiji?" Anasuya (early orphaned) exclaimed, "Oh, he was my mother!" But the most universal answer to the question as to what one felt around him was: "In his presence *one could not tell a lie.*" Such exclamations, childlike in the best sense, were typical also for men who by their early contact with Gandhi had been propelled into the power structure of modern India and had learned only too well how to respond politely and vaguely to inquisitive foreigners. When asked about their first meeting with Gandhi, they would, if only for a moment, sit back with the expression of an imaginative child and remember the beginning of it all. On visiting the Vice President, Zakir Husain, I had to make my way through a resplendent cortege, reminiscent of both the Moguls and the British Raj, which was waiting at the gate and in the arching driveway of his villa to take him to a cabinet affair, for he was acting President at the time. I felt almost guilty when, under such circumstances, my question as to what Gandhiji had meant to him when he was a student seemed to make him forget the present. Recalled, as it were, by an aide, he arrived at the meeting, I later learned, with an enigmatic smile and the pre-occupied remark that he would have preferred to talk some more to "the American professor."

And yet, Zakir Husain (now President of India) is typically a man who speaks of the Mahatma as a man and with the objectivity born of respectful disagreement. Only with utmost caution can one approach unreconstructed Gandhiites for information, for they not only repeat in perpetuity what Gandhiji or Bapuji or Mahatmaji said at one time or another but also insist that they know exactly what he would have said were he still living—a brazen assumption habitual to the faithful followers of all great men but especially disconcerting in individuals who should remember how eminently surprising Gandhi's utterances and decisions could be—at the time. But this kind of preconception is the fate of any "ism" as I, a Freudian, should know. The "truest" Gandhiites I met, although the exclusive owners of so many original facts of Gandhi's life, were also the least helpful in elucidating the Ahmedabad Event for me, unwilling or hesitant as they were to believe that a presence such as Gandhi's, in order to remain alive or indeed to become alive for mankind beyond India, must be retold in terms of a new age. They wanted to retell it, over and over, the way it had come to seem to them.

But then, this was true for all informants: the closer I came to asking for simple facts, the more they mistrusted me, as if I were trying to get "behind" the sacred appearance. On the other hand, cautious as I was, or indeed mindful simply of getting at necessary data, my informants would sometimes open up with very personal confessions and, indeed, with memories, dreams, and fantasies which I had in no way solicited or expected.

But then, what was I looking for? I was a psychoanalyst, my informants knew, and men of my kind do not merely ask for facts that can be put on the dotted line but really want to discover hidden meanings within the facts and between the lines. Some had met psychoanalysts, bona fide ones and quacks, and had been subjected to interpretations of both Gandhi's unconscious and their own. A psychoanalyst studying an historical event could, on the basis of the very history of his field, mean to them only a clinician looking for the neurosis in the greatness of a man and searching for case histories among his followers—case histories in which he could find verification for Freud's theories or his own. And it would have been both unjust and useless to treat such apprehensions as altogether unfounded.

There is no doubt that to any trained clinician a man's conflicts represent what he "really" is, and this not only because clinical know-how is set to gauge conflicts but also because clinical curiosity is sanctioned by the endeavor to cure and to help. In transferring clinical insights to historical persons and events, however, the clinician all too easily makes himself believe that he is engaged in "therapy" on a larger (social, historical) scale. Therefore, any reluctance on the part of his informants to provide him with the necessary data is, to him, a "resistance" analogous to the one expected in patients who so perversely protect themselves against the very insights which might rid them of their symptoms. In fact, we must first free the term from the connotation of a conscious, insincere, and fraudulent reluctance to tell the truth. The term resistance was, in fact, adopted by Freud not as a moral opprobrium but as part of the physicalistic vocabulary of his time: some "resistance" is in the nature of all response to inquiry. Just as one would not expect to encounter electricity except in a medium which, depending on its structure, "resists" conduction, so we would not or should not expect the possibility of a totally "free" communication of memories or motives: they, too, have to "pass" a medium. While one might expect a word such as "resistance" to carry the connotation of a conscious refusal to comply, it means (even on its clinical home ground) exactly the opposite, namely, an involuntary, necessary, and inherent difficulty in any communication offered under the special condition of being the subject of an inquiry.

The psychoanalyst-turned-historian, then, must adapt himself to and learn to utilize a new array of "resistances" before he can confidently know that he is encountering those he is accustomed to. There is, first of all, the often incredible or implausible claim of having lost memorabilia—a claim which can be variably attributed to simple carelessness on the part of witnesses, or to a lack of awareness, or, indeed, an absence of candor. Deeper difficulties, however, range from an almost cognitively a-historical orientation—ascribed by some to Indians in general—to a highly idiosyncratic reluctance to lose the past by formulating it. Here the myth-affirming and myth-destroying propensities of a post-charismatic period must be seen as the very stuff history is made of. Where mythmaking predominates, every item of a great man's life becomes or is reported as a parable, while those who cannot commit themselves to this trend must disavow it with destructive fervor. I, for one, have rarely met anybody of whatever level of erudition or information, in India or elsewhere, who was not willing and eager to convey to me the whole measure of the Mahatma as based on one sublime or scandalous bit of hearsay. And some formulas sanctify him in a manner which dispose of a true man just as totally as do the formulas which define him by what he was not—not a saint or not a statesman, not a true Indian or not a literate man. One begins to sense that we now live in the aftermath of the Mahatmaship even as the Event to be retold in this book appears to have taken place in the lull before it: it is as though a man had passed by who simply made too great demands on all as well as himself and must, therefore, be disposed of somehow. Thus, the funeral pyre which consumed his remains to ashes often seems to be an elemental act of pity and charity compared to the totem meal by which his memory is now being devoured by friends and adversaries alike: many feed on him, deriving pride from having owned him, from having intelligently disposed of him, or from being able to classify the lifeless pieces. But nobody thereby inherits (for this is the archaic illusion of a totem meal) what held him together and what gave him—and through him, millions—a special kind of vitalizing aliveness which does not seem expendable in this world.

There are those whose lives became part of their leader's and who therefore had to incorporate him into their self-image. They must consider his image as well as their own an invested possession to be shared only according to custom and religion, personal style—and stage of life. Here it becomes especially clear that a man in the wake of great events will want to divest himself of his past only in order to cure, to purify, or to sell himself; wherefore the psycho-historian may do well to clarify his informant's general purpose—as well as his own.

# The Counterplayer

BECAUSE Ambalal Sarabhai was Gandhi's prime counterplayer in the Event, and because I found interviewing him a strangely upsetting experience, I will report my difficulties in some detail in order to indicate the kind of ambivalences which may enter historical work. If in this I spare neither myself nor my respondent, it must be remembered that, from a psycho-historical point of view, there can be no historical evidence without an encounter between reviewer and recorder, and no encounter without ambivalence.

In his letter to the press regarding his fast in the mill strike, Gandhi wrote:

. . . I cannot conclude this letter without mentioning two names of whom India has every reason to be proud. The mill-owners were represented by Mr. Ambalal Sarabhai who is a gentleman in every sense of the term. He is a man of great culture and equally great abilities. He adds to these qualities a resolute will. The mill-hands were represented by his sister, Anasuyaben. She possesses a heart of gold. She is full of pity for the poor. The mill-hands adore her. Her word is law with them. I have not known a struggle fought with so little bitterness and such courtesy on either side. This happy result is principally due to the connections with it of Mr. Ambalal Sarabhai and Anasuyaben.[5]

Such enthusiasm for his principal adversary in the Ahmedabad episode did not exactly serve to diminish the widespread suspi-

cion that the strike had ended with a Bania deal and that the
national and international cause of labor had been sold down the
Sabarmati. But more about this later.

In the first chapter, I suggested briefly the difference in the
life styles of this brother and sister. But, in all their difference,
they seem to have lived close to each other in a relationship of
mutual respect and familial loyalty which began when they
were early orphaned together and which certainly survived the
years of Anasuya's work on behalf of Ahmedabad labor. Ambalal, it seems, always considered it Anasuya's right as a woman
and her privilege as his sister to help the workers establish a labor
organization with and against which he could bargain forcefully.

The Sarabhai profile shared by most of the sons and daughters
does not seem to come from their father but from their mother,
whose dignity and energy I have described earlier. Ambalal's
features and physical appearance are on the whole undistin-
guished except for lines of a delicate strength which, one can
believe, could be quietly tough in the pursuit of his economic
rights as well as determined in the defense of those whose civil
rights he had made his own. Both he and his wife give the
impression of being stubborn and somewhat righteous people,
made tolerant, however, by what they themselves have suffered
from the orthodoxies of their respective castes and their social
milieus. At public functions they seem somewhat isolated from
their peers, whether they keep aloof, or whether they are being
avoided. I observed that whenever, at a public function, the
governor of the state of Gujarat would appear, he would single
them out for the first *namastes* (greetings). They both dress
simply and exquisitely, he usually in the finest raw silk and Jain
cap, she in immaculate khadi. At the time of our interviews he
was still being driven to his office almost every morning, although he was slightly stooped, dragged one leg, and slurred his
speech—the evidence of a number of small strokes.

I have described Ambalal and Saraladevi's unconditional help-
fulness at the time of Joan's illness; and I will (getting far ahead
of my story) quote here a passage from one of the last chapters
of Gandhi's Autobiography concerning an experience a few

months *after* the strike when he fell severely ill from despair, it would seem, as much as from exhaustion.

. . . The exhaustion brought on a delirious fever. The friends got more nervous, and called in more doctors. But what could they do with a patient who would not listen to them?

Sheth Ambalal with his good wife came down to Nadiad, conferred with my co-workers, and removed me with the greatest care to his Mirzapur bungalow in Ahmedabad. It was impossible for anyone to receive more loving and selfless service than I had the privilege of having during this illness.[6]

As hosts, the couple were truly gracious, and over an after-dinner cigar Ambalal offered on our first visit many small confidences including what Gandhiji used to say on this occasion or that and, in fact, a number of stories which had stimulated my interest in the Event. So I had every reason to believe that I could count on him to help me in elucidating his relation to Gandhi.

A marked change had come over him, however, when I returned about a year later for a more formal inquiry and when he learned that I might be writing a book. Although I was staying in a small house on his estate, put at my disposal by his son Gautam, Ambalal now insisted that to see him, I would have to come to his executive office in the Calico Mills. There he sat behind his big desk in a Western business suit, asking me softly but sternly what I wanted. I told him that I had read the references to him in Gandhi's Autobiography and that he had often mentioned Gandhiji in our conversations; that I would like to explain to Western readers some less well-known aspects of Gandhi's personality and of the inception of Satyagraha in India; and that, since he and Gandhi had shared such a memorable capacity to be good opponents, I hoped he would help me by letting me check a few points with him. He waited, somewhat coldly, for the first point. I mentioned the mural behind the Birla House in Delhi, but he would not confirm that he was the man about whom Gandhi said in his Autobiography:

One morning [this must have been in late 1915 or early 1916 and thus well *before* the strike] shortly after Maganlal had given me warning of our monetary plight, one of the children came and said that a Sheth who was waiting in a car outside wanted to see me. I went out to him. "I want to give the Ashram some help. Will you accept it?" he asked.

"Most certainly," said I. "And I confess I am at the present moment at the end of my resources."

"I shall come tomorrow at this time," he said. "Will you be here?"

"Yes," said I, and he left.

Next day, exactly at the appointed hour, the car drew up near our quarters, and the horn was blown. The children came with the news. The Sheth did not come in. I went out to see him. He placed in my hands currency notes of the value of Rs. 13,000 and drove away.

I had never expected this help and what a novel way of rendering it! The gentleman had never before visited the Ashram. So far as I can remember, I had met him only once. No visit, no enquiries, simply rendering help and going away! This was a unique experience for me. . . . We now felt quite safe for a year.[7]

Now I had expected and still assume that in the heat of controversy during the strike rather unsavory things happened which Ambalal would be loath to deliver to an inquisitive foreigner. But it was surprising to see how he hesitated to admit items which we would consider perfectly decent, and which furthermore were already common knowledge. I asked him for an explanation of this. The identity of the donor, he told me, soon became known, and his wish to remain anonymous had been promptly misinterpreted: he was accused of having wished to escape the criticism of his caste. The implication of Ambalal's telling me this was clear: he much preferred remaining anonymous to having "lower" motivations attributed to him, a tendency which was and is, I can attest, the wont of some Ahmedabadis. And (this he did not admit at first) what could one expect of a psychoanalyst, even if one trusted him personally, the moment his professional interest entered the relationship?

I found out only much later that Ambalal had been recently exposed to a (non-clinical) situation in which a foreign psychoanalyst had offered interpretations which had seemed gratuitous to the industrialist. In retrospect I am glad that I did not know of this specific experience, for my ignorance forced me to view our relationship on its own terms. On the other hand, Ambalal had, as I knew from our after-dinner talks, an intense curiosity concerning psychoanalysis. Decades ago when he happened to be in Vienna, he had, in fact, visited Freud to see what kind of man he was and whether he could be trusted to help one of Ambalal's relatives; there, too, he had refused to give his name. I would not expect Freud to have taken kindly to such a refusal if, indeed, he cared.

His passion for anonymity, however, made me feel uncomfortable. I had been this man's guest, had sat and worked on his terrace, and had let him protect me against the stark facts of Indian life. And yet, how much does the presence of money—just plain More-Than-Enough-Money—do to the relationship between one who has it and one who has never had it? I realized how often I myself had sat behind *my* desk and all *it* symbolized, asking a moneyed individual: "What do you want from me?" in a tone indicating that I could not be bought and yet expecting him, if I did accept him as a patient, to pay for a considerable percentage of the living standards to which my profession had accustomed me. And here sat this man, implying that he had been glad to support my plans in general, but why should I—in return—pry into his past? What, indeed, *did* I want? I knew (as he knew) that if I were worth the salt of my training, I would be unable *not* to use the power which was my gift and vocation, namely, to read between the lines of whatever he would tell me, and that in future publications I intended to use any new insight which would bring me whatever name and money it was worth. Suddenly, the sense of therapeutic duty and medical tradition which had always helped restore my equanimity when I worried about having to publish clinical observations for the sake of advancing theory or technique—suddenly that sense of justification left me.

But Ambalal was preoccupied with his own discomfort. His very power of speech withdrew behind a whisper, which undoubtedly was a symptom of a slight paralysis, aggravated when he was fatigued, and yet also served as a screen which protected him against being understood—and misunderstood. "At any rate, don't mention the ashram scene in your book," he said. I told him again of the mural (which he had not seen), and I suggested that I would be perfectly satisfied if he would simply consent to verify or correct what was already known. He then went freely into other well-known facts which will find their place in my eventual narration of the strike.

When I left, he said with a not-very-relaxed smile, "So what have you learned now?" and I answered truthfully that I had learned to understand a bit of what Gandhi had been up against with him—and he with Gandhi. Although this remark was not made entirely without anger, or maybe because it was, it cleared the air, and Ambalal laughed. In the evening I found myself writing:

. . . The first interview kept to well-known facts, which Ambalal does not seem to know (or pretends not to know) are well known. The overall impression is of a man who considers even his historical role as private property.

But even as I was writing this, he telephoned me from his mansion (which I could see through the trees where I sat) to ask me not to mention a particular story he had told me that afternoon—a story which I had heard from several others and which, again, attested entirely to his courage and benevolence. I told him that the facts were well known. "Well," he said, "don't say I mentioned it." I laughed and then and there gave up trying to understand or fight Ambalal's reluctance to be quoted. As I write this, I know that by describing how he did *not* want to be quoted, I quote him almost vociferously; but I also hope that it will become clear that in doing so, I illustrate the fact that there is always a personal rock-bottom in any interviewing which must be accepted and respected, even if the focus of study is an event, not a man. And any attempt to analyze the man rather than his participation in the event is not only unfeasible outside the psychoanalytic setting but dangerous to the main undertaking.

Only after a while, however, did I realize how right I had been in telling Ambalal that the first interview had taught me something about him and Gandhi, although I should have added: and about myself, too. For no doubt my initial consternation had been due to a certain parallel between Gandhi's and my relationship to the mill owner. For had not Ambalal been my benefactor as well as Gandhi's? Had I not gladly accepted the wealthy man's hospitality when I was a newcomer to India—a haven of friendship and sanitary safety from which to venture out into an unknown land? Had not Gandhi gladly accepted his financial support when he came back from South Africa, in many ways a newcomer to India after twenty-five years of absence, and nearly abandoned by men of caste? And had not Ambalal treated Gandhi as an intruder when, instead of taking care of his ashram, he had made it his business to investigate labor relations even as I had now turned historian on Ambalal? The common factor which interests us here is, of course, the matter of that ambivalent kind of transference which we know so well from our clinical work. Transference is a universal tendency active wherever human beings enter into a relationship with others in such a way that the other *also* "stands for" persons as perceived in the pre-adult past: he thus serves the re-enactment of infantile and juvenile wishes and fears, hopes and apprehensions, and this always with a bewildering mixture of affects—that is, a ratio of loving and hateful tendencies which under certain conditions alternate radically. This phenomenon plays a singularly important role in the clinical encounter, and not only in the dependent patient's behavior toward the clinician but also as part of what the clinician must observe in himself; for he, too, can transfer onto different patients a variety of unconscious strivings which come from *his* infantile past. What I want to emphasize here is, in fact, my transference to Ambalal. For one harbors an unconscious transference onto any host, that is, the attribution of a father or older-brother role to anyone in whose home one seeks safety or in whose influence one finds security. I should add that in my case this theme seems to be anchored in the childhood experience—and, strictly speaking, this alone makes a true transference out of a mere thematic transfer—of having been a fatherless child who found a loving stepfather in a foreign country.

One ingredient of Ambalal's life history, however, was also a principal ingredient of his relationship to Gandhi and is, in fact (as I will show later), typical of the Indian scene and of the general atmosphere around Gandhi wherever he was. Behind Ambalal's obvious mixture of shyness and drive for power, of benevolence and severity, there are strong contending emotions of maternal solicitousness on the one hand and of an (almost dutiful) business sense on the other. This mixture could make him offer money to a not-yet-famous man such as Gandhi who seemed willing to be a failure and an outcast for mercy and for principle, and yet would permit him to protect the interests of industry when Gandhi seemed to be encroaching on them. It had made it possible for him to be a most considerate host while I was his guest, and yet to guard his privacy against my inquiry until he could be sure what *my* business proposition was and whether I intended to assail or to undermine his position. It was, then, only a gesture of a certain propriety that, for this kind of purpose, he insisted on my coming to his office.

In Ambalal, I (like Gandhi) was up against a man, who in some ways seemed to belong to feudal days and in others was always ahead of his time. Ambalal, for example, was willing to give—and then to give unexpectedly and overwhelmingly—when he was fully motivated to do so and never for any other reason. Such "motivation" has a somewhat special quality in an Indian, for it includes, beyond what may seem to Westerners a merely selfish reason for doing good, the question of what seems right and proper in the sense of *dharma*, that is, that wider propriety within one's total fate which does not always yield to the differentiation between egotism and altruism in the Calvinist sense—either in Ambalal's mind or in Gandhi's.

Heinrich Zimmer summarizes the meaning of *dharma* thus:

The correct manner of dealing with every life problem that arises, therefore, is indicated by the laws (*dharma*) of the caste (*varna*) to which one belongs, and of the particular stage-of-life (*asrama*) that is proper to one's age. One is not free to choose; one belongs to a species—a family, guild, and craft, a group, a denomination. And since this circumstance not only determines to the last detail the regulations for one's public and private conduct, but also represents (according to this all-inclusive and pervasive, unyielding pattern of integration) the real ideal of one's present natural character, one's concern as a judging and acting entity must be only to meet every life problem in a manner befitting the role one plays. Whereupon the two aspects of the temporal event—the subjective and the objective—will be joined exactly, and the individual eliminated as a third, intrusive factor. He will then bring into manifestation not the temporal accident of his own personality, but the vast, impersonal, cosmic law, and so will be, not a faulty, but a perfect glass: *anonymous* and *self-effacing*.[8]

These are high Western terms for intrinsic Eastern patterns. But one could err grievously by letting this ancient world-mood explain what is also determined by personality, vested interest, and (possibly) neurotic idiosyncrasy. The seminar, at any rate, had taught me how difficult it is to differentiate between stubborn and superstitious remnants of an orthodox world-image, personal and conscious emphases and omissions, and repressions and denials coming from irrational recesses. The fact is that none of these can be separated, for in any given life they have become intertwined, even as in any cultural situation economic fear, neurotic anxiety, and existential dread are always aggravated and alleviated—together.

Once I fully understood that Ambalal could take our encounter to be only that of two individuals with allegiances to their respective occupational *dharmas*, things became easier, and he eventually expressed his full confidence in my work. In conclusion, then, I believe that Ambalal's relationship to Gandhi and Gandhi's to Ambalal in all its "natural" ambivalence harbored a mutual respect for their *dharmas*. As Gandhi might well have expressed it himself: he was in the saint business and genuinely so, while Ambalal considered himself to be in the textile business, eager to make the most of it in all possible directions, and not letting anything interfere with the soul of business, which is business.

As to my relation with the mill owner, Ambalal seemed to feel—along with many educated Indians—that a different *dharma* gives one a different sense of causality, and he had sensed and resisted the radical determinism with which psychoanalytic interpretation reduces matters to a core of infantile and neurotic motivation. He later admitted this freely, but typically in a *social* situation when one of his daughters-in-law had joined us in the garden. There he told us what he thought a psychoanalyst *might* think was behind his maternal solicitude for members of his family and his many secret acts of benefaction. His explanation sounded insightful and well taken, although I had to insist that in his self-analysis he was more surgical with himself that I would have cared to be.

As for Ambalal's public image—which must interest us here—I believe that in acting within his *dharma*, he wished to be called neither softhearted and hardheaded, nor hardhearted and softheaded. He told me, for example, how he had opened eye clinics for his workers. The immediate "reason" for such generosity had been, he said, not an upsurge of humanitarian feeling, but rather the fact that one day at luncheon he had seen his wife and small daughter suffer under acute conjunctivitis, only to become aware on his drive back to work how many children along the road had trachoma. So he acted without delay. But once when he gave a large sum to the Labor Association (so one of the labor leaders told me), he said curtly, "Understand, this is not charity, just good business," and I dare say there is much self-respect and respect for the workers in such a statement. It *is* a feudal, as well as a personal, trait to extend a certain narcissistic and hypochondriac overconcern to one's family and then by further extension to others who become somehow (and sometimes quite accidentally) associated with them. Since this was one of Ambalal's traits, we shall see how Gandhi benefited from it, because (as always) he recognized and tried to utilize it—for the good of *his* cause.

In the meantime it may help to know that the enigma of Ambalal's shyness is one which goes back at least to the days of the strike. In the spring of 1918, a plague again broke out in Ahmedabad, and the Ahmedabad magazine, *Praja Bandhu*, reported at length on Ambalal's establishment of a plague hospital in a wing of his own home.

The Sarala Devi Plague Hospital—mark the name—Sarala Devi is the wife of the benevolent donor of this hospital. Even in such a simple matter as the christening of the hospital the act proclaims the man. A young Hindu gentleman does not thus parade the name and fame of his wife. But Mr. Ambalal is nothing if not thoroughly modern in all his ideas. He belongs to a sect of the Jains who, though living in the heart of Hinduism, have had the rare boldness to discard some of those pernicious customs of the Hindus which hang like a millstone round the neck of this great community. His home life has been singularly happy. He firmly believes that he has found inspiration for whatever good he has been able to accomplish in the love and devotion of this lady, and the naming of the hospital after her is a delicate tribute to her beneficent influence. . . .

Two redeeming features stand out predominantly from amongst the mass of disappointing failure which marked the progress of the disease, the one remedial, the other preventive, viz. The Sarala Devi Plague Hospital and Mr. Chatfield's [the highest ranking Englishman in Ahmedabad] institution of inoculation in the latter stages of the epidemic. The former was ushered into being, contrary to the prevailing custom, without any noise at all, without the pomp and circumstance which usually attends upon such functions in these days of advertisement. Almost everything connected with this hospital is indicative of the character of the founder, its birth especially. It is reminiscent of the high walls which surround Mr. Ambalal's dwellings, the spirit which is buried in lime and concrete is the spirit in which this institution was launched upon its career of usefulness. No flourish of trumpets proclaimed its advent, no opening ceremony blessed its birth. He would do things only to satisfy his conscience, not to gain applause. He believes in doing good stealthily, not in proclaiming his good intentions from housetops. And truly if any man . . . shuns public notice as he would shun poison, it is this man. And yet the irony of the thing is that at the present moment he is the best known man in the city, nay, far beyond the confines of the city.[9]

So Ambalal's "shyness" was a lifelong habit, indeed, and was present at the time when Gandhi entered the strike story as his antagonist, forcing this 25-year-old spokesman of an industry to match Gandhi's cunning and determination. But as to Ambalal's public image, one can well imagine what a competitive community may have made of this double display of conspicuous charity (naming, against all custom, the donor's wife) together with the wish to remain anonymous. And high walls, of course, exclude as well as include.

For the story to be told in this book, the assumption of an underlying pervasive ambivalence on Gandhi's part toward the mill owner is inescapable. Yet, their relation is also an example of a mutual and manly acceptance of the Hindu *dharma*—that is, of the assignment to each man of a place within the world order which he must fulfill in order to have a higher chance in another life. If, as Gandhi would put it, "fasting is my business," then making money was that of the mill owner; and Gandhi could not have fulfilled his role of saintly politician (or, in his words, "a politician who tried to be a saint") had he not had the financial support of wealthy men. This, the Marxists might say, corrupted him, while the Hindu point of view would merely call for a clean division of roles within a common search for a higher truth: a division which, Gandhi must have felt, had been blurred by the circumstances of his fast. The Freudian point of view, however, would suggest that such a situation might also cause an unconscious "transference" to the present of unresolved conflicts of the past. Young Gandhi—as we shall see—had, in varying ways, forsaken his caste and the memory of his father when he left home to become an English barrister; and later, when he had chosen to become a reformer, he had forsaken his older brother who had wanted him to join him in legal work. Such deviations from one's ancestral *dharma* pose grave problems in the lives of many creative Indians. At any rate, when he returned and settled down in Ahmedabad, the city in which both his native language and the mercantile spirit of his ancestors had reached a high level of cultivation, and when he again deviated grievously by taking a family of Untouchables into his ashram, the mill owner alone had continued to support him. The mill owner, thus, had become a true brother; and anyone familiar with Gandhi's life will know how desperate at times was the "Great Soul's" never requited and never fully admitted search for somebody who would sanction, guide, and yes, mother *him*. This is a complex matter, and it will be enough to indicate here that without the assumption of such a transference of the prime actor in my story to the principal witnesses, a brother and sister, I could not have made sense of the meaning of the Event in Gandhi's life—and of his wish to "play it down."

I went over the strike story also with Ambalal's sister, saintly

Anasuya (and I use this designation in this book only for her and for Kasturba, Gandhi's wife). Two exclamations will tell the story of her as a witness. When we went over the fact that she, as a concerned young woman long before the Event, had presided at a meeting of the warpers on the Sabarmati sands under one of the bridges and had exhorted them to strike, she said gaily, "And I must have made a speech!" That speech, in fact, had started organized labor in Ahmedabad. But to her it was not an event more likely than unlikely. In regard to her more personal history, she spoke more freely with Joan Erikson. But Joan, too, was sympathetically taken aback when Anasuya, having for a while given ample answers to her questioning, suddenly sat back and smiled at her with her round kind face: "Why all these old details? Why not let the ripe fruit fall?"

CHAPTER
# III

# Four Old Indians

---

To ILLUSTRATE A FEW OF the varieties of styles displayed by interviewees in India, I will describe my encounter with three, even though, in sketching my discussions with them, I may have to mention data which will make historical sense only as we proceed.

Shankerlal Banker at the time of the strike was already a ripe old twenty-nine; he was already in his late seventies, then, when I met him. For many hours we talked on a sun porch in the cool bright mornings of the Indian winter, looking out on the fabulous garden which Ambalal had planned, for Shankerlal shares Anasuyaben's house. He is hard to describe. At times defiantly gay and childlike (and defiantly toothless as Gandhi probably was), he almost seems to dissimulate what once was no doubt a complex personality with a great deal of nervous energy. All this made Shankerlal an excellent informant. The residues in him of an entrepreneurial impulse made him feel, I think, that my book should be written, even though he could be most reticent in volunteering what I had to elicit from him. Also, he took something of a truly Gandhian pleasure in the humorous truth; in fact, I sometimes heard Gandhi chuckle in the background. With his high-pitched voice Shankerlal, at the beginning of our meetings and especially when we had not met for awhile, always started again to raise some pseudo-philosophic smoke screen, by quoting Gandhi or whomever. But he never minded, and in fact chuckled appreciatively, when I interrupted him sharply, asking for names, small details, and exact meanings; and nothing would please him more than to catch somebody (and especially himself and me) in the trickery of some double talk. The stories he told of Gandhi—once he stopped quoting the Gandhian scriptures— were always refreshingly actual because, in fact, he had never surrendered to Gandhi unconditionally and had never joined him in his ashram. From Shankerlal, above all, I received an impression of Gandhi's Franciscan gaiety, which persisted even when the two were locked up for a year together in prison at a time when Gandhi was not treated with all the special consideration awarded him later. The stories he told of their companionship in jail revealed the deeply concerned and yet always mutually challenging and teasing relationship Gandhi could have with other men—intimates, strangers, or officials.

But Shankerlal also made a good informant because he always wanted to understand himself better in the act of giving me information; and being a Bania himself, he would never hesitate to indicate when it was time for me to tell him a little more of what I had figured out about him: on occasion he would simply go on strike and make *me* talk. He insisted on calling me "doctor" in a somewhat mocking fashion, tentatively transferring to me some of the respect he had felt for learned men in his culture. In fact, his uncle-mentor had been a medical man. Shankerlal had gone through one or two emotional crises in his life which he wanted to clarify as we went along. One aspect of his life, however, he quietly and stubbornly refused to discuss, namely, what is described (or rumored) by others as a markedly masculine, even *bon vivant*, and entrepreneurial period in his young manhood. Only once did he show me an old photograph of himself, young, handsome, energetic, in a British business suit. His old and widely hailed organizational energy appeared only when he detected that I needed a reference or might profit from seeing a particular individual: the next day the reference would lie on the tea table, or the individual would appear without warning to have midmorning tea with us. I was often annoyed about the ease with which Indians improvise an interview or a meeting in well-intentioned disregard of one's own plans; but in India if one is always prepared for just about anything, one is always apt to learn something. I might explain here in passing that this is the reason why it is difficult for a stranger to visit the poorer quarters or to stay overnight at a nearby village without being greeted as an official or foreign personage: the *visitor* is being gazed at. I do not know whether it was Shankerlal's doing that, on what was to be a discreet inspection trip to the Untouchables' quarters in Ahmedabad, Joan and I found ourselves the center of a small ovation. Led up to the end of a wretched little street, we were cornered by an eager crowd and seated at a covered table bedecked with flowers, to be joined presently by a candidate for City Council who asked me to speak and then translated what I said (or said he did). Yet I could not even be sure that he spoke the language of these people well. At any rate, it was only too clear that Shankerlal, this "passive" man, was trying to run our interviews and sometimes did so only too efficiently. But one could always count on a thoughtful kind of truth. In fact, the struggle in him between pragmatic efficiency and meditative passivity (certainly a conflict in the all-Indian identity of today) appeared to be a conflict of a kind which Gandhi, as we will see in detail, would always spot immediately and exploit superbly.

In Delhi, I met two men who had not exactly been witnesses to the Event, but who had both started to serve Gandhi in the early days of the Textile Labor Association and had advanced to national leadership—two men as dissimilar in personality as in the mandates which they assumed as the heritage of Ahmedabad: Gulzarilal Nanda, the Home Minister, and Indulal Yagnik, a fiery opposition leader in Parliament.

When I first visited Gulzarilal, as he is called affectionately or derisively, then India's Home Minister in the enormous ministry built by imperial England, I had to wait for quite a while in the small and cluttered outer office. The atmosphere was tense; there had been riots in Kashmir and in Calcutta, and Nehru was more incapacitated by his stroke than the public knew. Nanda, as the senior minister in the cabinet, was in line to be acting prime minister in the case of Nehru's death or total infirmity; and there was even some chance of his becoming prime minister if the Congress Party failed to settle on another candidate. When I finally got to see him, the tall and thin but muscular Punjabi looked utterly exhausted, and I begged him to send me away. But upon hearing from his secretary what my interests were (I had submitted them in writing), he asked me to stay while he answered messages and inquiries. Then, suddenly, he told his secretary and aides to leave him absolutely alone with me for exactly ten minutes. Under such turbulent conditions I felt that ten quiet minutes could be a significant span of time: after all, one can sleep, dream, and awake refreshed in ten minutes. And indeed, Nanda threw his head back and reclined, half relaxing and half collapsing, took his glasses off, and rubbed his eyes. "All right," he said, "what do you wish to ask me?" I said that I had just come from Ahmedabad, had seen the place where he had then lived and where he had started in his service to Labor and to India, and I had wondered: How far *was* it from the Textile Labor Association in Ahmedabad to the Home Ministry in New Delhi? Now completely reclining, he laughed amusedly and thought for a moment, as if refreshed by the challenge. "Not very far at that!" he exclaimed. "When I first met Gandhiji, I was quite young, twenty-three years old to be exact; and when I offered my services to him, he said, 'I can use you if you will promise always to go where you are most needed.' I promised; and you see—now I am needed here." Everywhere he went, Gulzarilal created organizations—he even organized the Sadhus. He then inquired what details I was after, and I told him of my study, hoping against hope that I would see him again. By then the ten minutes were up. Yet I felt strongly that he had expressed, in one minute, the theme which Gandhi had imposed on his life—no doubt as intuitively tuned to this young man as he was to so many others—for I learned that Gulzarilal, indeed, had already taken over much of Nehru's work. And the next day, at the Independence Day Parade, I could see how irreversibly sick Nehru was as he arrived, pale, bent, and limping. It was obvious that Nehru had had decidedly more than a "light stroke," which was the official version.

When I saw Gulzarilal a year later, he was again very busy and proved to have forgotten that we had met. He asked me to explain who I was, and I said, "Mr. Home Minister, I saw you for ten minutes the last time. If you will give me ten minutes a year, I think we can get some things straightened out." Again he laughed disarmingly and relaxed but this time retained a secretary who took notes; for conditions demanded that he not be misquoted. I recovered my *dharma*, and as I asked my question, the same glow came over the minister that I had seen earlier in the Vice President: the glow of a youthful memory, the memory of the beginning of a mission, a mission sanctioned and led by a great spirit. But he did not remember anything at all about the strike of 1918. He had kept a complete diary of the strike of 1923 when he was in charge of the Textile Labor Association while Gandhiji and Shankerlal were in jail, but he hastened to add that these diaries were lost at the time of the Association's move to new headquarters. (In the preservation of data, *my* data, I could not help thinking, the Millowners' Association and the Labor Association were evenly matched.) Otherwise Gulzarilal obviously looked back on this early accomplishment as a miracle—the miracle of Gandhi's confidence, which in its energy-producing power was the equivalent of a conversion for most of our witnesses. Unfriendlier observers felt, I knew, that such conversions to a sense of being irreplaceable in a historical mission often lead to an obsessive continuation of job occupancy which may look like love of power even in Gandhiite office holders. But again, there was time for only one question, and knowing that he was in charge of the country's police force, I asked him what he thought of the nonviolent discipline which had been the ideal of conduct in "the old days." "Nonviolence," he said with a deep and, I felt, somewhat tragic pensiveness, "will be the weapon of choice wherever democracy itself has made issues so opaque and complex that a return to an utter simplicity of approach becomes mandatory—as is the case now

in your country." We will return to this formulation when we
come to discuss the Ahmedabad events in detail. It implies that
nonviolence is best employed where it can make the simple logic
of historical actuality prevail over pious legalities, crafty compli-
cations, and invested power. I felt touched by the man's momentary simplicity and thoughtfulness; but I could not help wondering whether this powerful and controversial minister, who could
be so relaxed and simple, had now been caught himself in the
confusion of democracy (or rather of a one-party bureaucracy)
and that "the next time" nonviolence might well be used against
him and his establishment. He may have had such a thought
himself, as he looked on his present position again with the eyes
of the twenty-three-year-old. For he added that the over-all
importance of the Ahmedabad episode had been the emergence
and the investment of an almost spiritual belief in reconciliation
as a ritual. By then, he had given me twenty minutes.

EXCEPT for the elongated thinness which they have in common,
no two men could be less alike than were the Home Minister
of the Government of India and the oppositional firebrand,
Indulal Yagnik. The first represents Gandhian reconciliation in
power, and thus something Gandhi himself considered an inner
contradiction—wherefore he had never sought office and had
advised Congress after independence to become a social agency
in the widest sense rather than a political party. The other
typifies the relentless labor movement which is determined to go
beyond the reconciliation of the classes under the reign of industrial feudalism as established in Ahmedabad. I had been eager to
meet Indulal in order to gain at least a glimpse of the man who in
Ahmedabad personifies the historical question as to who is the
true representative of revolutionary advance—he who modestly
continues the work of a giant and adapts it to less heroic circumstances, or he who continues to flex his muscles to see whether
he may prove to have gigantic measurements himself. At any
rate, I had heard sedate citizens of Ahmedabad nominate Yagnik
as the one-man danger to the Ahmedabad Labor Peace which
the manufacturers consider the heritage of the Gandhian spirit.

Some called him "a communist," and, at any rate, considered
him the instigator of the riots which had occurred in Ahmedabad in the middle sixties. I was, then, most eager to meet this
man to see how *he* would look back on the Ahmedabad of 1918,
although my friends in Ahmedabad seemed not especially eager
to have me come face to face with him. On his 75th birthday he
was shown in the papers sweeping the streets of Ahmedabad in
true Gandhian fashion, if with more sinister implications. But
once in Delhi, I found him quite easy to contact and eager to
express his views. He was living alone in small quarters in an
otherwise fashionable apartment house. He was extremely simply dressed and responded with alert and almost piercing eyes in
a very fine, long, bony face—one of the best profiles and a pair
of the most direct eyes that I had seen in India. He spoke both
precisely and incisively, with eminently fitting, idiosyncratic
expressions, and none of the flowery Macaulay phrases I had
become used to. But he could not listen. He merely asked me to
confirm what I had told him on the phone and then launched
into a very systematic account of his student days in the years
after Gandhi had returned to India. He, the active politician, did
not hesitate for a moment to answer the question about what
impressed him first and foremost in Gandhi with the statement:
"He was a consummate politician," a side which I then needed
desperately to have spelled out for me because Gandhi's friends
always emphasized the inspired or even revelatory way in which
the Mahatma would go about his business; and yet without a
political awareness not only of the Indian masses but also of the
Russian revolution, Gandhi's activities of 1918 simply made no
coherent psychological sense. Indulal's emphasis too, no doubt,
was one-sided and a projection of the speaker's own self-image.
But is not every version of Gandhi—"truthful," "kingly,"
"crafty"—such a projection? And is it not the genius of the
leader that he can elicit a variety of such projections, each true,
and yet none exclusively so?

Otherwise, I soon realized that Indulal was telling me almost
word for word what was recorded in his autobiography; and
since it had not been translated into English (a friend had ab-

stracted for me some salient passages), he could do so with a feeling of telling me "news." And yet these memories now seemed to be fixed and had become representative of one type of early encounter with Gandhi: the potential follower is a young man so rebellious, and yet so dependent on an uncle figure of some kind; so upset (Yagnik speaks of "mental anguish") in a way which we today would characterize as alienated from his family, from his country's indigenous strivings, and from its colonial condition; and so fanatically concerned that Gandhi at first seemed to promise too much with too small a voice. But then after trying to listen to others, and then again to Gandhi, the young man, typically, would hear the dead earnest honesty and persistence of the man, and what one might call a cumulative conversion suddenly becomes irreversible.

Yagnik now musingly described how he had met Gandhi early after his return from South Africa. Gandhi was (these are all Indulal's phrases) a "probationer" then, "in a way sincere" and quite aware that "everything had to change," but deliberately remaining "a closed book" for a year or two while "gathering an entourage" that would help him change things. This description obviously fits Yagnik's own sense of mission at the moment, for he thinks everything must change, from Gulzarilal Nanda down to ATLA; but a closed book Yagnik was not.

His original meeting with Gandhi took place in Bombay, where he and Shankerlal went to school together; he was twenty-four years old. Indulal, the impatient activist, now laughs about old retired Shankerlal, but not without some indication of respect for his long-ago-discarded persona of organizer. A firebrand already then, Indulal was at first rather disappointed in Gandhi, learning to listen only gradually to the quiet power ("without flourish or shouting") of his factual and yet impassioned discussion of indentured labor. At the Congress meetings of 1915, he remembers, Gandhi was sitting "in the last seat in the last row" on the leaders' platform: we shall see how Gandhi deliberately kept in the background until he was drafted into the very foreground. Indulal claims that he, an official of the Gujarat Sabha, invited Gandhi to give the Gokhale memorial

speech in February 1917.[10] It was afterward in Poona, during
an informal discussion, that Indulal suddenly recognized the
Mahatma. Gandhi had discussed the necessity of setting a definite date for the end of the Indian Government's collaboration
with the system of "indentured labor" abroad. Gandhi was
"quietly chewing his groundnuts" when, as Indulal relates, he
suddenly said with a cheerful smile and without any change in
his tone of voice that if and when a date was set, "we must be
prepared to die" in order to make it stick. Everybody felt that
Gandhi *meant* this after-dinner chat—and was struck "as by a
thunderbolt." The implication was that, especially around
Poona where many young firebrands were ready to kill and be
killed in the fight for independence, the quiet readiness to die at
the time and for the purpose of one's own choosing meant
"meaning it." No doubt, for many, such simple readiness seemed
to suddenly fuse, in a moment, traditional and modern identity
elements into a workable whole. In his "widening search for
system and symbol," Indulal thought, Gandhi seemed in no
hurry at all—a consummate lawyer, politician, and diplomat. To
Indulal, then, my contention that Gandhi had selected the
Ahmedabad site as part of a grand scheme which had to include
workers *and* peasants seemed not sacrilegious at all. And he
added that Gandhi could choose the time and the place of his
commitments anywhere in India because in South Africa he had
learned to deal on a reduced and well-circumscribed scale with a
cross-section of India, with Madrasis as well as Gujaratis, with
Muslims as well as Hindus, so that when he had chosen to settle
in his native Gujarat, he could travel anywhere and immediately
seem somewhat at home.

Indulal also insisted that he, as well as Vallabhbhai Patel, had
invited Gandhi to speak at the great Educational and Political
Conferences, at which he made a truly national name for himself.[11] In all of Gandhi's utterances at that time, two themes
stood out, new in the independence movement: never start what
you have not clearly circumscribed in your own mind or what
you are not ready to suffer for to the very end. What impressed Indulal most is that Gandhi was "a twenty-four-hour

man" (what an American way of putting it, I thought). While
Patel always remained a bit sceptical ("we already have too
many mahatmas"), Indulal, the younger man, committed himself totally to Gandhi. During the Kheda campaign, Indulal
covered five districts of Gujarat as an agitator. He himself was at
that time not interested so much in labor as in the poor, for he
had, so he said, (and here the smart politician anticipated an
interpretation which I had come to apply if ever so cautiously to
some of the early Gandhiites) a "mother complex." I could not
help thinking that he could afford to see this so clearly because
he had worked the "complex" through—and had *remained* a
rebel, identified with Gandhi's more masculine traits, while refusing to join the communal bosom of the ashram. Of the early
days in Ahmedabad, in fact, he did not wish to speak. No, he
never lived on the former Sarabhai compound in Mirzapur, but
on Mission Road; and he stated this with the air of one who does
not want to acknowledge his old colleagues in Ahmedabad and
least of all any connection with the Sarabhais. The Association is
"making a job of it," he said contemptuously, referring to the
Textile Labor Association, and he obviously meant "a corrupt
job." So he provided me with a necessary corrective. Paranoid
(as some say) or not, fanatic (as all say) or not, Indulal seemed
to me to represent something of that continuing momentum
which is the very soul of a revolution—a soul which, in its refusal to admit any tiredness, any aging, seems permanently
enthused. During the Event, Indulal was in Iraq.

In the next chapter we shall trace the early path of this man
Gandhi himself, from his childhood in Rajkot to the time when
he met all these young men and women: what, in his own development, had prepared him to become their Mahatma? Here, the
Autobiography will once more be our basic material. However,
Gandhi's own account of his childhood has quite recently been
amplified by a man who heard much from Gandhi's own lips—
and noted it down—and who did exhaustive research on the
Kathiawar peninsula where Gandhi grew up. This man is Pyarelal Nayar. Pyarelal had met Gandhi only the year after the

strike, so he is not strictly speaking one of our witnesses. But since we shall use the result of some of his research in our review of Gandhi's "first fifty years," Gandhi's biographer and secretary for nearly three decades becomes a prime witness. It so happened that he put the finishing touches on the first volume (*The Early Phase*)[12] of his monumental biography in 1965 in Ahmedabad. Since we then lived across a field from the Navajivan Trust (the owner of all of Gandhi's works), and since Pyarelal seemed to like to check certain items with us, there was for about two weeks some lively traffic across the empty field, which taught us much about the tricky problem of the role of English in the historical identity of India. Pyarelal's task was a difficult one, for the last two volumes of his inclusive biography, *The Last Phase*,[13] had already appeared, so that to work on the introduction to the first volume meant to make a suitable beginning for what had already found its printed conclusion. Pyarelal has amassed an astounding number of facts; his brilliant chapters on Gandhi's study of Tolstoy and on the condition of India at the time of his return from South Africa will occupy us later. But here the question arises of how much we can trust the style, even of an Indian who was thoroughly and for a long period intimate with Gandhi, to convey to us a psychological sense of the man. The problem seems indefinable, often ludicrously so. An erudite Indian's attempt to express himself in the best of the King's English often leads him to write in the Queen's—Victoria's, that is. It is painful, for example, to see Pyarelal, this devoted old friend of Gandhi, quoting *Kipling*, of all people, in order to find the right words for the kind of man *Gandhi* was ("If you can dream—and not make dreams your master,") or using such chapter headings as: "A Whiff of the Romantic Past" for historic Kathiawar and "A Tale of Two Cities" for Porbandar and Rajkot. These titles, like some of the text at times, almost convey a questionable authenticity, for they express even everyday Indian experience in a colonial imagery which suggests an enforced transvaluation of values. How important it would seem for Gandhi's biographer to find terms as close as possible to the vernacular! For example, in the history of

Gandhi's youth we find a small-town Muslim boy (we shall meet him presently) quoted as having said to him, "Observe my physical prowess and daredevilry!"[14] One can only wonder, then, how much of the literary consciousness of India, employing as it must the imagery of the Empire, fails to express the very best of the native mood. This is, of course, what men such as Tagore attempted to rectify, and one realizes why Gandhi insisted on writing and speaking in Gujarati. But alas, even Gandhi's *Collected Works*, painstakingly and soberly effected under the auspices of the government he helped create, must offer the writings of the Mahatma in a language made on foggy North Sea islands. I know how unfair this critique must sound, coming as it does from one who is a stranger in India and an immigrant in his own country. Maybe for this very reason one searches for authenticity. The fact is that we almost wept when Pyarelal and his sister Sushila (then Minister of Health) arranged for us to listen to Gandhi's own voice and diction on recordings. Indeed,

My hesitancy in speech, which was once an annoyance, is now a pleasure. Its greatest benefit has been that it has taught me the economy of words. I have naturally formed the habit of restraining my thoughts. And I can now give myself the certificate that a thoughtless word hardly ever escapes my tongue or pen. I do not recollect ever having had to regret anything in my speech or writing.[15]

Throughout this book I must let this voice speak in what at times may seem inordinately long quotations.

However, Pyarelal had not begun to review his material on Gandhi's "Middle Period"—he did not seem to be familiar with Mahadev's *Righteous Struggle*—and little light was thrown on the Ahmedabad Event in many hours of otherwise vivid conversation. He telephoned the ashram, which now boasts of a splendid new library with large, comfortable reading rooms, and requested them to have the file for 1918 ready for inspection. When at last we drove out, we were greeted by an ever-so-reverent reception committee but found nothing but a few of the leaflets distributed under the Babul Tree. I was glad enough to hold these simply and beautifully printed sheets in my hand,

but they were in Gujarati and available elsewhere in translation.
And there was not a single document or letter. Gandhi himself
seems to have destroyed them before he left Ahmedabad.

These then were men and women through whom I received
some clarification of what the available documents say about the
Ahmedabad Event. As time went on, I was glad of my decision
to take my chances with this one Event. As Gandhi used to say:
"God never occurs to you in person but always in action." And
so does a special person manifest himself only in events which
are of his making. But here we owe it to ourselves to ask what it
may have been in his nature and in his background, in his childhood and in his youth, that fashioned him in such a way that he
grew up to be one who would make history.

# PART TWO

## The Past

---

WE SHALL NOW RETRACE some major steps in Gandhi's life from Moniya's friskiness to Mohan's gloom and from the unsure student days in England to young man Gandhi's firm householdership in South Africa. We shall be seeking the clues to how the boy and the man grew into his historical role, and inquire into the personal origins of militant nonviolence.

Data which owe their very survival to a previous generation's sense of the momentous can never be used quite convincingly to reconstruct what has become relevant to our generation; for we might not have preserved the same kind of data. Gandhi's "Experiments," as we have seen, are marked both by the stage in his life when he recorded them and by the era for which they were written, and they must therefore be read as part of a long series of adventures for which B. R. Nanda in his eminently readable biography finds the following formula:

. . . What was extraordinary was the way his adventures ended. In every case he posed for himself a problem for which he sought a solution by framing a proposition in moral algebra. "Never again" was his promise to himself after each escapade. And he kept the promise.[1]

But the question arises as to the nature of an aging man's "experimentation" with (I almost said "transference" to) his own childhood. How far must he adapt his early memories to the moral needs of approaching old age? Or could it be that toward the end of life the man and the child meet each other in mutual recognition—a kind of mental euthanasia? Gandhi concludes the introduction to his Autobiography with these words:

. . . It is an unbroken torture to me that I am still so far from Him, who, as I fully know, governs every breath of my life, and whose offspring I am.[2]

Later in this book we shall come to review again the whole question of the relationship of an "original" man to the man who originated him and to "Him whose offspring" they both are. Here we are concerned with the reconstruction of a man's childhood as part of what he became. For what a man adds up to must develop in stages, but no stage explains the man. Above all,

. . . How all this happens—how far a man is free and how far a creature of circumstances—how far free will comes into play and where fate enters on the scene—all this is a mystery and will remain a mystery.[3]

In case histories we have learned to trace the beginnings of human conflict further and further back into childhood, and I have characterized as *originology* the habitual effort to find the "causes" of a man's whole development in his childhood conflicts. By this I meant to say that beginnings do not explain complex developments much better than do the ends, and originology can be as great a fallacy as teleology. But in addition, the psychiatric origins of our approach have trained us to think in traumatological terms, that is, to discern not only origins but traumatic ones at that—trauma meaning an experience characterized by impressions so sudden, or so powerful, or strange that they cannot be assimilated at the time and, therefore, persist from stage to stage as a foreign body seeking outlet or absorption and imposing on all development a certain irritation causing stereotypy and repetitiveness. In applying my traumatological métier to Luther, I tried to understand his conflicts and his failures, attempting, however, not to underestimate the fabulous restorative energy of youth which gave his native genius the vitality to renew and restate Christian faith reaffirmingly. For that youthful energy, in fact, I called the book *Young Man Luther*. Since then, the application of traumatology to life histories has become standard practice. And because on occasion it is applied with more or less explicit reference to my work, I must try to be circumspect in this matter; for I consider any attempt to reduce a leader of Gandhi's stature to earlier as well as bigger and better childhood traumata both wrong in method and evil in influence—and this precisely because I can foresee a time when man will have to come to grips with his need to personify and surrender to "greatness."

Gandhi himself does not make such circumspection easy. He, like Luther, often presents himself as a case study, and he does so with an uncanny eye for conflicts which psychoanalytic insight would, indeed, consider both critical and universal in man. But in the long range of human awareness, Freud is both a successor to Luther and a contemporary to Gandhi. It could well be, then, that we must look at the self-inspection practiced by such men in public as part of an "evolutionary" trend in man to break through to new kinds of awareness. If a case for such a trend can be made, it must wait for the end of this book; in the meantime we must see what kind of case the man under scrutiny makes for himself.

In America we too have a father of the country who did not tell a lie, but we delegate the proof of such excellence to one little story suitable for children—and probably apocryphal! The inventory of Gandhi's scrupulosities, however, is deadeningly repetitious for all except those readers to whose condition he speaks: he was not a good student, he tells us, but he was somehow doing quite well and, at any rate, was obedient and most watchful of his own character and especially of truth. He was very shy and withdrawn, unable to be critical of his elders, and given to fantasies and stories which extolled only devotion to parents. Married too early, he was driven by a carnal desire which might have debilitated and even killed both him and his wife had they not lived separately for prolonged periods. Eager to teach his stubborn child bride to read and write, and yet feeling desperate over what turned out to be a lifelong failure, he likewise was trying desperately to reform a Muslim boy who, in turn, went to unbelievable lengths to make young Mohan eat meat and prove his manhood in brothels. Incidents of smoking and stealing and a spurious "suicide attempt" are followed by the crowning tragedy: the father whom he had nursed diligently died in an uncle's arms while the negligent boy lay with his (pregnant) wife. Perhaps some day we will have a translation of the Autobiography in which the didactic tone of the original is not confounded by excessive literalness. Then, maybe, the humor which one suspects is in the original (and which I have verified for myself by checking some passages with a highly educated young Gujarati) will be free to shine through. In the meantime, the peculiarities of the Autobiography must be underlined, particularly because of the barrier which the monotonous references to "lust" creates between the originator of Satyagraha and today's and tomorrow's fighters for peace. This treatment of sexuality prejudices the future relationship of creative nonviolence to an enlightened eroticism (including the enlightened sacrifice of it) which men of the future will consider their sovereign choice not to be surrendered to what we shall discuss later as the inner violence of dogmatic moralism.

If Gandhi selects, even from his childhood, events which could qualify as moral experiments, I will apply to them the theory that a man like him is early and painfully conscious of a special mission, a direction which must lead to all or to nothing. And yet, being a child with a given schedule of maturation, he (like anybody else) must make do with the limited equipment of a child and an adolescent as he tests the world impulsively and yet maintains throughout a certain inviolacy of spirit. This inviolacy, I believe, escapes all our attempts to test and to standardize a child's development or, at any rate, to think that a child is the sum of his testable traits. For a child, I am sure, is, at distinct and important moments, much more perceptive and mature than he can afford to be at all times: therefore, he reserves great dreams of both triumph and defeat for later enactment. A moral "experiment" in this sense can only mean that a precocious self-awareness makes the experimenter undergo

situations in which the unavoidable weakness and dependency of
childhood seem to be in painful contrast to an equally precocious conscience. A child like Gandhi (and since there are so
few "like" him, I should say that I have in mind such men as St.
Augustine, St. Francis, and Kierkegaard) in all his early vul-
nerability seems to involve the very persons he must depend on
in an intimate struggle in which he attempts to wrestle from
them all possible strengths without losing any of his precocious
inviolacy; and he will, painfully early, reverse positions and become the giving and judging and, in fact, the *parental agens*. In
regard to Mohandas's obsession with a "jealous watch over his
own character," Pyarelal emphasizes the defensive wish to be
untainted and unsmudged; and this obsessive part of Gandhi, no
doubt, remained lastingly and, to some extent, destructively
effective. But I believe that Gandhi meant to convey something
else also. Mere character could be, as it were, a cold chimney,
nothing more than an encasement. A fireplace is not worth more
than the fire it can hold and the warmth it can generate; and a
man like Gandhi, I would surmise, early knew that he had to
contain a superior energy of destructive, as well as benevolent,
forces, an energy which he later called Truth Force and endowed with a discipline.

Without such assumptions, Mohandas makes little sense to me,
certainly not as the predecessor of Gandhi. With these assumptions, he makes a certain dynamic sense which I will try to spell
out in a number of strategic respects. And here, even the most
fragmentary material contains a number of correctives: for one,
whatever is said of a growing human being should be consistent
with and at any rate not improbable in the terms of his stage of
life and of his particular condition at the time. I will call this
*developmental probability*. At the same time, it should be consistent and certainly not incompatible with analogous moments
throughout the span of his life. Take what we may call Gandhi's
*experimental existentialism:* this we should (and will) see at
work early in life in a form commensurable with the condition
of being a child or an adolescent or a young man and yet also
with a certain pervasive quality which matures throughout life.

If, as we shall see, the teasing of people and animals in childhood was one of the outstanding ways in which Moniya tested his family and the world of Porbandar, we shall recognize many somberly reported stories of his later life as animated by a subtle teasing perceived by all those present at the time. We shall then see little Moniya and his father reappear in the story of how the Mahatma teased the British Viceroy. Now while teasing as a habit underlies certain psychodynamic vagaries recognizable in case histories, its successful employment throughout a life history demands an investigation in which it will be important to show why, for example, little Mohandas got away with his teasing in the home of his stern father-official as well as in the British Viceroy's palace, got away with it in supreme adaptation to historical actuality *and* according to the logic of personal development. Neither his father nor the Viceroy, neither his home nor the British Empire were ever the same after they had come up against his mixture of humor and deadly determination.

Gandhi's Autobiography alone, then, is a poor guide to the question as to how Moniya's and Mohan's, Mr. Gandhi's and the Mahatma's propensity for teasing makes sense in terms of what we today know something about, namely, *developmental probability* and *social relativity*. The leader *was* once a child, and the saying, "the child is father of the man," makes new and particular sense for special men: they, indeed, *have* to become their own fathers and in a way their fathers' fathers while not yet adult. This spells special conflicts and special tasks, and I will attempt to circumscribe these by putting together as well as I can what Gandhi reports in his old age, what Pyarelal and B. R. Nanda have gleaned from personal observation and from contemporary sources, and what my insight into the stages of life has taught me to consider probable.

# CHAPTER
# I

# Childhood and Youth

## 1. MONIYA AND HIS MOTHER

THE EARLIEST available photograph of Moniya makes it quite plausible that the small child "had a cheerful, sweet face and lovely eyes." Pyarelal's description omits, however, the big and protruding ears which help to "round out" the little boy's face but later would rob the Mahatma's countenance of its proportions, especially when he laughed in his toothless way. That all through life he loved to laugh and make others laugh, later pictures, too, make plausible; and even in the somber days of his young manhood, he would write in his diary that he could always console his mother by making her laugh heartily. So we gladly believe Pyarelal—gladly, not the least, because what is a saint without gaiety?—that Moniya had a hearty ringing laughter, and that everybody liked to fondle him.

The youngest and last son of a young mother (25) and an aging father (47), Moniya was born into a large family crammed into a big house with many small rooms in the port city of Porbandar on the Arabian Sea coast of the peninsula of Kathiawar. Thus, like many great leaders, he was born on the periphery of his future "domain" and in a setting which would provide a strong regional identity to start with. Porbandar is a fishermen's and a sea traders' world, renowned for its toughness and shrewdness, for from here as from the larger nearby port of

Cambay, the ships went back and forth between India and Arabia and the east coast of Africa—down to South Africa, where the man Gandhi later would "find his vocation."

For all those who know only the stereotyped Gandhi of the "Experiments," it may be difficult to imagine the little boy roaming about in the sensuous and populous setting in which he grew up. Porbandar is a town which

> with its narrow lanes and crowded bazaars, surrounded by massive walls which have since been largely demolished, is no more than a stone's throw from the Arabian Sea. The buildings, though by no means architecturally distinguished, are built of a white soft stone which hardens with the years, shines like marble in the sunlight, and has given to the town the romantic name of the 'White City.' The streets are dotted with temples; the ancestral house of the Gandhis was itself built around two temples. But the life of this port was and is necessarily centred on the sea.[4]

Moniya was born and grew up in a three-story ancestral house which in photographs looks imposing and roomy enough, but was shared by his father with his five brothers and their families. The suite allotted to his father, the head of this clan and prime minister of the small princely state of Porbandar, "was on the ground floor and had, besides a tiny kitchen and veranda, two rooms, one of which was 20 feet long and 13 feet wide and the other 13 feet long and 12 feet wide." Six generations of Gandhis were home ministers or prime ministers on the Kathiawar peninsula, which counted an abundance of princely "states," some larger than a fairly large estate, some smaller. The "sovereignty" of these states, fostered by the British as long as it suited their policies, helped to preserve a certain regional, feudal, and professional pride which—in all its precariousness—would be of great importance to Gandhi's original world-image. But it was of equal import that in the days of his youth the British rather abruptly concluded that these political and cultural conclaves had become expendable—and with them their prime ministers. But more about this later.

As is the custom in India, a joint family builds on (and *in*) wherever space permits, adding small rooms to accommodate the

newlyweds of each generation. Thus small, stuffy, and darkened rooms are created, such as the "kitchenette," in which even
two persons could hardly sit comfortably, and where mother
Putali Ba passed her whole later life. It was in this room that
Moniya was born. The lying-in bed was owned jointly and lent
to whatever sub-family was in need of it. Behind this room was
another apartment, even smaller. Here the grandmother lived
with her sixth son, Tulsidas.

The oppressive narrowness of these appointments, however,
was compensated for in good weather by open doors and courtyards, where the whole joint family would congregate on festive
occasions and where on an ordinary day the prime minister's
dinner guests would assemble—rarely fewer than twenty.

If Gandhi's mother is always described as an ideal housewife,
"the first one to rise and the last to go to bed," eating only
"when she could manage it," then it must be remembered that
she, as well as her husband, emulated ancient models whose
conduct was strictly regulated. And it should be immediately
obvious that certain impressions recorded earlier regarding joint
family life apply here: if the mother, for example, "never made
any distinction between her own children and other children in
the family . . . ," then her children may at times have been
forced to share more than they could afford emotionally. If they
also learned "to live *for*, as well as *in*, mankind"—a felicitous
phrase well applicable to the style of life Gandhi would later try
to institute in his ashram—they did not learn it only from the
mother. The father, Kaba Gandhi, had to look after the wellbeing of every member of his clan, whether they were ready to
get married, settle down, or assume jobs. He is even said to have
helped Putali Ba in household work:

It was a familiar sight, which the people of Porbandar still remember, of
him sitting in the Shrinathji temple day after day, peeling and paring the
vegetables for his wife's kitchen, while he discussed with his visitors and
officials affairs of the State.[5]

The total image is one in which it is difficult to allocate
masculine and feminine identifications.

One of the best and most instructive passages in Pyarelal's work describes the life of a joint family, for once stating bluntly the sources of bitter ambivalence:

. . . Where so many people with diverse tastes, habits, and temperments are cooped up day and night in a narrow space from week to week, month to month, and year to year, it requires no little diplomatic skill, delicacy, tact, especially on the part of the head of the family, to maintain a healthy and sweet atmosphere. The members on their part have to develop the attitude of mutual help and regard, the capacity for give-and-take, and adjustment to one another's idiosyncrasies. A single tactless remark, a slip or oversight, an uncouth habit, heedlessness or disregard of another's feelings may set people's nerves on edge and make life hell for the whole family. Competition in this narrow world is keen; even the youngsters feel the edge of it; little things assume big proportions; the slightest suggestion of unfairness or partiality gives rise to petty rivalries, jealousies, and intrigues. To smooth them requires infinite patience, resourcefulness, and knowledge of human nature. Delicate and conscientious care in the minutiae of everyday life or its lack can make in the narrow confines of the joint family all the difference between peace and discontent, happiness and misery.[6]

Undoubtedly, all this contributed to the style of living later created by Gandhi in his ashram: a life of mutual observation and intricate discipline hard to grasp and harder to condone for the uninitiated. If Putali Ba provided the ideal of womanhood later fostered in the ashram (and one could add facetiously, fostered in the men as well as in the women), then we must also acknowledge that the typical experience of joint family life may have helped the ashramites to find safety and inspiration in a style of living in parallel isolation and joint service.

A passionate founder and habitual head of ashrams, however (and who can imagine Gandhi ever as an inmate in somebody else's ashram), must have experienced a more complex early life in a joint family than was typical. And, indeed, Moniya seems to have had the capacity to insist on special relationships. No doubt being the last child of a young mother and an aging patriarch gave him a central place in the family and one conducive to "spoiling." He seems to have cultivated this advantage in developing that quality of tenacious and clever attachment which made his parents feel that their relationship to him was a unique one and made him in turn, feel that his was the fate of an elect being. While he always felt relatively isolated in groups, his was the most intense search for one-to-one relationships, until in South Africa he found a professional and political style of being one-to-one with a community—of followers. Since, I believe, this is an important prerequisite for some styles of "greatness," we must try to envisage how a series of unique relationships was allocated, first to his mother and father, then to his child bride, and finally to his "evil" childhood friend—allocated each time with oppressive trust, intense conflict, and the eventual bitter insight of one who felt early that he was experimenting for extremely high stakes.

That, in his youth, Mohandas temporarily despaired of his uniqueness—a despair which was the model for repeated depressions in later life—should not blind us to the high probability that Moniya also harbored an early sense of originality and, in fact, superiority. For while our clinical era might see in his confessions only an admission of having been possessed by irrational guilt, the Mahatma does not stop there. He *experimented*, so he means to emphasize (and so, I believe, he was read by his countrymen), with the devils of shame and doubt, guilt and inferiority: he challenged them and won. And if we suspect that no *great* child would make sense without such a challenge, maybe we should go all the way and say that *no* child would, and that greatness depends on the preservation and continued corroboration of something which most ex-children lose. But it is equally important to see that his parents had enough humor to "suffer" him to test them instead of spoiling the game by over-emphasizing the occasional sadism in his testiness. For a child is easily overcome by the fear of his own initiative and curiosity, while the native strength of his personality cannot as yet match the precocity of either his brashness or his sensitive conscience. Thus Moniya seems to have been lucky in the choice of his parents; and defeat came to Mohandas only when he faced in all-too-young years the marital encounter with another and equally stubborn child.

Outstanding also, all his life, was Gandhi's locomotor restlessness and energy. It is said even of men and women whose greatness was grounded in the contemplative life (such as St. Francis or Kierkegaard) that nobody could keep up with their locomotor velocity and vigor. Gandhi's enormous perambulatory vigor in later years is well known.*

The described closeness of elbow room and air in the Gandhi brothers' mansion would make this restlessness, paired with insatiable curiosity, a fortunate method of getting out and away, although this tendency in Gandhi imposed quite a job on those who were supposed to keep an eye on him while his mother was busy. His older sister seems to have been the chosen victim. When she was ninety, this sister described Moniya as "restless as mercury"and "full of curiosity." He would try to make friends with animals, sometimes by "twisting dogs' ears" and this apparently with such nonviolent cunning that he was never bitten. (One young man of my acquaintance still found it hard to forgive the Mahatma for having twisted *his* ear rather painfully, while a well-known photograph shows Pyarelal's niece as a baby not too happy with the fact that the Mahatma insisted on rubbing noses with her.) But it was good to get Moniya out of the house, for when his father was not there, he was inclined to usurp strange rights. He would remove the image of the ruling Prince from its customary stool and put himself in its place, a habit of pretending to be his father's master of which we shall make all we can. He also used to scatter the utensils of worship and to "write" on the floor. When his mother tried to forbid this, he (in Pyarelal's words) "stoutly dissented,'" in what may have been the ontogenetic origin of the sit-down. On the other hand, he strongly dissented also from any necessity of being watched outdoors. His sister says that she was told by their father

* That he could outwalk anyone has also been said of Freud, whose best and least known pictures show him in Alpine attire; but we are impressed by the locomotor vigor of such meditative men as, say, Kierkegaard, who so loved to converse while perambulating that he used to crowd his partner first into the house on one side of the street and then, when the victim tried to free himself by changing places, gently pushed him across the street into the house walls on the opposite side.

to keep out of sight when watching Moniya, a consideration at variance with the assertion that the father wanted to squelch the child's adventuresomeness. When found high in a mango tree, Moniya gave an excuse which attests to an early combination, so characteristic of the mature Gandhi, of locomotor restlessness and the obsession for taking care of others: he was bandaging the mangoes, he explained.

But while he was playful and without fear when he could set his own pace, he proved uninterested in all organized games. For this he blamed his "shyness"; yet he did not hesitate to take the role of peacemaker when the playmates quarreled among themselves. This, Pyarelal says, was the "passion of his life."[8] And, indeed, from his childhood in Rajkot to his maturity in Indian politics, he would never "play" unless he was in a position of such moral dominance that he could convince himself and others that the power game of his mediatorship was "for their own good." And (not unimportantly) it often turned out to be just that.

To convince parents of this while one is still a child, however, is a special feat. Yet it is not an uncommon one in uncommon men and women. The feat is that of maintaining the prerogative of a child and yet of first pretending to be and then actually becoming so nearly the parents' counterplayer in more and more serious encounters that one acquires their strengths through significant interplay. Whether or not, later on, one succeeds in doing the same with counterplayers in pursuits of ever-wider public importance—that eventually determines objective greatness.

Most interpreters emphasize Putali Ba's religious observance, if not obsession, and some insist on blaming her for Gandhi's propensity for fasting at critical moments. We will later discuss the many aspects of fasting in India (or anywhere) which range from the purest of self-purifying endeavors to pious and impudent blackmail. But I have read of no incidence which would indicate that Putali Ba used fasting as punishment, except insofar as a deep-seated resentment over her manifold duties may have induced her to insist on one sphere of privacy: that of worship and self-abnegation. Putali Ba's children seem to have watched her anxiously.

... Once she vowed not to have food without seeing the sun. We children on those days would stand staring at the sky, waiting to announce the appearance of the sun to our mother. Everyone knows that at the height of the rainy season the sun often does not condescend to show his face. And I remember days when, at his sudden appearance, we would rush and announce it to her. She would run out to see with her own eyes, but by that time the fugitive sun would be gone, thus depriving her of her meal. "That does not matter," she would say cheerfully, "God did not want me to eat today." And then she would return to her round of duties.[9]

On the other hand, she was an utterly undogmatic religious person of a kind who wished to pursue only what made her feel right and clean. Indeed, she imbued her little son with a tolerance for any religion as long as it cultivated a deep sense of communion with the unseen and silent. Moniya, in fact, seems to have had a kind of humorous understanding with his mother that some religious restrictions were a bit of bunk, teasing her, for example, by saying that on the way home from school he had touched an Untouchable and then admitting that he was just joking; or, more seriously, pestering her into giving him food on days when religious custom forbade it. He related to Pyarelal,

I was my mother's pet child, first because I was the smallest of her children but also because there was nothing dearer to my heart than her service. My brothers were fond of play and frolic. I found not much in common with them. I had no close bond with my sister either. Play had absolutely no fascination for me in preference to my mother's service. Whenever she wanted me for anything, I ran to her.[10]

Always when *she* needed *him!* Never an intimation that *he* may have needed a *mother*—never, that is, until in his seventies, not long before his assassination, when he would shiver at night so desperately that he would ask some of his women companions to lie down close to him and warm him. But even then he would proclaim it was all just to test his manhood—that is, in Indian terms, his capacity to control it so that he could use this vital essence to bolster his waning political power.

Pyarelal even claims that little Moniya taught his mother a lesson in *ahimsa*, by telling her that she should keep the older brothers from beating him rather than encouraging him to beat them back. But the unbearably stilted Macaulayism, "Should you not, mother, prevent my brother from beating me instead of asking me to imitate him?" indicates the mythologizing that goes on in the writings of the true followers.[11] No doubt, however, neither Moniya nor Mohan nor the Mahatma could ever face the "natural superiority of women" without a competitive attempt at becoming more maternal than the most motherly of mothers. If nursing was another passion of his life, then it all started when in his own unique "oedipal" arrangement, he became a mother to his father—a mother who always had time for him. But the Westerner would do well to see in Gandhi's protestations of motherliness more than an emotional inversion: the primary power of motherliness (symbolized in the cow) is an ancient and all-pervasive ingredient of Indian tradition. When this boy appointed himself his father's nurse, there was a drive in it which later would suffice for the care of all India as well as of Untouchables and lepers, of mankind as well as of an ashram.

No doubt a certain basic religiosity—the undogmatic sense of being carried along by a demanding and yet trustworthy universe—was first personified for Moniya in his mother. I must leave it to others to elaborate on those traditional values of the Vaishnavite religion and the Jain culture which surrounded Moniya: vegetarianism and periodical fasting; cleanliness and purification; the making of confessions and the taking of vows; and above all: *ahimsa*, avoiding harm to living beings. But it is equally important to realize that Putali Ba belonged to a small sect which prided itself on having unified the Koran with the Hindu scriptures and which abhorred any regression to the idolatry of either, to the point of allowing no images at all in its temple. His mother's religion was of that pervasive and personalized kind which women convey to children; but it also prepared the boy for the refusal to take anybody's word for what anything meant, either in the Hindu scriptures which he rediscovered only in his youth with the help of Western writings, or in the Christian gospels, the essence of which he tried to resurrect in Eastern and modern terms, having as a child abhorred the missionaries about town. But as we shall see, a certain ambivalence would pervade those reforms in diet and daily living, which he would claim he "owed" to his mother, and which yet would betray in their exaggeration, in their coerciveness of others, and in their occasional self-destructiveness, a remnant of suppressed rebellion. But even the most glaringly neurotic aspects of all this must not blind us to his often successful attempts, born of his relation to his mother, to unite the feminine and the masculine aspects of religiosity—and to convey this unification to the masses. And Moniya, indeed, survives not only in the willfulness of later "experiments," but also in the deliberateness with which passing errors and even major mistakes are later sovereignly admitted—with a queer mixture of owning up to them and yet claiming them to have been experiments, as if part of a gigantic game. This at times must have had a manic quality, true counterpart to the depressive side of Gandhi's nature, which we shall discuss next. Gandhi, no doubt, had days when he acted gaily on a scale which would make his followers and adversaries gasp with awe and apprehension. But this does not exclude the other aspect, the Autobiography's overconscientious side, from also being there rather early; the Autobiography only authenticates the depressive trends which haunted the child no less than the pubertal boy, the youthful man no less than the aging autobiographer. These self-critical trends were to have sinister consequences aggravated by the man's tendency to dare himself and others: but it would be impossible to understand the Mahatma's stature and influence without knowing that he once was Moniya, and that the Moniya in him helped at strategic moments to free inner resources in himself and in his followers and to gauge, with a child's random sure-footedness, the actualities of the historical situation.

## 2. MOHAN AND HIS FATHER

THERE ARE photographs of Mohan, as he was then called, at the ages of thirteen and fifteen which are more easily reconciled

with the Mahatma's description of his youth (and with the interpretations based on this description) than is the earlier
image of Moniya. Yet Mohan seems so much stauncher, so much
more exquisitely put together than one would gather from the
sum of the stories told about him by the Mahatma. Who can
describe, who "analyze" such a young man? Straight and yet
not stiff; shy and yet not withdrawn; intelligent and yet not
bookish; willful and yet not stubborn; sensual and yet not soft:
all of which suggests that integrity which is, in essence, unex-
plainable—and without which no explanation is valid. We must
try to reflect on the relation of such a youth to his father, because the Mahatma places service to the father and the crushing
guilt of failing in such service in the center of his adolescent
turbulence. Some historians and political scientists seem to find it
easy to interpret this account in psychoanalytic terms; I do not.
For the question is not how a particular version of the Oedipal
Complex "causes" a man to be both great and neurotic in a
particular way, but rather how such a young person, upon per-
ceiving that he may, indeed, have the originality and the gifts
necessary to make some infantile fantasies come true in actuality,
manages the complexes which constrict other men. This one
cannot learn from Freud because he primarily described the conscience which inactivates ordinary people, and neglected to ask
aloud (except, maybe, in a cryptic identification with Moses)
what permits great men to step out of line. He was content to
demonstrate the unconscious restoration of mastery over our
inner complexes by nightly dreaming, but he neglected to dwell
on the question of what additional mastery made it possible for
him to understand his own dreams. This, like morality, he took
for granted.

We have heard about the kind of prime minister's court
which Moniya's father, administrator of one of the Kathiawar
princes, held daily in his home in Porbandar. His profession and
function, then, was no secret to the little boy, who playfully sat
himself in the prince's place. And, indeed, for twenty-eight
years of his life Karamchand, Gandhi (called Kaba) was an influential and, it seems, eminently respected man. The height of

his career coincided with Mohan's childhood and was reflected in a sovereign leniency toward his favorite son, which may have permitted the son to entertain benevolent fantasies of emulating him and yet to feel all the more guilty. But toward the end of Moniya's first childhood decade, his father was induced to leave Porbandar and the coast for Rajkot, in order to become the Prime Minister of the "Thakore" there—a more powerful potentate, it seems. Thus both the boy and the father lost their milieu; while, in addition, the father's career and health began to decline. The ruler of Rajkot was so imprudently proud of his new prime minister that he soon "lent" him to a neighboring ruler, who in turn proved so unreliable that Kaba left him within the year, not without declaring a hunger strike in order to be released. There is a story that on leaving, Kaba refused a generous monetary settlement because it did not correspond to the original terms. "You will not find another ruler who will offer you such a generous sum!" the prince exclaimed, to which Kaba replied: "And you will not find another Karbhari who is too proud to take it." The story is, somehow, Gandhian, if only in the pride of saying no. But it is of interest also because the ruler is said to have used the argument that Kaba might need the money for sending Mohan, then ten years old, to England for studies. This would indicate that the ruler and the father were already then aware not only of Mohan's gifts but also of the fact that only a son with a higher education obtained in England would in the future be able to defend the rulers *and* their prime ministers against the British agents.

Even to begin to understand the child and the youth who was going to be Gandhi and the Mahatma—so I have indicated—it is necessary to assume that he emerged from the love and care of his relationship with his mother as one given to one intense relationship at a time and this a relationship of service, nay, salvation of the other. When, as all children must, he had to abandon the fusion with his mother (in a joint family, as we saw, a most tenuous fusion at best), he could only relive, in line with his personal growth, a series of equally intense and yet "experimental" encounters with a selected cast of primary counter-

players: father, wife, and boyhood friend. Maybe such biblical
refusal to let the other go and to wrestle with him for a blessing
is also a sign of greatness; and if Gandhi later transferred such
insistence to corporate counterplayers—India, the Empire, mankind—this is by no means a mere matter of "transferring" infantile energies and goals onto a widening reality of concerns. A
crank, a fanatic, a psychotic can "transfer," but only a political
genius can master the minute and concrete interplay by which
he succeeds in arousing from powerful collectivities responses
fully as unique as those which he had established in a smaller
circle at home.

It was at his aging father's insistence, never to be forgiven by
the son, that the family decided to combine Mohandas's marriage
to Kasturba with the planned marriages of an older brother and
of a nephew. Mohandas, then thirteen, had already been engaged
by family contract for the third time. His first two fiancées had
died, but he probably did not know or care to know of either
their existence or their death. These were matters for the parents
to settle, and Moniya had probably played for years with strong-
willed Kasturba, who lived in the immediate neighborhood in
Porbandar. The multiple marriage was contemplated primarily
for economic reasons, but it also seems that the father wanted to
be sure he would live to be present at Mohan's marriage. And as
things developed, his presence became the central fact for Mohan, whose wedding picture shows him to be a rather scared
boy. Yet, he is said to have enjoyed the proceedings to a point,
while making it quite clear how far he would go in the usual
ceremonial show: he was not, for example, going to be paraded
through the streets on a decorated horse. Otherwise, he seems to
have anticipated the more intimate companionship with his child
wife as a mixture of exclusive playmateship and the total possession of (and service to) one who would belong to him by rights.
The sexual act which he knew was expected of him could not
have remained a secret under the living conditions of a joint
family and the semirural closeness to animals around such provincial towns. Also, one was coached in such matters by solicitous
relatives, and one could at any rate, as the Mahatma wrote, count

on knowing what to do from the knowledge acquired in previous lives—the Hindu counterpart of the concept of "instinct."

But if there was a tendency in the to-be-wed Mohan to enjoy
the marriage playfully, this and the whole festive character of
the occasion were marred by the fact that his father had a nearly
fatal accident on the way to the wedding: a kind of curse in
the son's life. The father's carriage overturned, and he was
actually hurt more seriously than it at first seemed:

My father put on a brave face in spite of his injuries and took full part in
the wedding. As I think of it, I can even today call before my mind's eye
the place where he sat as he went through the different details of the
ceremony. Little did I dream then that one day I should severely criticize
my father for having married me as a child.[12]

These words betray the bridegroom's awareness of his father,
maybe greater than that of his child bride. And, indeed, after
their return home, he divided his intensely intimate attention
between his wife and the care of his father. His skillful maternal attention to Kaba could now replace, as well as fuse
with, his service to his mother, for it freed her from the nursing
duties which otherwise would have had to supersede all else. But
the Mahatma confesses to having thought of his wife when
massaging his father and of his father when being with his wife,
while both marriage and nursing meant a neglect of his studies.
No wonder that his account of his life suggests a certain frantic
rush from one to the other, from wife to father and father to
wife and to and from both, to and from school; and one may
well assume this to be the model for later alternations between a
manic mobility and a transitory settling down—always in the
service of somebody or something that *needed* him. At any rate,
a true account of Mohan's youth (and here good fiction would
be truer than any composite of the tendentious "facts" available) would have to show him from day to day in the over-
lapping and yet also deeply conflicting duties of attending
father, wife, and school and (the reader will be almost glad to
hear of it) experimenting with a bit of juvenile delinquency as
well.

Let us first dispose of school life, for it seems to have meant least to him. As Pyarelal puts it (and we know this of other boys of future prominence), "learning unrelated to life and its duties had little attraction for him." But I would also surmise that no teacher came on the scene to whom it was worth attaching himself with the intensity that would make any unique intimacy worthwhile. The Mahatma later made light of his teachers as well as of his school. Always willing to take the blame, however, he would simply call himself a mediocre student, who was "astonished" when he won prizes and scholarships and let it go at that—with one exception: when in the exigencies of school life, his *moral* character was in doubt.

But I very jealously guarded my character. The least little blemish drew tears from my eyes. When I merited, or seemed to the teacher to merit, a rebuke, it was unbearable for me.[13]

To remain unblemished, then, is described as *the* overweening emotional necessity; but beyond this the Mahatma documented (without admitting the slightest malice) how he taught one of his teachers a lesson. Once when the Educational Inspector visited the school, the teacher noticed a mistake on Mohandas's spelling sheet and, eager to present a perfect record, hinted to him somehow that he could copy the exact spelling from his neighbor.

. . . It was beyond me to see that he wanted me to copy the spelling from my neighbour's slate, for I had thought that the teacher was there to supervise us against copying. The result was that all the boys, except myself, were found to have spelt every word correctly. Only I had been stupid. . . . Yet the incident did not in the least diminish my respect for my teacher. I was by nature blind to the faults of elders.[14]

One would like to subsume *that* much goodness on the part of a schoolboy under the formula that it was all part of the message the aging autobiographer meant to convey. But this, no doubt, would mean to neglect a lifelong trend which, in fact, found its climax in the Autobiography. This trend has its own developmental logic—a logic which Gandhi's life has in common with the lives of other saints. Here an overweening conscience can

find peace only by always believing that the budding "I" harbors a truthfulness superior to that of all authorities because this
truth is the covenant of the "I" with God, the "I" being even
more central and more pervasive than all parent images and
moralities. This I would consider to be the core of a *homo
religiosus*, and the burden of the story just told is not that
Mohan was a good boy but that he dared to stand unprotected
by frail authority between absolute evil and absolute truth. But
such a boy often appears, of course, too good to be true.
Pyarelal quotes (with a shudder not typical for a Gandhian
writing about Gandhi) from a letter which the Mahatma wrote
to his seventeen-year-old son Manilal many years later:

> Fun and frolic are permissible only during one's years of innocence, i.e.,
> up to the twelfth year. As soon as a child attains the age of discretion, he
> must learn to go about with a full sense of his reponsibility and make a
> ceaseless, conscious effort to develop his character. . . . I remember
> when I was less than your age, my greatest joy was to nurse my father. I
> have not known what fun and frolic are since my twelfth year.[15]

To judge such a statement, one would want to know the
occasion which elicited it. And, of course, one would also want
to know the traditional tone of paternal letters: for in the Hindu
scheme of life one was supposed to be an ascetic student at
seventeen, and therefore, as Gandhi says in the same letter,
something comparable to a Sannyasin at least in the matter of
refraining from all sensual levity. And we shall substantiate later
that Gandhi's letters to his sons are often moralistic in a vindictive way, as though his sons had to be doubly good for having
been the issue of that early marriage.

In the Autobiography the Mahatma recounts the myths and
plays he remembers most intensely from his youth. Of all the
holy pictures publicly displayed by itinerant showmen, it was
the one of "Shravana carrying, by means of slings fitted for his
shoulders, his blind parents on a pilgrimage" which left, he says,
the most indelible impression on him. "Here is an example for
you to copy," he reports having said to himself. But as if to
atone for what vanity may have been suggested by the son's
power, Shravana died, and "the agonized lament of the parents

over Shravana's death is still fresh in my memory. The melting
tune moved me deeply, and I played it on a concertina which
my father had purchased for me." If the modern observer is
inclined to see in this a sentimental denial of the wish to be
stronger than his father, we must remember that not even Freud
considered it desirable or possible that the Oedipus theme be
conscious. In fact, to think that one *can* be conscious of it because one now has a name for it could be a cheap substitute for
suffering it through with all one's being and in terms of both
ancestral mythology and changing technology.

At about that time, Mohan had secured his father's permission

to see a play performed by a certain dramatic company. This play—
*Harishchandra*—captured my heart. I could never be tired of seeing it.
But how often should I be permitted to go? It haunted me, and I must
have acted *Harishchandra* to myself times without number. "Why should
not all be truthful like Harishchandra?" was the question I asked myself
day and night. To follow truth and to go through all the ordeals
Harishchandra went through was the one ideal it inspired in me. I *literally believed* in the story of Harishchandra.* [16]

The story, in all brevity, concerns a king of uncommon goodness and virtue. The gods decide to test him. They send a
Brahman to him who at first asks for alms, then for more and
more. The king, true to his *dharma*, gives him all he has including his kingdom. He becomes a slave and his wife leaves him,
taking with her their son, who soon after dies. As a slave,
Harishchandra is put in charge of the local cremation grounds.
His wife reappears with the body of her son and requests
cremation. Harishchandra, following his new *dharma*, dutifully
insists on the customary fee, which his wife cannot pay. She
pleads with Harishchandra, "But he is your son!" But at last the
gods intervene and restore to Harishchandra his kingship and his
family. If we could understand what Gandhi meant by saying
that he "literally believed" such a story we would come much
closer to understanding him and his attitude toward his own
history. In my own terms, I can only surmise that to him the

* Italics mine.

parable had an intrinsic *actuality* much superior to any question of *factual* occurrence, while he later strove towards—and, indeed, succeeded in—living on the level of parables while engaged in the most concrete activities.

In reading the letter to his son, however, we realize with an additional shudder that the period of his disavowal of all "fun and frolic" includes all the years of his early marriage with that willful and playful young girl and, in fact, makes all his puerile and adolescent escapades a matter of deadly earnestness: was there ever an *Antevasin*, one is tempted to ask, whose apprenticeship was a more naked, a more lonely confrontation with the existential categories of sonhood, manhood, selfhood? Here another lifelong trend is indicated: while others may accept deprivations in order to be worthy of the support of traditional teachings and the sanction of certified teachers of the traditional, young Gandhi had to *create* a new tradition.

The nursing care of the father is pictured as the one endeavor superior to all other purpose: was this a parable in which the son not only atones for his own sins but also forgives the father for *his* too? For, no doubt, by forcing the son into an early marriage, Kaba had in a significant way upset something in the son's *dharma*. Gandhi's sexuality, by omission or commission, became permanently marred by what to him was juvenile excess, depleting his power of spiritual concentration. His wife, as long as they lived in lust and begot children, came to personify a threat to higher loyalties, even as all loss of semen was traditionally perceived as a drain on a higher vitality. The strength of such tradition undoubtedly varied in different regions and castes and was vigorously counteracted in some with an almost obsessive erotic flourish. But that higher brain power is enhanced by the physical sexual substance which is lost in ejaculation but can be saved in continence and pumped up to the brain—that seems to be a traditional Indian model of a theory of sublimation. Where such imagery is dominant and some obsessive and phobic miserliness is added, as is universally the case in adolescents convinced that ejaculations are draining them, all sexual life assumes the meaning of depleting a man's essence. Here, then, Mohan

faced a conflict which undermined all spontaneity and playfulness, even in a sexual life legitimized by convention and
"ordered" by his father; and at the end only total abstinence
could give back to him—and to his wife—the sense of humor
which can mark the triumph of self-mastery.

Mohandas' child bride accepted his sexual demands, whatever
their quality, intensity, or frequency really was, because that
was a Hindu girl's lot. But in trying to absorb her into his
adolescent black magic, he met his first (and many feel, lasting)
master: her simplicity and dignity were not to be impaired. She
was, he admitted, initially superior to him in physical courage
and she remained unafraid, unyielding to his frantic efforts to
make a more worthwhile human being out of her by teaching
her to read and write. She would become the all-admired Ba, but
*never* literate: and she could always, as Pyarelal puts it, "make
him feel absurd . . . by just one simple, devastating home-truth
for which she had a genius." But she managed gradually to
assent to a life of sacrifice which she could not escape. Shankerlal asked her in her old age what had happened to her girlish
desire for nice things to wear, and she said: "The most important thing in life is to choose one direction—and to forget the
others." But, of course, she would never discuss the intimate
aspects of her early marriage—not even, one gathers from some
of Gandhi's remarks—with her husband. And from the Mahatma we have only unalleviated Augustinianisms. "If with this
devouring passion there had not been in me a burning attachment to duty, I should either have fallen a prey to disease and
premature death or have sunk into a burdensome existence."[17]
He congratulates himself and her on the fact that in India "the
child wife spends more than half her time at her father's place,"
and he later considered his trip to England at the age of eighteen
"a long and healthy spell of separation." How "passionate" such
a boy or man really is becomes a moot question, for we can only
know of the quantitative threat which he feels the need of confessing. But one thing is devastatingly certain: nowhere is there
any suggestion of joyful intimacy. Later when he had given up
all sexual activity, Gandhi obviously was able to find a certain

erotic-aesthetic gaiety in a kind of detached physical closeness to both women and men. But all genital desire remained a stigma and all yielding a catastrophe: which puts quite a burden on the children who are the accidental issue of such transgressions. As we shall see, this whole matter of Gandhi's fatherhood of natural and of spiritual sons came to a head in the very period of the Ahmedabad Event.

It must be obvious, by now, why much of Moniya's playful and mischievous teasing went sour in his adolescence. And yet I would not concede that his capacity for laughter became totally subdued just because the autobiographic chapters on his youth might as well have been entitled "Experiments with Sin." It probably is true for many, if not for all children, that truly childlike playfulness stops where play with the fire of sexuality begins, if for no other reason than for that factor which Anna Freud describes as the relative weakness of the adolescent ego in the face of pubertal pressure. But in Mohan's case, one suspects, it was the inability to reconcile the sexual demands of his early marriage with the overweening need to use those closest to him for moral encounters. Compared with that, the sexual act was nothing but humiliating contumescence, and in all his writings there is never a suggestion that even as a procreative experience sexual closeness could lift the intimacy between a man and a woman to the level of joyful generativity.

Clinically speaking, one can only conclude that Gandhi *had* to save his kind of playfulness, intimacy, and creativity from a sexuality which had offended him in the biblical sense and that he was fortunate in his capacity to derive eventually a sense of gaiety from plucking it out. But we shall see that some vindictiveness, especially toward woman as the temptress, survived in him and made him insist on absolute chastity as a necessary condition for leaders in nonviolence. There are good institutional reasons for making the love of ashramites or of the inmates of any holy order a love of brothers and sisters. But the disavowal of all phallicism offers only two avenues of sublimation: a transcendence to a "higher" plane of all that is playfully and yet forcefully aggressive and intrusive about the joyful use of the phallus (and this, no doubt, Gandhi would transfer to the more provocative phases of his nonviolent approach); and a regressive emphasis on the eliminative character of detumescence, and an obsessive insistence on cleanliness. Here a life-giving substance is reduced to the status of a dirty and dirtying one which must be contained and counteracted by avoidance and purification. This has powerful and yet highly contradictory antecedents in Indian tradition, and there is no doubt that Gandhi's fanatic dislike of filth and contamination eventually served to direct public attention to the fatal carelessness of Indians in matters of human waste: for acts of spiritual purification can coincide (as in the Ganges) with a total recklessness in matters of hygiene.

One should not rush, then, to interpret such notions as mere products of a personal and neurotic quirk. The question must be recognized as an age-old one: For the sake of what goals, and by what methods, will man learn to contain his excess of instinctual activity? And interestingly enough, *The Story of My Experiments with Truth*, no less than *The Interpretation of Dreams*, assumes that in order to make sexuality amenable to mastery by either "experiment" or "analysis," a man must confront his childhood and, above all, give an account of his conflicts with his father.

### 3. THE CURSE

THE FIRST and only childhood item reprinted in Gandhi's *Collected Works* is a letter which he wrote at the age of fifteen in order to confess to his unsuspecting father the fact that he "had removed a bit of gold from his brother's armlet to clear a small debt of the latter." According to his sister's account (as told to Pyarelal when she was ninety), he first confessed to his mother, who said: "Go and tell your father." "Would father thrash me for this?" he asked. "He won't," the mother replied, "why should he? Has he ever done so?"[18] This, if correctly remembered, at least confirms that the otherwise short-tempered father never laid hands on *this* boy. Gandhi himself continues:

I decided at last to write out the confession, to submit it to my father, and to ask his forgiveness. I wrote it on a slip of paper and handed it to him myself. In this note not only did I confess my guilt, but I asked adequate punishment for it, and closed with a request to him *not to punish himself* [not to take the punishment on himself] for my offence. I also pledged myself never to steal in future.

I was [my hand was] trembling as I handed the confession to my father. He was then suffering from a fistula and was confined to bed. His bed was a plain wooden plank. I handed him the note and sat opposite the plank.

He read it through, and pearl drops trickled down his cheeks, wetting the paper. For a moment he closed his eyes in thought and then tore up the note. He had sat up to read it. He again lay down. I also cried. I could see my father's agony. If I were a painter, I could draw a picture of the whole scene today. [Even today] it is still so vivid in my mind.

[The love arrow of] those pearl drops of love cleansed [pierced] my heart and washed my sin away—[I became pure]. Only he who has experienced such love can know what it is. As the hymn says: "Only he who is smitten with the arrows of love [Rama] knows its power."

*This was, for me an object-lesson in Ahimsa. Then I could read* [see] in it *nothing more than a father's love*, but today I know that it was pure Ahimsa. When such Ahimsa becomes all-embracing, it *transforms everything* it touches. There is no limit to its power. [It is hard to measure this power.]

This sort of sublime forgiveness was *not natural* [basically unnatural] *to my father*. I had thought that he would be angry, say hard things, and [probably] strike his forehead. But he was so wonderfully peaceful, and I believe this was *due to my clean confession*.

A clean confession, combined with a promise never to commit the sin again, when offered before one who has the right to receive it, is the purest type of repentance. I know that my confession made my father feel absolutely safe about me and *increased his affection* for me beyond measure.[19]

My italics mark those passages in which the son, at the age of fifteen, is exquisitely aware of his power to induce in his father an extraordinary state of mind. If such "sublime forgiveness" was "basically unnatural" to his father and if the whole matter nevertheless turns out to be "an object-lesson in Ahimsa," then it is the son who with the spiritual will embodied in his "clean confession" purified the father. For old Kaba did not hit his son (something he seems to have done quite "naturally" to others), nor did he "take the punishment upon himself" by hitting himself on the forehead—an Indian custom which can be most resounding and utterly disconcerting to all within earshot. Instead, there was peace. All of which is emphasized here not only for its intrinsic importance in the development of Gandhi's sense of a superior destiny but also because the story has a certain "typical ring"—a resonance with the lives of other leading individuals with a premature conscience development and an early assumption of moral responsibility for a parent—a responsibility which they subsequently extended to mankind itself.

It seems fitting here to digress in the service of one of the dimensions of biographic interpretation. Even an item as idiosyncratic as Mohan's confession can be fruitfully compared with analogous items in the lives of comparable figures of world history, thus revealing a "typical" experience at least among those who write autobiographies. Let me offer for consideration two items from widely different settings.

Here is a famous passage from Kierkegaard:

Once upon a time there lived a father and a son. Both were very gifted, both witty, *particularly the father*. . . . On one rare occasion, when the father looking upon his son saw that he was deeply troubled, he stood before him and said: poor child, you go about in silent despair. (But he never questioned more closely, alas he could not, for he himself was in silent despair.) Otherwise, they never exchanged a word on the subject. Both father and son were, perhaps, *two of the most melancholy men* in the history of man.

And the father believed that he was the cause of the son's melancholy, and the son believed that he was the cause of the father's melancholy, and so they never discussed it. . . . And what is the meaning of this? The point precisely is that *he made me unhappy*—but out of love. His error did not consist in lack of love but in *mistaking a child for an old man*.[20]

Again, I have italicized the phrases which illustrate what I have in mind, namely, that such encounter is possible only where the father-son relationship has assumed a very special peculiarity. In a patriarchal era a son with a precocious conscience and a deep sense of superior mission could, while still a child, feel spiritually equal to—nay responsible for—a father who, by his own desperate neediness, made it impossible for the boy to hate him. I would venture to suggest that certain kinds of greatness have as an early corollary a sense that a parent must be redeemed by the superior character of the child, and we shall see presently what "sin" it was that Mohandas felt he had to redeem in his father.

But in order to indicate the whole range of this problem, we will shift the scene radically to the autobiography of a woman and modern American and a bearer of a quite different kind of greatness. In Eleanor Roosevelt's life the overweening theme of owing maternal care to all of mankind, as well as to special groups and individuals, manifested itself most decisively and most proudly in the support which she, a previously most undecisive young woman, determined to bestow on her stricken husband. Here is the account of Eleanor's last meeting with her father.

. . . I remember going down into the high ceilinged dim library on the first floor of the house in West 37th Street. He sat in a big chair. He was dressed all in black, looking very sad. He held out his arms and gathered me to him. In a little while he began to talk, to explain to me that my mother was gone, that she had been all the world to him, and now he only had my brothers and myself, that my brothers were very young, and that he and I must keep close together. Some day I would make a home for him again; we would travel together and do many things which he painted as interesting and pleasant to be looked forward to in the future together.

Somehow it was always he and I. I did not understand whether my brothers were to be our children or whether he felt that they would be at school and college and later independent.

There started that day a feeling which never left me—that he and I were very close together, and some day would have a life of our own together. He told me to write to him often, to be a good girl, not to give any trouble, to study hard, to grow up into a woman he could be proud of, and he would come to see me whenever it was possible.

When he left, I was all alone to keep our secret of mutual understanding and to adjust myself to my new existence.

On August 14, 1894, just before I was ten years old, word came that my father had died. My aunts told me, but I simply refused to believe it, and while I wept long and went to bed still weeping, I finally went to sleep and began the next day living in my dream world as usual.

My grandmother decided that we children should not go to the funeral, and so I had no tangible thing to make death real to me. From that time on I knew in my mind that my father was dead, and yet I lived with him more closely, probably, than I had when he was alive.[21]

Here it must be added that her father was an alcoholic and had been put away for years in a sanitarium. He was, in fact, permitted to see his daughter only on singular occasions—such as that of the mother's death. Yet here too the image of the guilty and suffering parent becomes an indelible secret possession and a source of a lifelong and very special strength. In a biographic study[22] Joan Erikson makes a convincing case of it that Eleanor, as the wife of FDR, suddenly lost all her shy undecisiveness when she realized that her husband, then crippled by infantile paralysis, was to be put away, as her father had been at a time when she had been too young to prevent it. Thus Eleanor became great as a president's nurse, companion, and helper and later as a principal trustee of his spiritual-political estate and a co-author of the UN charter of human rights.

In the case of a maternal son, the element of ambivalence looms, of course, very much larger wherever the son is fanatically preoccupied with the care (physical or spiritual) of the father. And, indeed, at the very beginning of his Autobiography, Gandhi refers to his father not only as short-tempered (and we have seen how the son cured him of that) but also as possibly "given to carnal pleasures." For the father's marriage to his mother had been his fourth: and he had married the eighteen-year-old girl when he was already forty. Gandhi records that his father had lost all previous wives by death, but this does not seem to be correct: his third wife was, in fact, still alive, although hopelessly invalid, when Gandhi's father married Putali Ba—a not altogether negligible circumstance in a gossipy community's view of a prime minister's life. It may, in fact, have weighed heavily on Putali Ba. At any rate, that Gandhi, the master of *Brahmacharya*, on the first page of his Autobiography refers to his father as possibly oversexed, and this because he married his mother and fathered him, is a rather fundamental statement of the generational dilemma. For it contains, I believe, the further accusation that the father, by insisting on the son's early marriage, had cursed the son with his own carnal weakness—certainly a powerful ontogenetic argument for the Augustinian stigma of primal sin. Kaba, by exposing his son to sexuality so early, also made him a father before the son could know what he was doing. Kierkegaard, like many a man devoted to the problem of existence as such, thanked God for the fact that He had saved him from becoming a father. If the Mahatma's eldest son would eventually take exquisite revenge on his father by dying a destitute's death, we recognize in Gandhi's life a son-father and father-son theme of biblical dimensions.

This will prepare us for the second, final, and fatal encounter with the father which the Mahatma recorded with such devastating vividness in his Autobiography. It has been quoted so often and overinterpreted so much that I cannot bring myself to reprint it yet again in full. Enough: One night his sick father was fast sinking; but the young son left the nursing care to the father's favorite brother and went to his bedroom to join his (then pregnant) wife. After a while, however, somebody came to fetch him. Rushing to the sickroom, he found that his father had died in the uncle's arms—"a blot," Gandhi writes, "which I have never been able to efface or to forget."[23] A few weeks later his wife aborted.

This experience represents in Gandhi's life what following Kierkegaard, I have come to call "the curse" in the lives of spiritual innovators with a similarly precocious and relentless conscience. It is indicative of an aspect of childhood or youth which comes to represent an account that can never be settled and remains an existential debt all the rest of a lifetime. But it must be clear that one single episode cannot be the *cause* of such a curse; rather, the curse is what we clinicians call a "cover memory," that is, a condensation and projection of a pervasive childhood conflict on one dramatized scene. In individual cases this may seem to be the cause in childhood of a set of dangerous and pathogenic developments in later life; but we may do well to ask what the propensity for such dramatization may mean in phylogenetic development. A dark preoccupation with the death of the old seems unavoidable in a species which must live

through a period of infantile dependence unequaled in length
elsewhere in nature, which develops a sensitive self-awareness in
the very years of immaturity, and which becomes aware of the
inexorable succession of generations at a stage of childhood
when it also develops the propensity for intense and irrational
guilt. To better the parent thus means to replace him; to survive
him means to kill him; to usurp his domain means to appropriate
the mother, the "house," the "throne." If such guilt is, as religions claim, of the very essence of revelation, it is still a fateful
fact that mankind's Maker is necessarily first experienced in the
infantile image of each man's maker.

This curse, clinical theory would suggest, must be heir to the
Oedipus conflict. In Gandhi's case the "feminine" service to his
father would have served to deny the boyish wish to replace
the (aging) father in the possession of the (young) mother and
the youthful intention to outdo him as a leader in later life. Thus
the pattern would be set for a style of leadership which can
defeat a superior adversary only nonviolently and with the
express intent of saving him as well as those whom he oppressed.
Some of this interpretation, in fact, corresponds to what the
Mahatma would have unhesitatingly acknowledged as his conscious intention.

It is of little help, then, to submit Gandhi's confession to such
pseudo-clinical formulations as that "Gandhi in his inner being
was quite the reverse of the filial model he defends in his Autobiography." This is too nonspecific an assertion to explain the
magnitude of his confessed conflict—and what he did with it. It
purports to unmask something which Gandhi, in fact, was aware
of to a fault. The question is, rather, why certain men of genius
can do no less than take upon themselves an evolutionary and
existential curse shared by all, and why other men will be only
too eager to ascribe to such a man a god-given greatness surpassing that of all others.

The question is a threefold one: how does the child and the
youth come to develop the capacity to take on such a fate, and
the man, the determination to honor it; what motivation makes
the multitudes wait for such a man, eager to consider him holy;

and how does he learn to make their motivation and his converge in events which release creative, as well as destructive,
energies of great magnitude?

While Gandhi's Autobiography pictures him as a child and as
a youth totally obsessed with matters of guilt and purity and as a
failure in the ways of the world, he, of course, "somehow" acquired at the same time superior powers of observation as well as
an indomitable determination. But I believe that just because
Mohandas was early (if only darkly) aware of the unlimited
horizon of his aspiration, his failure to preside mercifully over
his father's death and thus to receive a lasting sanction for his
superior gifts was, indeed, the curse of his life. But this, as we
saw, is (typically) a shared curse, for if "carnal weakness" was
to blame, it was the father's weakness which had become the
son's.

The ontogenetic version of this childhood curse remains fateful. The theme of nursing a stricken (and ambivalently loved)
superior adversary reappears in Gandhi's later life both literally
and symbolically. We shall meet it in the role of one who twice,
although an adversary of British policy, recruits for an ambulance corps in support of British war efforts when the Empire
was in danger. And we shall find it in the conviction of the
Satyagrahi that in fighting nonviolently, he is really taking care
of his adversary's soul and its latent "truth."

Yet this theme of nursing a stricken father, too, must and can
be seen in historical perspective. One would not wish to overdo
the parallel, but it is thought-provoking that in Freud's reported
dreams the conviction of having been of medical assistance to his
dying father looms large as a dream-wish counteracting his guilt
over his medical ambitions.

In order to illustrate this, again, with an analogous scene from
a different background, let me turn to the writer Lu Hsün, who
is often quoted with veneration by Mao as the founding father
of modern China's revolutionary literature. His famous short
story, "Diary of a Madman" (1918), the first literary work
written in vernacular Chinese, is a masterpiece not only (we are
told) in the power of its style but (as we can see) as a very

modern combination of a precise psychiatric description of paranoia (Lu Hsün had studied medicine in Japan) and a night-marish allegory of the fiercer aspects of traditional and revolu-tionary China. In an essay entitled "Father's Illness," Lu Hsün combines a historical theme—namely, the discrepancy between Western and Confucian concepts concerning a man's last mo-ments—with the ambivalent emotions of a son.[24] He had spent much of his adolescent years, he reports, searching for herbs that might cure his ailing father. But now death was near.

Sometimes an idea would flash like lightning into my mind: better to end the gasping faster . . . and immediately I knew that the idea was im-proper; it was like committing a crime. But at the same time I thought this idea rather proper, for I loved my father. Even now, I still think so.

This is the Western doctor speaking; but at the time a Mrs. Yen, a kind of midwife for the departing soul, had suggested the application of some traditional magic actions and had urged the son to scream into his father's ear so that he would not stop breathing.

"Father! Father!"
His face, which had quieted down, suddenly became tense. He opened his eyes slightly as if he felt something bitter and painful.
"Yell! Yell! Quick!"
"Father!"
"What? . . . don't shout . . . don't . . ." he said in a low tone. Then he gasped frantically for breath. After a while, he returned to normal and calmed down.
"Father!" I kept calling him until he stopped breathing. Now I can still hear my own voice at that time. Whenever I hear it, I feel that this is the gravest wrong I have done to my father.

Lu Hsün was fifteen at the time (to Gandhi's sixteen). His forebears, like Gandhi's, had been high officials whose fortunes were on the decline during the son's adolescence. At any rate, his story clearly suggests that in his life, too, a desperate clinging to the dying father and a mistake made at the very last moment represented a curse overshadowing both past memory and fu-ture redemption.

It is not enough, however, to reduce such a curse to the

"Oedipus Complex" reconstructed in thousands of case histories as the primal complex. The oedipal crisis, too, must be evaluated as part of man's over-all development. In its habitual connotations it is only the infantile and often only the neurotic core of an existential dilemma which (less mythologically) may be called the *generational complex*, for it derives from the fact that man experiences life and death—and past and future—as a matter of the turnover of generations. Yet, this human crisis is obviously shared by all men, and to highlight it retrospectively in the case of an uncommon man would seem to be a rather minor triumph of ingenuity, if one cannot clarify what makes the man and his complex uncommon.

It is, in fact, rather probable that a highly uncommon man experiences filial conflicts with such mortal intensity just because he already senses in himself early in childhood some kind of originality that seems to point beyond competition with the personal father. Often, also, an especially early and exacting conscience development makes him feel (and appear) old while still young and maybe even older in single-mindedness than his conformist parents, who in turn may treat him somehow as their potential redeemer. Thus he grows up almost with an obligation, beset with guilt, to surpass and to create at all cost. In adolescence this may prolong his identity confusion because he must find the one way in which he (and he alone!) can re-enact the past and create a new future in the right medium at the right moment on a sufficiently large scale. His prolonged identity crisis, in turn, may invoke a premature generativity crisis that makes him accept as his concern a whole communal body or mankind itself and embrace as his dependents those weak in power, poor in possessions, and seemingly simple in heart. Such a deflection in life plan, in fact, may crowd out his chances for the enjoyment of intimacy, sexual and other, wherefore the "great" are often mateless, friendless, and childless in the midst of veneration and confound further the human dilemma of combining the responsibilities of procreation with those of individual existence.

But not all highly uncommon men are chosen; and the psycho-historical question is not only how such men come to experience the inescapability of an existential curse, but how it comes about that they have the pertinacity and the giftedness to re-enact it in a medium communicable to their fellow men and meaningful in their stage of history. The emphasis here is on the word *re-enactment*, which in such cases goes far beyond the dictates of that "repetition compulsion" which characterizes symptoms and irrational acts. For the mark of a creative re-enactment of a curse (and here we may recall King Oedipus on the stage) is that its communal experience becomes a liberating event for each member of an awe-stricken audience. Some dim awareness of this idea must be the reason why the wielders of power in different periods of history appreciate and support the efforts of creative men to reenact the universal conflicts of mankind in the garb of the historical day, as the great dramatists have done and as the great autobiographers do. A political leader like Mao, then, may recognize a writer like Lu Hsün not for any ideological oratory, but for his precise and ruthless presentation of the inner conflicts that must accompany the emergence of a revolutionary mind in a society as bound to filial piety as China. In a man like Gandhi the autobiographer and the leader are united in one person but remain distinct in the differentiation between re-enactments in writing and re-enactments in action. In all re-enactment, however, only the transcendence of an infantile curse by an adult deed marks the man. But as we trace the curse through the stages which prepare the deed, we remind ourselves of that great fact in human life which bridges infantile guilt and adult action: playful enactments in childhood. Seasoned playfulness is long in developing, and I think that in Gandhi's life it can be shown to have alleviated his moral precocity and to have added a significant dimension to his evolving personal and political style. It even seems to be an essential ingredient in nonviolence.

### 4. MOHANDAS AND HIS EVIL FRIEND

How THIS prematurely conscientious boy managed at the same time to "experiment" with delinquency offers one of the most difficult problems of interpretation to anyone—including the Mahatma as witness on his own behalf. But one reads with some relief that Gandhi *could* write with a touch of humor about his youthful escapades—at least the earlier ones. He even reports (with his Gujarati tongue in cheek) a "suicide attempt" which sometimes is reported without quotation marks. I will quote Pyarelal's version, for Pyarelal manages better than other writers to see the preadolescent testing so common in such conspiracy. The boys had talked one another into the conviction that boys should be permitted to smoke. They felt that their

> . . . lack of independence was intolerable. Even death was preferable to it. They decided to commit suicide, made a suicide pact, sealed it by a visit to Kedarji Mandir [a temple], lighted a light to the deity to bless their enterprise, and proceeded to a lonely spot with the seeds of the poisonous *dhatura* (belladonna) in their pocket. They swallowed a few seeds each. But then their courage deserted them. Surely, the lack of independence could be put up with for a little while longer, they thought, till they were grown up and had means of their own. They would then smoke and smoke openly.[25]

But the freedom to be grown up—grown up enough to light a cigarette—often comes only when the disapproving parent is dead; and in India as well as elsewhere even middle-aged men of otherwise independent stature are known to have avoided smoking in the presence of their aged fathers. And so at least in regard to a later crisis when meat-eating was at stake, the Mahatma reports a more outspoken anticipation of the parents' demise on the part of Mohandas: "When they are no more and I have found my freedom, I will eat meat openly, but until that moment arrives I will abstain from it."[26]

The theme of meat-eating brings us to an important figure in Mohandas's life, his "evil genius" or even "the tragedy of his life," as the biographers continue to call him obediently and humorlessly—Sheik Mehtab. There is some social irony in the fact that this boy, who tried to ruin the son of the Vaishnavite prime minister morally, is said to have been the son of the Rajkot police chief—a Muslim. As such, he was a fitting counterpart to Mohan's only other school friend, the younger brother of one of his teachers. Whether or not their powerful relatives provided some background assurance, these two boys are said to have protected Mohan against the bullies who would have tried to test the mettle of a boy who habitually told on others in the name of "truth." But Mehtab's role in Mohan's life was obviously one of elemental significance, not only because the young Muslim was such a "devil," but because Mohandas chose him and stubbornly held onto him in order to test, I believe, the devil in himself.

If Mohandas had ever welcomed his child bride as someone who might free him from a certain enslavement to his parents (and his passion was now "entirely centered on one woman"), she obviously failed him, because unwittingly she became associated with the threat of a worse, a carnal, enslavement. And if his boyhood friend Mehtab in turn was to guide him in an escape from his wife *and* from his parents, Mehtab likewise would fail, because he could not avoid being in sinister league with other enslaving drives. Poor Mehtab was a resourceful and systematic tempter, only to be damned in the very titles of two whole chapters of the Autobiography as "A Tragedy" and "A Tragedy (contd.)." Nobody seems to have a sympathetic word for the boy, whom Gandhi, long into the South African years, not only refused to relinquish but whom he also defended against all detractors. Mohandas, one must conclude, was somehow addicted to Mehtab. And while it is understandable that the Mahatma later had to warn youth against such a friend and to make an evil example of him, it is also clear that Mehtab would have had to be invented if he had not existed. A more insightful and just era may yet build Mehtab a small monument somewhere in Kathiawar. For Mehtab played perfectly the personage on whom to project one's personal devil and thus became the personification of Mohandas' *negative identity*, that is, of everything in himself which he tried to isolate and subdue and which yet was part of him.

Gandhi claims that he befriended Mehtab in order to "reform" him. Ironically, however, Mehtab had himself become a tool of what at that time was widely referred to as "*the* reform," that is, a liberalization in Hindu life which would strengthen and free Indian energies for the task of gaining independence from the British. This reform was aiming to make militant men out of Indians by overcoming certain restrictive taboos such as that against the consumption of meat, which obviously had made British muscle so tough and rosy. One can well see why the two "reforms," pitted against one another, provided that ideological controversy which corresponded to a deep ambivalence within Mohan: for if he managed to become tougher, he might not only some day fight the British and show Indians how to be masters in their own homes, but he also might prove to his wife that he was master of *his* house (or their room within his father's house)—and of her. Mehtab, as is the wont of evil reformers, apparently considered it necessary to make his friend crudely jealous of his wife, fanning the passionate old wish to possess one person totally. But with masculine logic he also encouraged him to be unfaithful and arranged for him to visit prostitutes in order to prove to himself that under favorable conditions, he was really quite a man. And so the tragicomic scene ensued of a prostitute throwing an impotent Mohan out of her house, one of the scenes immortalized in the mural behind the Birla house. Gandhi was gentleman enough to state later that the woman "naturally" lost patience with him. And he did not claim that all such visits ended with his being saved in the same way.

Experiments with truth? Yes, I believe (with that folksy mural) that some such experimentation was necessary for the future leader, for the young man was just about to become the slave of his precocious conscience and all too much addicted to the haughty and habitual use of a tone of moral superiority. It is unthinkable that a man of Gandhi's ethical stature could have remained (or remained only) a moralist who would never face his negative identity. By choosing Mehtab as a friend, he unconsciously tested himself in order to prove to himself that he *could* sin—and test the limits of that experience, too. For the same reason he could not dismiss Mehtab until much later, when as a young reformer Gandhi had found his identity. There is even a suggestion that Gandhi respected and enjoyed the flair of the man Mehtab as Mohandas had admired his boyish courage—and his muscle. We will later report how the men parted.

That this relationship involved a passing experiment with homosexuality, I doubt. Gandhi would have said so, although at the writing of the Autobiography, Mehtab was still alive, and Gandhi admitted later that aside from the boy's name he had left out a number of facts. But any intense friendship among men which excludes and demeans women cannot be without a homosexual element. At any rate, a curious scene, typical for the most pathological phase of an acute identity confusion, occurred when at the end of his eighteenth year Mohandas was ready to leave for England. An important errand was to be done in Porbandar.

An hour before the time of my departure, a serious accident took place. I was always quarreling with my friend Sheikh Mehtab. On the day of departure I was quite engrossed in thinking about the quarrel. We had a musical party at night. I did not enjoy it very well. At about 10:30 P.M. the party ended, and we all went to see Meghjibhai and Rami. On our way I was buried in the madcap *thoughts of London on one side and the thoughts of Sheikh Mehtab on the other.*

Amidst thoughts *I came unconsciously in contact* with a carriage. I received some injury. Yet I did not take the help of anybody in walking. I think I was quite dizzy. Then we entered the house of Meghjibhai. There I again *came in contact with a stone unknowingly* and received injury. I was quite senseless. From that [time] I did not know what took place, and after that, I am told by them, I fell flat on the ground after some steps. I *was not myself* for five minutes. They considered I was dead. But fortunately for myself the ground on which I fell was quite smooth. I came to my senses at last, and all of them were quite joyful. The mother was sent for. She was very sorry for me, and this caused my delay, though I told them that I was quite well. But none would allow me to go. . . .[27]

Much can be made of this somnambulistic occurrence. It certainly is the most "malignant" condition reported by Gandhi. He did not yet speak English well when he wrote this; and yet the phrases he uses can be said to be typical of a "borderline" state in which a loss of control is imminent: "I came unconsciously in contact," "I came in contact with a stone unknowingly," "I was not myself." It has been suggested that this state

ensued from a kind of homosexual panic induced by the anticipation of being separated from Mehtab. Some such latent element cannot be excluded, especially in view of Mohandas's passionate relationship to all his single counterplayers to whom he
gave more of himself than he could afford and from whom he
wanted he knew not what. But I would ascribe this occurrence
to an acute conflict reported one paragraph earlier in the diary
we have quoted. He had visited a leading lawyer, Kevalram, in
order to consult him about his plans to go to England. Kevalram
had not only refused to support a possible scholarship but had
added:

"You will have to set aside all your religious prejudices, if any. You will
have to eat meat; you must drink. You cannot live without that. The
more you spend the cleverer you will be. It is a very important thing. I
speak to you frankly. Don't be offended; but, look here, you are still very
young. There are many temptations in London. You are apt to be en-
trapped by them." I was partially dejected by this talk. But I am not a
man who would, after having formed any intention, leave it easily.[28]

His mind, then, was made up; but I would venture to suggest
that Kevalram had touched on Mohandas's "experimental" propensity with words reflecting Mehtab's earlier and probably
now renewed advocacy of meat-eating and promiscuity. This
was in the center of Mohandas's inner and (not unimportantly)
public conflict. Inner conflicts, at a time of an acute identity
crisis, are always aggravated to the point of panic by sexual
temptation. And as for others, his mother had so far withheld
her full consent to his trip to England, and his whole caste were
opposing his trip as sinful and untraditional; a Vaishnavite Bania
does not cross the "black water"—except, as young Gandhi was
to argue with the council of his caste at Bombay, to Aden and
for business' sake. At any rate, he and his whole family were
threatened with excommunication. If Mehtab's voice and his
own inner temptations were now in not-too-unconscious alliance, he could not be sure that he would be able to meet and
oppose the leaders of his caste with moral conviction. And, indeed, at the very beginning of his youthful diary from which we
have quoted, young Gandhi admits to his adventurous spirit:

. . . Before the intention of coming to London for the sake of study was actually formed, I had a secret design in my mind . . . to satisfy my curiosity of knowing what London was.[29]

What "London was" covers a multitude of possible sins, and I would say that Mohandas was sorely tried by the tempting anticipation, once in England, to make new experiments not only with sexuality but also with diet and tradition. He finally settled the conflict with himself and with his mother by letting her take him to a Jain monk, with whom she had discussed her apprehensions; and there he took a vow to abstain from meat, women, and wine. This alone could safeguard his stay in England and make of it a true moratorium, a period of apprenticeship between the childhood that was over and a future leadership of unforeseeable dimensions.

His childhood had now taught him a decisive lesson which the Mahatma could spell out in sentences as clear and pregnant as they had been dearly bought:

. . . I have seen since that I had calculated wrongly. A reformer cannot afford to have close intimacy with him whom he seeks to reform. True friendship is an identity of souls rarely to be found in this world. Only between like natures can friendship be altogether worthy and enduring. Friends react on one another [affect one another]. Hence in friendship there is very little scope for reform. I am of opinion that all exclusive intimacies are to be avoided, for man takes in vice far more readily than virtue. And he who would be friends with God must remain alone or make the whole world his friend.[30]

This was to be the moral of morals. At the time, however, there is no indication that young Gandhi left with anything but a deeply angry, probably quite confused, but also utterly determined decision to free himself from all intimacies which might penetrate his peculiar need for inviolacy without bringing him nearer to true intimacy with anyone. But neither did he "break" with anyone who did not try to interfere with his departure.

Mehtab was among those who saw him off in Bombay. Being literate, he was to receive and deliver all the letters Mohandas would write to his stubbornly illiterate wife: what an arrangement for endless, fateful mischief! For when Mohan went to England, he left behind not only a wife but also his first-born son, Harilal. And Harilal, no doubt, would not only hear from his father through Mehtab the messenger, but would also become aware of the continuing complaints from grandmother, his mother Putali Ba, and his uncle Tulsidas (the head of the family) that his father continued to trust Mehtab, whom his whole family detested. What else did Harilal see or know of this evil man who had become such a strategic go-between? And in the case of the oldest son of a great man later so righteous in private and so exalted in public, chances always are that nothing is left for the son to correct or to complete, nothing to live out which in the old man's life remained recognizably unlived as a mourned and abandoned potential—except the old man's negative identity, his "murdered self." It may be that Harilal found in Mehtab the ingredients for that rebellious role with which he later faced his father. At any rate, Harilal later became a Muslim and a derelict who within a year after the Mahatma's assassination, was found in a coma "in some locality."[81]

Other experiments followed: Mohan's "delinquent" role was superseded by that of a London dandy, high white collar, silk "chimney-pot," and all. If the Mahatma's description of these roles with their monomaniac emphasis on spotlessness and near-contamination sometimes causes a mild nausea in the reader, he must always remember that it is the man himself who exposes them with a minimum of apologetic ornament. And while it would be easy to call him all kinds of clinical names, from phobic to obsessive to psychopathic, it is also clear that there was a superior self-guidance in it all which permitted the young man to lose himself in petty deviations and, one sometimes feels, in outright deviousness, without losing the over-all direction of one who would, once he found his identity and his "vocation," wield an exceedingly rare power.

# CHAPTER
# II

# From Vow to Vocation

## 1. THE INNER AND THE OUTER MAN

WHEN YOUNG Mohan sailed for England in September of 1888 —then a boat trip of fifty days—he was a quite provincial Kathiawadi. Even to Ahmedabad, the closest cultural and administrative center, he had traveled for the first time only the year before to take the matriculation examination. His attempt to get a government grant from the Administrator of Porbandar had been his first serious encounter with an Englishman. He had, in fact, never even read an English newspaper. And only shortly before leaving for England had he seen the metropolis of Bombay, where he had to seek special dispensation from the elders of his caste to cross the ocean. He faced them with a courage which probably surprised him even more than it did them; but this was a matter of survival—the survival of identity, that is. His inner voice had begun to tell him when and where rebellion is superior obedience in the service of a direction to be implemented by knowledge not yet acquired, by techniques to be learned and opportunities to be recognized. In the meantime he would leave the field clear for the inner voice by first implementing the necessary avoidances, among which the consumption of meat would prove dominant because it was in the center of the whole ambiguity of mere physical survival and spiritual perdition.

To eat or not to eat meat, then, became the first question. In sketching the variable answers, I do not mean to belittle the question itself: the eating of animal flesh, an easy matter of course for most men unless made complex by ritual warnings, may yet turn out to be a problem of psycho-social evolution when mankind comes to review and reassess the inner and outer consequences of having assumed the life of an armed hunter, and all the practical and emotional dead ends into which this has led him. Only then will it be possible to separate the superstitious, neurotic, and faddish aspects of vegetarianism from its possible ethical persuasiveness. At any rate, Gandhi's humor smiles through when he reports the passengers' comments:

They said I would require it [meat] after leaving Aden. When this turned out untrue, I was to require it after crossing the Red Sea. And on this proving false, a fellow passenger said, "The weather has not been severe, but in the Bay of Biscay you will have to choose between death, and meat and wine." That crisis too passed away safely.[82]

But it seems quite apparent that the young man invited many, if not all of these dire predictions, by demonstratively isolating himself in his cabin and room, by worriedly scanning menus and plates, or by simply leading every conversation to the vow he had given to his mother—and this apparently in such a childish fashion that one report speaks of a vow "taken at his mother's knee." And a kind of mother transference seems to have induced the young man to challenge the women, the restaurants, and the societies in London to help him to honor the vow, while he challenged every man to repeat Mehtab's sinister warnings.

This young man, then, would soon stand in the lobby of the Victoria Hotel in London on one of the last foggy days of October attired in a white flannel suit and feeling pierced by what were probably rather indifferent British eyes. One thinks here of the thousands of young Indians who, for the sake of learning Western ways, leave the familiarity and closeness of their joint families to endure an English winter in drab lodgings or to sidestep the dirty ice on the streets of Cambridge, Massachusetts. There are a few, of course, who adapt quickly, probably because they have been used to foreigners at home. But Mohan's not atypical letters to the English administrator in

Porbandar, and then to the political agent of Kathiawar, seem as unpersuasive as they are demanding:

. . . from two months' experience in London I find that . . . in order to live here comfortably and to receive good education, I shall require an extra help of 400 pounds . . . during the late rule of H. H. the Rana Saheb, very little encouragement was given to education. But we can naturally expect that education must be encouraged under the English Administration.
. . . I have very little doubt that you will take the same interest [that you took in my father] . . . and I feel confident that you will try your best to procure me some substantial help which would facilitate my course of study in this country.[33]

In the meantime, the white flannel suit represents much more than the wrong choice of clothing by an innocent young traveler; for as we shall see throughout this chapter, Gandhi was always highly aware of the significance of clothes as uniforms which might identify at least one's aberrant identity fragments—until he learned to be himself, near-naked.

What to take in, then, in order to keep the inner man uncorrupted, and what to wear in order to present to the world the outer man that might represent this inner man—these would prove to be engrossing experiments in the years to come. But here again, the lines between shy withdrawal and the need to tease, between meek adaptation and the need to mock, between abject failure and inner triumph will often be hard to distinguish.

Yet these alternatives provide a kind of formula for reading the Mahatma's account of his student days and for looking behind what otherwise often arouses among the most sympathetic readers some tedium or even aversion: I mean his seemingly self-pitying tone, which is echoed by some biographers ("The Slough of Despond and the Shadow of the Valley of Despair").[34] We now know the motive of the aging autobiographer—namely, to impress on young India the fact that the long wide road of evil begins with the first inch of temptation not recognized as such. And if we remind ourselves that he who wants to "experiment with truth" must also experiment with untruths, we can follow young Gandhi in his deadly-serious and yet half-mocking attempt to become "more English than an Englishman." But again, insofar as there is propaganda in all famous autobiographies (most brazenly so in that of another well-known vegetarian, Adolf Hitler), it is to demonstrate that the writer in his youth had proved to himself that he had mastered every danger and, yes, every ridicule, in such a way that as an adult he would be able to call all his virtues and all his values *his own*. The Mahatma's central chapter on British vegetarianism is appropriately called "My Choice," a title which points to the essence of young adulthood: for he who is tied by a promise which he cannot assent to intellectually or ethically, or he who obeys only out of fear or out of a sense of guilt or sin, is neither free nor a believer. By facing the whole meat-eating issue in all its tragicomic irrelevancies and exaggerations, the future Satyagrahi had to learn to *choose actively and affirmatively what not to do*—an ethical capacity not to be confused with the moralistic inability to break a prohibition.

There appear to be, on first sight, rather blatant contradictions between the Autobiography and young Gandhi's statements at the time: in an interview in 1891 in London, the young law student, when asked what had brought him to England, unhesitatingly exclaimed "Ambition!";[35] while the old man, looking back on that young student, spends ten chapters on the history of his temptations, moral triumphs, and near failures, and then starts the eleventh with the sentence: "I have deferred saying anything up to now about the purpose for which I went to England, viz., being called to the bar. It is time to advert to it briefly."[36] And whereas he had belittled his interest in school, he now concludes, "I passed my examinations, was called to the bar . . . but . . . I did not feel myself qualified to practice law." Such a man never admits that he has learned anything essential from anybody, except where he chooses to ascribe to somebody else what he has already figured out for himself. This and many similar contradictions, however, far from canceling each other out, are "all true," and it is our task to sketch their psychological truth with the conceptual means at our disposal.

The young man, as we would say in our terminology, was now in his *moratorium:* away from home and not as yet constrained to become self-sufficient, head of a family and a citizen, he can test, take chances with, and reassert his childhood identifications. We have already met the main contestants for Gandhi's lasting identifications: Mother, Father, and Evil Other. He now is free of them geographically, but he has brought them with him as his soul's baggage, and even while learning the different roles available to a young Indian student in the London milieu, he must test what he has brought along. His father, of course, is dead; and yet some deep determination to compete with his memory by wielding power in a new way will and must emerge only gradually. That, in fact, *is* the important delay granted by what I have called the adolescent moratorium. But his mother and his negative alter ego he brings with him in all their mutual exclusiveness. His vow now ties him like an elastic band—to be stretched to the limit of endurance—to mother, motherland, and mother-religion, while the male voice of temptation challenges him to snap it—and be "free."

This vow, of course, was more than a promise to behave himself. The greater the distance from home, the more it became the tangible tie to his mother—as if only by not eating meat could he preserve her within him; and he was mightily homesick, "haunted" by his mother's love. But he was also a great eater (a "trencher," as Pyarelal put it in conversation) with mighty oral needs. And Luther's example has taught us to expect as much from a future orator, even (and maybe especially) if his oratorical gift is inhibited in youth. And for a hungry Indian boy in England, it was not just a matter of eating non-Indian food devoid of all condiments, but of eating *English* food. His Scylla and Charybdis was the choice between breaking a vow and filling himself up with brussels sprouts boiled *à l'anglaise*. In this predicament the young man appealed to elderly women in restaurants and to the landladies of his lodgings, who undertook to look after him, only to find him forever "starving."

But at last he found a vegetarian restaurant (appropriately called The Center) on Farringdon Street. Standing before it, he experienced "the joy that a child feels on getting a thing after its own heart." Before rushing in to have his "first hearty meal since my arrival in England," he purchased by the door a book called "A Plea for Vegetarianism" by a Mr. Salt. Thus he had found simultaneously a place to eat well, the literature which would support his vow, and the company of "compatriots" in a wider realm of practical spirituality, for vegetarianism was then allied not only with such concerns as the abolition of vivisection but also with social programs as wide as those of the Fabian Society. And even as vegetarianism helped him to identify with his mother more deeply by inducing him to cook for himself nutritiously *and* economically, it also helped him to develop the householder's habits with which he would later take care of ever bigger things.

The vegetarian movement, however, was divided in regard to the definition of "meat." Did it include the flesh of all animals, and if so, fish as well? And did it also include what was taken from animals—eggs, milk? A young man of Gandhi's scrupulosity would soon find himself scanning the vegetarian menus and the plates on his neighbors' tables for signs of ingredients which he could not eat. And while he decided that "my mother's interpretation of meat was, according to the golden rule, the only true one for me," it is not easy to see where the golden rule comes in or whether he ever asked his mother for her interpretation of his vow under such totally changed conditions. At any rate, eggs were out, too.

We have spoken of the young newcomer's white flannels. The Mahatma later admitted that his "punctiliousness in dress" persisted throughout life; it is said to have been obvious to connoisseurs even in the carefully arranged folds of his shawl and loincloth. But by his chapter title, "Playing The English Gentleman," the Mahatma also characterizes the spuriousness of his Bond Street experiment. Here is a description of his appearance in the circle of the very man whose book he had bought before his first good meal in England:

. . . And in the very early days, an Indian in silk hat and black coat, walked in . . . sat among very affable and talkative people and asked where he could get dancing lessons. . . . Salt was kindness and understanding itself. "My name is Gandhi," he told them, "you have, of course, never heard of it." Salt made a note of a possible new member. Years went by and the name was forgotten.[87]

To the Bond Street clothes and the dancing lessons were added violin lessons as well as instruction in French and elocution; but when the future Indian orator heard himself ape a British model, such as Pitt, he "awoke." It took a kindly woman, his violin teacher, to encourage him "in the determination to make a complete change," by helping him to sell his violin, which he had impetuously acquired for three pounds.

A moratorium is also a period for meeting one's neurosis. True, activities are lightly chosen and easily discarded, imposed by chance and found irrelevant, but an experiment would not be a true one and would not yield answers if it were not taken very seriously at first. This can lead to many minor and a few major moments of panic which confront the experimenter with the choice of suppressing the anxiety or yielding to it as a valid warning. The Mahatma (rightly, it would seem to the psychologist) does not hesitate to do the latter—no matter how he may have felt at the time. "Shyness My Shield" for example, is the title of the chapter which describes, nay, dwells on his early failures in public speaking. He even congratulates himself, the future barrister, for "succeeding" in making himself ridiculous on occasions when lack of inhibition might have led to empty oratory. But while we gladly grant that the inhibitions and anxieties of the moratorium may protect the novice against false and premature successes, they also point to what may prove unresolved in the man and unresolvable in his teaching.

Young Gandhi's "shyness" seems to have been most pronounced in the presence of young women and on certain, but by no means all, occasions when he had to make a speech. Where young women were concerned, his descriptions are probably more humorous in Gujarati than in translation. They became self-caricatures in an effort to protect himself with an exaggerated display of confusion and ineptitude against what would seem to have been imaginary sexual dangers emanating from some sprightly young English women. Indeed, as he suggests, the Anglo-Saxon mores of overtly "free" but basically inhibited companionability may have been too new to him, and he may have wanted to warn young Indians against the danger of being colonialized by London ladies. But the mockery of it all becomes only too obvious in this scene reported by an autobiographer who as a child was an agile tree climber, and as a man could outwalk anyone:

. . . My landlady's daughter took me one day to the lovely hills around Ventnor. I was no slow walker, but my companion walked even faster, dragging me after her and chattering away all the while. I responded to her chatter sometimes with a whispered "yes" or "no," or at the most "yes, how beautiful!" She was flying like a bird whilst I was wondering when I should get back home. We thus reached the top of a hill. How to get down again was the question. In spite of her high-heeled boots this sprightly young lady of twenty five darted down the hill like an arrow. I was shamefacedly struggling to get down. She stood at the foot smiling and cheering me and offering to come and drag me. How could I be so chicken-hearted? With the greatest difficulty and crawling at intervals, I somehow managed to scramble to the bottom. She loudly laughed "bravo" and shamed me all the more, as well she might.[38]

It should be added that the young man had never intimated to these ladies that he had a wife back in India, and that he chose to make this fact a matter of dramatic confession only when he imagined himself to be the victim of intended matchmaking by his landlady.

Then there were the occasions on which young Gandhi had such anxiety attacks when he tried to speak in public that even the kind-hearted Vegetarian had to describe Mr. Gandhi's appearance as "rather nervous." The first occasion seems to be especially important, since it points to the kind of self-imposed task which induced the young man to speak in public in the first place and to the element within that task which seems to have disturbed him most. The president (and financial backbone) of the Vegetarian Society had urged a committee of which Gandhi was a member to expel a medical member (Doctor Allinson, by name) who publicly advocated birth control. Here, young Gandhi felt immediately called upon to represent the view that the object of the Society was "the promotion of vegetarianism and not of any system of morality"—certainly an early manifestation of the singleminded manner in which Gandhi later would hold his followers to one stated purpose at a time. For, no doubt, young Gandhi was not in sympathy with birth control—except by abstinence. Yet, he felt that the doctor's activities outside of the Vegetarian Society were none of the Society's business. And then again, his emotions were hopelessly tangled: he became so flustered that he had to have his remarks read for him. The doctor lost the day; nevertheless, the Mahatma is proud to register the fact that "in the very first battle . . . I found myself siding with the losing party."

One could accept this and similar episodes as memories in support of the Mahatma's proposed moral that a certain shyness is helpful in maintaining a high standard of oratorical chastity. Yet he *could* speak quite well. On one occasion when asked to do so impromptu at a meeting, he even had his wits sufficiently ready to quote Shakespeare:[39]

> Who can be wise, amaz'd, temperate, and furious,
> Loyal and neutral in a moment?

He thus quite courageously expressed himself against the multiplicity of causes and moods entertained by his vegetarian hosts. It becomes all the more clear that neurotic conflict was operative on the occasions when young Gandhi was acutely inhibited as a speaker. In the first instance the difficulty, one suspects, was over the fact that birth control would do away with much of the necessity for self-control; while, as we saw and will see, progeny is for a man of Gandhi's spiritual bent a living accusation of faulty self-discipline and of insufficient clarity in one's existential life plan. And, indeed, the theme of conception seems to have been present also on the last of the occasions in England when Gandhi failed in a speech. Here, in fact, he seems to have tried to come to his own rescue by telling a joke which (whether or not he had recognized it as the critical theme) makes a pun on the word "conception." Before leaving England, the young barrister gave a "brilliant and sumptuous" party for his friends at the fashionable Holborn restaurant, which went vegetarian for the occasion, at least in one of its rooms. He tried to overcome his shyness by referring to a well-known story, in which the politician, Addison (a name reminiscent of the controversial Dr. Allinson), on giving his maiden speech in the House of Commons, began with the words "I conceive," became flustered, and repeated the words twice, whereupon a helpful colleague arose to exclaim, "The gentleman has conceived thrice but has produced nothing." The laugh, however, was on young Gandhi, who could not finish *his* story and sat down with curt thanks.

Although, according to English Vegetarianism, health and vigor could well be associated with sexual freedom, for this young Hindu the prime significance of vegetarianism was that of avoiding evil. The young barrister summed up his concerns before leaving—with his vow still intact all around. Having admitted that Hindus are notoriously weak, he claimed that there were other causes for this weakness than mere abstinence from meat:

One of the most important reasons, if not *the* most important one, is the wretched custom of infant marriages and its attendant evils. Generally, children when they reach the great age of nine are burdened with the fetters of married life. . . . Will not these marriages tell upon the strongest constitutions? Now fancy how weak the progeny of such marriages must be.

There follows a strangely personal note:

. . . Then about six years after marriage he has a son, probably he has not yet finished his studies, and he has to think of earning money not only to maintain himself but his wife and child, for he cannot expect to pass his whole life with his father, and even granting that he may, he should certainly be expected to contribute something towards his wife's and his child's maintenance. Will not the mere knowledge of his duty prey upon his mind and thus undermine his health? Can anyone dare to say that this will not shatter a most robust constitution? But one may well argue that if that boy in the above example, had eaten flesh-meat, he would have kept stronger than he did. A reply to such an argument is to be found from those Kshatriya princes who in spite of their meat diet are very weak, owing to debauchery.[40]

But he did not leave his friends in England without an appeal for the Indian masses:

... In practice almost all the Indians are vegetarians. Some are so voluntarily, and others compulsorily. The latter, though always willing to take, are yet too poor to buy meat. This statement will be borne out by the fact that there are thousands in India who have to live on one pice (⅓ d.) a day. These live on bread and salt, a heavily taxed article.
The drinking of tea and coffee, by the so-called educated Indians, chiefly due to the British rule, may be passed over with the briefest notice. The most that tea and coffee can do is to cause a little extra expense, and general debility of health when indulged into excess, but one of the most greatly-felt evils of the British Rule is the importation of alcohol—that enemy of mankind, that curse of civilization—in some form or another. The poor [in India] as everywhere are the greatest sufferers. It is they who spend what little they earn in buying alcohol instead of buying good food and other necessaries. It is that wretched poor man who has to starve his family, who has to break the sacred trust of looking after his children, if any, in order to drink himself into misery and premature death. ... But what can the energy of one man, however powerful, do against the inaction of the apathetic and dormant Government?[41]

Was *he* "this man, however powerful" who might try to stir what was apathetic and dormant in his homeland and become the first all-India leader with a following? If so, his capacity for leadership, at the time, was still almost totally dormant. Yet we may ask what he had learned in England. The relative neglect of his studies of the law, which he cites in his autobiographic account and his summary ("I did not feel myself qualified"), are justified only if understood as part of a deeper success by which young Gandhi learned to be just enough of an Englishman to join an English identity element with the Indian one before subordinating *both* first to a wider British, and then to a truly universal identity. For in this period he had also learned something of the world religions, even reading his own people's Bhagavad Gita for the first time with two theosophist Englishmen. The martial and punitive Old Testament was abhorrent to him, but the Sermon on the Mount went "straight to my heart." He associated the command to turn the other cheek with the Indian "for a bowl of water give a goodly meal," but then this period *was* one preoccupied with food. All of this, however, was literary religion, and Gandhi was a very unliterary man. If any saying or song went "to his heart," it meant that it would eventually be translated into action. We shall see how, given his personal history and that of Indian tradition, he could be really free to lead others only after he had founded his own kind of religious order.

In the meantime his vow had helped him, beyond mere avoidances, to keep committed only to the religion of Putali Ba and his nurse, Rambha, or at any rate, to the folk religion of Mother India which enters a child's mind "with his mother's milk." To have kept that area free from encroachment by Western thought—and, yes, I would think, safe from white women who might invade a heart confused by wine and fun—that was the deeper meaning of the vow. That young Gandhi left England with this vow intact was a matter of enormous importance, not only in his own eyes, but later also for his ethical stature among his people. The clinician must add, however, that this victory also reinforced Gandhi's obsessional trends, set him against women and even against milk, and in no way furthered his capacity to appreciate or even tolerate sexual intimacy—a fact which will call for our most thoughtful attention later.

He left England having learned much that he could rely on later in adapting to the best in the British; but above all he left England an augmented Indian, and that means a stronger man as well as his mother's son. He still had to preserve this combination in the face of a sacred obligation—namely, the promise to reward his brother, his father's memory, and the family whose fortune he had spent in England with the success to be expected from a barrister made-in-England.

As to his over-all appearance, he now spoke English well and knew how to dress like an Englishman: in a last picture of the Vegetarian Society, the white handkerchief falls like a cascade over the rim of his breast pocket. But if in the next chapter we emphasize dress as much as we have dwelt on food intake here, it is due to the problem of identity: for what kind of attire will feel "like oneself," and what kind will make us outlandish in our own eyes—that question is not unimportant and assumes special significance in one who some day would wire Winston Churchill that it was his endeavor to be "as naked as possible." There was, and there would be, much vanity in his poverty, much conceit in his humility, and much stubborn persistence in his helplessness, until he would find a leverage to make—for himself and for the destitute Indians—out of poverty, humility, and helplessness a new strength and a new instrument: but that new hope would come only when the young man's search for his vocation had reached rock-bottom.

## 2. ARJUNA IN THE COURT OF SMALL CLAIMS

IT MIGHT SEEM appropriate to start an altogether new chapter at the point of young Gandhi's return home from England in 1891 and another at his departure for South Africa in 1893. But the story of transformation to be told here reaches a resolution only on a railroad trip from Durban, Natal, to Pretoria, Transvaal, where young Gandhi would find himself literally beaten down body and soul. Thus far, as we have seen, he had struggled to hold on to a vow, but he had not yet found a vocation, a call.

Young Gandhi went home because he had graduated; that he went home with the wholehearted intention of making good is quite unlikely. A soul that sensitive, proud, and self-centered can find a vocation only by *not* succeeding in ordinary ways, even if that means to perish. When the Mahatma later looks back, and on a number of different occasions points to specific events as having "changed the course of my life," the moral is obvious (and often implied in the wording) that he was waiting for and, in fact, even "setting up" some of the shocking events which would sanction a radical direction already well under way.

The first shock that awaited the young man at home, however, was one that unavoidably sealed his childhood. When on arrival he asked how was his mother was, there was an embarrassed silence, and the abrupt news that she had died. She had lived just long enough to hear, with tears, of his graduation. The fact of her death had been kept from the traveler as too unnerving; but although his grief was, as he put it, "even greater than over my father's death," he "took to life as though nothing had happened." We mourn most dramatically where, with the death of someone, an unlived chance of reconciliation and inner enrichment is gone forever. That, after all, is the meaning of the totem ritual; in fact and in spirit we want to be sure of having incorporated and assimilated what generative strength there was in the deceased.

His father's death had remained a kind of curse for young Gandhi. But his mother, it seems, he had taken along by way of his vow, and he had made her a part of himself in the process of sustaining it. His preoccupation with food had been and would be obsessive and faddish, and much of his deep ambivalence toward the "good" and the "bad" mother survived in his dietary scruples. For even as young Gandhi, the expert cook, "became" his mother, he also remained, throughout his dietary experiments, teasing little Moniya in relation to her. All semblance of an "experiment" is lost, of course, where the experimenter maximizes the inner split of self-observation the way Gandhi did throughout his life: one can get a touch of indigestion merely from reading how he would cook, eat, and then watch himself for signs of increased or weakened vitality. And more than once he made himself ill by trying to purify his inner linings with a "totalistic" fervor, while in the end he abjured even milk in order not to feel unduly erotized. But we must recognize his dietary struggle also as a fundamental solution to an existential problem. At the beginning when the mother is truly the matrix of survival, we can learn to trust the world and to develop the basic ingredient of all vitality: hope. Having tasted our mother's body with mouth and senses, we remain part of it and yet also become strong enough to part from it. Our first firmament is the mother's face, shining above the goodness of nourishment; and only the study of universal mythology and of the deepest mental pathology can give us an inkling of the sinister rages and the confused imagery which that early trust must help us to contain before we can emerge from the maternal matrix. Those moods and that confusion must often be lived through again in

breast-hope

adolescence—and this especially in passionate youths beset with a sense of sin—when the original trauma of separation from the mother's body is repeated in the necessity to leave "home"— which, as we have seen, may include motherland, mother tongue, mother religion. Young Gandhi's vow and the way he worried about it served to tide him over a period when his moralistic self-denial only gradually ripened into an ethical capacity to find his own formula for the ancient religion which he had absorbed in his childhood. But this process had long since transcended his individual mother: and I think he mourned less because he knew she was in him and was at the core of the best in him—the only immortality which a parent can claim.

I am not preparing the reader for an interpretation that Gandhi's identification with his mother was any more "important" than that with his father—as has been claimed. But the mother simply comes earlier in the cycle of life, and what is significant about her must be combined with the more complex, more competitive father identification; while what remains weak and conflict-ridden in both expresses itself in behavior sometimes more symptomatic than creatively unique. But there was a strong maternal aspect to Gandhi's creativity, and it is not unimportant, therefore, to attempt to spell out what his special characteristics of ambivalence toward his mother and to motherhood in general may have been. Gandhi's biographers, of course, usually deny him the right to harbor even as much ambivalence as is any human being's birthright, and Gandhiites go to unbelievable lengths to speak of their master as totally loving—so much so that one often yearns for an inkling of that ambivalence which makes love meaningful—or possible. Every child feels abandoned and betrayed by his mother, though often in a preverbal and later unconscious way. But Gandhi gives indications of a more extraordinary conflict. If, as he says, his father was "given to carnal pleasure," then his young mother was either the father's more or less willing conspirator or his victim; and the implication is that little Moniya is himself the living issue of what, perhaps, might better not have been. There are persistent indications, some already mentioned, that to a man like Gandhi "lust" as such meant both a cloacal pleasure and a thoughtless play with the fire of procreation. But where traditional Eastern concepts of birth and rebirth, of death and Nirvana enter, a Westerner must tread cautiously. No doubt Gandhi, like Socrates, came to regard a real death (that is, relief from rebirth) as a cure from life.

The relationship to the internalized mother, then, is highly complex: for here, the very hope for life as nourished in the infant by his mother must become faith in the possibility of *not* being reborn, of overcoming the necessity for rebirth through a love which is nondestructive because it transcends bodily existence and with it sexual differentiation. In this Gandhi seems to have felt supported by the memory of his highly religious mother. Had she not after his birth ceased to have children? He himself, then, had been the cause of her determination to let procreation come to an end—and lovingly so. In identification with this woman, Gandhi obviously learned to value the abstention from any but the most necessary food intake—a feat managed by many a successful dieter and yet, I would assume, rarely matched in the abstainer's capacity to feel nourished and vitalized by the smallest amount of the most highly selected food (as well as by short, but well-spaced, periods of sleep). And if the freedom from desiring meat also meant the freedom from any voracious and destructive oral attachment, then young Gandhi could count on a secret agreement with his mother which united them both as it emancipated both: where the mother who gives and the mother who denies thus becomes one benevolent agency, a rare energy of loving self-denial and self-denying love may well be a lasting emotional treasure.

In London, as we have seen, Gandhi could use his vow as a bridge to a vital contemporary movement, vegetarianism, and could thus combine a more intellectual approach with archaic aspects of Indian religiosity, which was still very much alive in the Indian masses—and in him. The vegetarian movement also brought him into first contact with such vital Christian and Western writers as Tolstoy, Ruskin, and Thoreau (although he claimed to have really read Thoreau only later, in jail in South

Africa) and, in fact, introduced him to some of the classical Hindu scriptures. In many ways, then, the internalized strength of his mother combined with a universal education would eventually strengthen in him a peculiarly Indian intuition and yet also a critical ability to empathize with the Indian masses, who, with their closeness to the superstitition of the soil and the imagery of the mother religions were, and remain in our time, the challenge of economic, political, and spiritual inventiveness.

To end on a clinical note: it is always difficult to say where, exactly, obsessive symptomatology ends and creative ritualization begins. But it must be clear that where the individual's dispositions and preoccupations help to release a new energy capable of awakening corresponding energies in others, what may at first look like a shared symptom can claim to approach the mutuality of fruitful ritualization. And Gandhi, as we shall see, was an inveterate ritualizer. This, then, seems to be the political meaning of Gandhi's identification with his mother: the maternal side of Bapu ("the father," as he was later called) attracted particular types of followers and inspired particular trends in the masses: almost as though he had provided in his own person a new matrix, had become India herself. But this could not come to fruition until he had integrated equally well his father's stubborn integrity and Bania pragmatism. What ambivalence remained in his maternalism, however, would eventually support a pervasive ambivalence toward him which would result in his whole image and his whole career being regarded as a massive hindrance to the democratic fraternalism and managerial rationalism of the industrial age.

But we must now attend to another important influence in Gandhi's prolonged identity crisis. It is significant that the chapter in the Autobiography which tells of young Gandhi's homecoming at the age of twenty-two and of his mother's death does not bear a title referring to either. The heading is "Raychandbhai."[42] This is the name of a man only a few years older than he, whom young Gandhi met on the evening of the very day he heard of his mother's death. Raychandbhai (as Gandhi affectionately calls one Rajchandra) was a deeply philosophical young man who came as close to being Gandhi's guru as anybody ever did—which, to tell the truth, was not *very* close. There was a literal transfer in this sudden attachment, by which I do not mean that it was merely "mother transference," for Raychandbhai's attraction as a person of saintly insight was widely recognized. In fact, this young man and his precepts were to become the anchor of young Gandhi's religious imagination during the very period of his life when he felt most lost, for he had to turn from the obedience to his mother to an affirmation of himself: from his vow, then, to his vocation. And *his* vocation meant to surpass and to renew the professional heritage of his father and his forefathers.

How a man (in Woodrow Wilson's words) "comes to himself" is superficially apparent in what he loves, or would love, to do because it augments his sense of genuineness—but it is also defined by what makes him feel "not himself" and by what can drive him "beside himself." We recognize at the beginning of the Mahatma's report on his homecoming one hope: that he may have been about to make contact with the heritage personified for the moment by Raychandbhai. But there are also three well-defined apprehensions. How would he meet the expected trouble with his caste which had excommunicated him and his family when he left for England; how would or could he settle down to a profession for which he felt in no way prepared, in spite of his English training, title, and manners? And how would he establish himself as a reformer? For he now had no doubt in his central competence: "I was a reformer."[43]

In reforming himself and others, he felt "himself"; but he was still a brother, a husband, a father, and—even if excommunicated—a caste member. And for the vast majority of Hindus, caste was an all-enveloping identity provider in this life as in all other possible lives. Yet when he had left for England, he had faced his caste elders with that "eternal negative" which he so often would express in the nonviolent phrase "I am helpless"— meaning his mind had made itself up, and he had to obey. But since his mother's dying wish had been her son's reconciliation to his caste, this matter had to be settled first. After a purification ceremony at a sacred shrine in Maharashtra and a caste dinner in Rajkot, the Rajkot division readmitted him, but the Porbandar and Bombay branches never did. Gandhi would preserve his self-respect and theirs by never asking any member of these branches to "even give me a glass of water." This, incidentally, excluded all his in-laws from social contact with him and cannot have made Kasturba's life any easier. He would, henceforth, make certain ceremonial concessions, but he would never mortgage his identity to caste; and, indeed, some of the caste members who shunned him ceremoniously at this time became at a much later date some of his most respectful political adherents.

The hopeful reformer, however, met the limits of his determination in his own home. For this he would partially blame himself in the old manner: "My lust came in the way"; he proved as "jealous" as before, whatever that meant. He would also blame Kasturba for being the cause of those states of being "beside himself" with rage which he would vent only on Kasturba and on his sons for years to come. Again, he sent Kasturba home (and across the caste barrier): for he could not come to terms with her until she would accept the fact that his family, to remain his family, would have to become part of a reform community reformed by him. The old question of what was the real "reform" still befuddled all issues; he attempted to introduce into his home a queer mixture of dietetic purification and English refinement, even forcing his family to eat with fork and knife and to adopt English dress, including what he himself would later consider a rather distasteful aspect of Western civilization transferred to a tropical climate, namely, sweaty socks. By the same token, he now tried to break Kasturba's resistance to literacy by assigning her the new role of the wife of a barrister made-in-England, which had no meaning whatever to her. It all ended with this ambiguous statement:

. . . and as I had now become her teacher, however indifferent, and helped her to make certain reforms, we both felt the necessity of being more together, if only to continue the reforms.[44]

Who was indifferent?

He also attempted to teach the children of the family what he had learned, from diet and calisthenics to "God Save the Queen." He came, in fact, to the conclusion, "I should make a good teacher of children." Since this never came to a full-time test, one has rather the feeling (confirmed only by a number of vague impressions gathered from photographs and witnesses) that Gandhi transferred his tendency to tease animals to that of teasing and provoking children, some of whom, no doubt, were highly entertained and some only politely tolerant. His meeting with children, one gathers, became a ritualization, too, and no doubt they felt important. As to the later education of his own sons, one would need to clarify what some of them learned in spite of him as much as through him, and what they learned during the frequent separations from him. At any rate, nowhere in this book is the analysis of Gandhi's conflicted attitudes toward his maturing sons to be interpreted as a reflection on their actual lives as adults—except, of course, in the case of the oldest, Harilal.

Reforming costs money, and although his status demanded that he charge ten times their fee, this highly trained professional knew less of Indian law than the untrained local *vakils*. He conceded, of course, that his brother had a right to expect of him a measure of professional success. Whether his brother still expected him to become a prime minister or whether he now aspired to such a position himself is not clear, and, at any rate, for Gandhi that kind of job had lost what glamour and integrity it had possessed in the years before their father's death. But it does seem that other available jobs did not measure up either to young Gandhi's English dignity or, indeed, to his enormously sensitive integrity. A stubborn inner voice obviously did everything to sabotage any success as a lawyer either in Rajkot or in Bombay. For such avoidance, too, a great man can count on a guardian angel.

Young Gandhi's first appearance in court ended in that scene which is immortalized in the mural behind the Birla house as a way station in the Mahatma's life. It was his first case, simple enough, and was expected to last no more than a day. But the young lawyer was "beside himself" with fright. It must have been a miserable scene. And yet, when the Mahatma writes of his shyness as a shield, he himself seems to recognize that what looked like failure may, in fact, have been a kind of triumph. But I submit that he implies more. For if his public nervousness in England is described with the words "my vision became blurred, and I trembled," is this not reminiscent of young Arjuna whose chariot has been drawn up between the two armies? "My limbs fail," Arjuna tells Lord Krishna (in Gandhi's own translation), "my mouth is parched, a tremor shakes my frame and my hair stands on end."[45] And how well does a courtroom fit the opening line of the Bhagavad Gita: "In the field of righteousness. . . ." True, the scene of the trembling young barrister committed to represent "one Mamibai" for thirty rupees in a Bombay small claims courtroom can hardly be compared with a setting where "stationed in their great chariot, yoked to white horses, Krishna and Arjuna blew their celestial conches." But when the Mahatma says that there in that courtroom "my head was reeling, and I felt as though the whole court was doing likewise. . . . I was past seeing anything,"[46] he again echoes Arjuna's condition, "I cannot keep my feet, and my mind reels." That the future Mahatma was smitten in the drabness of that court only signifies his style of leadership, for he would tend to seek out the smallest and most local situations as a great soul's proper battlefield.

But since this is a psychoanalyst's book, we must also take note in passing of that neurotic factor in the young barrister's confusion which had been apparent in previous "attacks." In the Vegetarian Society he had faltered in his defense of an advocate of birth control, and in the Holborn restaurant when he tried to speak humorously of a gentleman who had "conceived thrice." At the time of the court scene in Bombay, Kasturba was again pregnant. And years later when Gandhi's voice would fail him once more and for the last time in a large meeting, Kasturba would be pregnant with their last son. Symptoms, we say, are always "overdetermined" and cannot be reduced to one "cause." But the contributing causes converge on unitary themes. Here they combine to support the interpretation that to continue to generate children somehow meant to forfeit the grand scheme of this man's reform, and that the young householder and lawyer trembled over his *dharma*, as did the young prince and warrior before the battle.

At any rate, it is probable that high spiritual aspiration was more "real" to the "briefless barrister," the hapless husband, and the unwilling father than were his transitory failures. Arjuna's confusion in the Bhagavad Gita is resolved by caste membership: a Kshatriya must kill when necessary and die when the time comes, knowing that his personal identity is entirely determined by the identity of his caste and that by fulfilling both with detachment he transcends not only the limits of identity but also those of death, whether he inflicts it on others or suffers it. By the same token, Gandhi would become himself exactly at the moment when his personal and physical powers and limitations were transcended by the reformer's duty: selfless service.

This brings us back to Raychandbhai, the young *savant*, whose demeanor and words "went straight home to me." No doubt young Gandhi recognized in the twenty-five-year-old friend something of what he felt was his own essence, and while his other obligations weighed heavily on his moral sense, he found in this friendship the first affirmation of his as yet deeply inarticulate ethical direction; Rajchandra succeeded in translating for him the highly personal commitment of his vow into the ideological terms of the Jain community—a world that had enveloped and pervaded the whole religious scene in Kathiawar —including Putali Ba's special Vaishnava sect. Young Gandhi now could absorb Jain ideology without accepting any dogma or ritual whatsoever; and if he says in his Autobiography that, in addition to Rajchandra, Tolstoy and Ruskin had inspired him most, it must be clear that he accepted from all of these men only a sanction of and a vocabulary for what was becoming articulate in him. In the long run, young Gandhi would commit himself to nothing less than the stubborn intention of making out of religious precepts what he thought he recognized in the Gita: a "grammar of action."

Rajchandra, however, could not be a future activist's guru. True, he combined admirably the occupation of a diamond merchant and the vocation of a philosopher-poet, but to Gandhi's taste he bowed too much to the caste system in this world, while being so other-worldly that he forgot to take care of his body. He died at the age of thirty-one—as Gandhi thought, of self-neglect, a diagnosis which would prevent Gandhi later from accepting the only other candidate (Gokhale) as a true guru. But, if ever so fleetingly, young Gandhi had met a genuine seeker after truth, and we shall find essential elements of Jain thought in Gandhi's later ideology. And since there can be no identity without an ideology, and since this is exactly where gurus come in, it is important to note that he had found in Rajchandra the man who would gently advise the returnee from the West that there was nothing in other religions that Indian religion had not formulated more tolerantly and more practically—and long before the others.

If the Mahatma concludes all this with the remark that "the throne" of guru had "remained vacant" in his life even up to *Moksha* time, one could be tempted to follow the throne imagery in his life, from the time way back in Porbandar when little Moniya had sat himself in the place of Thakorji's picture, to all the real or symbolic thrones and top jobs he would come close to in one context or another. It would appear that he never occupied one and yet never bowed to one either. Any throne, or for that matter any prime ministership, was too sedentary a place for a pilgrim.

And, indeed, it seemed to be time to move again, especially after young Gandhi, in another highly confused scene, had demonstrated to himself and to his brother that there was no place in Kathiawar for a gentleman barrister of his kind. To make it brief: his brother had asked him to intervene on his behalf with the British administrator in Porbandar, whom Gandhi had met briefly in London. Young Gandhi knew he should not attempt to exploit that acquaintance for local and personal purposes, but he went anyway, was persistent, and was thrown out. This was another one of those episodes which he says changed the course of his life. The fact is that they supported his inner direction. And when an offer came to go to South Africa, he probably felt, against all immediate promise or evidence, that there was a better chance for him almost anywhere else than at home. And so begins the prophet's detour—twenty years and thousands of ocean miles long.

He was not sought out as a barrister in his own right but as a London-educated, English-speaking Gujarati who might help the local lawyers formulate a lawsuit started by an ex-Gujarati Muslim merchant in Transvaal. Gandhi knew he was a mere "servant of the firm of Dada Abdulla and Company," and yet in April 1893 he crossed the Indian Ocean first class and arrived dressed in a frock coat, shining boots, and a turban, which the Mahatma describes as an imitation of the "Bengali pugree." Maybe Gandhi learned slowly—or, maybe, he continued to test; at any rate, he reports that on this trip, in an unspecified port, another tussle occurred with a prostitute, in which he again remained "unscathed," although he had followed the ship's captain ashore for purposes which must have been obvious enough; again he apologizes in retrospect to "the poor woman."

On his arrival in Durban there was some mutual sizing up— Dada Abdulla not being at all sure what kind of man he had imported. On about the third day he took him to watch a court session. The judge tried to size up his strange appearance, and asked him to take off his turban—only to be greeted with the "eternal negative." The judge insisted; Gandhi left the court.

He was then told the whole fantastic story of race relations in South Africa. The judge had scrutinized his contrived appearance in order to classify him: if he were an Indian *Muslim*, then he could pass as an "Arab," a fiction which Indian, Dutch, and British had agreed to maintain. An Arab not being an "Asiatic," he could have kept his turban on as did his companion Dada Abdulla. If he had been an Indian *Parsi*, however, he would call himself a "Persian" and would not think of wearing a turban in the first place. So here he faced both a religious and a national identity problem. Still insisting on the role of the English barrister, he immediately offered to wear a high hat which he would *have* to take off in court. Ah, but that, he was told would make matters even worse, for only *Christian* Indians wore European clothes, and they were usually waiters and clerks: a class confusion, then. Thus the whole headgear issue which had come to represent the most snobbish aspect of his conflict between exhibitionism and humility had landed him in the middle of his people's identity confusion—or rather in the middle of the web of pretenses which were supposed to be its solution, at least in "adjusted" and moneyed circles. For the bulk of the tens of thousands of poor Indians in South Africa, there was not even the remedy of such cultural pseudologia, for they were the "indentured labourers" who had been shipped to Africa under an agreement that they would work in mines and fields for five years and then either be paid the return fare to India or be permitted to remain as "freed" Indians, only to be kept in a condition of semi-slavery in the British, as well as the Boer, states of South Africa. And since this largest and lowest class was called "coolie," the South Africans did what certain other Southerners have done; they lumped all "colored" folk together: all Indians in South Africa were called "coolie" or "sami." So Mr. M. K. Gandhi, erstwhile member of the "Inner Temple," was a "coolie barrister."

But how is it possible that Gandhi had never heard of his countrymen's condition in Africa? When one considers that the Indian Ocean was a much-traveled body of water linking India's West Coast with Africa's East Coast, then certainly the Gujaratis in Kathiawar and those in Natal were sharing a common world of trade and migration. How could such conditions remain unknown? On questioning his employers in Natal, Gandhi received the Bania answer he deserved:

"Only we can live in a land like this because for making money we do not mind pocketing insults. . . . *This country is not for men like you.*"[47]

I have italicized the last sentence because it will serve as a negative motto for Gandhi's emerging identity as the man who was needed. In spite of being a "coolie barrister," he saw the whole matter at first as an affront to his own class, which was learning to emulate the white man. The parallel with race relations in our country is obvious: the Negro middle class, too, had conspired with the whites in keeping the stark facts of discrimination hidden behind the claim that more and more educated and moneyed Negroes were doing already so much better that, for their sakes, gradualism deserved acceptance as a way of life. Our eyes, too, were opened to what was open to anybody to see, only when some of our young men put their "bodies on the line." And so the young barrister also became the conscience of his nation only when—inadvertently at first—he found his body on that line which marks the difference between retreat and irreversible commitment.

This moment came on the night of nights. After a week in Durban, Natal, it seemed advisable that Gandhi should proceed to Pretoria in the Transvaal. He traveled first class, of course. In Maritzburg, the capital of Natal, a white man entered his compartment and immediately refused to spend the night in a coolie's company. The conductor ordered Gandhi to third class. There followed the "eternal negative," and the arm of the law deposited him and his bags on the station platform. Since his bags were taken in custody by the station master, the young barrister found himself without an overcoat in a dark waiting room at an altitude of two thousand feet. It was during that wintry night that he resolved that South Africa was, indeed, a country for him—if only he could learn to be the man for that country. He decided,

The hardship to which I was subjected was superficial—only a symptom of the deep disease of colour prejudice. I should try, if possible, to root out the disease and suffer hardships in the process.[48]

There is every reason to believe that the central identity which here found its historical time and place was the conviction that among the Indians in South Africa he was *the only person equipped by fate* to reform a situation which under no conditions could be tolerated.

This conviction was immediately put to a test. For on this very trip he would be beaten for the first time in his adult life.

To get from the railroad system of Natal to that of the Transvaal, young Gandhi had to travel for some stretch by stagecoach. He refused to take the "seat" assigned to him on a piece of burlap at the feet of the conductor, who began to "belabour" the pretentious "sami." The other passengers eventually spoke up for him and invited him in, whereupon the place of humiliation was assumed by a Hottentot servant. So far, so good—at least within the racial pecking-order. In Johannesburg the Grand National Hotel was "all full up" when he tried to register; so he spent the night with a Gujarati Muslim. The next day he managed to get a first class ticket by appearing "in faultless English dress" before a station master who turned out to be a "Hollander, not a Transvaaler." The whole tragicomic trip came to its fitting conclusion when, on arrival in Pretoria, he found that nobody had come to welcome him because he had been expected the night before. And who should approach him but an American Negro, who took him to "Johnston's Family Hotel." Mr. Johnston at first offered him a room only if he would consent to eat by himself but immediately felt, bless him, ashamed of himself. So he arranged with the other guests for the Indian visitor to have a good meal—vegetarian *and* integrated— in a clean dining room.

Within the first week the young barrister told the leading Indian merchant of his

intention to get in touch with every Indian in Pretoria. I expressed a desire to study the conditions of Indians there, and asked for his help in my work, which he gladly agreed to give.[49]

That was Gandhi. There would be times (for example, in Ahmedabad, in 1918) when such investigative determination on his part meant trouble for everybody involved; for no matter what he found, decided to do, and managed to accomplish, the situation would most likely be reformed—lastingly and significantly.

The twenty-three-year-old newcomer called a meeting of all the Indians in Pretoria in order to confront them with a "picture of their condition in the Transvaal." Stressing truthfulness in

business, he suggested the formation of an association in which
all Indians ("Hindus, Musalmans, Parsis, Christians, Gujaratis,
Madrasis, Punjabis, Sindhis, Kachis, Surtis, and so on") were to
be welcome. He had no trouble whatever in speaking up and in
making himself clear—in English, of course, for that was the
only language all these regional Indians had (more or less) in
common.

### 3. THE ONLY ONE AVAILABLE

ON LEAVING Pretoria somewhat less than a year later, Gandhi
could boast that there was in that city "no Indian he did not
know or whose condition he was not acquainted with." But only
after having assumed the over-all identity of a "public worker,"
that is, the pragmatic guise of a reformer, had he been able to
become a lawyer after his own heart—and a successful one at
that. His professional style was set, and we shall see it at work
from Pretoria to Ahmedabad:

I acquired such a grasp of the facts of the case as perhaps was not
possessed even by the parties themselves, inasmuch as I had with me the
papers of both the parties.[50]

First the facts and then the truth; let lawyers and clients laugh,
but

Facts mean truth, and once we adhere to truth, the law comes to our aid
naturally.

He managed to convince both parties to settle out of court in
order to avoid impoverishment by lawyers' fees. An arbitrator
was appointed, and Abdulla won. But Gandhi knew that the
deal would ruin Abdulla's opponent, a Meman from Porbandar,
and that there was an unwritten law among those people that
"death should be preferred to bankruptcy." This kind of law, he
argued with Abdulla, had to be respected, too, and he convinced
him that he owed it to his defeated opponent to let him pay in
comfortable installments. And here is the Bania lawyer's final
accounting: "I lost nothing thereby—not even money, certainly
not my soul." I would add that he proved, in fact, to have
gained that congruence of affirmative strivings, native tempera-

ment, and trained capacities which is the sign of a man's "having come to himself."

He also continued during this first year to take care of his soul, letting it remain, however, what today we would call "open-ended." When some Christians tried to convert him, he gave their creed some very serious consideration but found the dogma that Christ was God's *only* son entirely unacceptable. He came to a conclusion worthy of young Luther:

I do not seek redemption from the consequences of my sin. I seek to be redeemed from sin itself, or rather from the very thought of sin. Until I have attained that end, I shall be content to be restless.[51]

And if, at the end, Tolstoy's "The Kingdom of God is Within You" seemed to be the answer, one can only recall Luther's formula according to which man, if he only knew it, was already saved by faith.

Identity, however, becomes most evident in unhesitating commitment—when the time is ripe. Having concluded his case, Gandhi went back to Durban to board a steamer for home. In view of the unresolved problems which awaited him there, it is not wholly surprising that by another one of those coincidences "which changed his life," he chanced to see during a farewell dinner given in his honor by leading Indian citizens "a paragraph in a corner of a newspaper." This paragraph referred to a bill called the Franchise Amendment Act, which had already passed a first reading in the Natal Legislature and was to have its second reading the very next day. The bill was revoking the right of the very descendants of the "leading citizens" who were his hosts that evening ever to vote in Natal. He asked them what they knew about this, and they confessed they neither knew nor cared about such matters; whereupon, he exclaimed that this bill "strikes at the root of our self-respect!" Our! he had said, and the shrewd Muslim merchants immediately seized on the obvious and asked him to stay on—just for a month. In that moment political passion seized the young lawyer; he devised a campaign which would reach the Legislature the next day, and the Colonial Secretary in London within a fortnight, not to speak of the fact that it was to arouse public opinion in India in a way he could never have effected by going home. In July 1894 he sent to Dadabhai Naoroji, then not only a leading Indian nationalist but also a member of the British Parliament

A word for myself and for what I have done. I am yet inexperienced and young and, therefore, quite liable to make mistakes . . . *I am the only available person who can handle the question.* You will, therefore, oblige me very greatly if you will kindly direct and guide me and make necessary suggestions which shall be received as from a father to his child.[52]

I have italicized the words which, to my mind, express the core of his freshly gained identity, for which he was seeking sanction from the "grand old man" of the nationalist movement.

In his childhood, we remember, he was the only person who could take care of his sick father, the only son who would, in his family's opinion, continue the glorious line of Kathiawar prime ministers. Henceforth, only as the only one could he be himself. But such a man would not hesitate to *create* a situation for the handling of which he was the only available person. The young lawyer outlined that situation for his hosts that night in words which would echo in the *Times* of London as well as the *Times* of India, in the Colonial Office as well as the Indian National Congress.

While it will be entirely impossible even to list the widening issues with which Gandhi concerned himself within the two decades which as yet separate us from the Event in Ahmedabad, it may be worthwhile to sketch here this first issue in which the young lawyer recognized a personal, an existential, and a political obligation.

Natal, originally settled by Boers having "trekked" north from Cape Colony, had been occupied by the British in 1893. Now it had been granted "responsible government" by the British Crown and had immediately begun to enact the legislation which caught Gandhi's attention. This bill was designed to disenfranchise all Indians in the future, although about 250 Indians, mostly of the merchant class, were already on the list of voters on the legal basis of either owning immovable property worth at least 50 pounds or of paying an annual rent of at least 10 pounds. There were then 46,000 Indians in Natal—one thousand more than there were Europeans, who, of course, panicked when the Indians began to outnumber them, although (as Gandhi would prove, calmly and statistically) the chances were nil that any of the 16,000 as-yet-indentured Indians or many of the 25,000 "free" Indians in Natal would ever live up to the requirements for franchise which, in fact, were met only by less than one fourth of the Europeans!

But these were legalistic quibbles. For both Indians and whites were outnumbered ten to one by hundreds of thousands of Natal Zulus. The Indians, of course, considered themselves to be closer to the whites than to the blacks, both as descendants of an ancient civilization and as adherents to three world religions. But to the whites they were nonwhites and therefore a cultural and political wedge for the masses of blacks. And as everywhere, it was the poorer whites, the petty white traders, and even white labor, whose fears were most vociferous, while the wealthy and landowning class in their economic and political fortresses could well afford to be open-minded in order to keep the influx of Indian labor coming. The law, of course, reflected the sense of threat shared by the majority of whites and had long since begun to control all nonwhites in a web of demeaning police ordinances.

When the leading Indians of Durban told Gandhi that they did not know and did not care about this bill and that their exclusive interest was trade, it stung him with the very proof of what the press was saying:

The Asiatic comes of a race impregnated with an effete civilisation with not an atom of knowledge of the principles or traditions of representative Government. As regards his instinct and training he is a political infant of the most backward type from whom it is an injustice to expect that he should . . . have any sympathy with our political aspirations. He thinks differently and reasons in a plane unknown to European logic.[58]

This was the reasoning behind the bill, the first exclusively racial act of state legislation. But the paper went further, warning prophetically that:

If these people suddenly found themselves endowed with these new and strange privileges, there were grounds for believing that they might become propagandists of agitation and instruments of sedition in that great country from which they came.

One can imagine the (nonviolent) gleam in Gandhi's eye. To retell the story briefly: literally overnight the Indian merchants found themselves organized. By morning, a petition had been drafted by Gandhi and recorded (for Gandhi's handwriting was ever illegible) by a "Syrian" Christian calligrapher. Among the Indians invited to an emergency meeting the next day, there were, on Gandhi's insistence, representatives of Indian Christian youth, in whom he had recognized the best educated and potentially the most activist segment of the Indian population, although they seemed at that moment totally "alienated from their Indian background." Five hundred signatures were collected in one day for the first petition in the history of Natal; and when the bill came up for a third reading in the Legislature, the Strangers' Gallery was invaded (another "first") by what the press called "Arabs and Hindus," who appropriated the front seats and promptly betrayed their utter unworthiness of the franchise by not rising to yield these seats to white ladies, who "not being content to sit in the back, naturally had to retire." The bill, of course, was passed, but it needed the Queen's assent to become law. Within two weeks Gandhi and his friends (old Muslim merchants in carriages and young Christians on foot) had collected ten thousand signatures which were affixed to a petition sent to the Colonial Secretary. While the matter was under consideration, Gandhi founded the Natal Indian Congress, directly intended to be a counterpart to the Indian National Congress, the organizational spearhead of nationalism in India. Not until September 1895, however, was there a clear indication that the Queen might withhold her assent to the bill on the grounds that

It draws no distinction between aliens and subjects of Her Majesty or between the most ignorant and most enlightened of the natives of India. Among the latter class there are to be found gentlemen whose position and attainments fully qualify them for all the duties and privileges of citizenship.[54]

And not until March 1896 was a new Franchise Bill passed by the Natal Legislature, according to which

. . . no persons shall be entitled to franchise in Natal, who "not being of European origin" were "natives or descendants in the male line of natives of countries which have not hitherto possessed elective representative institutions, unless they shall first obtain an order from the Governor in Council exempting them from the operation of this Act."[55]

Gandhi, of course, had stayed on and had decided to see the matter through. He applied for admission to the bar of the Natal Supreme Court. There was an attempt by the lawyers' association to exclude him, but this aroused some of the press against the association rather than against Gandhi: for he had begun to impress the wider community with his candor. He was accepted and sworn in. When, on that occasion, the Chief Justice requested him to take off his turban, this time a turban signifying his admission to the Bombay Bar, he did so without hesitation. And when he argued his first case, there was not the slightest "nervousness." In fact, in his legal briefs, as well as in his public announcements, Gandhi now displayed a combination of such good English, clear thinking, and ruthless honesty that within a year he had established himself as a model as well as a force. When the prime minister of Natal finally introduced the new Franchise Act, he said he would not go so far as to admit that the petition was the "emanation or production of one man— M. K. Gandhi." But he warned:

Members might not be aware that there was in this country a body, a very powerful body in its way, a very united body, though practically a secret body— . . . the Indian Congress. That was a body which possessed large funds, it was a body presided over by very active and very able men, and it was a body the avowed object of which was to exercise strong political power in the affairs of the Colony.[56]

When the substitute bill was passed, Gandhi advised his friends to accept it. That the Indians had succeeded in preventing the Queen's assent to the first act, which was a purely racial one, seemed to him sufficient for the moment; the second one applied to all British subjects, and Gandhi was as yet far from challenging the Empire—or speaking for the masses. In fact, taking on legal retainers from twenty merchants, he settled down to the practice of law—as he saw it. Pyarelal describes his domicile:

Beach Grove Villa . . . in Durban was an unpretentious, semi-detached, double-storeyed building with an iron front gate, a side entrance with a passage, and a verandah under the balcony facing the Durban Bay. Harry Escombe, the Attorney-General, lived next door. All the neighbors were Europeans. . . .

It was not lavishly furnished. In the lounge, which was carpeted, were a sofa, two arm chairs, a round table with a cover, and a bookcase. Conspicuous in the bookcase were the writings of Tolstoy, Madam Blavatsky and Edward Maitland, publications of Esoteric Christian Union and the Vegetarian Society, the *Koran* and the Bible, literature on Chrisitan, Hindu, and other religions, and biographies of Indian national leaders. The dining room had an oblong table, eight bent-wood chairs, and a corner what-not. Two out of the five bedrooms upstairs were furnished with wardrobes. There were only hard wooden beds to lie on—no springs, nor mattresses, only bare board.[57]

It was into this setting that he planned to bring his family when in June 1896 he set out at last to fetch them from India. But before he left, there was a scene with which we may well conclude the history of Gandhi's identity struggle. We have spoken of the new and astonishing alignment of the young man's gifts and strengths, now so safely secured in the positive aspects of his identity. We last discussed young Gandhi's "negative identity" when I claimed that he had "projected" it, like the driven devil, on his alter ego, his Muslim friend.

Now we learn that all these years Sheik Mehtab had remained close to Gandhi. He had, in fact, been the first to join Gandhi as a "companion" in the new and comfortable house in Durban. Needing a kind of major-domo who would supervise his staff of servants, Gandhi, it appears, had put in a call for his friend in Rajkot, trusting that at last he had been reformed. But alas, the scoundrel in his celebrated way set servant against servant and finally had been caught bringing prostitutes into the house when

Gandhi was in his office. When told of this by an informer, Gandhi rushed home and threw Mehtab out, not without threatening to call the superintendent of police and being threatened, in turn, with "exposure"—of what, one wonders? Mehtab, to the last, seems to have considered himself part of some kind of conspiracy; but he had now become expendable and, in fact, a threat to the new establishment as well as to the owner's consolidated identity. Thus, identity solutions can lead to the dissolution of friendships. Yet, once on his own, Mehtab seems to have become "reformed" after all, and a loyal follower of Gandhibhai.

# CHAPTER
# III

# Householder in South Africa

## 1. SOMEBODY

YES, ESTABLISHMENT IS THE WORD. For in contrast to the most widely held image of Gandhi as an occupational failure who would come into his own only as a professional revolutionary and saint, there was a decade and a half in his life when he was a Householder in every sense of the word: in the simple fact of presiding over a prosperous household in South Africa; in the Hindu sense of a defined stage of life, concerned with family and immediate community; and in the literal sense of one who learns to know and to "household" the facts of life. In ancient imagery, the center of his territory is a man's "house," be it a home or a farm, a firm or a family, a dynasty or a church; and his "city" marks the boundary of all the houses associated with his.

Gandhi now settled down to occupational tasks; and he consolidated into one way of life his legal competence, his passion as a reformer, and his religious sense of a universal truth. For a young man in the years of his apprenticeship can only transform but cannot discard the essential elements of the world-image he has absorbed. Rajchandra put this world into words for him: and the most essential of all Jain truths thus to pervade his legal and political work was the "manyness" of outlooks which today we would call relativity. This truth Gandhi came to live long before he could formulate it, not without being accused of being opportunistic in his relativism and evasive in his apologetics.

In the Hindu life cycle, a profession becomes an intrinsic part of the stage of Householder which, in turn, is a necessary ashram or way-station, an indispensable step. It is, therefore, not enough to consider Gandhi's need to be "established" only as a need for British respectability. This explanation, which he had furthered by characterizing part of his identity struggle as "playing the English gentleman," undoubtedly has kept many admirers from acknowledging Gandhi's householding years as a genuine and essential part of his life. This is doubly unfair because such selectivity keeps us from understanding the man in the context of the human life cycle, and most of all, because it denies him the logic of the Hindu life cycle by which one can get established in one stage in all sincerity and thoroughness—and then disestablish oneself in order to enter another stage. Thus, if Gandhi in the following decades was to become a new kind of religious revolutionary, this development is neither in psychological nor in ethical contrast or contradiction to his householdership; and it even serves him in applying to a wider community the lessons of householding in small and acute matters. We have seen how Gandhi learned to pay meticulous attention to his health; and while in his scrupulosity he would sometimes upset his health as well as the good will of others, he learned to household his body and to derive from it a flexible strength and resolute energy. Equally meticulous was his attention to bookkeeping and to the use of available funds. True, he would later accept wealthy patronage with sovereign detachment, and yet he was always scrupulous in his detailed accounting. We are already prepared for the fact that, unable as he was to household equally well what Freud has called a man's "libido economy," he would, for the very sake of emotional economy, within a decade abjure sexual activity altogether. But then, this would come about within the total context of the endeavor to transform his "house" from a home for his family to a hostel for co-workers and followers, and eventually into an agrarian settlement with many characteristics of a religious order.

And if St. Francis' householdership began with God's admonition: *"Va, Francesco, ripara la mia casa che, come vedi, va in rovina"* ("Go, Francis, and repair my house which, as you can see, is in ruins"), the "house" to be repaired meant a single chapel as well as the Church in the City of God. But for Gandhi, "repairing" came to mean curing, teaching, reforming, governing—that is, any context in which one can remain a religious craftsman. Gandhi's widest acceptance of power would wait for the time when he also accepted the Indian masses as his family and nothing less than an independent India as his city. How Gandhi consolidated himself as a lawyer and a family man and *then* began to envisage a more inclusive "house" and a widening "city"—that is the story of his young manhood.

On his short visit to India in 1896, Gandhi found himself recognized as a young leader worthy of appearing on one platform with two of the great nationalists of that day, Lokamanya Tilak and Gopal Krishna Gokhale. His cause, however, was well circumscribed: he had made a politically conscious community out of the Indian élite in South Africa, and he had made the world conscious of the plight of the Indians there. Only Gokhale, a wise and energetic leader, had recognized the potentialities in the now twenty-seven-year-old Gandhi and the wider implications of the South African issues; from here on, he would watch the young man, and the younger man would look upon him as the *"political* guru" who would eventually guide his return to India as a prophet in his own country.

But when Gandhi at the end of 1896 brought his family to that suburban house in Durban, Kasturba in an elegant sari and the boys (including his widowed sister's son) in Parsi outfits, in order to start a law practice which, given his special experience and training, could be expected to become singularly lucrative and eminently respected, the meticulously dressed lawyer (again recognizable, as he admits, by his very special turban) was nearly lynched on arrival. This is what happened: While in India, he had aroused public opinion with speeches and pamphlets which detailed the sufferings of the Indians in South Africa; he had said little, if anything, that he had not already

told the South Africans to their faces. But this time the world
press had appropriated his utterances and had wired them with
sensational exaggeration to the corners of the earth—including
South Africa. This made him overnight the best known and the
most hated Indian there. And it so happened that he not only
arrived on a "coolie ship" filled to overflowing with "coolie
immigrants," but simultaneously with another ship similarly
loaded. To the whites, then, he was brazenly leading a symbolic
invasion into a country he could claim as his own, even after
having maligned it. Using the recent outbreak of bubonic plague
in India as an excuse, the Durban port authorities did not permit
the two ships to dock for three weeks. During the Christmas
celebration on board ship, when Gandhi was asked by the
captain what he would do if he were faced with a lynch mob, he
said he hoped he would forgive them. And he was given an
opportunity to prove his Christian sentiments. When at last they
landed, Gandhi sent his family on ahead and, following the
advice of the Attorney General himself, remained on board. But
when he finally went ashore, he was recognized by the mob and
badly beaten up—to be saved only by the Police Chief's wife, a
Mrs. Alexander, who took him under her parasol (which, being
part of a lady's gear, was sacred to the crowd) and protected
him at least against head blows until the constables arrived to
accompany him to the house of his friend where his family were
waiting. But now the mob knew where he was, and even as he
was being stitched up, they surrounded his house and demanded
his extradition so that they could hang him. Now Mr. Alexander
sprang into action: standing in the doorway, he entertained the
crowd by even lustily singing along with them "Hang old
Gandhi on the sour apple tree," until Gandhi had escaped
through the back door in a policeman's uniform—an act, we
may be sure, to which Gandhi consented only for the sake of the
families inside. (This, incidentally, continues the history of
headgear in Gandhi's life: this time a helmet was improvised out
of a tin pan held on the head by a shawl.) When the wily chief
told the crowd of the escape and invited a delegation to confirm
it, the crowd could not help laughing with him; and when, after

a few days of waiting it out in police custody, Gandhi had been cleared by the press of the worst quotations attributed to him, he was unmolested. He had, in fact, earned the respect of the community by refusing to name his assailants, although the Colonial Secretary had wired to demand their arrest.

All this served to create and publicize an image of a man with noble and nonviolent intentions, but it confirmed Gandhi only as an upper-class Indian. For the Natal Indian Congress was, we must remember, as yet an élite group more intent on "quality than on quantity." Quality here meant intelligence, devotion, and willingness to volunteer work; but it also meant money, for it cost three pounds to be a member, and nonpayment brought exclusion.

As suggested in the description of my seminar in Ahmedabad, in "my book" Householdership coincides with two stages of life: the stage of Intimacy, when work relations and sexual life will define for a man whom and what he can love in mutuality; and the stage of Generativity, in which he will find himself to be the parent of children, the producer of works and goods, and the originator of ideas, and will increasingly be defined by the extent and the quality of his ability to *take care* of all these.[58] Intimacy and Generativity, then, will inexorably commit him to a place or a niche in the cultural and economic consolidation of his day: this (unless he is alienated through malaise or lonely giftedness or both) will define his "reality," that is, that ideational consensus which characterizes a particular cultural consolidation. "Reality," of course, is man's most powerful illusion; but while he attends to this world, it must out-balance the total enigma of being in it at all. If the Hindus assign to the "maintenance of the world" a circumscribed stage in the middle of life, they insist that it be preceded by a meditative apprenticeship and followed by a meditative renunciation. All this was in Gandhi's "bones," but he was also a modern man and a great innovator.

I would call Gandhi a solicitor. This is what he called himself at times, but he was a kind of roving solicitor in more than a professional way. He was solicitous (if I may play with this

word) even then, and with all his overdeveloped meticulousness,
of many individuals and occurrences which he could comfortably have ignored. He would redefine the area of concern for a
practicing solicitor, and he would continue to consider his guar-
anteed income only a mandate to work ceaselessly first for the
disenfranchised and then for the altogether poor. At any rate, to
consolidate one's powers within the powers of the existing
establishment meant to him to affirm the earthly consolidation of
his historical time and place only in order to disestablish some of
its ills and inhumanities, while remaining aware of the tempo-
rality of all rebellion as well as of all consolidation. But the
borderlines between consolidation and reformation and between establishment and religiosity are often tragically blurred;
and nobody could even begin to play with them, who would not
feel or come to feel a humility which Ruskin inadvertently
formulated for Gandhi in the phrase: "Unto This Last." It was
now clear to him that no dogma could claim to be in the exclusive possession of historical revelation. To him that religion was
most meaningful which would help him formulate the revelatory essence of daily experience and action. And here Rajchandra's rewording of old Jain precepts seemed to speak to him
directly: "I very much like this doctrine of manyness [anekant-
avad] of reality," he would write many years later. "It saves me
from attributing motives to my opponents or critics . . . today
I can love them because I am gifted with the eyes to see myself
as others see me and vice versa."[59]

In a few pages we could not possibly trace all the details and
detours of the whole course just sketched. Since our concern is
with the origins of the political tool of militant nonviolence, we
will briefly concentrate on Gandhi's personal experience with
violence. Here, again, it is not for the sake of playing with
words that I must point out that even somebody who is well on
the way to becoming *some*body, still is a *body*, and that nothing
could quite remind him so forcefully of nobodiness as the experience—so vividly described by our Negro writers—of finding
that neither the nobility of the inner man nor the class aspira-

tions expressed by the outer man save a body from being kicked around as a detestable thing as if marked by the stigmata of a lower species.

The mass of Indian laborers in Natal were indirect beneficiaries of the work of the Indian élite, but then neither in India nor in South Africa were the masses as yet conscious of even the possibility of any kind of political dignity and freedom. Slavery, it must be remembered, was a historical habit with the white man; and when public conscience had done away with it as an institution, interested groups such as the plantation owners in the Caribbean and the growers of tea, coffee, and sugar in South Africa attempted by every device possible to continue the practice while calling it something else. When the British Indian Government proved ready to let poor and illiterate Indians sell themselves to the agents of South Africa as *indentured labor*, the whole new institution came very close to slavery, indeed, while proving ever so much more profitable. For Indian tradition had made hard work a matter to be taken for granted in most castes, while the Negroes, although stronger in body and ever so much more numerous, worked for others only under pressure and threat. This tradition, of course, made "free Indians" (who, in contrast to those who had never been indentured, were really the *freed* Indians) much more dangerous competitors as small farmers, petty shopkeepers, and roaming vendors. For white prudence, then, there could be only one policy, divided in itself: bring into the country as many indentured laborers as you can and then force out as many freed ones as possible. In the meantime the lives of the laborers were marked by the demeaning aspects of all slave labor: they could be beaten with impunity, arrested without recourse, restricted to given areas, and (most demoralizing) separated from their families. Thus, in some areas all semblance of family or community life broke down and, with it, what health, legality, or loyalty had been characteristic of communal life in India.

Gandhi gives to his first shocking acquaintance with a *physically abused* laborer the prominence of a whole chapter in his Autobiography. Even the name of the man became a symbol:

Balasundaram.[60] This shows how solicitous Gandhi felt at that time for the semi-slaves, and it demonstrates his ability to dramatize their dilemma in order to impress the public with a new kind of Indian history, with new kinds of martyrs and new kinds of heroes. But there was no thought then of organizing these people and of offering them a choice and a means to their own liberation:

Probably it did not occur to anyone to enlist their support; if the idea did suggest itself to some, there was in their opinion, the risk of making matters worse by allowing them to join the movement.[61]

Gandhi learned to know the violence of *warfare* in the Boer War. This, it will be remembered, was the result of the never-quite-subdued antagonism between the English and the Dutch settlers in South Africa, and of the question of the distribution of power between these groups under the political unification which was, in the long run, unavoidable.

His book *Satyagraha in South Africa* (written to be sure, much later) is introduced with a characterization of the Boers so glowing that one would think Gandhi had been their partisan or, at any rate, had been converted to their kind of belligerence. Here, it is worth quoting at length:

Every Boer is a good fighter. However much the Boers may quarrel among themselves, their liberty is so dear to them that when it is in danger, all get ready and fight as one man. They do not need elaborate drilling, for fighting is a characteristic of the whole nation. General Smuts, General de Wet, and General Hertzog are all of them great lawyers, great farmers and equally great soldiers.

. . . Boer women are as brave and simple as the men. . . . [They] understood that their religion required them to suffer in order to preserve their independence, and therefore patiently and cheerfully endured all hardships. Lord Kitchener . . . confined them in separate concentration camps, where they underwent indescribable sufferings. . . .

. . . But when the cry of agony raised by the women in the concentration camps reached England not through themselves, not through their men—they were fighting valiantly on the battlefield—but through a few high-souled Englishmen and women who were then in South Africa, the English people began to relent. . . . Real suffering bravely borne melts even a heart of stone. Such is the potency of suffering or *tapas*. And there lies the key to Satyagraha. . . .[62]

It is clear that Gandhi here was telling Indians that fortitude is indispensable for a Satyagrahi: without any "fight" in them, they cannot be nonviolent either—a theme to which we shall return more than once. But in the meantime, and in the "many-nesss" of events, Gandhi organized an Indian Ambulance Corps for the British. And since here Jain relativism and nonviolent legalism first appear wedded in one of those ambiguous official positions for which Gandhi is famous (and, to some, infamous), it seems important to see his point of view clearly. Luckily for him and his cause, his loyalty to the Empire was not tested by the offer of service as combatant: even the ambulance corps was accepted by the British only when the war seemed to be going against them. Gandhi's reasoning behind his offer of service, however, was (and would be) that although he was in opposition to a particular government on the grounds that it did not let him (or his people) participate in the benefits of constitutional principles, he would nevertheless have to defend the Empire whenever and wherever it seemed to be in danger. For the Empire promised to all British subjects what I would call a wider identity of powerful political actuality; and opposition to what was worst in the Empire made sense only on the assumption that the best in it would eventually guarantee more good to more people than any other existing or available political system. At any rate, the words with which Gandhi in *Satyagraha in South Africa* defends his noncombatant participation in the Boer War are worth repeating here—for our time:

> . . . if any class among the subjects considers that the action of a government is immoral from a religious standpoint, before they help or hinder it, they must endeavour fully and even at the risk of their lives to dissuade the government from pursuing such a course. We have done nothing of the kind. Such a moral crisis is not present before us, and no one says that we wish to hold aloof from this war for any such universal and comprehensive reason. Our ordinary duty as subjects, therefore, is not to enter into the merits of the war, but when war has actually broken out, to render such assistance as we possibly can.[68]

Since under the circumstances he could and would offer only non-combatant assistance, Gandhi recorded with pride that "a

*to actualize a wider*

_used on father_

large and splendid Corps composed of nearly eleven hundred Indians left Durban for the front"—and among them, it should be noted, several hundred freed Indians. Almost eager to enter the danger zone, they yet saw only two months of service. But Gandhi himself acquired another headgear—a sergeant major's felt hat with a wide brim smartly turned upward on one side and fastened with a cockade. He posed proudly enough for his photograph. One might add that thus even Gandhi became one of those non-commissioned "corporals" who assumed charismatic power in a number of great countries after World War I.

At the time, however, Gandhi's passing pride in his uniform and in his presence in the danger zone was important for the history of Satyagraha: for the Boer War permitted Gandhi to include the front soldier in his imagery of established roles. The image of the Satyagrahi eventually would transcend, not bypass, that of the soldier: and it is on this basis that he continued to admire the militant Boers. This sympathy would soon find a new historical reinforcement: for once the British had defeated the Boers and had taken over their republics they established a kind of postwar rule of British ex-army officers (including officers once stationed in India) which endeavored above all to serve the veterans who wished to remain in the Transvaal, while enforcing and reinforcing all those existing laws and statutes which kept the Indians in their place. For the British thus to go back on the promises seemingly implicit in the whole idea of the Empire; to go back on one of their announced war aims, namely, greater internal justice in South Africa; and to reward with contempt such loyalty as was symbolized by his ambulance corps—all this, in Gandhi's eyes, was much more inexcusable than were the Boer's semireligious and simple-minded prejudices.

## 2. NOBODY

IN 1901, between the Boer War and the Zulu Rebellion, Gandhi "visited" India again. Actually, he went home once more fully prepared to settle down. He took his family with him; and it now seemed as though he were both emotionally and

_potential of identities_

professionally prepared to establish a law practice in Bombay—combined of course with "public work" on a large scale.

It is fascinating to see how—as if in a second identity crisis—the temptation to maximize his opportunities as a professional and a leader was at this moment opposed by the determination to escape the establishment and to reduce himself ever more to that "zero" position which alone would provide the Archimedean point for total national renewal. During this stay in India, Gandhi participated in an annual session of the Indian National Congress (in Calcutta, in 1901). We must sketch briefly here the ascendance of the two leaders who represented that thesis and antithesis of Indian leadership which Gandhi would eventually synthesize. At the time when Gandhi was just beginning to organize the Indians in South Africa, at home in India Bal Gangadhar Tilak had already succeeded in creating and popularizing a militant Hindu brand of nationalism, thus creating a basis for an *extremist faction* within the Congress party, and winning the popular title of Lokamanya—"one revered by the people." Gopal Krishna Gokhale, in turn, had become the principal spokesman for the moderate position of *constitutional reform* and was respected in England as well as at home. Both men were Brahmans from Maharashtra, and as Stanley A. Wolpert phrases it, "legatees as well of the heroic traditions of the last great Hindu state to flourish in South Asia before the advent of British rule."[84] Tilak was Gokhale's senior by ten years and Gandhi's by thirteen. There could not have existed three more different aspirants to Indian leadership. Gokhale, while slight in build, was adorned with a walrus mustache and is usually pictured with Maharashtrian headgear but otherwise in Western garb. His hair was long, and he wore eyeglasses: the very image of the professor which, in fact, he was. Tilak was shorter, darker, tougher; he also wore a bushy mustache but was otherwise distinguished by the traditional Brahman tonsure and topknot. In modern terms, Tilak was a religious fundamentalist and revivalist, a fanatic revolutionary not disavowing violence and terror, and a nationalist visionary who sounded, at times, fantastic. Gokhale, however, was the rationalist intellectual, a pro-

gressive committed to strictly constitutional changes and a reformer given to gradualism. One can see where he and Gandhi
could agree—for a while:

"Our young men must make up their minds about it that there is no
alternative to British rule, not only now, but for a long time to come, and
that any attempts made to disturb it, directly or indirectly, are bound to
recoil on our own heads. Moreover, they have to recognize, if they want
to be just, that this rule, in spite of its inevitable drawbacks as a foreign
rule, has been on the whole a great instrument of progress for our people.
Its continuance means the continuance of that peace and order which it
alone can maintain in the present circumstances of the country."[65]

Tilak's political imagery could harbor surgical and violent
phrases which (whether he meant it literally or not, and this
would never become quite clear) were judged by the British, as
well as by some Indian youths, as propaganda for terrorism. He
was also given to an adoration of Hinduism, weakly disguising as
"strict" science what were mythological delusions concerning
the divine origins of the Aryan race and of Vedic religion. His
conviction that "hero worship is at the root of nationality, social
order, and religion" led to the ingenious superimposition of
nationalist rituals on traditional holidays. All in all, then, Tilak
originated a philosophy and a mode of action which—at least in
its florid suggestiveness—came as close to Nietzsche and even to
Hitler as a good Hindu could manage. Gandhi, no doubt, respected him, in the "manyness of things" and even out of some
dialectic sense, as a necessary and in some ways great leader and
organizer. Gokhale, in turn, remained a politically conflicted
man throughout his public life. Not only was he "a rationalist
who believed in astrology, a statesman who founded a monastic
society, a poet who taught mathematics"; he also "maintained
the dual role of responsible administrator and external agitator.
While functioning in either one of these capacities, he could not
forget his obligations to the other and was to this extent denied
the pleasures of single-hearted loyalty."[66]

These two leaders, over the years of Gandhi's absence, had
come to represent and serve as spokesmen for the two moods
which dominated—and divided—nationalist politics until Gan-

dhi returned to India to stay. It will become clear later
that although both the secular constitutionalism of the "moderate" Gokhale and the radical Hindu populism of the "extremist" Tilak had their day in modern Indian history, neither
was destined to provide the eventual solution to political independence. What in the meantime brought Gokhale and Gandhi
together was a common interest in rural reform. And here
Gokhale could teach Gandhi much, for he was an excellent
economist as well as a statesman—and he recognized the desperate need for nationwide public health measures.

These, then, were Gandhi's "elders," by dint of the fact that
they held power a generation before he did and also because he
would systematically conceal his own aspirations until he was
ready to take over. He avoided any deal with the two extremes
and grimly held to the lowest common denominator in order to
avoid the danger of forgetting the least and the last among the
masses on his way to power. Later, his critique would be
scathing, "The Congress would meet three days every year and
then go to sleep," the meetings themselves only sanctioning
"democratically" what had already been decided in committee.
At the same time, the Congress was the monopoly of an élite of
Brahmans and other urban professional castes; and among them,
there was, to Gandhi's mind, wasteful indulgence in caste and
regional competition—as if India could become "free" and independent merely by severing the bonds with England. His immediate action, right there at that annual meeting of Congress
luminaries, took the form of service of the "Untouchable"
kind:

There was no limit to insanitation. Pools of water were everywhere.
There were only a few latrines, and the recollection of their stink still
oppresses me. I pointed it out to the volunteers. They said point-blank:
"That is not our work; it is the scavenger's work." I asked for a broom.
The man stared at me in wonder. I procured one and cleaned the
latrine.[67]

Remaining determinedly anonymous, he was delighted in the
confidence placed in him when he was permitted to take on the
job of acknowledging minor Congress mail in the secretariat:

even this service, so common among dedicated political workers today, was initiated by Gandhi. But he also "loved" to button the shirt of one of the secretaries, who "did not mind my doing little acts of personal service for him." All of this is to prove that "my regard for elders was always great":[68] Moniya and Mohan all over again—testing, teasing. And, indeed, the Mahatma speaks of "his childlike intellect" at the time and of his wondering "where I should be in that vast assemblage." Almost deliberately he regressed again, and all the "facility for speaking that I had acquired in South Africa seemed to have left me for the moment."[69] Some of this, however, must have appealed to Gokhale, who invited him to his house and "treated me as though I were his younger brother." We should be prepared to find that no older brother had even a chance to make *this* younger one fulfill the hopes invested in him in any anticipated manner; Gandhi eventually would justify the trust of all of his older brothers only by becoming great his own way. And no more than Rajchandra could Gokhale have been his true guru, and this for the same reasons: he did not household his physical energies, and he accepted the establishment as the given territory for his otherwise most commendable activities. So Gandhi now staged what was in every sense of the term a dress rehearsal for his future activities in India. No doubt with an eye to teaching Gokhale a lesson in what he later, in Ahmedabad, would call "Indian leadership Indian style," Gandhi set out on a simple pilgrimage. He had seen enough of the varieties of Indian life: from Maharajas

bedecked like women—silk pyjamas and silk achkans, pearl necklaces round their necks, bracelets on their wrists, pearl and diamond tassels on their turbans and, besides all this, swords with golden hilts hanging from their waistbands.[70]

to the flocks of sheep being driven through the streets of Calcutta to be sacrificed to the goddess Kali. Now before settling down, he would make a tour through India—third class. So

I purchased a canvas bag worth twelve annas and a long coat made of Chhaya wool. The bag was to contain this coat, a dhoti, a towel, and a shirt. I had a blanket as well to cover myself with and a water jug. Thus equipped, I set forth on my travels.[71]

Gokhale was so fascinated that he came to the station ("I should not have come if you had gone first-class," he teased), and brought him a metal box filled with sweets. This trip initiated the future style of the pilgrim on (third-class) wheels.

The low point of Gandhi's descent into the life of the masses came in Benares when he was taking "his ablution in the Ganges in the proper orthodox manner." Playing the poor pilgrim and testing the worth of humility, he offered a penny at the Well of Knowledge but was told that such niggardliness would land him in hell. God, he concluded, had "laid down the law and, as it were, retired."

And yet—once more he returned to Bombay and rented "chambers in Payne, Gilbert and Sayani's offices," as well as a "fine bungalow" in Santa Cruz. He in fact admits pointedly:

I took a first-class season ticket from Santa Cruz to Churchgate and remember having frequently felt a certain pride in being the only first class passenger in my compartment.[72]

But again, a cablegram changed the course of his life, calling him back to South Africa. Aware that the center of the struggle had now shifted to British Transvaal, Gandhi lost no time in applying for admission as an attorney of the Supreme Court and in opening an office in Johannesburg. Here he found not only a newly created Asiatic Department at work, manned almost exclusively by army officers previously stationed in India, but a political philosophy which included the intellectual Darwinism of such men of otherwise high character as General Smuts. This is the way Gandhi paraphrased it later:

. . . the very qualities of Indians count for defects in South Africa. The Indians are disliked in South Africa for their simplicity, patience, perseverance, frugality, and otherworldliness. Westerners are enterprising, impatient, engrossed in multiplying their material wants and in satisfying them, fond of good cheer, anxious to save physical labour and prodigal in habits. They are therefore afraid that if thousands of Orientals settled in South Africa, the Westerners must go to the wall. Westerners in South Africa are not prepared to commit suicide, and their leaders will not permit them to be reduced to such straits. . . . The problem is simply one of preserving one's own civilization, that is, of enjoying the supreme right of self-preservation and discharging the corresponding duty.[78]

While Gandhi, for two years, merely attempted to "resist the inroads of the Asiatic Department," his way of life remained both practically and symbolically divided between the newly created farm in Phoenix and his establishment in Johannesburg. Phoenix he had founded in 1904 after one of his new friends, Henry Polak, had given him Ruskin's *Unto This Last,* a book which (as he understood it) gave clear and concrete confirmation of what was developing in him—even though Cecil Rhodes, Gandhi's clearest philosophical and practical antagonist on the South African scene, had also used Ruskin's text as a sanction for *his* colonialist policies. At any rate, during a "night on the train," Gandhi read Ruskin's book, and it became another of those nights which "marked a turning point" in his life. In Phoenix all his precepts of the simple life were put into practice with the help of his new "family," which included young people he had brought with him from India and the new intimates he had found in some (mostly Jewish) soul mates among white South Africans. At the same time, his practice in Johannesburg was at its peak.

Two events finally induced him to break altogether with the identity remnant of the well-dressed, highly educated, and fair skinned "coloured" citizen of the British Empire: a new war, that of the British against the rebellious Zulu, and a new law, the so-called Black Law. Still a citizen of Natal, Gandhi again felt that in time of war his loyalty called for noncombatant participation, and he organized a small ambulance corps which saw only very brief service. But this gave him an opportunity to give up his house in Johannesburg, and he later thanked God for opening his eyes once and for all to the impossibility for any nonwhite to think of himself as anything but black—and to start anew from there. Let me quote him:

It was no part of our duty to nurse the wounded after we had taken them to the hospital. But we had joined the war with a desire to do all we could, no matter whether it did or did not fall within the scope of our work. The good Doctor [Dr. Savage] told us that he could not induce Europeans to nurse the Zulus, that it was beyond his power to compel them, and that he would feel obliged if we undertook this mission of mercy. We were only too glad to do this. We had to cleanse the wounds of several Zulus which had not been attended to for as many as five or six days and were therefore stinking horribly. We liked our work. The Zulus could not talk to us, but from their gestures and the expression of their eyes, they seemed to feel as if God had sent us to their succour.[74]

It was on the front, too, that two ideas which had been "floating in his mind" became "firmly fixed" and "united in one vow": *celibacy* and *poverty*. Only this combination, he now became firmly convinced, would assure that he would not shrink from "undertaking the lowliest of duties or the largest risks."

This decision, at long last, brings us back to Kasturba. On that first and stormy arrival in Durban, she had been pregnant and in May of 1898, she had given birth to son Ramdas. Another son, Devadas, had followed in 1900. In line with his general insistence on "natural" methods, Gandhi had acted as midwife. He was "not nervous" he said. After 1900 (that is, when he was thirty-one years old), he had attempted, with his wife's consent, to abstain from sexual intercourse; but he seems to have succeeded only after having taken—during the Zulu rebellion—a formal vow; and he would henceforth consider vows essential in the lives of Satyagrahis. It is of importance here that he gave up sexual intimacy for a wider communal intimacy and not just because sexuality seemed immoral in any Calvinist sense. The sexual life (at least for him) seemed to becloud the sense of unerring craftsmanship needed for the creation of the new instrument of peace, Satyagraha.

We come now to the period in Gandhi's life in which all the modern methods of nonviolent militancy and loyal noncooperation were developed one by one. For those who would wish to study this whole period in Gandhi's life more comprehensively than is possible here, it would be necessary to compare *The*

*Story of My Experiments with Truth* with *Satyagraha in South Africa,* to see what the Mahatma selected for one or the other publication and in what sequence.

In 1924, when he began to record the emergence of Satyagraha in South Africa, Gandhi was in jail. The peacefulness which this gave him is reflected in descriptions of the land and the people of South Africa, a sensuous quality which differentiates this book so markedly from the Autobiography. It was dictated, incidentally, to his cell mate, Indulal Yagnik, whose exquisite gift for language I have mentioned earlier: and one wonders what he (as well as the translator) contributed to a style so much more vivid than much of the Autobiography. The *Experiments,* of course, describes Gandhi's moral and spiritual itinerary rather than historical chronology; there his account of his renunciation of sexuality precedes the Boer War and follows that of his children's education. He tries to justify the determined way in which he himself designed their upbringing, although he must admit that his oldest son later "broke away from me." For this, however, he blames his own early period of "indulgence and inexperience" which the boy, impressionable as he had been, "naturally" considered as the brightest period in his father's life. The Mahatma's account here is full of concern; and he did come to consider, as Freud did during approximately the same period, that infancy matters. Gandhi's conclusion, however, is that "the physical and mental states of the parents at the time of conception are reproduced in the baby" and that therefore married couples should have intercourse only when they "desire issue." And he ends on a note which stresses the issue and the stage of Care:

I think it is the height of ignorance to believe that the sexual act is an independent function necessary like sleeping or eating. The world depends for its existence on the act of generation, and as the world is the play-ground of God and a reflection of His glory, the act of generation should be controlled for the ordered growth of the world. He who realizes this will control his lust at any cost, equip himself with the knowledge necessary for the physical, mental and spiritual well-being of his progeny, and give the benefit of that knowledge to posterity.[75]

At any rate, the Mahatma states clearly that his main object in giving up sexual intercourse "was to escape having more children" and (in line with the book's emphasis on *Moksha*):

that if I wanted to devote myself to the service of the community in this manner, I must relinquish the desire for children and wealth and live the life of a *vanaprastha*—of one retired from household cares.[76]

Gandhi's account in the Autobiography, then, presents the personal side of the matter, while his brief reference to his final vow in *Satyagraha in South Africa* specifies the value of the vow as one of the tools of Satyagraha.

Neither of the two books alone gives an adequate account. Furthermore, one feels that in spite of all the Mahatma's candor, some connecting themes are missing which fit neither into the style of the *Experiments* nor into that of *Satyagraha*. These themes, were they to be clarified, might more directly connect the two decisions of avoiding both sexual intercourse and killing. For it would seem that the experience of witnessing the outrages perpetrated on black bodies by white he-men aroused in Gandhi both a deeper identification with the maltreated, and a stronger aversion against all male sadism—including such sexual sadism as he had probably felt from childhood on to be part of all exploitation of women by men. For this, however, we can quote adequate evidence only when we come to discuss the strange document *Hind Swaraj* which Gandhi wrote during his last years in South Africa.

In the meantime, not even the most convincing "dynamic" explanation of how a man comes to live with the fact of death can fathom the genius of religiosity—namely, that striving for ethical clarity in the face of the one fact which gives all humanity a joint identity and yet is denied by each subspecies in its own way. Religiosity is the consciousness of death, the love of all men as equally mortal, and the charitable insight that men hate other men "mortally" in the hope of gaining a sense of immortality out of the vaingloriousness of their own pseudo-species. For this reason the truly religious man must avoid, or at least gain insight into, all incentives to vanity, including those of parenthood. The very course of human life seems to decree that man, between a certain romantic, or heroic, or morbid consciousness of death during adolescence—when he faces the question of "To be or not to be" (to which I would add the word "himself")—and the acute certainty of death in old age, must participate in that mutual consolidation of identities and solidarities, capacities, and opportunities which the Hindus call Householdership. Such consolidation is the very foundation for the pseudo-species, for it traditionalizes the illusion that particular styles of life and particular castes or classes, nations or churches can provide a certainty, security, and reality of a higher order, superior to the fact of death. This sense of safety, mightily supported by the evidence of man's procreative and productive capacity, can and in some ways must lead to a collective narcissism and especially also to an exaggerated belief in the utopian potentials of one's children, who by their mere growth and unfolding validate their parents' sense of immortality. Religious ritual attempts to sanction the involvement in this world by offering at regular intervals ceremonial confrontations with ultimate concerns which both reveal and hide the fact of death through the formulas of dogma; and religions attempt to gather into priesthoods and monkhoods those driven to religiosity and fit to serve as the craftsmen of ritual. They decide in their very adolescence to remain poor and chaste in order to serve those occupied with the "maintenance of life" as living bridges to an eventual clarity of existence, or at least to a sense of consolation which makes it possible to produce, create, and serve without debilitating despair. Craftsmanship, however, tends to become crafty, and all ritualization and consolidation leads eventually to rigidity, hypocrisy, and vanity. This, in turn, is felt with deep indignation and passionate concern by those men who are the true *homines religiosi* of their age.

Gandhi, as we have seen, was and felt deprived by his early marriage of the choice to devote his life to monastic or, at any rate, to singlemindedly spiritual pursuits. To tell the truth, I think that, like Luther, Mohan would have been a failure as a monk without politics, just as he was a failure as a barrister without reformatory zeal. We have sketched (we could do no more) the gradual consolidation of his professional, economic, and political capacities in an over-all identity of service. He could have spared himself much agony by becoming a missionary of some kind. But all his accounts of his deepening involvements reveal that this man never tried to cheat destiny by *not* getting involved in what he felt drawn to, whether this might lead him to active affirmation or to stubborn negation. When such a man comes to the decision that only he who neither procreates nor kills can comprehend the clarity of death and the resultant responsibilities to life, then, one feels, he has "earned" his position the hard way; and at any rate, such a man's rare effect on others will immediately validate the genuineness of his position.

As always in Gandhi's life, however, political emergency stalked his spiritual decisions. While still at the Zulu front, Gandhi heard about the proposed "Black Law," and his immediate reaction was that it would be far better to die than to submit to such a law:

But how were we to die? What should we dare and do so that there would be nothing before us except a choice of victory or death? An impenetrable wall was before me, as it were, and I could not see my way through it.[77]

The name "Black Law" suggests the fantastic ambiguity in the connotations of the color black. In the Autobiography, two chapters called "The Black Plague" precede the account of his struggles with the Asiatic Department: here black means death. In the period of the Zulu rebellion, Gandhi began to refer to all non-whites, including himself, as black, as is now becoming the proud and unflinching custom in America. Yet the idea that a light skin is clean and a dark one dirty is deeply embedded in man's psychogenetic evolution. What is darker and hairier comes to symbolize what is tempting as well as degrading and thus a danger to higher aspirations as well as to life itself. One can see, then, why Gandhi, in all his preoccupation with sexuality and with dirt, with race and with poverty, gradually recognized the fact that civilized man can overcome his pride in his pseudo-species only by learning to differentiate rationally and compassionately between matters of unhygienic contamination and matters of mere symbolic uncleanness—a modern sense of discrimination which would no longer reject India's Untouchable castes upon whom all dirtiness had been ritually projected for centuries. But he also saw that "cleanliness," once it becomes a matter of pious compulsion, can be as dirty as its opposite, even as hypocritical moralism can be as immoral as sin. Thus, to wash compulsively in dirty water can make one feel virtuous and clean, even as today hygiene by detergents can contaminate the very water which is supposed to provide a clean source of health: for man ignores what it really means to be clean because of his vain satisfaction in having *acted* "clean." It was, then, as important for him to be scientific and fearless in handling filthy waste and leprous disease without flinching, as it was for him to become free of any color prejudice—against black or white. We will have occasion to return to these matters in more than one context, and ultimately in connection with the outbreak of the plague in Ahmedabad. The Black Act, however, was "black" because according to its provisions all Indians in the Transvaal, men or women, and even children above the age of eight, had to register and be finger-printed. They would have to carry a certificate of registration on their person at all times and to produce it on request, or be fined, jailed, or deported. It is clear that the purpose of this law was the prevention of illegal immigration, but it is obvious also that it treated Indians, and only Indians, as potential criminals. It should be added that the Indian Muslims were particularly incensed because of the possible invasion, by police inspection, of their women's religiously sanctioned seclusion. On this score, they were ready to kill—and it was now Gandhi's job to convince them that to kill and to be killed was relatively easy: to know how to die without killing and to make one's death count for life—that was the question. Thus, from this rock-bottom of racial indignity, Satyagraha emerged, step by step.

Gandhi, the people's solicitor, was now widely known and

purity—power
soul force
spirit power
indomitable spirit

affectionately addressed as Gandhibhai, which means something like brother Gandhi—an appellation more congenial to him than the eventual designation of Mahatma.

## 3. INSTRUMENT OF PEACE

SATYAGRAHA was the Sanskritic combination Gandhi later chose as a name for his way of life and of action—"Truth" and "Force," in literal translation. Yet for quite some time Gandhi continued to use what was easily the most unsuitable rendition of his term in English, namely, "passive resistance." This dilemma has never been resolved: "Truth force" as a term has nowhere come close to having the power of a slogan in the West. "Militant nonviolence" (the term, I think, preferred by Martin Luther King) is at least descriptive of the attitude and the action of the Satyagrahi, but it fails to suggest the spiritual origin of nonviolent courage in Gandhi's "truth." I will speak of the "leverage of truth" when, in addition to truth and force, I want to suggest the skillful use of a sensitive instrument. For it must be obvious that it is the challenge of our generation to understand, as far as psychological assumptions permit, what Gandhi calls truth as an actual force in mental life, the kind of force that "moves mountains." A lever, I admit, is a hopelessly primitive analogy in an electronic age. But whatever we will do with it in future settings, Satyagraha did have its origins in a technological imagery in which the body was still part of the tool; and it will be seen that even today the more direct uses of Satyagraha always include the body and the meeting of bodies: the facing of the opponent "eye to eye," the linking of arms in defensive and advancing phalanxes, the body "on the line": all these confrontations symbolize the conviction that the solidarity of unarmed bodies remains a leverage and a measure even against the cold and mechanized gadgetry of the modern state.

At the beginning of an age, then, when man is apt to sacrifice the threefold instrumentality of his body, his mind, and his soul to the clever complexity of his own inventions, Gandhi, as we shall see, strove for the naked clarity of all three. How he did this in given moments I can only try to illustrate in a series of

scenes in which essential parts of the new instrument were
created so that later, in describing the Event in Ahmedabad, we
will be fully aware of the meaning of each action taken there,
trivial as it may seem and simple as, in the nature of things, it
had to be.

## Oath

September 11, 1906: The Empire Theatre in Johannesburg,
popularly known as the "Jewish theatre," was filled to the brim
with Indian delegates from all over the Transvaal. An old and
eminent Muslim business leader presided; Gandhi, as usual, sat in
the background. He was waiting for the fourth resolution, of
which he was the author, to come up for discussion. The resolution called for all present *to vote* that they would rather suffer
all penalties than submit to the Black Act. Gandhi claims that he
himself did not quite understand every implication of this resolution, although he could "read in every face the expectation of
something strange to be done or to happen." This is a perfect
setting for an improvisation Gandhi style: he did not quite know
yet what he was going to do, but he had already created an
expectancy from which he would take his cues. His moment
came when one Haji Habib, in Gandhi's words, "imported the
name of God into the resolution." The "vote" was thus in
immediate danger of becoming an oath, and an oath was Gandhi's business, "possessing as I did much experience of solemn
pledges and having profited by them." He immediately asked for
the rostrum and, in a phrase reminiscent of the American Declaration of Independence, declared that "it would be, indeed, in
the fitness of things" to take an oath on this occasion. But an
oath, he warned, cannot be passed by majority vote: each
individual takes it, facing not his neighbor but his God. Nor
should it be taken in order to gain power over anybody but
oneself, for the power of an oath is defined by what one man
can promise to do, and what he is willing to suffer: insult,
incarceration, hard labor, flogging, fine, deportation, and even
death. "But I can boldly declare, and with certainty," he said
"that so long as there is even a handful of men true to their

*solomn oath - piskis*

pledge, there can only be one end to the struggle and that is victory."[78] Gandhi would often repeat this faith, and it is hard to believe that at that time he was not familiar with Thoreau's statement that

I know this well, that if one thousand, if one hundred, if ten men whom I could name—if ten *honest* men only—ay, if one *honest* man, in this state of Massachusetts, ceasing to hold slaves, were actually to withdraw from this copartnership, and be locked up in the county jail therefor, it would be the abolition of slavery in America. For it matters not how small the beginning may seem to be: what is once well done is done forever.[79]

At any rate, all present raised their hands and took an oath with God as witness. He knew, Gandhi said later, that "some new principle had come into being," to which he at first gave the name "passive resistance." The immediate result of the overpowering scene was a new and strong sense of solidarity which called for implementation by action. Yet, as so often, there followed a paralyzing period of waiting: waiting for all constitutional means to be exhausted, including even an appeal to the Crown to withhold its approval of the Act. Waiting, however, permits second thoughts; and before leading a delegation to England, Gandhi asked for written affirmations of the oath taken, and found, of course, a decrease in the number of the fervently committed.

The scene of action then shifted from the Empire Theatre in Johannesburg to the drawing room of the House of Commons and one of those promotional dinners, at which wine was served —a "barbarous custom," according to Gandhi, and one from which only a "crooked" compromise could emerge. The Secretary of State for Colonies declared himself staunchly opposed to the Act but slyly informed the government of Transvaal that since "responsible government" was to be conferred on them as soon as January 1, 1907, they were free anyway to act after that date. And, indeed, the new parliament lost no time in passing the "Asiatic Registration Act," which differed from the Black Act only by one concession: women were to be exempt. The Act was to take effect on July 31. It was now time to organize, and the "Passive Resistance Association" was formed. The oath was readministered "for safety's sake," and this time no defections were noted.

### Jail

July 1907: Henceforth, the meetings of the Satyagrahis were so well attended, sometimes by more than two thousand people (out of a total of ten thousand Indians in Johannesburg and Pretoria), that they had to be held on the grounds of the Pretoria Mosque. There, one evening, one Ahmad Muhammad Kachhalia spoke. The description of this man is typical of the "folksiness" of *Satyagraha in South Africa*:

Mr. Kachhalia was being deeply moved. His face reddened, the veins on his neck and on the head were swollen with the blood coursing rapidly through them, his body was shaking, and moving the fingers on his right hand upon his throat, he thundered forth. "I swear in the name of God that I will be hanged, but I will not submit to this law, and I hope that every one present will do likewise." So saying he took his seat. As he moved his fingers on his throat, some of those seated on the platform smiled, and I remember that I joined them in their smile.[80]

The affection shining through this description is typical also of other accounts, such as that of the volunteer pickets (from age twelve upwards) who later warned Indians to stay away from the registration offices, or who (holy Satyagraha) escorted potential registrants through their own picket lines to demonstrate that to register or not to register was a man's private decision. But in spite of the ugly threats from more pugnacious Indians, and the government's offer to have registrants come in the dark of night to private homes, in the end, only five hundred men registered in all.

The first man arrested was a Hindu who "had a brave look and was endowed with some gift of the gab. He knew a few Sanskrit verses by heart."[81] This apparently had earned him among his people the "learned" title of Pandit. The government meant his arrest to be a warning. But he was led to jail by a celebrating crowd and received parcels of delicacies from the community while locked up. After his release he was garlanded and feted. He became the envy of the community and famous over all South Africa. But suddenly he disappeared. An ex-indentured laborer, he was (it turned out) a fugitive from the (criminal) law, and his very fame had resulted in an unhealthy state of affairs for him.

And, finally, it was Gandhibhai's turn. Having been ordered out of Transvaal, he remained and was arraigned to appear in the prisoner's box in the very court in which he had pleaded cases as an immaculately dressed counsel. In the audience were colleagues as well as brethren. He not only confessed, but pleaded with the Magistrate for a heavy sentence as agitator and ring-leader. He was not granted such courtesy and was unceremoniously locked up in a cell. There, for a moment, he lost heart. What if his followers failed to fill the prisons in order to make the government's position untenable? The spell of gay rebelliousness would be broken. But he reprimanded himself: "How vain I was! I, who had asked the people to consider the prisons as His Majesty's hotels!"[82] He then, for the first time, donned a prison uniform and was locked up in a large cell—in the "Nigger Block." Before long, however, laughing Satyagrahi prisoners began to arrive in droves—150 of them. The prisoners arranged for exercise drills led by a Pathan, a

compatriot of ours named Nawabkhan, who made us all laugh with his quaint pronunciation of English words of command. He rendered "Stand at ease" as "Sundlies." We could not for the life of us understand what Hindustani word it was, but afterwards it dawned upon us that it was . . . only Nawabkhani English.[83]

All this gaiety was part of a new and invincible spirit which did not escape the country's and the government's notice. One day Gandhi was taken by the Superintendent of Police himself from his cell to the office of General Smuts. Here the two London barristers worked out a "gentlemen's agreement." Smuts offered to repeal the Act if the Indians agreed to undergo *voluntary* registration. Gandhi agreed, was released on the spot and, given the train fare to Johannesburg, held meetings the very next day in which he impressed his followers with the principle that a Satyagrahi is never afraid to trust his opponent.

The majority of the Indians raised their hands and pledged to register, but the martial Pathans, of whom only fifty lived in the Transvaal, decided to put the gay Satyagraha discipline to a severe test. They, it will be remembered, came from the rugged Hindu Kush in India's northwest, where later, under the leadership of the towering, bearded "Red Gandhi," Ghaffar Khan, Satyagrahis would take over the city of Kabul, induce crack British units to lay down their arms, and prove to the world that martial men, in fact, may make the best Satyagrahis. But here they were in the minority, and in their customary suspiciousness were sure that Gandhi had turned traitor. As Gandhi remarked:

The Pathans are an unsophisticated and credulous race. Brave they are as a matter of course. To kill and get killed is an ordinary thing in their eyes, and if they are angry with anyone, they will thrash him and sometimes even kill him.[84]

And, indeed, one of the two Pathans present threatened to kill the first man who would dare to register. As was predictable that first man would be Gandhi himself.

### Card-burning

February 1908: When the certificates of registration were ready, Gandhi set out from his office for the Registrar's office less than a mile away. The Pathans were waiting for him. Asked where he was going, he offered them, truly, a Bania deal:

"If you will go with me, I will first get you a certificate with an impression only of the two thumbs, and then I will take one for myself, giving the [ten] fingerprints."[85]

He had only time to cry out *He Rama!* before the blows felled him. Taken to the home of a Baptist minister, he was stitched up and forbidden to speak, but he insisted on having the certificate brought to him. Gandhi refused to testify, but since there had been European witnesses of the assault, the Pathans were sentenced to hard labor.

General Smuts graciously validated the voluntary registrations; he did not repeal the registration law. Gandhi accused him not only of a breach of promise but also of behavior unbecoming a gentleman.

The Indians then sent to the government what Smuts called an "ultimatum" because it set a time limit for a reply, and because the only acceptable reply, it was made clear, was the repeal of the Asiatic Act—and the only alternative a mass burning of the certificates of voluntary registration. That the members of the Transvaal Assembly "reddened with rage" and promptly "unanimously" and "enthusiastically" passed Smuts' new version of the bill, was only welcome to the Satyagrahis, who now shared one mood: they wanted action. And so two hours after the expiration of the time limit, the largest caldron to be found in Johannesburg was on the grounds of the biggest mosque, ready to receive two thousand cards for burning. If the government could "tear up" a pledge voluntarily given, the citizens, united, could burn up certificates voluntarily signed. And the assembled Indians were not to be disappointed. The Government's negative answer, delivered by a volunteer on a bicycle, was greeted with cheers. As Gandhi put it, "the opportunity of burning the certificates did not after all slip out of their hands." Yet he seems to have questioned "the propriety . . . of such a feeling of gladness," since, after all, something had to be destroyed as a symbolic burning of the last bridge. Thus had the burning of the Papal Bull initiated the Reformation; and at least one London newspaper compared the card-burning with the Boston Tea Party. A party it was, and the Pathan who had tried to kill Gandhibhai apologized publicly and received with a warm handclasp the renewed assurance that there was no ill feeling.

### "Passive" Resistance?

For the aggressive phase of the first "passive" resistance in history, we have Gandhi's account in *Satyagraha in South Africa*. No doubt in the early nineteen-twenties, when that book was begun, the principles of Satyagraha appeared much more sharply defined than they had in the first days of improvisation.

And yet Gandhi's account conveys on every page some of the gaiety <u>and pride</u> of a man and a people who truly felt that in improvising new methods against an overweening government, they were obeying some destiny dictated by some divine truth. Gandhi himself seems to have felt liberated by the fact that he, the coolie barrister, had faced physical injury and professional oblivion for having trusted a powerful gentleman like Smuts. Somehow he could now let himself be guided again by the spirit of little Moniya: he and his people, by teasing and testing, could make the great adversary—the Transvaal government, the British government, *all* government—acknowledge the power of the weak. The difficulty of finding the right terminology for a nonviolent "weapon," which pervades the whole Gandhian literature, including that contributed by English-speaking writers,[86] commenced then and there. Gandhi, almost as if teasing, would switch in mid-paragraph from the imagery of "soldiers" to that of "pilgrims," while calling himself a "general" at one time and a "scavenger" at another. Conversely, he would alternately call his people's attempts to cross forbidden borders "pilgrimages" and "Asiatic Invasions"—the last term, of course, mocking the powerful Europeans who were so ungallantly afraid of an "invasion" from India, after having themselves imported the Indians as slaves when they needed them.

As for the gradual involvement of the masses of South African Indians in Gandhi's campaign, I cannot give even a curtailed outline here: we are still so far from Ahmedabad. I can only indicate how Gandhi, always allowing events to coerce him into doing what his grand strategy had long committed him to plan, followed the "punches" of a government which seemed committed to breaking again and again whatever promises it had appeared to hold out. Thus, the fact that even those Indians who had been admitted because they had been able to pass some special educational tests were to be barred from free interstate travel promptly secured for Gandhi the important collaboration of the *literate* part of the Indian community—which rounded out this following among the privileged élite.

In 1912, Gokhale visited South Africa and (as seems to be the

wont of that government even today), as a distinguished and
foreign representative of an otherwise despised race, was treated
with utmost courtesy by the South African government. Inadvertently, he played a role somewhat comparable to that of
Neville Chamberlain of peace-in-our-time fame. In his conversations with the ministers, Gokhale thought he had been assured of
the repeal of the three-pound yearly tax imposed on ex-indentured laborers. The government denied having given this assurance, but Gandhi seized on the opportunity to include such a
repeal among his minimum demands, thus with one stroke giving
the masses of *Indian workmen* an immediate stake in the long-
range campaign.

As for Gandhibhai, when Gokhale came to visit Tolstoy
Farm, his host was "foolish enough to imagine that Gokhale
would be able . . . to walk about a mile and a half from the
station to the Farm."[87] Gandhi had always teased Gokhale about
his lack of exercise and his habitual use of a horse carriage. At
any rate, it rained, and Gokhale caught a chill. Thoroughly
good-natured about it, he refused all personal help: "I will bear
any amount of hardship," he said poignantly, "but I will humble
your pride."

In supporting Gokhale's triumphant tour through South
Africa and in taking with mock seriousness his assurance that the
three-pound tax would be repealed for sure, Gandhi seems,
again, to have been playing the role of one who professes inability to think ill of his revered elders, but who quietly lets them
live out their style of élitist leadership, which he fully intends to
replace with what we would call a grass-roots campaign. And,
indeed, thus far

Satyagraha had not been so much as mentioned among the indentured
labourers; still less had they been educated to take part in it. Being
illiterate, they could not read *Indian Opinion* or other newspapers. Yet I
found that these poor folk were keen observers of the struggle and
understood the movement, while some of them regretted their inability
to join it. But when the Union ministers broke their pledged word, and
repeal of the 3 pound tax was also included in our programme, I was not
at all aware as to which of them would participate in the struggle.[88]

Mass following and political momentum now supported the gradual crescendo of newly improvised methods with which the Satyagrahis could challenge the government—methods which have since become familiar to the scene of protest around the world. In South Africa, the most aggressive of these was to court arrest by "invading" borders closed to Indians and thus to fill the jails. This forced the government to do *something;* and whether the government employed police action or let the aggressors pass, it could only lose face.

Before describing these now-classical events, we must take note of a fateful question: what were the foci of the Satyagrahis' demands—what were their limits? For the masses of Indians now ready to follow Gandhi, the answer was clear: they wanted *all* their grievances settled. But Gandhi knew that a Satyagraha campaign, in order to exert its full momentum, must be clearly defined, step by step. The Satyagrahi, ready to die if necessary, must first define, for himself and his opponent, the irreducible minimum for which he will offer his life in any one campaign. If, instead, he intends to raise his demands every time he has gained a little ground, he gives his adversaries a chance to obscure the truly elemental nature of the struggle and demeans the spirit of self-suffering. Nothing less than the very nature of the instrument is at stake here, for surely a tool that can be blunted after only one or two uses does not appear reliable or durable:

Satyagraha offered on every occasion seasonable or otherwise would be corrupted. . . . And if any one takes to Satyagraha without having measured his own strength and afterwards sustains a defeat, he not only disgraces himself but he also brings . . . Satyagraha into disrepute by his folly. . . . For in Satyagraha the minimum is also the maximum and as it is the irreducible minimum, there is no question of retreat, and the only movement possible is an advance. . . . No matter how strong we were, the present struggle must close when the demands for which it was commenced were accepted.[89]

And yet, at the very beginning, Gandhi found his cause prejudiced by historical fact. Indentured labor, he knew, had been a historical blunder in the first place, and he was by no means opposed to an eventual total embargo on it. Yet neither did he

see any advantage in an unrestricted immigration of uninden-
tured Indians, least of all to the point where they would become
an aggressive political power in South Africa—as the South
Africans feared. Rather, he objected to all legislation incompatible with the self-respect and social health of Indians caught
up in this historical dilemma—in South Africa or elsewhere. To
this purpose, any further deterioration of public morale had to
be prevented at all cost.

In 1913, a justice of the Cape Supreme Court provided additional incentive. He invalidated all marriages not concluded
according to Christian rites or recorded with the Registrar of
Marriages, as Indian marriages were not. Apart from the difficulty of invoking Satyagraha against a court opinion, this
affront to both womanhood and motherland, as it was interpreted in India, gave Gandhi an opportunity to declare the
"propriety of sacrificing" *Indian women*, too, on what he referred to as the "firing line" of Satyagraha. It is obvious that
without the gradual addition first of the intellectuals, then of the
workers and the women, the first Satyagraha campaign would
never have been the popular movement and grass-roots instrument which it in fact became. In the meantime, Gandhi had
acted as a leader who, as the mind and conscience of the movement, must exert on himself and on his followers what he called
the "progressive self-restraint" of a major Satyagraha campaign,
while his lieutenants, the strategic sense organs and nerves of the
campaign, must in contrast be permitted to test, through small
and improvised confrontations, the extent of the popular readiness to become involved and to endure.

### Asiatic Invasions

1913: We now come to the history of the progressive "invasions" which were to tease and test the first government that was
exposed to Satyagraha. This history is also that of an all-Indian
list of new heroes; we shall hear more of them during the
Ahmedabad episode, for there Gandhi would hold these men
and women up to the textile workers as embodiments of a new
typology of heroism, almost a new religious pantheon. The first

was a Parsi by the name of Sorabji. Gandhi, who always emphasized the possible weaknesses in each type of coworker only to
show, of course, that Satyagraha made reliable heroes out of
them all, was not quite sure whether this man could "stand to his
guns in critical times." Yet Sorabji was chosen to enter the
Transvaal at Volksrust illegally, that is, as an educated man no
longer admissible. Volksrust is a small town on the Transvaal
side of the border with Natal, a town which "had no way of
knowing the strange scenes it would witness and the role it
would play in the history of India and of civil disobedience."
The government, however, simply was not sufficiently provoked, and it displayed what Gandhi called a "masterly inactiv-
ity." So the Satyagrahis had to devise new methods of needling
it. A larger group of wealthy traders and educated men, among
them Harilal Gandhi, constituted the first "invasion" of the
Transvaal. They were arrested, tried, and deported back to
Natal, but they immediately re-entered to be sentenced to three
months' imprisonment with hard labor. The popular reaction
was this:

The Transvaal Indians were now in high spirits. If they could not
compel the release of their Natal compatriots, they must certainly share
their imprisonment. They therefore cast about for means which would
land them in jail.[90]

The game was now underway—with people of education and
means hawking on the streets without a license so as to be
arrested: one was described by Gandhi as one "who had a Malay
wife and a horse carriage," another as a graduate of Cambridge
University who stood on a corner with a basket of vegetables.
Hawking was a matter of local ordinances, however, and before
the government could act,

things came to such a pass that anyone who wished could get himself
arrested. Jails began to be filled, "invaders" from Natal getting three
months and the Transvaal hawkers anything from four days to three
months.[91]

Gandhi himself was arrested and enthusiastically took on cooking for his seventy-five Indian companions in the Volksrust jail.

To chasten him (and maybe also to safeguard his jailmates' health), he was put in solitary confinement.

A teased government, however, becomes brutal until it learns to respond parsimoniously to a new weapon. The oldest counter-weapon, of course, is the filling of jails. Then there was deportation, which at first meant dumping Satyagrahis over the state lines or into Portuguese East Africa. But the government soon realized that the very worst threat was that of deportation to the "motherland," where many of these Indians no longer had any ties, or where, indeed, they had never been—this threat combined with the threat that they would have to leave behind in South Africa what family or property they possessed. But by deporting them, the South African government only aroused public opinion in India and the Empire and thus inadvertently supported a long-range goal in Gandhi's strategy, namely, to make Satyagraha in South Africa the opening campaign for a review of the position of Indians in other parts of the Empire—and, indeed, in India itself.

It is remarkable that Gandhi managed at the same time to assume leadership in these expanding issues and to cultivate his householdership in a new kind of community which now had clearly replaced and absorbed his personal family. As already mentioned, Tolstoy Farm had been bought for the Satyagrahis by the wealthy architect and erstwhile German Jew, Kallenbach,[92] and had been so named to mark its affinity with the great Russian's ideas of the basic moral value of physical labor and of natural (and here meatless) diet. One wonders how much Kallenbach was aware of the kibbutz movement which at that time, not without Tolstoyan influence, was opening Jewish settlements in Palestine; but the difference between a kibbutz and this model for future ashrams is immediately and well defined by the fact that in the Tolstoy Farm men and women lived separately. At any rate, Kallenbach had visited a Trappist monastery near Durban and had learned sandal-making there—he taught it to Gandhi, who apparently was already then thinking of an early retirement to a rural setting, even while he was learning to make himself at home in jail cells as well as at ministerial conference tables.

The women were now solidly equal as Satyagrahis; and two groups, the "Tolstoy sisters" and the "Phoenix sisters," (names indicative of Gandhi's monastic aspirations) served in the novel shock troops whose mission was to cross forbidden state lines. The "Phoenix sisters," who were to cross from Natal into Transvaal, were at first the more successful. Most of them were Gujarati, and five were Gandhis—including Kasturba herself, whom Gandhi had at first studiously ignored so that she would not feel coerced into heroism by the fact that she was his wife. Nor did he hide his ambivalent discomfort:

. . . if you began to tremble in the law court or were terrified by hardships in jail, I could not find fault with you, but how would it stand with me? How could I then harbour you or look the world in the face?[83]

She, of course, remained firm. The party refused to give their names to the border guard, assuming that the police would not knowingly arrest such a collection of Gandhis. They succeeded in getting tried and sentenced to three months' hard labor.

The "Tolstoy sisters," all from Madras, had not been so "successful" with their first invasion. They crossed into Transvaal, but maybe because six of them had babies in their arms, the border guards were reluctant to arrest them. Their next orders were to cross back into Natal and, if not arrested, to proceed to the coal mining center of Newcastle, there to start agitating for a strike in protest against the three-pound tax. That would get them arrested for sure! And, indeed, this plan worked so well that the government as well as the Satyagrahi headquarters would come to wish the sisters had been arrested at the border: for the miners proved quite unexpectedly ripe for a strike and immediately left their work by the hundreds, and then by the thousands. They were almost all Madrasi Tamils, and the women's native oratory hit home. Gandhi, "as much perplexed as pleased," immediately proceeded to Newcastle without the slightest idea of what to do. Not only were "the masses" on the move, but the news of the women's incarceration with common criminals immediately became international news. Thus the decisive test of his leadership and his style of action had been forced upon him. And in all its grimness, the whole matter developed with a kind of Franciscan gaiety on a mass scale. The mine owners cut off the utilities in the strikers' company houses. Gandhi fearlessly advised that "the only possible course was for the labourers to leave their masters' quarters, to fare forth in fact like pilgrims." They should sell their belongings, he told them, and take nothing with them except the clothes on their bodies and blankets. But where would they go and who would feed them? Gandhi was staying in Newcastle with a man named Lazarus, a middle-class Christian from Madras who owned a small house and plot. His tiny establishment became a "caravanserai" for a continuous stream of pilgrims who "retired from the household life to the houseless one." Luckily, the weather was favorable, and the traders of Newcastle provided cooking pots and bags of rice and dal. Spirits were excellent; Gandhi and the health authorities, however, viewed the gathering with mounting alarm. The Madrasi strikers' ideas of sanitation had not improved with indentured proletarization, and some of them had turned tough with frightening records. But somehow, everybody seemed to "grasp the gravity of the situation." And as was Gandhi's wont, he would not only insist on hygienic and social restraints but would preach to this group the basic ethical rules for the forthcoming march:

None was to touch any one's property on the way. They were to bear it patiently if any official or non-official European met them and abused or even flogged them. They were to allow themselves to be arrested if the police offered to arrest them.[94]

Even in his fifties, when recording this situation, Gandhi gives us a candid account of his highly mixed rationale for the next step. These thousands (he could not count them) of men, women, and children had to be "safely deposited"—somewhere. They could not be taken by rail, for there was no money, and furthermore, Gandhi could not supervise such mass transportation. The Transvaal border was thirty-six miles away: two days' march. The miners accepted the idea of a march, for they could see that "it would be some relief to poor Lazarus," and the Newcastle authorities had to be prevented from taking stringent measures for the prevention of a possible plague. But I would add to all these reasons the possibility that Gandhi played with the idea of an Indian Trek as an indigenous gesture of manly protest which might reverberate in South African hearts. For, as we have seen, Gandhi was deeply impressed with the Boers' fortitude in leaving their homesteads for the freedom of the open spaces; and it may well be that the famous Boer Trek provided one heroic model for the great March and for many marches since.

### The Great March

On October 28, 1913, the Great March began. Gandhi had, of course, warned this invading force (as he had conscientiously warned all the smaller ones) of the great dangers and hardships ahead of them and had told them that he could promise only a pound and a half of bread and an ounce of sugar to each "soldier" a day. Yet, on November 6, the day set for crossing the border, Gandhi counted 2,037 men, 127 women, and 57 children. He scrupulously co-operated with the health authorities on the way (shaming his followers into cleanliness by "scavenging" himself) and had prevented the most likely unrest by taking personal charge of (and responsibility for) the distribution of food, which proved to be plentiful, if necessarily ill-cooked.

There is a bewildering passage in *Satyagraha in South Africa* in which Gandhi expresses his respect for the spirit of this new kind of pilgrim army by comparing it with that of mythological and historical models:

The men and women in Charlestown held to their difficult post of duty in such a stoical spirit. For it was no mission of peace that took us to that border village. If anyone wanted peace, he had to search for it within. Outwardly the words "there is no peace here" were placarded everywhere, as it were. But it is in the midst of such storm that a devotee like Mirabai [fifteenth-century bhakti poetess beloved throughout Gujarat] takes the cup of poison to her lips with cheerful equanimity, that Socrates quietly embraces death in his dark and solitary cell and initiates his friends and us into the mysterious doctrine that he who seeks peace must look for it within himself.

With such ineffable peace brooding over them the Satyagrahis were living in their camp, careless of what the morrow would bring.[95]

This passage follows an account of how two of the "pilgrim" women had lost their babies on the way, one by dropping it into a river and hopelessly seeing it driven downstream: but both women had refused to be dejected and had continued their march. Peace beyond progeny!

This passage, however, probably reflects the mood of the reminiscing chronicler more accurately than that of the historical moment. At the time, Gandhi probably had little time to reflect. He tried to prevent disaster by writing, wiring, and even phoning General Smuts to the effect that if he repealed the three-pound tax, the miners would return to work and be released from the Satyagraha campaign. But while the Europeans along the way unexpectedly restrained all possible violence from *their* side and, in fact, proved friendly and helpful toward the peaceful marchers even in the face of all the nuisance such a march entailed, the government insisted on settling the matter with police measures. Gandhi was arrested three times, each time, as he wryly noted, by an official of higher rank. Twice he posted bail and returned to the front of the advancing column. But, finally, the Principal Immigration Officer of the Transvaal himself came to take him into custody. Gandhi wanted to leave last instructions, but the officer forbade any speeches. The Mahatma comments in retrospect:

The officer knew that for the time being I was master of the situation, for trusting to our non-violence, he was alone in this desolate veldt confronted by two thousand Indians. He also knew that I would have surrendered to him even if he had sent me a summons in writing. Such being the case, it was hardly necessary to remind me that I was a prisoner.[96]

The plan now was that the "pilgrimage" would proceed to Tolstoy Farm (a further march of eight days) and there settle down to agricultural work and to the building of mud huts before the rains came. But in Balfour, near Johannesburg, three railroad trains awaited the marchers, and in Gandhi's absence Mr. Polak was the one to persuade them to entrain without resistance. To the last, the metaphors were mixed:

It would ill become soldiers to claim to elect their commanders or to insist upon their obeying only one of them . . . jail was the pilgrims' goal, and they should therefore appreciate the Government's action when they were ready to arrest them.[97]

The workers' apprehensions would prove only too justified. The government had in the meantime transformed the mine compounds in Newcastle into concentration camps (a term first used during the Boer War) and had appointed the European employees as deputy wardens. This (brutally executed) attempt to match the Satyagrahis' nonviolent inventiveness with methods of officially sanctioned slavery was only another instance of the often-observed fact that a government unnerved by nonviolent opposition inadvertently plays into the hands of its opponents; for overnight it made "the South African question" the burning topic of the day in India and throughout the Empire. Strikes broke out in other parts of Natal, and the ensuing police brutality only involved the government deeper and deeper in a situation in which any further escalation of state violence could only result in a demonstrable justification of the Satyagrahis' aims and methods.

The end, like the beginning, was Gandhian in method—or rather, in the seeming lack of it. The government appointed a commission. Since the commission did not include any Indians, the Satyagrahis boycotted it and, in fact, began to make plans for a new march as soon as Gandhi was released. But then the railway employees of the whole South African Union for reasons entirely their own went on a strike of such serious proportions and implications that the government had to declare martial law. If the railroad workers, in seizing this moment, were deliberately exploiting the government's predicament, the Satya-grahis would not do likewise: Gandhi informed Smuts that he was going to interrupt his campaign until the government had settled its affairs on that other front—a decision both magnani-mous and wise, if for no other reason than that Satyagraha needs the center of the stage.

The commission's report was, on the whole, favorable to the Indians, and the subsequent debate in the Union Parliament of a proposed "Indian Relief Bill" was "long and pleasant," no doubt largely because of the good impression the peaceful march had made on the public. According to Gandhi's summary, one part of the bill validated such marriages (although only one per man) as were held to be legal in India. In a final letter to General Smuts, Gandhi concluded:

As you are aware, some of my countrymen . . . are dissatisfied that the laws . . . have not been altered so as to give them full rights of resi-dence, trade, and ownership of land [as well as] full interprovincial migration. . . . They have asked me that all the above matters might be included in the Satyagraha struggle. I have been unable to comply with their wishes. . . . I shall hope when the Europeans of South Africa fully appreciate the fact that now the importation of indentured labour from India is prohibited, and the Immigrants Regulation Act of last year has in practice all but stopped further free Indian immigration, and that my countrymen do not entertain any political ambition, they, the Europeans, will see the justice and indeed the necessity of my countrymen being granted the rights I have just referred to.[98]

In July 1914, Gandhi left South Africa for good. There he had spent twenty-one "sweet and bitter" years in which he "had realized his vocation in life." In the long run, his campaigns proved to be no more than skirmishes in a war which the Indians of South Africa have, as of this date, lost. Yet, today, the stub-born government of South Africa finds itself outside the Em-pire; and, as Gandhi wrote half a year after his return to India,

We fought to keep the theory of the British Constitution intact so that practice may some day approach the theory as near as possible. . . . Passive Resistance . . . is at present inapplicable, its application being confined to grievances which are generally felt in a community and are known to hurt its self-respect or conscience. . . . Our grievances . . .

may any day advance to that stage. . . . Till then, only the ordinary remedies of petition, etc., can be and are at present being applied.[99]

And Gandhi did succeed, during his first year back in India, in having the practice of indentured labor stopped once and for all—anywhere.

### 4. MANIFESTO

WE HAVE NOW described some of the main components of the instrument which Gandhi forged in South Africa. Its wider applicability would become apparent during the years to come. Similarly, the ideas which Gandhi formulated in that period and compressed into one terse manifesto would capture the attention of India and of the world only very gradually.

In 1909, on his return from a most discouraging trip to England, where he had found that the Imperial Government was half helpless and half unwilling to support Indian self-respect either in South Africa or in India, Gandhi wrote *Hind Swaraj* or *Indian Home Rule*,[100] a rather incendiary manifesto for a man of peace. Written on a steamer in less than a week, it staked out a sphere of leadership reaching from utterly personal and local concerns to the very limits of India. The motto is: Home Rule equals Self Rule and Self Rule equals Self-Control. Only he who is master of himself can be master of his "house," and only a people in command of itself can command respect and freedom. The pamphlet is written in the form of questions by a "reader" and answers by an "editor" and is vaguely reminiscent of a Socratic dialogue; and, indeed, Plato's account of Socrates' death is one of the works listed in the bibliography, together with six of Tolstoy's books, and two each by Thoreau and Ruskin. The "reader" is obviously a composite of all those young Indians whom Gandhi had just met in London and had found so eager to employ Western methods of emancipation, including terrorism, which at least in the British Press had come to be identified with Tilak's style of nationalism. In *Hind Swaraj*, however, Gandhi only alluded to Tilak as "one of the best sons of India, now in banishment." In fact, Gandhi uses his "reader's" questions to set up for himself an opportunity to dispose of India's leaders, one by one.

He avoids, of course, head-on critique: each leader is defined as an indispensable step in history, but a step to be transcended. Take Gokhale:

> We believe that those, who are discontented with the slowness of their parents and are angry because the parents would not run with their children, are considered disrespectful to their parents. Professor Gokhale occupies the place of a parent. What does it matter if he cannot run with us? . . . His devotion to the Motherland is so great that he would give his life for it, if necessary. Whatever he says is said not to flatter anyone but because he believes it to be true. We are bound, therefore, to entertain the highest regard for him.
>
> Reader: Are we, then, to follow him in every respect?
> Editor: I never said any such thing.

Or take Congress as a whole:

> . . . the Congress gave us a foretaste of Home Rule. To deprive it of the honour is not proper, and for us to do so would not only be ungrateful, but retard the fulfilment of our object. To treat the Congress as an institution inimical to our growth as a nation would disable us from using that body.[101]

Yet, Tilak's shadow seems to hover over the whole panorama of leadership; and, indeed, Tilak had been the first to make a national slogan of Home Rule ("Swaraj is my birthright; and I shall have it!") while Gandhi here adopts it (as he did throughout his life with the ideas of others) in order to transform it. In doing so, he does not avoid sounding much like Tilak:

> We are day by day becoming weakened owing to the presence of the English. Our greatness is gone; our people look like terrified men. The English are in the country like a blight which we must remove by every means.[102]

Nor does he refrain from encouraging a kind of mystical nationalism, which might absorb some of Tilak's emotional success and utilize it for a nonviolent movement. All this leads to one conclusion: every Indian leader, himself excepted, wants to make India free by un-Indian methods and for the sake of an un-Indian future:

> . . . we want English rule without the Englishman. You want the tiger's nature, but not the tiger; that is to say, you would make India English. And when it becomes English, it will be called not Hindustan but *Englistan*. This is not the Swaraj that I want.[103]

There follow sweeping denigrations of the British Parliament and of the "free" press, of civilization in general and the railways in particular, of lawyers and doctors, all of whom are said to prostitute, infect, weaken, and cheapen the Indian people, who enjoyed Home Rule in the ancient past:

> It was not that we did not know how to invent machinery, but our forefathers knew that, if we set our hearts after such things, we would become slaves and lose our moral fibre. They, therefore, after due deliberation decided that we should only do what we could with our hands and feet. They saw that our real happiness and health consisted in a proper use of our hands and feet. They further reasoned that large cities were a snare and a useless encumbrance and that people would not be happy in them, that there would be gangs of thieves and robbers, prostitution and vice flourishing in them and that poor men would be robbed by rich men. They were, therefore, satisfied with small villages.[104]

"Prostitution" is a word used rather often in this document; and clinical judgment can not overlook the fact that at the time Gandhi was again returning from the metropolis of temptation. At any rate, a peculiar state of mind seems to have induced him to write a document with such irrational overtones that it may well serve to reveal the remnants of Moniya's and Mohan's conflicts in the man's ideological style. There are, at any rate, two passages in *Hind Swaraj* which capture the eye of a reviewer sensitive to the inroads made by the irrational into an intellectual or ideological discourse. One of these passages uses and demeans the word *mother*, and the second, *father*. Thus, the British Parliament is first referred to as the Mother of Parliaments and then derided as no better than a prostitute or an otherwise "sterile woman." To justify such a comparison the pamphleteer uses rather strange metaphors. The Parliament, he

says, is like a prostitute—"under the control of ministers who
change from time to time." The word "under" appears again
and again in what is in all probability not a conscious pun:
"Today it is under Mr. Asquith, tomorrow, under Mr. Balfour,
and the day after it will be somebody else." Rather than being
"under one master all the time," then, Parliament is used by a
series of prime ministers who exploit this institution for their
purposes without making it fertile, with the result that "its
movement is not steady but it is buffeted about like a prostitute."[105]

One cannot escape the impression that the whole imagery
evoked here harbors a fantasy of the kind which usually breaks
through in a dream, and one wonders whether the sea-voyage
did create a special state of consciousness in the writer. At any
rate the fantasy is that of a once-trusted mother, revered by
many as "the mother of them all" who, however, demeans
herself by letting herself be used and "buffeted." And if this
outburst links "mother" and "prostitute," a few pages later an
equally surprising passage links "father" with "thief." Gandhi
makes his imaginary questioner ask how he would deal nonviolently with a thief in the house. He answers:

I do not agree with you that the thief may be driven out by any means.
If it is my father who has come to steal I shall use one kind of means. If
it is an acquaintance, I shall use another; and in the case of a perfect
stranger I shall use a third. If it is a white man, you will perhaps say you
will use means different from those you will adopt with an Indian thief.
If it is a weakling, the means will be different from those to be adopted
for dealing with an equal in physical strength; and if the thief is armed
from top to toe, I shall simply remain quiet. Thus we have a variety of
means between the father and the armed man.

At first, then, the father appears to be only a random example,
or rather, a figure marking the greatest contrast to a strong-
armed man. But Gandhi gets more and more deeply involved in
what now begins to read almost like a daydream:

Again, I fancy that I should pretend to be sleeping whether the thief
was my father or that strong armed man. The reason for this is that my
father would also be armed and I should succumb to the strength

possessed by either and allow my things to be stolen. The strength of my
father would make me weep with pity; the strength of the armed man
would rouse in me anger and we should become enemies. Such is the
curious situation. From these examples we may not be able to agree as to
the means to be adopted in each case.[106]

The sentence, "The strength of my father would make me weep
with pity," seems especially mysterious; and equally mystifying
is the method which Gandhi now suggests should be employed
against the robber after the deed.

Instead of being angry with him, you take pity on him. You think that
this stealing habit must be a disease with him. Henceforth, you, therefore, keep your doors and windows open, you change your sleeping-
place, and you keep your things in a manner most accessible to him. The
robber comes again and is confused as all this is new to him; nevertheless,
he takes away your things. But his mind is agitated. He inquires about
you in the village, he comes to learn about your broad and loving heart,
he repents, he begs your pardon, returns you your things, and leaves off
the stealing habit. He becomes your servant, and you find for him
honourable employment. This is the second method.[107]

This, then, is the answer to the question of what a Satyagrahi
should do when robbed; but it must be admitted that the route
from the question to the answer is indeed circuitous, bringing in
a father where he did not exactly advance the argument. This
serves to underscore the fact that in Gandhi's imagery father,
son, and theft are combined in a lifelong theme, as we saw in one
of his principal childhood memories—the confession of a theft
to his father—and as we shall see at the height of the Ahmedabad events, when Gandhi reports an analogous dream to his
youngest son. In a psycho-historical context it seems important
to hold to the dictum that such an emergence or breakthrough
of the past into the present always depends on two factors,
namely, the undiminished actuality of the past (in this case, the
father-son-thief theme), and something in the actuality of the
present which literally "recalls" that past in the very convergence of infantile and adult themes. The convergence here, I
think, is that of the possible usurpation of political power, which
brings a man face to face with those whom he must displace,
replace, and surpass in adult actuality, and which therefore

revives in him the imagery of the child's first power struggles—namely with mother and father—and the resulting identification with one or the other or both. In the Mahatma's rendition of his boyhood confession we recognized a tendency to show himself spiritually superior to a father before whom he was overtly prostrating himself; and we have indicated that in order to have the courage to surpass his father, the prime minister, Mohan had to strive to become a new kind of leader in whom paternal and maternal identifications coincide. The imagery employed in *Hind Swaraj* strongly suggests a transcendance of all male models: besides the benevolent critique of Indian leaders as respectable relics there is the more pugnacious criticism of particular professionals such as prime ministers, lawyers, and doctors (and here Gandhi confirms that he once had wanted to be a doctor himself).

On the other hand, as Gandhi later wrote in a letter to Maganlal Gandhi: "Nobility of soul consists in realizing that you are yourself India. In your emancipation is the emancipation of India. All else is make-believe."[108] It must be understood, then, that an imagery which exposes the Mother of Parliaments as a prostitute in the service of successive prime ministers not only bespeaks those infantile emotions which may have made Moniya feel that his mother was both the sexual victim and the co-conspirator of his much-married father; it also speaks to the condition of all the sons of a colonialized country. For the obvious suggestion is that if the English government can prostitute Parliament—the guardian of British constitutionalism—what will it do to India? Thus, the image of Mother India, victimized by successive invaders who exploit her resources with the claim of "civilizing" her, engages not only the leader's emotional resources but also something in the emotional core of the restless masses as well as of the rebellious élites. And Gandhi makes the simile quite explicit:

So understanding and so believing, it behoves every lover of India to cling to the old Indian civilization even as a child clings to the mother's breast.[109]

It should be noted in passing that such sexual imagery is by no means Gandhi's specialty: it erupts in other nationalists too, albeit in each according to his ideology and style of leadership as well as his personality. For example, as could be expected, Tilak would habitually emphasize the Hindu male's pride and privileges. Thus, violently opposed to any laws postponing the legal marriage age of Hindu girls, so many of whom would find themselves in their early teens the victims of ruthless sexual exploitation, he could exclaim:

. . . they make a statement condemning our entire country because of a few examples of rape committed on small girls, and they ask us to apply to the government to change the law. What better proof is there of our emasculation?[110]

In the spirit of preserving the Hindu man's prerogatives he gives his full consent to what he calls the "common rule"

for intercourse to take place on that very night when she has the first menstruation after having performed the *homa* sacrifice. This custom has been practiced for at least 2,500 years since the ancient era of the *sutra*.

Civilized Gokhale, in turn, at least once let a sexual issue of propagandistic value upset his usually reliable self-restraint. In 1897, having been certified by official London as a true Indian gentleman, he suddenly insisted that two Indian women had committed suicide after having been violated by British soldiers. This does not seem so remarkable in itself as was his reaction to the fact that (in this instance) he was proven wrong and felt forced to apologize. Nothing could have demeaned him more in the eyes of Tilak's followers than that apology. Yet as Wolpert reports:

He withdrew into a deep depression, confessing soon after he returned home that "recent events . . . have distracted me so far that my mental equipment has been for the present seriously impaired."[111]

One can only conclude that here both the statement and the apology had personal as well as political significance.

There is, then, an obvious strong and often painful link between the traditional, the personal, and the infantile meanings of a man's propagandistic imagery and its public resonance. A passion for defending the purity of mothers against vile intruders, foreign and domestic, may have been an emotional prerequisite for many future liberators (from Bolívar to Hitler). But the time and the place, the power, and the method of the liberatorship demand an acute sense for actualities and, above all, a simultaneous mobilization of the leader's emotional resources and those of the led. And Gandhi's gambit, both personally and propagandistically, was the ambition to personify a purified India and to overcome with the means of Satyagraha all thieving prime ministers—without, we must add, ever seeking to replace them in their defined authority. Like other charismatic leaders of his time who, unlike Napoleon, avoided usurping the roles of either kings or presidents, Gandhi in power would never be separated from the people by the pomp of a traditional office. But more, Gandhi insisted on entering into the mission of liberating his country with a set of demands on himself which represented his unique combination of political leadership with selflessness and even sexlessness. As he wrote on the "Kildonan Castle":

When a husband and wife gratify the passions, it is no less an animal indulgence on that account. Such an indulgence, except for perpetuating the race, is strictly prohibited. But a passive resister has to avoid even that very limited indulgence because he can have no desire for progeny. . . .

After a great deal of experience it seems to me that those who want to become passive resisters for the service of the country have to observe perfect chastity, adopt poverty, follow truth, and cultivate fearlessness.

Real Home Rule is possible only where passive resistance is the guiding force of the people. Any other rule is foreign rule.[112]

Unfortunately (some think), Gandhi's militant turn from English to Indian ideals was expressed also in a sweeping condemnation of the machine age. He concludes a chapter with

In our own civilization there will naturally be progress, retrogression, reforms, and reactions; but one effort is required, and that is to drive out Western civilization. All else will follow.

And another chapter opens with

Machinery has begun to desolate Europe. Ruination is now knocking at the English gates. Machinery is the chief symbol of modern civilization; I am convinced that it represents a great sin.[113]

And since we are now about to follow Gandhi to the mill-city of Ahmedabad, we must pay special attention to this programmatic statement:

We cannot condemn millowners; we can but pity them. It would be too much to expect them to give up their mills, but we may implore them not to increase them. . . . They can establish in thousands of households the ancient and sacred handlooms and they can buy out the cloth that may be thus woven. Whether the millowners do this or not, people can cease to use machine-made goods.[114]

But then, in view of the nuclear age which we have since entered, Gandhi's seemingly naive references to man as the armed animal must be read with renewed care:

Formerly, when people wanted to fight with one another, they measured between them their bodily strength; now it is possible to take away thousands of lives by one man working behind a gun from a hill.

Our difficulties are of our own creation. God set a limit to man's locomotive ambition in the construction of his body. Man immediately proceeded to discover means of overriding the limit.

What do you think? Wherein is courage required—in blowing others to pieces from behind a cannon, or with a smiling face to approach a cannon and be blown to pieces? Who is the true warrior—he who keeps death always as a bosom-friend, or he who controls the death of others? Believe me that a man devoid of courage and manhood can never be a passive resister.[115]

Here was a man, then, who was about to formulate a new conscience of action or rather to totally renew a very ancient one:

No man can claim that he is absolutely in the right or that a particular thing is wrong because he thinks so, but it is wrong for him so long as that is his deliberate judgment. It is therefore meet that he should not do that which he knows to be wrong, and suffer the consequence whatever it may be. This is the key to the use of soul-force. . . . Passive Resistance blesses him who uses it and him against whom it is used.[116]

Finally, a message to the British:

Only on condition of our demands being fully satisfied may you remain in India; and if you remain under those conditions, we shall learn several things from you and you will learn many from us. So doing we shall benefit each other and the world. But that will happen only when the root of our relationship is sunk in a religious soil. . . . If there be only one such Indian, he will speak as above to the English and the English will have to listen to him.[117]

# PART THREE

# The Event

---

# CHAPTER
# I

# A Personal Word

MAHATMAJI,

As far as I can gauge it, I am now about midway through this book and as eager as any of my readers to follow you to India and to that period of your life which was shared by my witnesses. But first I must say a word about your accounts of the period now to be left behind. I will put my critique into words which I hope I would have had the courage to address to you were you alive. My justification for approaching you would have been the conviction that psychoanalytic insights happen to complement your kind of truth by a strange reversal of the traditional roles of East and West: for you are now a model of activism in our culture, while Western thought has provided a new technique of introspection.

You have given me a perfect opening in a passage of the Autobiography which, on re-reading, I must take *very* personally. In a chapter called "Intimate European Contacts,"[1] close to the middle of your book, you suddenly interrupt yourself, aware of a critical voice other than your "inner voice":

What things to mention and what to omit regarding the English friends of whom I am about to write is a serious problem. If things that are relevant are omitted, truth will be dimmed. And it is difficult to decide straightaway what is relevant, when I am not even sure about the relevancy of writing this story.

I understand more clearly today what I read long ago about the inadequacy of all autobiography as history. I know that I do not set down in this story all that I remember. Who can say how much I must give and how much omit in the interests of truth? And what would be the value in a court of law of the inadequate *ex parte* evidence being tendered by me of certain events in my life?

And then you turn on an imaginary reader (and that is where I come in):

If some busybody were to cross-examine me on the chapters already written, he could probably shed much more light on them, and if it were a hostile critic's cross-examination, he might even flatter himself for having shown up [make the world laugh by revealing] the hollowness of many of my pretensions.

But this outburst against uninvited interpreters does not seem to have alleviated a deeper doubt within yourself:

I, therefore, wonder for a moment whether it might not be proper to stop writing these chapters. But so long as there is no prohibition from the voice within, I must continue the writing. I must follow the sage maxim that nothing once begun should be abandoned unless it is proved to be morally wrong.

And then you say something about your method of writing which makes a psychoanalyst feel unduly at home because it seems to resemble the method of "free association" which we use to tap the autobiographic propensities of our patients:

I write just as the Spirit moves me at the time of writing. I do not claim to know definitely that all conscious thought and action on my part is directed by the Spirit. But on an examination of the greatest steps that I have taken in my life, as also of those that may be regarded as the least, I think it will not be improper to say that all of them were directed by the Spirit.

If I did not believe something of this kind, I would not be writing this book. But I must now confess that a few times in your work (and often in the literature inspired by you) I have come across passages which almost brought *me* to the point where I felt unable to continue writing *this* book because I seemed to sense the presence of a kind of untruth in the very protestation of truth; of something unclean when all the words spelled out an unreal purity; and above all, of displaced violence where nonviolence was the professed issue.

So far, I have followed you through the gaiety and loneliness of your childhood and through the experiments and the scruples of your youth. I have affirmed my belief in your ceaseless endeavor to perfect yourself as a man who came to feel that he was the only one available to reverse India's fate. You experimented with what to you were debilitating temptations and you did gain vigor and agility from your victories over yourself. Your identity could be no less than that of universal man, although you had to become an Indian—and one close to the masses—first. Your profession could only be that of solicitor for the masses. Your "house" could only be a hostel for believers, your family only an improvised religious order, and your "city" only the whole Empire as long as it promised to play host to an all-human identity.

For these very reasons, however, I cannot accept the way you try to dispose, no doubt half humorously, of your moment of doubt:

I am not writing the autobiography to please [satisfy] critics. Writing it is itself one of the experiments with truth. One of its objects is certainly to provide some comfort and food for reflection for my co-workers. Indeed, I started writing it in compliance with their wishes. . . . If, therefore, I am wrong in writing the autobiography, they must share the blame.

No, Mahatmaji, you could not write for followers alone. But neither—so I now realize—can I interpret your self-revelations only for those who already share my clinical vocabulary.

My task in this book is to confront the spiritual truth as you have formulated and lived it with the psychological truth which I have learned and practiced. This truth, I believe, must supplement your work as it spreads, in many unforeseen ways, beyond India and into the future. To do this I will first apply clinical insights to your work, and then compare your kind of insight to ours—a task which I can complete only at the end of this book.

First, then, your self-interruption. To experience such a moment is one thing, to describe and publish it, another. In an autobiographical account it becomes a confession to the reader, a testament in the form of a query for future generations. And a reader of my generation and my training cannot overlook the fact that the disruption of your autobiographic endeavor follows a chapter which is called "A Sacred Recollection and Penance," and which relates some of the chagrin with which your wife responded to your determination to open your house to strangers (including Europeans) sympathetic to your cause. In this chapter you declare that it required no special effort at tolerance on your part to accept men and women of all races and creeds as part of your "family" in Durban. But it was difficult for your wife to open her house to all the world—and "all the world," here as elsewhere, meant a motley bunch of stray individuals out of whom only you could make the men they eventually became, and a variety of faddish ideas out of which only you could forge one truth. At any rate, your whole doubt as to what you should and would reveal about your European friends is intricately related to the question of whose house your house was. Yours *and* Kasturba's?

And the "sacred" confession is an account of how you literally showed your wife the door. This was, of course, an old habit from the early days of your marriage as children in India, but there she had had parents to go to and the excuse of a well-established custom to rejoin the folks, for prolonged periods. I do not recount this story in order to draw the nonsensical conclusion which is always greeted with mirth by our intellectuals, namely, that Kasturba was "more of a saint" than you were—for what do intellectuals know about saints? But I would like to get the story straight. I understand that your house in Durban was equipped with chamberpots; that you wished to do away with any vestiges of the ancient Indian system which considers the handling of human waste a matter for Untouchables only; that most of your "family" understood this and would take care of their own waste, but that in the case of some uninitiated newcomers, you had to share this task with your wife; and that your wife usually accepted this, although it went against her "grain"—and tradition. On this occasion, however, the waste to be discarded was not only a Christian's (by religion) but also an Untouchable's (by caste); and she made a face indicating that *this* combination was too much, whereupon, you demanded that she do the chore *cheerfully*. And as she exclaimed almost biblically, "*Keep your house to yourself and let me go!*" you showed her the gate, and she broke down in despair and righteous anger.

You settle this incident with one of those subdued statements by which you often express true intimacy:

If my wife could not leave me, neither could I leave her. We have had numerous bickerings, but the end has always been peace between us. The wife with her matchless powers of endurance has always been the victor.[2]

Such a statement can dispense with the word love because it is pervaded by it.

But there are instances where it would seem to an observer that you use the word *love* in order to clothe other propensities. I will, therefore, take issue with you only where I perceive a certain false pedagogic tone pervading the very kind of apologetic statement which you are apt to use in order to explain, for example, your attempts to impose literacy on your child bride:

But I was a cruelly kind husband. I regarded myself as her teacher and so harassed her out of my blind love for her.

It is this cruel love which is in need of clarification. As Tendulkar reports, you once told a theosophists' gathering in Johannesburg that if

they were to analyze their minds, they would find that they had very little reason to think ill of others, and would begin to think ill of themselves; for they would find that they harboured within themselves robbers and murderers—terms used by them so glibly in connection with others.[3]

But it is not enough to counter such self-deception with a moralistic exhortation to think ill of themselves, for there is, as we now know, a clear connection between the murderousness with which righteous man attacks his enemy and the cruelty with which moralistic man views himself. Too long, in fact, has man excused his cruelty to others with the claim that he does not spare himself.

Here, I submit, the future of Satyagraha is at stake, and this not because you "pretend" a love which you do not feel, but rather because you seem either unaware of—or want to wish or pray away—an ambivalence, a co-existence of love and hate, which must become conscious in those who work for peace. Your sadism sometimes comes through in those utterances in which your revulsion against sensuality turns, for example, against woman as a source of evil, against food intake as no better than defecation, and against milk as a "dangerous substance." If you have said (to a friend of mine) that one should steer away from beautiful women as a driver steers away from the gutter, the "association" between woman and gutter may be indirect. And if you recommend a well-known co-worker by praising the fact that she is beyond childbearing, you meant to honor her. But for the future it is important to affirm unequivocally that what you call Satyagraha must not remain restricted to ascetic men and women who believe that they can overcome violence only by sexual self-disarmament. For the danger of a riotous return of violence always remains at least latent if we do not succeed in imbuing essential daily experiences with a Satyagraha-of-everyday-life. It is in daily life and especially in the life of children that the human propensity for violence is founded; and we now suspect that much of that excess of violence which distinguishes man from animals is created in him by those child-training methods which set one part of him against another.

It is not enough any more—not after the appearance of your Western contemporary, Freud—to be a watchful moralist. For we now have detailed insights into our inner ambiguities, ambivalences, and instinctual conflicts; and only an additional leverage of truth based on self-knowledge promises to give us freedom in the full light of conscious day, whereas in the past, moralistic terrorism succeeded only in driving our worst procliv-

self-acceptance

ities underground, to remain there until riotous conditions of uncertainty or chaos would permit them to emerge redoubled.

What you suspect that busybodies like me might call *pretensions*, however, we simply consider unavoidable and mostly unconscious *ambivalences*, the propensity for which is part of the human equipment. Ambivalence means, of course, that an act, which is seemingly guided by one conscious emotion is, at the same time, unconsciously co-determined by the opposite emotion: an act of love by hate, an act of kindness by vindictiveness. To recognize ambivalence in such pious phrases as "cruel kindness" and "blind love" by which you characterize the long story of your remaining a forever frustrated teacher in your own house is, today, easy; and to take it for granted almost too easy. But for the sake of Satyagraha, we must take a good look at the formulation with which you conclude the story of Kasturba's failure as your student:

I am no longer a blind, infatuated husband. I am no more my wife's teacher. Kasturba can, if she will, be as unpleasant to me [scold me] today as I used to be to her before. We are tried friends, the one no longer regarding the other as the object of lust. . . . The incident in question occurred in 1898 when I had no conception ["no command" in the original] of *brahmacharya*. It was a time when I thought that the wife was the object of her husband's lust, born to do her husband's behest, rather than a helpmate, a comrade and a partner in the husband's joys and sorrows.[4]

This statement seems to seal the dogmatic assumption that a wife can be "a helpmate, a comrade, and a partner" in the husband's joys and sorrows only if she is not joined with him in a sexual relationship. And a doubter may, indeed, consider it a strange fruit of ascetic comradeship that you must confess:

It is likely that many of my doings have not her approval [liking] even today. We never discuss them, I see no good in discussing them. For she was educated neither by her parents nor by me at the time when I ought to have done it.

Does this not make it only too clear that you took revenge on her for her illiteracy by deciding unilaterally what she would and would not be able to discuss with you? In fact, this confessional statement covers a by no means rare vindictiveness toward Kasturba, who would not become your "intellectual" equal. And yet did she not (and did not even your destitute son, Harilal) also represent an important part of yourself, namely, an unwillingness to learn from *anybody anything* except what was approved by the "inner voice"?

However, with the phrase, "the one no longer regarding the other as the object of lust" you win: for wherever one considers the other a mere "object" of anything, there, of course, truth in any sense is excluded from the relationship. And here is the point: not once, in all of your writings, do you grant that a sexual relationship could be characterized by what we call "mutuality." This is by no means a capacity easily developed or sustained without self-control and sacrifice, but as an approximation and a goal, it describes the only kind of sexual relationship in which the other person does not become a mere object either of sexual or aggressive desire. I say "mere object," for I am not so delusional as to think that there is any healthy sexual relationship in which there is not also a reciprocal sadism for the sake of satisfying such desires "on" each other as are usually expressed in four-letter words; nor is there a healthy sexuality which does not *also* include a certain pleasure in the closeness of the sexual function to the evacuative organs and their modes. The point is that mutual consent and artful interplay truly disarm what debasement and what violence there is in merely taking sexual possession of one another. Nor do I deny that the highest forms of joint involvement in public—not to speak of religious—service may, under certain conditions, induce an enlightened couple to forego sexual relations for the sake of another form of joint affirmation. There is an old principle, not easily discarded, in your statement:

I hold that believers who have to see the same God in others that they see in themselves, must be able to live amongst all with sufficient detachment.

But I submit that "sufficient" detachment on both sides is possible only where the renunciation, too, was chosen by both—

and not based on the vindictive insistence of one partner. In your life, apparently, three extreme circumstances came together: Your precocious sexual life, combined with your moral scrupulosity, could not contain and, in fact, aggravated a sense of sadism in your sexuality. Your aspirations, and your gifts (fed by the historical situation) led you to envisage a life of service to humanity on a level which called for a self-discipline of a rare order. And, finally, Kasturba's strength of renunciation was, if anything, more consistent than yours. In your own life, therefore, it makes supreme sense that you should have resolved your sexual conflicts by making it a matter of will, sealed by a vow, that as you would not attack an inimical person with weapons, you would not attack a loved one with phallic desire; and that you would not cause new beings to be born where you had decided to take upon yourself the responsibility of self-aware existence.

Kasturba was an adult who could take care of herself, and your relationship to her is a modern saga just because you did not hesitate to reveal the way exalted issues became tragi-comic bickerings in the daily life of your marriage, too. So I have written to you about your marriage only because you yourself refer to that "sacred recollection" in the very context of your sudden doubts.

A SECOND INCIDENT reported by you is not an accident on the way to Satyagraha, but one committed (I have no other word for it) during a period in which you remember your faith and your courage to have been at their highest—that of the establishment of Tolstoy Farm. And this incident concerns very young people.

Here I must quote you in full:

This was my experiment. I sent the boys reputed to be mischievous and the innocent young girls to bathe in the same spot at the same time. I had fully explained the duty of self-restraint to the children, who were all familiar with my Satyagraha doctrine. I knew, and so did the children, that I loved them with a mother's love. The reader will remember the spring at some distance from the kitchen. Was it a folly to let the children meet there for a bath and yet to expect them to be innocent? My eye always followed the girls as a mother's eye would follow a daughter. The time was fixed when all the boys and all the girls went together for a bath. There was an element of safety in the fact that they went in a body. Solitude was always avoided. Generally I also would be at the spring at the same time. . . .

. . . One day one of the young men then made fun of two girls and the girls themselves or some child brought me the information. The news made me tremble. I made enquiries and found that the report was true. I remonstrated with the young men, but that was not enough. I wished the two girls to have some sign on their person as a warning to every young man that no evil eye might be cast upon them, and as a lesson to every girl that no one dare assail their purity. The passionate Ravana could not so much as touch Sita with evil intent while Rama was thousands of miles away. What mark should the girls bear so as to give them a sense of security and at the same time to sterilize the sinner's eye? This question kept me awake for the night. In the morning I gently suggested to the girls that they might let me cut off their fine long hair. On the Farm we shaved and cut the hair of one another, and we therefore kept scissors and clipping machines. At first the girls would not listen to me. I had already explained the situation to the elderly women who could not bear to think of my suggestion but yet quite understood my motive, and they had finally accorded their support to me.

And while you are speaking of cutting, you conclude:

This act of mine was not without its effect on the entire life of the settlers on the Farm. As we had intended to cut down expenses to the barest minimum, we changed our dress also.[5]

Call me a busybody, but I cannot overlook this sequence of "cutting off" and "cutting down"; for to pluck out what offends one—and to pluck it out in *others*—is so often the impulse of a despairing moralism. But the "noble girls," you continue, eventually "came round after all," and as you put it so self-consciously, "at once the very hand that is narrating this incident set to cut off their hair." Having then explained your act to the children, you say, you never "heard of a joke again." Who would not believe that?

It does not take much to see, Mahatmaji, that there is some violence in this. But I would like to explain why I think that here, in one brief episode, you illustrate what remained an existential conflict, if not at times a curse, in your whole undertaking. It concerns the relation of earthly progeny to divine truth—always a central issue in religion, but multiplied in a life like yours where pedagogic and political care were directly associated with religious transcendence. That your words (from "as a mother's eye would follow a daughter" to "the very hand that is narrating this") seem to betray some pretension may be partly attributable to the translation. And my job is not to pierce the pretension but to ask why it is necessary at all. Permit me, then, to review some of the content, for there are good reasons to believe that the themes of this story continued to haunt you to the bitter end of your long life and will haunt your image in the eyes of many, even the friendliest, critics.

That an educator must become, in varying combination, both father and mother to his students stands to reason. This, however, is so natural when it is there, and so complex when it is absent, that an act of will or penance cannot enforce it. How any man can make his eyes follow some young girls going down to the spring with strictly "maternal" eyes, that—at least to a Westerner—seems hard to comprehend and rather unnecessary to pretend. Is it because you feel a father might be aware of a daughter's attractiveness as a female? Would not the father or teacher who is aware of young curves but devoted to the growth of the person be better equipped to guide and protect his daughters than the one who "sterilizes" his own eyes?

The whole first part of the story can only impress the modern reader with the probability that here a guardian was following the "mischievous" boys and the "innocent young girls" to the spring with the moralist's secret hope that they *would* show some of the interest which had aroused the guardian's all-too-hungry curiosity. And, indeed, some unspecified boys "made fun" of two girls who henceforth remain the focus of the guardian's scruples and plans, although they are described as the mere victims of the boys' jokes. The news makes the guardian tremble—with what? Rage? Anxiety? Instinctual tension? Whatever the mixture of emotions, he emerges with an astonishing wish which is in no way explained:

I wished the two girls to have some sign on their person as a warning to every young man that no evil eye might be cast on them, and as a lesson to every girl that no one dare assail their purity.

The question which kept him awake all night, then, was "what mark should the girls bear to sterilize the sinner's eye?" But note that it is now one sinner's eye which must be "sterilized"—a word with any number of connotations, not the least that of preventing progeny. So you suggested "gently" and pleaded persistently that the girls' hair must go "by the very hand" which, in writing about it twenty years later, still feels strange, almost depersonalized, like the instrument of something terrible, or sacred, or both.

"Experiments such as I have placed on record," you now remember to explain, "are not meant for imitation." One could thank God for that, were it not that the cutting off of women's hair is an age-old ritual which receives its very meaning from "imitation"—imitation, that is, within a ritual context. Throughout history, such context might be judicial, and the denuding of the head could mean a punishment decreed by some form of ritual or popular sentence—as was true, for example, for girls who had sinned with enemy soldiers. Or the context might be religious, in which case a whole class of women, having offered their prayerful consent, are shorn by the representatives of a church or dogma so that whatever individual perversity there may be in the act of cutting or being cut would be contained in a communal setting and be given a symbolic meaning. Thus did St. Francis cut off the hair of St. Claire, a symbolic act which sealed a spiritual friendship. Your act, then, was not only personally idiosyncratic but it was also an abortive monastic ritualization: for you, Mahatmaji, have always tried, and sometimes desperately so, to tie together the loose ends of your restraints and restrictions in a communal pattern which would provide a new kind of "order." If in this you often seem to a Western observer to have acted arbitrarily and in a fragmentary manner, he should remember that your religious tradition always permitted a perplexing multiplicity of petty rules and small rituals.

Yet your own criterion for the moral soundness of many of
your edicts became a communal one: you were right wherever
you could give to your arbitrary decisions a pervasive meaning
enhancing Satyagraha and involving others in a clear and self-
chosen mutuality, and you were dangerously wrong where you
indulged in perverse arbitrariness. And here the vital pedagogic
question arises as to whether an act like the one described here
would make young people better Satyagrahis in the long run, or
only serve to convince them of the self-righteous folly of those
who usurp spiritual power.

The incident itself remains inconclusive. You do not say,
Mahatmaji, who the older women were who finally consented to
your intention: was Kasturba one of them? And as you dismiss
the boys, so you ignore the men, although males were in the vast
majority in your community, and being Satyagrahis and having
committed themselves to self-suffering, they surely should have
had a voice in the selection of the method by which male eyes
were to be "sterilized." Nor do you wonder what the girls'
parents would have said. But then, throughout your life you
appropriate other people's children unconditionally for your
way of life with a truly dictatorial combination of maternalism
and paternalism. Yet nowhere do you indicate that you cared to
understand what your usurpation of motherhood meant to the
children—or, indeed, to the mothers. Now, I do not know what
happened to the young people whom you brought up, and I
know very well that one incident alone almost never harms
young people unless it is prototypal for repeated traumata.
Young people for the most part tolerantly accept the spirit in
which a mistake is committed by their elders, or they can
sovereignly forgive and forget even an occasional lapse of spirit.
After all, God is with them, too. So the question is only what
may be the long-range meaning of this publicized incident. You
remembered it, Mahatmaji, and you recorded it; you above all
must have wondered about it.

Truth, you once said, "excludes the use of violence because
man is not capable of knowing the absolute truth and therefore
is not competent to punish." This is the crux of Satyagraha,

*/only amends*

whereby daily living becomes an "experiment in truth." For
what you call the relative character of truth, or what I, as a post-
Einsteinian and post-Freudian would call the *relativity of truth*,
reveals itself from generation to generation above all in the
meeting of adult and child, and teacher and student—both
trusteeships, as you would put it. But trusteeship means a mutuality between leader and led, in which the leader is guided by the
actuality of the led. I can see in your example little, if any, of
that mutuality which would have arisen from true persuasion—
and certainly no "self-chosen" suffering.

Demonstrative self-suffering on the part of adults is always a
dubious weapon to use against children, and your own mother
may well have gone to the very limit with it. You have given it
more dignity in those examples where you dealt with transgressions in the younger generation by your own fasting: once, on a
later occasion in Phoenix, by fasting for a week, you brought to
the attention of three "sinners" (a girl and two boys) "how much
you were suffering and how deep they had fallen." The girl
fasted with you and had her hair cropped short (not by you, it
seems). But she was twenty years old. On another occasion your
twenty-year-old son was "assaulted" by "a married woman"
(according to Fischer's strange phrasing).[6] Here you fasted for
two weeks, and again the woman had her hair cropped. As far as
propriety or pedagogies are concerned, these occasions, I feel,
were your business as well as that of the young people and of
the community. But as to the dynamics involved, such acts could
contain an ambivalence as wide and swampy as the Great Rann
of Kutch (to match your own reference, in another context, to
your "Himalayan miscalculation"). The ambivalence would
arise with the possibility that here self-suffering could harbor
the despotism of a cruel (if "cruelly kind") father who, by his
self-suffering, hurts ever so much more vindictively, and ever so
much more unfathomably than an outright angry one; whereupon the children feel punished, if not "crushed"—but by no
means persuaded.

That living progeny carry with them the curse of procreation—that association is often suggested in your utterances.

During the very year when you took the vow of Brahmacharya, you also wrote to your brother that "for the present, at any rate, I have ceased to think of [Harilal] as a son," and this, because Harilal wanted to get married.[7] Harilal was then in India, and you could expect your threat to reach his ears, but how can a son cease to be a son "for the present, at any rate"? And to rub it in, you—not untypically—refer in the same letter to somebody else's son as one "like Prahlad in spirit. He is therefore dearer to me than one who is a son because so born." And here, as so often, the figure of Prahlad assumes a central symbolic position. You, Mahatmaji, love the story of that boy prince who would not accept the claim of his father, the Demon King, to a power greater than God's, not even after the boy had been exposed to terrible tortures. At the end he was made to embrace a red-hot metal pillar; but out of this suggestive object stepped God, half lion and half man, and tore the king to pieces. You call that prince the first Satyagrahi. His often-exhorted example, it would seem, put your sons in a terrible predicament, because you (acknowledging neither their natural ambivalence nor your own) exhorted them to be truthful like Prahlad but repeatedly threatened to disavow and to disown them when their truth meant rebellion against you. Would it be too farfetched to say that what was activated in you and (maybe dimly) perceived by the young in such moments of wrath was, in fact, a facsimile of the very Demon King whom Prahlad resisted?

Some of your outbursts are, of course, just patriarchal bad manners. They merely signify how much you were inclined to treat those closest to you as possessions and whipping-posts. Those of us who have ourselves become fathers in a patriarchal era which only now is reaching a demise in universal unrest, dissent and violence have a right to single out your acts only where you rationalize them with ambivalent phrases and principles. And even then, we must admit that you could not possibly have known of the power of that ambivalence which we have now learned to understand in case histories and life histories—and indeed, through the painful analysis of our own symptomatic behavior as parents, having ourselves resisted such guilty insight as long, as illogically, and as meanly as we could. It is, therefore, not without compassion that I must point out that your lifelong insistence on the "innocence" (meaning sexlessness) of children is matched only by your inability to recognize the Demon King in yourself. And this *must* be pointed out because the demons triumph in all hidden and disguised ambivalences: however and wherever we let our children down, we become their demons. If, then, in order to fathom the truth we must hold on to the potential of love in all hate, so must we become aware of the hate which is in all love. Only if we accept the presence of ambivalence in the most loving human encounters does truth become just what you mean by it, namely, that which supports evolving humanity in the antagonisms of divided function, be it in the context of inequalities of size, age, sex, or power. For all these inequalities call for conscious insight rather than for moralistic repression. And it is here, I feel, that your attempts at enlarging human awareness, and Freud's, complement each other.

Sigmund Freud was, in fact, the only other man in our time who offered to the reading world such candid descriptions of small events in his life as you revealed of yours, and this not in the now-fashionable form of literary self-exhibiting, but strictly for the sake of a theory and a technique of truthfulness. In discussing the pedagogic incident at Tolstoy Farm, I applied what I have learned from him to one of your free confessions. Now I should like to point out in all brevity why I believe that the psychoanalytic method itself, by dint of always being a self-analysis paired with an attempt to understand another man's inner conflicts, is a counterpart to your Satyagraha, because it confronts the *inner* enemy nonviolently. Both you and Freud knew (as did other great confessors who expanded man's awareness) that human insight begins in oneself: and as you in your "Experiments" probed your own motivations, so Freud began by dealing "scientifically" with his own dreams as well as those of his patients.

In studying your method of Satyagraha, I have become increasingly convinced that psychoanalysis, not if judged by its physicalistic terminology and theory but if understood as it is practiced and lived according to the rules and the intentions of its originator, amounts to a *truth method*, with all the implications which the word truth has in Satyagraha. This, I submit, is more than a vague analogy; it is a correspondence in method and a convergence in human values which may well be of historical, if not evolutionary, significance.

Let me tell you briefly what the Viennese doctor refused to do to his patients and what he chose to do instead. Dr. Freud was approaching middle age when he faced the probability that his hysterical patients, far from being degenerates as his colleagues believed, suffered from an oppressive education and a resulting inner repression: they had developed a mortal prejudice against themselves in order to internalize the edicts of their Victorian parents. Furthermore, he concluded that the very doctors who were to free these patients from their inner repressions added to their unfreedom by imposing on them authoritative suggestions often given under induced conditions of dependence or hypnosis. This, Freud felt, did violence to what alone can free a man from inner compulsion, namely, the conscious acceptance of certain truths about himself and others. And this doctor in his consultation room made a decision analogous to the one you made in your South African proving ground, namely, that the instrument of enlightenment to be forged by him would have to include self-analysis, that is, the acceptance of himself as a person who shared his patients' inner mechanisms: the truth could cure the patient only insofar as the doctor had faced the corresponding truth in himself.

He decided, then, on a method which would permit the patient to relax his resistance to his own thoughts and feelings and, instead of censoring them, learn to let his repressed ideas and affects come to word. At the same time, the doctor would learn to relax both his condemnation of the patient and the condemnation of feelings aroused in himself by the patient's "free association." But in doing so, he replaced moral suppression with the belief that truth has enough force to make the patient reveal what he had repressed, and that this, in turn, would permit the doctor to recognize and to interpret what the patient could not understand by himself.

Freud thus called for a strict equality between patient and doctor, with the dictum that only as long as this nonviolent equality is maintained can the truth emerge. Given the probability that the patient could abide by a contract of truthfulness, the doctor would protect him from such slurs as inferiority or dishonesty and would deal with all inner hindrances in the process of truth-finding as "natural" resistances to be explained, not condemned. But the "basic rule" imposed on the patient to say what comes to mind without censoring it also called for some disciplined self-suffering on the part of the therapist.

To give you an example of how we *earn* our right to be busybodies in other people's lives, let me point out in passing that the patient's resistances often take the form of accusations and suspicions of the doctor, who is obliged to accept and explain them without anger or argument. In fact, he must encourage their verbalization once they have entered the patient's mind—an encouragement sacrificing all traditional protection of customary propriety. For the most part, of course, such attacks are transparently irrational, seasoned as they are with the ambivalence of a dim past which can and must be recognized as the primal "cause" of the patient's pathology. Yet there is a disconcerting propensity in even the sickest patients on occasion to see through their doctor with almost vicious poignancy, laying bare what he himself neither had seen before nor can quite deny now. Yet the doctor's exposure to self-suffering does not end here. The same patient on other days may passionately adore and glorify him; whereupon the doctor would not be permitted to let himself assume that these flattering reports reveal the truth any more rightly than do the critical ones. For the only truth that matters is the unconscious origin and meaning of the patient's affects, symptoms, and distortions. Maybe all this will convince you that the doctor has amply earned his license—and, within reason, his fees.

There was, in the early days of psychoanalysis, even an element of *Brahmacharya* in the method. Freud at first felt that a

a social contract
of unfreedom & untruth

psychoanalytic treatment was best conducted under conditions of total sexual abstinence—the patient's to be sure, and yet in part also the doctor's, for whatever sexual tension was aggravated in therapy, whatever sexual imagery or temptation revealed in all detail, the doctor had to be prepared to understand rather than to act upon his own reaction, whether it consisted of self-indulgent indignation, inadvertent sexual response, or mysterious guilt.

It is interesting that in the world's early evaluation of psychoanalysis, as well as of Satyagraha, the *passive* aspects were the first to be emphasized; and compared with the patriarchal methods of the clinicians of the day, the psychoanalytic technique did, indeed, look more like morbid co-meditation than a manly professional activity. The training analysis, in which the therapist tasted patienthood, seemed to be a strangely masochistic undertaking, especially considering the fact that it trained the doctor to confront and understand his own unresolved conflicts, of all places, in his work—a man's usual reserve and escape from his private weaknesses. No wonder psychoanalysis began as a scientific underground movement and for decades had to flourish outside the medical schools.

But all of this only begins to indicate the nature of the psychoanalytic process. Only the full story of a psychotherapeutic event—as detailed as this psycho-historical study of a historical Event—could convey a sense of how an interpretation emerges as the joint experience of a truth which relieves and restores as it enlightens, and how the truth thus revealed could emerge and can be contained only in a joined effort marked by a new kind of ascetic discipline—ascetic not in the repudiation of the erotic facts of life, but in the insistence on a rigorous truthfulness toward them. Thus—and this is my main point—we are somehow joined in a universal "therapeutics," committed to the Hippocratic principle that one can test truth (or the healing power inherent in a sick situation) only by action which avoids harm—or better, by action which maximizes mutuality and minimizes the violence caused by unilateral coercion or threat.

On some occasions of despair and illness you too, Mahatmaji, unknowingly came to join the Freudians in the conclusion that you should stop terrorizing yourself and approach your own body with nonviolence. Indeed, in many ways you were always very undogmatic and, in fact, antidogmatic in your judgment of various moralisms; the Old Testament with its violently "jealous" God did not suit you at all. Up to a point (namely, the point at which your own moralism won out), you understood that dogmatism induces the fanatic religionist to split himself into a cruel judge and a hopeless sinner, and to derive from this the license to view and to treat others as if they were no better than the worst in himself—whether these others are his own children or such classes of dependent men and women as he judges to be "no better than children." I have counterpointed your pedagogic examples and our insights, then, because we have learned to see in the encounter of adult and child the terrible challenge to anyone who wants to cure man of any of his irrational violence. For this cure it is essential—in your context and in ours—that the moral adult, so easily given to moral vindictiveness, should learn to educate without violence, that is, with a recognition of the inviolacy of the counterplayer even if, and especially when, that counterplayer is a child. But the mere avoidance of physical cruelty as such is not enough; it can, in fact, lead to a parental self-inhibition that abrogates all indignation as it pretends to sacrifice all force: this, we have learned, is little progress. We also "do violence" to children and arouse inner rage in them wherever we withhold from them a guidance without which they cannot develop fully—or force on them decisions for which they are not ready. No life history has ever illustrated this better than your own, for your early marriage did violence to you. But you, Mahatmaji, were one of the rare men who could overcome the impotent counterviolence aroused in his childhood by combining tradition and personal fate, religion and politics, in a method scrupulously—and sometimes tortuously—nonviolent.

Pedagogically speaking, I should say that *ahimsa* must come to include, beyond the insurance of another's physical inviolacy, the protection of another's essence as a developing person. It is, then, because one loves another for his potentialities as a person that one sacrifices some momentary consummative impulse or fantasy, not because the impulse or fantasy is wicked or forbidden. Only in this way can self-abnegation become self-affirmation and a tool of truth rather than a weapon of revenge. I know these are high-sounding words of the kind one should not use unless one has seen these phenomena occur quite wordlessly and un-self-consciously in the ethicality of everyday life—as I think I have. Then one also knows how much of what we used to ascribe to the Devil's wiles or to the id's inexorable demands can be tolerated, if absorbed by love rather than negated by violent moralism.

SOMEWHERE, Mahatmaji, you report with stark suddenness that a Protestant minister once asked you whether you believed in original sin and that you answered, "Yes, I do." To that question I would give the same answer in the improbable case that anybody would care to ask me the same question. But as a psychologist I would add, "Yes, I am sorry to say I do," for I believe it is part of man's curse that he cannot believe otherwise. For that very reason, however, I should ask the questioner immediately whom and what he may have specifically in mind. For few men can envisage the problem for very long in its existential enormity. Most people (more or less consciously) believe that all men bear a share of original sin, but that others bear more than they do. Thus Mr. Kruger, the President of the Transvaal, would unhesitatingly tell a deputation of your friends:

You are the descendants of Ishmael and therefore from your very birth bound to slave for the descendants of Esau.[8]

It is obvious, then, that this question, too, must be faced in its psychological as well as its religious dimensions, for it, too, makes killers of us. To kill sinners for a "just cause," to become a hero in taking the chance of being killed in the act of so killing, and to venerate such heroism as absolute in the eyes of God—all this frees us from the common human burden of living guiltily and absurdly. And yet we cannot become one species without assuming, together, that burden.

Clinically, so to speak, there can be little doubt that ideas of basic sin may be very much aggravated by personal fate and historical circumstance, and are rarely faced existentially. I have indicated ("in all modesty," as you would say) that at times such was the case with you. That moral absolutism which at times you found to be a necessary weapon against your own instinctuality made you see an irreversible curse in any and all instinctual indulgence. And so you do not hesitate to call "sources" of evil those items which become evil only by man's thoughtless exploitation; nor do you hesitate to claim, with a clear reference to your oldest son, that a child may be doomed by having been conceived in an embrace which did not deliberately intend him. To even the score, let me say that this kind of thinking is so universal that in clinical work, too, we always find ways to blame a curse in early childhood—if not a constitutional "cause"—for man's neurotic inferiorities. Yet, none of us has a right to foreclose as evil, sick, or doomed what we have not confronted in a radical spirit of risk and experiment: for this, in fact, you have offered the model of Satyagraha for some areas of life, as Freud offered psychoanalysis for others. And yet the sternness sometimes displayed in your letters to your children bespeaks an appalling sense of doom, as if they, as the product of your sin, had no chance for salvation except as partners in your renunciation. Here I must admit that we clinicians have cultivated an analogous curse in that our "genetic" approach led us to reconstruct a child's development as if it were nothing but the product of his parents' virtues or vices. But I think that we, too, would be more true, as well as more helpful, if we would admit that each child is potentially a new person as well as a product of others, and that we have no right to burden him with an abstract curse, unless the clinical data clearly point to a concrete defect. In regard to the procreative act, however, the important ques-

tion is whether Satyagraha will remain irretrievably tied to such
ascetic idiosyncrasies as your followers cultivate, or whether it
will prove valid anew in a future in which a better knowledge of
the role of sexuality and sensual pleasure in the energy household of men and women (and this with an advanced technology
of planned parenthood) will, maybe, incline more people to true
peacefulness. Whether it will also incline them to be willing to
suffer in defense of the right of others also to live a livable
life—that, I admit, I do not know.

In fact, if you, Mahatmaji, could reply, you could well remind
me of some sexual and hedonistic excesses which have spread
over some of the most civilized parts of the Western World,
often in the name of Freud. I must concede this; and it is not for
a cheap comeback in such tragic matters that I remind you, in
turn, of the riots which followed your nonviolent campaigns,
although only very remotely in your name. The point is that
excess and riot follow repression and suppression when the
moral restraints are lifted, precisely because of the autocratic
and blind nature of these restraints. Here, too, I can only re-state
my original point: nonviolence, inward and outward, can become a true force only where ethics replaces moralism. And
ethics, to me, is marked by an insightful assent to human values,
whereas moralism is blind obedience; and ethics is transmitted
with informed persuasion, rather than enforced with absolute
interdicts. Whether the increasing multitudes of men can ever
develop and transmit such an ethical attitude I do not know; but
I do know that we are committed to it, and that the young are
waiting for our support in attempting it.

Satyagraha in social conflict, however, we can say with assurance, will have little chance to find its universal relevance unless
we learn to apply it also to whatever feels "evil" in ourselves and
makes us afraid of instinctual satisfactions without which man
would not only wither as a sensual being but would also become
a doubly destructive creature. For man can find what peace
there is in this existence only in those moments when his sensual,
logical, and ethical faculties balance each other: this all cultures,

at their best, have striven to achieve, and this a world-wide technological culture must help make universal at least as an ideal to be envisaged in a spirit of faith and realism. There is no doubt, however, that in the world of today a severe disbalance of sensual, logical, and ethical experience is upon us.

BUT as we now follow you back to India, in the year 1914, I cannot hold back a question, which I know has been asked vindictively and contemptuously by some of your countrymen. Was not Hinduism at its best rather free from the Calvinist sense of sin? And did it not for that very reason offer a logic of the life cycle which permitted gradual detachment *after* a full involvement in life? If "nonattachment to the fruits of action" is the central theme of the Bhagavad Gita, was it not wedded to the other theme, namely, that the fruits themselves must first ripen? When Krishna convinced Arjuna that he had to live out the *dharma* of the warrior, Arjuna was not about to "act out" some impulsive aggression: he was an expert warrior and a man. To the extent to which men remain inexperienced and incomplete in any stage of life or in the craftsmanship implicit in their technological identity—do they not to that extent also forfeit their chance of "detachment" and existential freedom? I may not understand this; but without such fulfilment, would a man not, to some extent, vindictively transmit the curse of unlived potentials to coming generations? Here it seems of utmost significance that you, in attempting to be both spiritual and political, detached and activist, create an impossible dilemma with your implicit vilification of procreation. For without an alliance with the Hereness of women as the guardians of an earthly order dedicated to an optimal hospitality toward planned progeny, man would have to re-create Satyagraha, ever again, out of conflicts so morbid (because so crudely male) that only crime, riot, and war could relieve the unbearable pressure. And because I have, in my clinical work, endeavored to recognize in the suffering of the young their parents' distance from truth, I cannot help concluding (what I know you later recognized) that such passionately suicidal sufferers as your son, Harilal, in the perverse way of a world not mythological but generational, are, in fact, the Prahlads of their parents.

At the end, your candid revelations about your temper, in relation to your wife and children, only express concretely and nakedly an ambiguity inherent in all genius and, maybe, especially so in religious genius. For a religious genius, even more than other originators, faces not only the problem of whose son he is but also whose father. For even as he was originated by one earthly man and was born out of one woman's womb in a defined place and moment, and even as he cannot act without advancing or destroying the actuality of living, his soul is ever jealous in its search for *the* father and *the* son who might match the enormity of existence. In the meantime, your involvement in the life of your people brings it about that, in protesting "namelessness," you come to be a name on everybody's lips; in being zero, you aspire to be everything for everybody; and, by the same token, in trying to be free of all familial bonds, you usurp motherhood along with fatherhood.

But all this, God help me, is not by way of an accusation or even a clinical judgment. I can only view with awe a man who (making himself more transparent than any of the saviors and saints of the mythologized past) improvised every item in the inventory of saintliness—nakedness, poverty, silence, chastity, and charity—without being baptized or ordained in any traditional investiture; and who attempted to apply the power of that position in every waking minute to the Here and the Now as lived by the masses of men. The sacrifices which you imposed on yourself and on others devoted to "national service" made you, on your return to India, ready for the masses as no man in history had been or has been since. So I can only humbly accept what you wrote on your return, to Mr. Lazarus, your and the miners' long-suffering host in Newcastle:

Games . . . may have their place under certain circumstances. But I feel sure that for us who are just now so fallen, they have no room.[9]

Having told you all this, I can now simply narrate, without argument or discussion, the years of your ascendance to the job of a prophet in his own country. And I can conclude this letter more truthfully: with abiding and affectionate respect, yours as ever.

CHAPTER
II

# Prophet in His Own Country

---

## 1. WHY AHMEDABAD?

FROM THE MOMENT in January of 1915 when Gandhi set foot
on a pier reserved for important arrivals in Bombay, he behaved
like a man who knew the nature and the extent of India's
calamity and that of his own fundamental mission. A mature
man of middle age has not only made up his mind as to what, in
the various compartments of life, he does and does not *care for*,
he is also firm in his vision of what he *will* and *can* take *care
of*. He takes as his baseline what he irreducibly *is* and reaches
out for what only he can, and therefore, *must do*. We will now
show how Gandhi went about consolidating himself in all of
these respects. Without further vacillation he made it a point to
appear amidst the "dazzling splendor" of the reception with
which his countrymen meant to honor him in the simple outfit
of a "Kathiawadi rustic," that is, a native of his own province.
Offering without delay "what might be called a little Satyagraha," he addressed the dignitaries at public functions in his
native Gujarati. He told his countrymen off in a manner so
taunting as to be worthy of little Moniya, and yet with the soft-
spoken sincerity of a man who not only meant every word he
said but also meant to follow it up with deeds—or perish. And
the response of the public soon "emboldened me to think that I
should not find it difficult to place my new-fangled notions

before my countrymen." He obediently, if half-mockingly, accepted Gokhale's advice to lie low for a while in matters of public politics, but he never hesitated to speak up in such a way that *his* program for a reformation, Indian style, would unfold with methodical certainty.

But first he had to make clear who he was. When presented, on the second day after his arrival, with an address enclosed in a silver casket with fetters made of gold, he described the gifts

as somewhat unsuitable to a person who had neither a roof over his head nor locked doors to his house. Fetters, whether of gold or of iron, were the same to him, as they were fetters after all. A function like the one they held, he said, was most uncongenial to him. . . .[10]

To the élite of Bombay, who appeared six hundred strong at a reception, he confided that he and his wife

during the three days that they had passed in Bombay, . . . had felt—and he thought he was voicing the feelings of his wife, too—that they were much more at home among those indentured Indians, who were the truest heroes of India.[11]

And when the people at Rajkot greeted him with a meeting presided over by the Dewan, he admitted that with all these gatherings his health was "going down badly"; he only hoped that they would keep up the love they were showing that day when in days to come they saw him really work and maybe fail. His own caste community's reception he accepted as a blessing, but only when the "testing time" came could he know whether their love was sincere or whether they had gathered together "blindly, like so many sheep."[12]

Losing no time, then, Gandhi set everybody's sights on an untested future. But being the son of an agrarian age, he proceeded with equal devotion to get "settled," to sink permanent roots into native soil before branching out into every region of India and into every aspect of her immediate dangers and promises. He soon found the place for a resettling of the "Phoenix family" near Ahmedabad by the Sabarmati River. The story to be told, then, is how, having settled down in this city and having explored the four corners of India, he chose Ahmedabad for what we shall describe as the first full application of the instrument of Satyagraha.

There were (it must be stated), and there still are many Indians who never forgave Gandhi for being a Bania in the first place and for settling down in Gujarat into the bargain. But least forgivable in their eyes was his getting involved with the Ahmedabad mill owners. And even among those who admit that Gandhi, with all his peculiarities, was a powerful tool, if by no means the driving force in the independence movement, there were and are many who suspect that his reaffirmed Bania nature was what blinded him to the potency of certain elements then emerging: the unique grandeur of Hinduism and the manly ideology of its martial castes, the political potential of the intellectual and artistic renaissance which began in Bengal, the nationalist awakening of Maharashtra, and behind it all, the truly revolutionary potential of the Indian peasant proletariat. And since, as we saw, his Autobiography plays down the Ahmedabad episode, we must be interested in trying to understand why he did choose a spot across the Sabarmati River for his Satyagraha ashram and why he came to offer his first fast for a public issue in a struggle with, of all things, the textile industry.

"Settling down" of course always remained for Gandhi a matter for quotation marks, and the years between his return to India and the Event were, in fact, years divided between the endeavor to establish a "home" for his "family" and an almost manic rushing around the subcontinent by railroad. And if his settlement served prayer and reform, it also became the headquarters for a national campaign; and while traveling was to serve him for the gathering of the greatest diversity of first-hand information, it also became the vehicle for the widest possible propaganda. He did adhere to his promise to Gokhale and declared himself everywhere as "on probation" as a politician. Exploiting his original fame as a true friend of the poor, he became a pilgrim in loincloth, but he was a pilgrim on railway wheels, spending every fourth night on the train—third class, of course. And what a scene, worthy of a modern Giotto: the slight "Kathiawadi peasant," almost falling asleep while standing and swaying all night in a rattling railway compartment, because he was unwilling to wedge himself between the impudent passengers who had spread themselves on the seats and on the floors. "How can you take it," somebody exclaims, "what is your name, anyway?" "My name is Mohandas Gandhi"—and the compartment comes to its feet. Soon also the secret police would follow him, and passengers would note with disgust how they harassed "the poor Sadhu" by requesting to see his papers over and over again. And again the passengers would ask with mixed awe why he "took it" and who was he, anyway? This was folk fame on a very low and very broad level.

But before we record the altogether new kind of national campaign he would wage whenever and wherever he detrained, let us ask: why Ahmedabad in the first place, why the "Manchester of India"?

I think I know. But then, Ahmedabad is the only city in India with which I am somewhat acquainted through having had at least a temporary function in it: the seminar. One always senses something unique about a city to which one has to adapt "functionally," and one learns to grasp in a short time what it would be impossible to observe in a longer and less challenging contact. But one also acquires prejudices which will determine one's conception of that city in all future. My preconception was that I had happened to come to a city of just the right size and structure to be comprehended in its function through the centuries, although it was built neither around a palace nor by a harbor. It simply was, and in all memory had been, a true city. It breathed, if one may say so, the logic of mercantile life, for its industry had grown from native crafts to small enterprises and to a large industry by an uninterrupted process so consistent that it could truly be said to have a corporate identity. This gave it a character both solid and limited, both strong and ingrown, both alive and isolated, by which it had been able to household through the centuries a remarkable energy now renewed in the personalities of my hosts and in the institutions of research, management, and education. Which is not to deny that Ahmedabad displays, in addition to the squalor typical of all Indian cities, the noise and the smog of an industrial establishment which consists not only of factories, but of all the plants for processing and printing, packing and shipping. But (as in Pittsburgh) a single-minded industry also means an over-all orientation and a comprehensive life-view for hundreds of thousands of people. These people managed, furthermore, to maintain some ethnic community life and to keep in lively contact with the surrounding villages and even the more distant ancestral homes. The Mahatma, in retrospect, states simply:

I had a predilection for Ahmedabad. Being a Gujarati I thought I should be able to render the greatest service to the country through the Gujarati language. And then, as Ahmedabad was an ancient centre of handloom weaving, it was likely to be the most favourable field for the revival of the cottage industry of hand-spinning. There was also the hope that, the city being the capital of Gujarat, monetary help from its wealthy citizens would be more available here than elsewhere.

Gandhi, then, first of all emphasized the factor of *language*. The Gujarati-speaking people comprise not more than one-tenth of all Indians, but they were his people. And one of the first requirements for a free man, he felt, was the ability to express himself well in the language of his childhood. If Gandhi later made unacceptable and ineffective suggestions for a solution of the truly abysmal language problem in India, it is clear that he was right in principle, and India today is the poorer for the fact that no leader followed him who had enough vision and authority to approach the language dilemma with equal propagandistic zeal and vigor. All that the apostle of truth could do was to set a personal example and to awaken his people to a national calamity. For truth becomes a hazy matter indeed where most official business and much of the everyday life of a people must be transacted either in a stilted and often broken English or in a multitude of idioms offering no more than an approximation of intended meaning. And since this fact, in the long run, makes it both impossible and unnecessary to say what one "really" means, it supports a form of habitual half-truth such as the English had come to consider "inborn" in all Indians.

When Gandhi chose Ahmedabad, then, it was the city where

an official Gujarati had always been spoken, studied, and cultivated in commerce and in colleges; and then, it was an ancient seat of *hand-loom weaving*. For besides the incurable split between regional languages and official English, Gandhi blamed the disruption of native crafts for the deterioration of Indian identity. He was soon to elevate the spinning wheel to significance as an economic necessity, a religious ritual, and a national symbol. It is a typically Gandhian paradox that Ahmedabad, of all Indian cities, had become, in fact, the seat of the most modern methods of spinning and weaving. We shall see that in regard to Indian textiles, too, Gandhi proposed solutions which were effective on a large scale only for a limited period, wherefore he was to be accused of being a machine-wrecker and a craft romantic. But here, too, he was in principle profoundly right; and while there were many who were concerned about the future of a textile industry in competition with millions of private spinning wheels, I have not met a single Indian industrialist who did not see a mutual enhancement rather than competition in a coexistence of a vigorous textile industry with a reborn hand-loom culture in the villages. At any rate, Gandhi wanted to settle down where both tradition and available materials would permit him and his followers to build a community around the cultivation of spinning and weaving. And he was right (up to a point) in assuming that some of the wealthy Jain merchants and industrialists would not hesitate to finance their "competitor."

For the weaving tradition in India meant much more than an indigenous way of producing goods; native crafts were deeply embedded in the whole system which makes *guild*, *caste*, and *religion* intimately interdependent. And in Ahmedabad, the various communities which served the financing, manufacture, and distribution of textiles had for centuries lived in mutual dependence and adaptation: in Ahmedabad caste structure had literally "worked" and had been little eroded by British ways. Gandhi had a dialectic problem before him which is all too easily belittled by Western ideologists who demand that he be found "consistent." He had to call for a rapid modernization of awareness and aspiration and yet also to acknowledge and even pre-

serve those aspects of the ancient social structure which alone
could provide irreplaceable elements of a traditional identity. So
Gandhi could do no better than to settle in a modern place that
had preserved some ancient structure, so that from there he could
travel and study what he later came to call the "four ruins" of
Indian identity.

And Ahmedabad must have been a mirage of power on the
horizon of Moniya's and Mohandas's world, as it had been for
many generations of his ancestors. Centuries before Moniya was
born, Ahmedabad had a strong name in the world of trade
routes and shipping lanes. The early Ahmedabad[18] furthermore—it seems incredible today—was famous for its wide
streets and tall trees and for the pleasure gardens laid out by
Sultan Ahmed's successors in the outskirts of the city (models,
no doubt, for the kind of "Retreat" built by Ambalal). But
what may well have impressed the visitors from Kathiawar, as
from all Gujarat, inclined as they were toward an almost "Protestant" combination of the religious and mercantile spirits, were
Ahmedabad's ancient guilds, which gave a firm and yet flexible
basis for the duties and privileges associated with caste, class, and
religion. This, no doubt, was an elaborate urban version of the
ancient jajmani system widely dominant in the villages. Traditionally, the head of the most influential guild, the merchants
and financiers, was also the head of the Jain community and the
"mayor" of the city; while the head of the cloth dealers was also
head of the Vaishnava sect and master of the market. Much of
the city was subdivided into "pols," that is, walled-in clusters of
houses each built around a quadrangle and temple: here the
castes and sub-castes lived together, and here for a long time the
wealthy insisted on living among their own people and taking
responsibility for the needy ones. Their wealth was displayed
inwardly in those periodic caste festivities which are the ritual
obligation of wealthy Hindus, and more lastingly in the elabo-
rately carved façades of their houses, depicting the usual multiplicity of intimate and sometimes erotic scenes. Such caste terri-
toriality kept growing families (and fortunes) within the city
walls and gradually resulted first in a kind of implosion of each

pol into every available space, and then in an expansion outward into the streets. The consequences of this process are best illustrated in the ordinance by which the British later found it necessary to regulate building codes and traffic laws: the roofs of the top floors extending into the once tree-lined avenues must be kept at least eight feet apart! Thus did a city become the architectural expression and the living symbol of an ingrown tradition.

Before the British extended their rule over Ahmedabad in 1817, there was a brief "dark age" which tested the durability of Ahmedabad's social networks. City life had deteriorated under the careless rule of conquerors, and the population had been decimated by famine and plague. But it soon appeared that the leading families and their capital had merely gone underground, for Ahmedabad soon regained its mercantile vitality and prominence, and this especially since British rule gave trade a new boost—opium. Some of the most respectable financiers seem to have refused, at impressive sacrifice, to take part in this; but it is said that Ahmedabad's Jain temple, the most impressive recent building in town (the older and finer architectural specimen being Muslim), was built with opium money. At any rate, in the nineteenth century, when competition with the Lancashire mills made mandatory the introduction of modern methods and ambitions, the old textile spirit remained intact, and Ahmedabad's uniqueness in India continued to rest on its traditional urban arrangements—the contractual system among finance, manufacture, and trade, and with all these, a style of commercial interdependency and monetary morality. Handicrafts flourished independent of princely subsidy, and a highly responsible, almost hereditary plutocracy was tuned to the welfare of the city as a whole. The British, in turn, were shrewd and discreet enough not to tamper with such a congenial urban phenomenon; British influence, the British seem to have realized, could have little play in such a close-knit society, and the military kept to its own compounds on the outskirts of the city.

Moniya as a child, furthermore, may well have heard the saga of *industrialization*. A shrewd old man (Ranchhodlal by name) had decided around 1860 to build a spinning mill to provide yarn for the city's weavers, but the ship carrying the whole equipment burned and sank while trying to come around the Cape. A new mill was ordered and at long last unloaded in Cambay, from there to be transported in appropriate chunks on oxcarts up to Ahmedabad. The English engineer who had preceded the equipment died of smallpox, and the assembling of the mill was a hazardous job all around. Yet the mill was put together, and it worked. And first slowly, then eruptively (especially after the opening of the railroad link to Bombay), industrialization began—although the real rise of the Indian mills had to await the free trade agreement of 1882, which ended the incredible tariffs by which both England and India had been "protected" from Indian textiles. In the meantime, the Ahmedabad mills could count on a steady labor supply from both the city and the surrounding countryside: there was a small Hindu "aristocracy" of warpers; there were the handloom weavers, mostly Muslim; and from the hinterland, a mass of landless laborers who (being Untouchables) remained confined to the spinning departments. This favorable labor situation and the indigenous élite of financier-managers became the strength of the Ahmedabad textile industry, and its main claim on the chance to compete with Bombay and its harbor. If Swaraj for all India was Gandhi's overweening aim and if Swaraj begins at home, then there could hardly be another instance in Indian history in which a potentially modern urban community also offered as unbroken a tradition of "home rule."

While Gandhi had been finding his vocation in England and South Africa, then, Ahmedabad had found its style as an industrial city. As for ownership, the mills were operated on the "management agency" system typical of much of Indian industry. This means that individuals or groups would run the mills on a commission basis for the "owners"; and such ownership in ingrown and interdependent Ahmedabad was infinitely shared not only among shareholders, but also among many small "depositors" who provided as much as 85 per cent of the capital in some mills; however, since some managing agents and their families were able to buy up both the shares and the deposits, they became, in fact, the recipients of both dividends and commissions, and thus came to be called "mill owners"—which is the reason why we have thus referred to Ambalal Sarabhai, whose grandfather purchased the right to manage the Calico Mills as an agent in 1880.

By the time Gandhi settled across the river on an outlying spot, Ahmedabad was the sixth largest city in India (after Calcutta, Bombay, Madras, Hyderabad, and Delhi)—and its population of about 250,000 included nearly 100,000 textile workers and their dependents. The first mill had opened with 2,500 spindles and 63 workers. There were now close to 100,000 spindles and 20,000 looms. Of the labor force, more than half had been born in the city and another quarter in neighboring regions, including Gandhi's native Kathiawar. For an understanding of his future relations with both owners and workers, it may be useful to refer to just one chart from the Census of 1921,[14] which is the closest we can come to 1918:

### Population of Ahmedabad in 1921

|  | % OF POPULATION | % OF LITERATES IN EACH GROUP | |
|---|---|---|---|
|  |  | IN ENGLISH | OTHER THAN ENGLISH |
| HINDUS | 72.5 | under 5 | 22 |
| MUSLIMS | 19.6 | 1 | 15 |
| JAINS | 6.3 | 10 | 55 |
| CHRISTIANS | 0.9 | 25 | 50 |
| ZOROASTRIANS | 0.6 | 40 | 80 |

It seems clear that among the Jain owners Gandhi met a highly literate, although by no means Anglicized, group, while among the workers he would address a largely illiterate and almost solidly Gujarati-speaking population.

The economic and cultural condition of labor will be discussed when we come to the moment Gandhi makes it his business to investigate it. In the meantime Ahmedabad labor seems to have profited from the fact that by the time the mills received machinery and technical advisors from England, the English industry had learned much about increased safety and better conditions of work. The Indian mills, furthermore, could afford to employ more operatives for each machine. Yet in 1916, just before the plague, the mortality rate in Ahmedabad was already considered extremely high, mostly because of the combination of dust from the river bed, coal dust, smoke from the mills, and a totally inadequate water supply. While Ahmedabad, then, was a uniquely well-put-together city as Indian cities go, it shared with the rest of the country and with the whole colonial world certain calamities which Gandhi was now investigating in width and in depth.

## 2. THE FOUR-FOLD RUIN

In January 1930, the Indian National Congress would present to the world a declaration of independence which contains the sentence: "We hold it to be a sin before man and God to submit any longer to a rule that has caused this four-fold disaster to our country."[15] I quote it here because both the word "sin" and the term "four-fold disaster" were obviously Gandhi's. And they mark the distinction from the American Declaration, which merely confirmed a separation from England already accomplished—and accomplished on the shores of a vast and as yet empty continent. In contrast, teeming India even in 1930 was still occupied by a foreign nation which, for all its enlightenment and high ideals, had exploited and "drained" the Indian subcontinent, so the nationalists charged, in four areas of national life: economic and political, cultural and spiritual. That these coordinates all meet in man's psychology was clearly seen by Jawaharlal Nehru—Gandhi's political heir and intellectually the most brilliant statesman of our time. He once said that what Gandhi had accomplished for India was "a psychological change, almost as if some expert in psychoanalytic methods had probed deep into the patient's past, found out the origins of his complexes, exposed them to his view, and thus rid him of that burden."[16] And if Nehru added that Gandhi had given back to India its "identity," he did not use that term in the loose way all too common today. For identity is (or so I have claimed) "a process 'located' *in the core of the individual* and yet also *in the core of*

*his communal culture,* a process which establishes, in fact, the
identity of those two identities."[17] Great leaders know this
definition instinctively, because they become great, and they
become leaders, precisely because they themselves have experienced the identity struggle of their people in both a most
personal and a most representative way. If, in the following, I
briefly abstract the "four-fold ruin," I know that mine is not the
historical reasoning which could present an "objective" critique
of the British Raj: on the contrary, I mean to emphasize what
Gandhi came to see as a nearly irreversible damage to a people's
identity wrought by colonial masters who often felt (and feel)
with justification that they have "advanced" their dependent
peoples in some important way. But it is the just fate of colonial
exploiters that they advance the very people whom they damage
in their identity to the point that some leaders among these
people can not only darkly feel but clearly perceive and diagnose the permanent harm done to them.

For some readers, it may be a vexing aspect of Gandhi's public
and private role that he equated service to India with service to
God—and by the same token considered any neglect of India a
sin. Such nationalist claims have all too often been used to justify
the exploitation and annihilation of other peoples *in majorem dei
gloriam.* Yet I think that in this unification of a political and an
existential task as a religious mission, Gandhi was on both good
psychological and (as far as I can judge) spiritual grounds. For
membership in a nation, in a class, or in a caste is one of those
elements of an individual's identity which at the very minimum
comprise *what one is never not,* as does membership in one of
the two sexes or in a given race. What one is never not establishes the life space within which one may hope to become
uniquely and affirmatively what one is—and then to transcend
that uniqueness by way of a more inclusive humanity. Thus was
Jesus a Jew. Gandhi, in his very development and in his emergence as a national leader, illustrates, because he lived every step
of it, that each man, as a leader and as a follower, must
somehow integrate the irreversible facts of his development as a

defined person within a given community in a particular geographic locus at a certain period of history so as to fulfill the potentialities of his existence. In a mankind not yet capable of an all-human identity, this means, of course, that every man, in the communal dimension of his identity, also lives in a condition which tempts him to exploit others and exposes him to exploitation by others: for any pseudo-species, besides fighting for territories and resources, always fights also for a dominant identity which permits it to consider itself the elite of the universe. Without such a feeling, man seems to consider himself inferior among men and beasts. But then, on rare occasions, a man appears who accepts the very nakedness and mortality of *all* men, without shirking his own historical identity.

While the British Empire may have promised to Indians and others a wider identity supervised by an élite of British choosing and training, it neglected to cultivate (as America neglected to do for the American Negro) those components of identity which neither a defined group nor an individual can do without—and this is a "criminal" neglect, indeed. It is the task of anticolonial revolutions to transvaluate such a condition so that identity elements which nevertheless developed, and which at the time seemed more or less accidental, ornamental, or expendable by-products of history, are turned into insignia of such pervasive dominance that to neglect them would be a sin in the face of existence. The case of India, then—or better, the case of England and India—is only the most extreme illustration of the historical trend known as colonialism: extreme in the magnitude of the population involved, in the distance between professed ideal and historical actuality, in the divergence of success achieved and disaster wrought, and in the perverse discrepancy of public glamour and degrading poverty.

Nehru, in a letter from prison to his young daughter (and eventual successor), wrote:

There can be few sights that are sadder than the sunken eyes of our *kisans* with the hunted, hopeless look in them. What a burden our peasantry have carried these many years! And let us not forget that we, who have prospered a little, have been part of that burden. All of us, foreigner and Indian, have sought to exploit that long-suffering *kisan* and have mounted on his back. Is it surprising that his back breaks?[18]

I am quoting this instead of enlarging on the obvious—namely, that the history of the four-fold ruin reveals "causes" to be found in the psychology of the colonized as well as in that of the colonizers, and that this history suggests that the "blame" must be shared among the various factions in each nation who conspired with and against each other in exploiting one of those transitory triumphs of human power and ingenuity for which always some have to pay. Only in this case more people had to pay more dearly, with a degradation both deeper and more lasting than ever before. We must understand, therefore, in terms of our time, what Gandhi felt he understood for his time.

In economic terms, then: as the British merchant-adventurers were defeating their European competitors in India, the ancient Mogul Empire was already disintegrating under the same pressures which had ended feudalism elsewhere. But when the servants of the East India Company took over the title as well as the capital and the dominion of that empire, they did not at once replace the old order with a new one; their original purposes were political only by implication. At first, the Company attached itself as a leech-like foreign body to an organism already weakened and decaying. For the economic conquerors, Nehru and other nationalist historians suggest, took over, wherever they went, the critical role of middleman and agent, not permitting, and indeed preventing, the creation of that new class which in other civilizations took over from feudalism: the great middle class which derived a pervasive mercantile identity from the enormous new power of trade.

When I first saw the title "Collector" which adorned the office of the chief English official in Ahmedabad, I was astonished at its bluntness, which seemed to suggest that the man was there not to govern and advise, but to collect and send off. And, indeed, the first title which the East India Company acquired from the Mogul Emperor in 1765 and which gave something of a fictitious legality to English occupation was that of "revenue

*to remove*

*economic fuel-assets*

farmer" in areas in which the Emperor's men had found it impossible to collect. And already ten years later, Adam Smith, in his *Wealth of Nations*, warned of the anomaly which was to be the economic basis of the great ruin:

The government of an exclusive company of merchants is perhaps the worst of all governments for any country whatever. . . . It is the interest of the East India Company considered as sovereigns that the European goods which are carried to their Indian dominions should be sold there as cheaply as possible; and that the Indian goods which are brought from there should be sold there as dear as possible. But the reverse of this is their interest as merchants. As sovereigns their interest is exactly the same with that of the country which they govern. As merchants their interest is directly opposite to that interest.[19]

For while the Company gave to the Emperor whatever revenue was due him, they took over some of his powers, not in order to govern but to plunder, being truly responsible only to the merchants and shareholders at home. For this, of course, they were superbly equipped, and within the moral vacuum of colonialism in the eighteenth century, we may even say that they did what they thought was right *and* British. But their national and occupational identity was that of a breed of middlemen whose vision did not extend beyond what the market of the moment would bear; for the most part, they had none of that instinctive self-restraint which might have governed the actions of a new class wanting to live and prosper tomorrow, too. It was hit-and-run exploitation.

We may now add that three of the five cities mentioned earlier as surpassing Ahmedabad's population today, namely, Calcutta, Bombay, and Madras, had all been founded by the English, while a fourth, Delhi, owed its life and size entirely to the administrative necessities of the Raj. It was through these three seaports that the native wealth of the nation was drained; while what was permitted to enter would poison and weaken it systematically. As Nehru recounted it in his prison correspondence with Indira:

The current which was flowing from India, bearing Indian goods to foreign countries, and bringing back gold and silver, was reversed.

Henceforth foreign goods came to India and gold and silver went out of it.

The textile industry of India was the first to collapse before this onslaught. As machine-industry developed in England, other Indian industries followed the way of the textile industry. Ordinarily it is the duty of a country's government to protect and encourage the country's industries. But far from protecting and encouraging, the East India Company crushed every industry which came into conflict with British industry. Shipbuilding in India collapsed, and the metal workers could not carry on, and the manufacture of glass and paper also dwindled away.

At first foreign goods reached the port towns and the interior near them. As roads and railways were built, foreign goods went farther and farther inland and drove out the artisan even from the village. The cutting through of the Suez Canal brought England nearer to India, and it became cheaper to bring British goods. So more and more foreign machine-goods came, and they went even to the remote villages. The process went on right through the nineteenth century and indeed it is going on to some extent still.[20]

Here it is of the essence to recognize that the merchants and their soldiers and administrators were, at first, not out for raw materials—an interest which might have led them to invest, to build, and to create new work for millions—but that they were after the goods already fashioned by ancient and contemporary craftsmen, goods that had symbolized both the traditional life of India and its identity in foreign eyes. Textiles especially, woven in millions of peasant homes and in tens of thousands of small-town industries, had through the ages not only supplemented agricultural production but had become a vast export. Not that the system here to be robbed of its fruit had not already been affected by a native blight: no doubt indigenous traders, as well as the alien revenue farmers, practiced their extortions where conditions permitted and custom did not restrain. The point is that under the early British occupation *all* custom began to fail, and with it all restraint in the exploitation of the artisans and the cultivators. Thus the identity-providing processes active in the previous system of society lost their native strength: for the skills necessary to produce excellent things are a prime source of identity only to the extent that the economic and legal system guarantees reward, status, and choice. Not only were artisans made to produce on demand, they also had to grant the Company's agents monopoly of delivery at set rates. All non-contracted activity was banned, and the ban re-enforced by the prohibition of even owning the raw materials and implements necessary for illicit production; this prohibition was, in turn, enforced by ruthless agents licensed to search homes and villages. "To this day in South India," Pyarelal reports, "the sight of a stray puff of cotton-wool lying about one's cottage is regarded by the villager as a sign of ill-luck."[21] To this enforced production and exportation was added the enforced consumption of what had been produced elsewhere, and always with an implied prohibition against replacing the old artisan identity with the new identities inherent in the new methods. From the most remote villages to the seats of government, Indians were more than discouraged from identifying with the conqueror, even when they wanted to and were willing to learn the necessary skills: we have seen in Gandhi's own case how desperately they could want to.

If Ahmedabad (as can now be more fully appreciated) had become one of the few strongholds of a post-feudal mercantile middle class in India which permitted the transition from native to industrial weaving and spinning with a minimum loss of identity, elsewhere the proletarization of artisans ruined both the life space and the identity of the cultivators. For jobless artisans became landless laborers in such masses that neither the land nor the economic system could support them. As Nehru, in prison, recalls:

. . . In 1834 the English Governor-General in India is said to have reported that "the misery hardly finds a parallel in the history of commerce. The bones of the cotton-weavers are bleaching the plains of India."[22]

For the cultivators' surplus over the barest home needs was to be exported, too, even though taxes were to be carried off no matter who starved or no matter how many of the infamous famines followed each other. This proletarization of the artisans and the cultivators was, as Nehru points out,

the foundation and the basis of the Indian problem of poverty. From this policy most of our ills have resulted. . . .

The little land each peasant household had was too small to support it decently. Poverty and semi-starvation always faced them at the best of times. And often enough the times were far from good. They were at the mercy of the seasons and the elements and the monsoons. And famines came and terrible diseases spread and carried off millions. They went to the *bania*—the village money-lender—and borrowed money, and their debts grew bigger and bigger and all hope and possibility of payment passed, and life became a burden too heavy to be borne. Such became the condition of the vast majority of the population of India under British rule in the nineteenth century.[23]

If Gandhi speaks of a four-fold ruin, however, he is diagnosing processes which aggravated each other; and in my references to the identity-eroding aspects of economic ruin, I have already indicated that psychologically, too, what was eroded here was the very essence of communal life. And that communal life, so incomprehensible and so unmanageable for those who wish to impose new patterns on it, did (and does today) still flourish; although, no doubt, narrow-mindedness, factionalism, and superstition had already then overtaken ancient customary patterns of commerce and government from the inside, making cultural and spiritual renewal long since mandatory. But whether or not the traditional life had the necessary resilience for further changes, the ancient system was all there was for new customs to build on, at whatever cost. Nehru describes Hindu Law:

Hindu law itself is largely custom, and customs change and grow. This elasticity of the Hindu law disappeared under the British and gave place to rigid legal codes drawn up after consultation with the most orthodox people. Thus the growth of Hindu society, slow as it was, was stopped. The Muslims resented the new conditions even more, and retired into their shells.[24]

Thus, as we would say in therapeutic parlance, whatever adaptive resilience there may have been now became defensive, and the defense often took the forms of either exaggerated compliance with or complete mistrust of those who, with superior force, introduced foreign ways into the ancient system. As Pyarelal describes it:

Before the British, land in India was not a commodity. It could not be mortgaged, distrained or auctioned for non-payment of dues or a debt incurred. A cultivator unable to meet his obligation might be imprisoned, tortured or otherwise oppressed by an arbitrary ruler, but he and his children could not be dispossessed of their source of living which land was to them. . . . Introduction of the English conception of landlordism by British Governors, who themselves largely came from the landlord class, coupled with the realisation of rent as a fixed amount in cash instead of a percentage of the produce, altered the whole picture. For the first time land became a commodity that could be mortgaged or distrained. The emergence of landlordism, to quote Jawaharlal Nehru . . . resulted in "the breakdown of the joint life and corporate character of the community, and the cooperative system of services and functions began to disappear gradually."[26]

We can now appreciate why Gandhi thought that the reintroduction of the spinning wheel in communities which had never made up for the loss of it, as either a tool or a symbol, might both answer a widespread economic need and serve as the symbol of a lost and regained identity. Later, when India was closer to political freedom and when Britain decided to support and invest in a new Indian industry, the wheel came instead to symbolize economic reaction. But when Gandhi first took over, the Indian masses had "sunk so low" (and here we come back to Nehru's letter to his daughter) that millions of parents day after day had to deny food to their hungry children and year after year in recurring famines had to let them die. Not infrequently they had to sell their children to pay off debts.[26] Where this happens, no basis of an identity is left to man or woman. And the famines, we learn, were not necessarily food famines, for even where the rains failed in some regions, a resilient system could have led to some redistribution, were it not for the fact that from many regions all "surplus" was carried off as per contract, even where neighboring millions starved to death. There seems to be little doubt that both the frequency of famines and the number of victims vastly increased rather than decreased under the foreign system of vast organizational powers.

But, of course, there were thousands of towns and many regions in India remote enough to have escaped the worst of the agricultural and manufacturing disaster—towns and regions, in fact, that could have lived on for a while under feudal systems (such as the seven hundred princedoms) propped up by the British in the middle of the historical decline of such feudal societies: in such small-town peace Gandhi did grow up. But as he would sense in his youth, propping up cannot keep alive an ancient identity which is losing its "natural" support in political and spiritual institutions. We must note, therefore, not only those glaring disasters and criminal deeds which comprise the all too visible colonial record nationalist historians dwell on, but also the quiet, almost benevolent methods of undermining the cultural and spiritual resilience of traditional institutions by legal and educational measures often administered, no doubt, by Englishmen who had both affection and some understanding for India.[27] Even Gandhi (like tens of thousands of equally serious and ambitious Indian youths) at first entertained the hope that the Empire would eventually grant, at least to an anglicized upper class, the right and the opportunity to become agents in administration, law, and education.

As for the concepts of law and legal truth—always key elements in any national identity and a necessary framework for individual identity—Sir William Sleeman, a Lucknow Resident, acknowledged the purely arbitrary relevance of British common law to village problems: "Our legal methods wrought more harm than all other evil agencies together."[28] And Sir Thomas Munro, Governor of Madras in the early nineteenth century, made one of those devastatingly honest confessions which makes one almost love the English for being able to do harm with *such* articulate and civilized self-criticism. "Our system," he wrote, "produces the litigation which we groundlessly impute to the character of the [Indian] people."[29] What he implies is that a system of justice imposed on a people brought up with entirely different concepts of reality and actuality makes liars out of the most scrupulous, especially if their language, in translation, seems to beg the very facts they try to render with accuracy. As Pyarelal puts it:

On all accounts, the *panchayat* justice was speedy, efficient and cheap. [It] fostered love of justice and fair play and encouraged the habit of truth-telling. The judicial machinery set up by the British in its place was inadequate, "obscure, complicated and pedantic." . . . Judges and magistrates were exclusively Europeans. They understood neither the language nor the customs and feelings of the people. The taking of oaths in the law courts was a thing which no respectable Indian could stomach, so much so that Frederick Shore, after long judicial experience, came to the conclusion that if any respectable Hindu gave evidence in a British court, it was "presumptive evidence against the respectability of his character."[30]

And we have more of the testimony of Sir William Sleeman, who declared in 1848 that there were no people from whom it was "more easy to get [truthful testimony] in their own village communities, where they state it before their relations, elders, and neighbours, whose esteem is necessary to happiness and can be obtained only by an adherence to the truth."[31] Yet he had to admit that the evidence of the same people in British Courts was "fantastically unreliable." But no Indian at that time was considered a reliable judge of the honesty of his own people, and the judges and magistrates in British India were all English.

Here arises the whole formidable question of the preservation or creation of a national identity among a people which is not  judged able to judge itself or to define the nature of fact or of truth in its native language. And as to the best educated and the most conscientious executors of any colonial power, in imposing their legal and linguistic logic on other peoples, do they wish to exclude those who strive to be like them or to offer them an avenue toward eventual inclusion? In no other respect in the Indian case did this question manifest its inherent ambiguity more flagrantly than in that of education. There were early suggestions that English schoolmasters be sent to India, although one all too farsighted governor general expressed the opinion that in case of full success in educating Indians, "we should not remain in this country for three months.' On the other hand, Mountstuart Elphinstone, early Governor of Bombay, wrote as early as 1824 it could be alleged with some justice that the government had

> . . . dried up the fountains of native talent, and that from the nature of our conquest, not only all encouragement to the advancement of knowledge is withdrawn, but even the actual learning of the nation is likely to be lost and the productions of former genius to be forgotten.[32]

The enormously influential Macaulay, however, in his "Minute on Indian Education" leaves little doubt about his fundamental views:

> . . . a single shelf of a good European library was worth the whole native literature of India and Arabia. . . . It is, I believe no exaggeration to say, that all the historical information which has been collected from all the books written in the sanskrit language is less valuable than what may be found in the most paltry abridgments used at preparatory schools in England. . . .
>
> . . . I think it clear that . . . neither as the languages of the law, nor as the languages of religion, have the Sanskrit and Arabic any peculiar claim to our engagement; that it is possible to make natives of this country thoroughly good English scholars, and that to this end our efforts ought to be directed. . . . We must at present do our best to form a class who may be interpreters between us and the millions whom we govern; a class of persons, Indian in blood and colour, but English in taste, in opinions, in morals, and in intellect.[33]

 But the absence or denigration of indigenous native schools is only one way in which the children of a colonized people or an exploited race are denied the right to assemble the elements of their historical identity into a world image of skills, facts, and ideas. Another is the pervasive perception, present in the smallest child and developed step for step throughout childhood and youth, of their parents' lack of faith in their future. Worse even, the more ambitious and gifted among the young (and the gifted and ambitious in each nation are the ones to bear the brunt of her identity crisis) can look forward to a future only by assuming a superimposed identity. As a historically minded Governor of Bengal put it:

By the middle of the nineteenth century a period of intellectual anarchy had set in, which swept the rising generation before it like a craft which has snapped its moorings. Westernism became the fashion of the day— and Westernism demanded of its votaries that they should cry down the civilization of their own country. The more ardent their admiration for everything Western, the more vehement became their denunciation of everything Eastern. The ancient learning was despised; ancient custom and tradition were thrust aside; ancient religion was decried as an outworn superstitition. The ancient foundations upon which the complete structure of Hindu society had been built up were undermined; and the new generation of iconoclasts found little enough with which to underpin the edifice which they were so recklessly depriving of its own foundations.[34]

The cultural assault was paralleled by the missionary offensive, which we need not describe here. Gandhi, it seems, attempted to absorb what Christ's teachings had to offer to the enlightened Hindu, while he defended himself and the youth of India against "Christianity without Christ."

The Indian Renaissance in Bengal and elsewhere permitted such families as the Tagores and the Nehrus to dream of an identity based on a recognition of Indian culture within an enlightened Empire. But the average Indian youth had no prospect of finding access to the governing circles in his own country. Until the second half of the nineteenth century, the Indian Civil Service was composed exclusively of Englishmen who intended only to return home when their service was up. Nehru describes these servants of the Empire:

They have been a curious set of persons. They were efficient in some ways. They organized the government, strengthened British rule, and incidentally, profited greatly by it themselves. All the departments of government which helped in consolidating British rule and in collecting taxes were efficiently organized. Other departments were neglected. Not being appointed by, or responsible to, the people, the I.C.S. paid little attention to these other departments which concerned the people most. . . . The British people filled all the high offices, but obviously they could not fill the smaller offices and the clerkships. Clerks were wanted, and it was to produce clerks that schools and colleges were first started by the British. Ever since then this has been the main purpose of education in India; and most of its products are only capable of being clerks.[35]

This is the closest the vast majority of young Indians had come to taking responsibility for themselves and for their country, when Gandhi set out to expose the four-fold ruin. And it should be clear by now why to Gandhi truth seemed essential to identity, and identity to self-government.

### 3. CONFRONTATION

GANDHI's every utterance in the years before his ascendance to leadership is characterized by its over-all relatedness to the apocalyptic combination of disasters—and by a direct, loving, and yet also shocking application of the themes just sketched to whatever audience was immediately in front of him. His wide-ranging addresses can well be compared to St. Paul's Epistles and to Luther's early pamphlets. St. Paul and Luther, of course, were greater writers and orators. St. Paul's message had to navigate from shore to shore and had to be sustained over the years by the promise of the next visit or the remembrance of the last one. Luther's pamphlets, in all their formidable formality, could count on the fast multiplication and distribution of printed matter—hot off the press. But Gandhi entrusted himself to the railroads, and while loudly complaining against the miserable conditions of third-class travel, he made the very most of joining the masses in motion, in stations, and especially in the compartments where they were thrown together most indiscriminately, often far away from home, and yet sure to return there or to arrive in new places with such news as spreads from rail centers to villages via oxcarts and camelback. And then Gandhi stopped and stayed and talked, a quiet, almost tender orator, but a man of the most intense and convincing presence, and a speaker who could make intimate contact with each particular audience. But one must hear samples of his talks, as  written down by him or reported on the spot, to appreciate how much his capacity to tease had matured into a relentless skill in challenging his audience in terms as fearless as they were often mildly humorous.

We have heard what he said on coming home to the old familiar places in western India. In April 1915, way across the

country, he addressed the Annual Dinner of the Madras Bar
Association—an exalted ceremony among the local members of
his old profession. To realize fully by what dramatic contrasts
he could impress his new style of leadership on a whole city, one
must visualize his arrival in Madras after three nights of travel.
Crowds of eager receptionists searched for him in the first- and
second-class compartments and were about to give up when
somebody discovered Gandhi and Kasturba in third class. A
loose shirt, soiled by four days of continuous travel, covered his
thin body, and a pair of trousers covered his legs. On seeing the
waiting crowd, Gandhi bowed. The Madrasi students who had
been waiting with a horse and carriage were persuaded by his
appearance to unyoke the horse and drag the carriage themselves.

The *Law Dinner* took place "in the open air under bright
moonlight on . . . extensive grounds." Gandhi was seated on
the left "of the Hon'ble the Advocate-General" and, lo and
behold, was asked to propose the toast to the British Empire.
Here is what he made his hearers swallow with their wine:

. . . I know that a passive resister has to make good his claim to passive
resistance, no matter under what circumstances he finds himself, and I
discovered that the British Empire had certain ideals with which I have
fallen in love, ("Hear, hear.") and one of those ideals is that every
subject of the British Empire has the freest scope possible for his energies
and efforts and whatever he thinks is due to his conscience. I think that
this is true of the British Empire as it is not true of any other Government that we see. . . . General Beyers, the trusted Commander of one of
the Forces of the British Empire, rose against that Empire in open
rebellion. It was only possible for him under that Empire and that
Empire alone not to have himself shot on sight. General Smuts wrote to
him in a memorable letter that he himself was at one time a rebel. He
wrote to General Beyers that it was only under the British Empire that it
was possible for him to save his life. Hence my loyalty to the British
Empire.[36]

The toast, so the papers reported, "was very enthusiastically
honoured."

In Calcutta, in turn, he spoke to a "stupendously large gathering" of the most militant Bengali *students* at the Students' Hall,

College Square. He spoke "On Anarchical Crimes." He saw no reason, he said, why students should not study *and* take part in politics. He told them that

he believed that that Government is the best that governs the least. But whatever his personal views were, he must say that misguided zeal that resorted to dacoities and assassinations could not be productive of any good. These dacoities and assassinations were absolutely a foreign growth in India. They . . . could not be a permanent institution here.[37]

And he concluded:

If they were prepared to die, [he] was prepared to die with them. He should be ready to accept their guidance. But if they wanted to terrorize the country, he should rise against them.

Back in Ahmedabad for a change, Gandhi was asked to speak at a small dinner honoring a friend who had been admitted to the Indian Civil Service, whose members were popularly referred to as *Civilians*. It may be questioned, he said,

whether, holding the views that I do, I should have come to a gathering such as this; it is still more open to question whether I should express them.

[The man you honour] has succeeded in gaining admission into the Indian Civil Service. . . . He deserves to be honoured for his hard work. . . . But I should not like other students to follow his example and enter the civil service. . . . [His] father spent Rs. 30,000 to make him a Civilian; I believe he could have put that money to better use instead. . . . Civilians have come to India in plenty, and many more will come; but it doesn't look as if they have been particularly useful to the country.[38]

To some *peasants*, in turn, gathered in a village square he had this to say:

When I started from Kathor in a small bullock-cart, I was in a hurry and as I wished, for the sake of my personal convenience, to reach here early, I did not mind when bullocks were struck with a goad. . . . I will have to answer for this in the court of the Almighty. When I come here again, it will make me happy to see that the sticks are no longer spiked. If I do not find that you have done so, I shall prefer going on foot rather than in the bullock-cart.[39]

A gathering of *economists* in Allahabad, in turn, found themselves lectured to ("perhaps you will treat my intrusion as a welcome diversion from the trodden path") on—Jesus:

"It is easier for a camel to go through the eye of a needle than for a rich man to enter into the kingdom of God!" Here you have an eternal rule of life stated in the noblest words the English language is capable of producing. But the disciples nodded unbelief as we do even to this day. . . . And Jesus said: "Verily I say unto you there is no man that has left house or brethren or sisters, or father or mother, or wife or children or lands for my sake and the Gospels, but he shall receive one hundred fold." . . . I hold that economic progress . . . is antagonistic to real progress. Hence the ancient ideal has been the limitation of activities promoting wealth. This does not put an end to all material ambition. We should still have, as we have always had, in our midst people who make the pursuit of wealth their aim in life. But we have always recognized that it is a fall from the ideal. It is a beautiful thing to know that the wealthiest among us have often felt that to have remained voluntarily poor would have been a higher state for them. . . . I have heard many of our countrymen say that we will gain American wealth but avoid its methods. I venture to suggest that such an attempt if it were made is foredoomed to failure. We cannot be "wise, temperate, and furious" in a moment.[40]

On another occasion Gandhi was scheduled to speak at the first political meeting ever held in Gujarat for petty *traders* and small *land holders*. The mighty "Lokamanya" Tilak was expected to preside but arrived late. Gandhi opened his speech ("Dear Brothers and Sisters") with the remark: "If one does not mind arriving late by three-quarters of an hour at a conference summoned for the purpose, one should not mind if swaraj too comes correspondingly late."[41] And he took the occasion of a Social Conference in a *low-caste community* to make his position on untouchability eminently clear, without speaking down to the Untouchables themselves:

. . . Where is the difference between us and this community? There is the same heart, the same nose, the same tongue, the same feeling—everything the same. . . . I do not know whether God was present at the political conference [where Untouchables were excluded], but I am sure he is here.[42]

But then, as was recorded by an operative of the Secret Police:

> A young *Dhed* then asked permission to speak. He came forward very
> nervously. He said that he was not an educated man. He was the son of a
> *Dhed.* . . . He gradually grew more confident and endeavoured to
> substantiate the claim of his community to be among the foremost ranks
> of the Rajput race.

> Mr. Gandhi rose at once to disillusion him of this, and advised him not
> to believe in such cock-and-bull stories regarding his ancestry. He ad-
> monished the *Dheds* to be content with their parentage and to rise by
> their own efforts, now that the higher classes had lent them a kindly
> hand.

But his most famous affront which, for once, ended in a
public scandal was reserved for the opening on February 6,
1916, of Benares Hindu University. Faced with a resplendent
audience which, besides members of the academic world, included aristocrats and dignitaries of both nations (including
Mrs. Besant), Gandhi addressed himself primarily to the students.[48] Formidably formal as the meeting had been up to then,
Gandhi relaxed:

> . . . I want to think audibly this evening. I do not want to make a speech
> and if you find me this evening speaking without reserve, pray, consider
> that you are only sharing the thoughts of a man who allows himself to
> think audibly, and if you think that I seem to transgress the limits that
> courtesy imposes upon me, pardon me for the liberty I may be taking.

So that his thought would be comprehensible as well as audible,
however, Gandhi had to think aloud in English! This was, he
said, a matter of deep humiliation and shame for him:

> Our language is the reflection of ourselves, and if you tell me that our
> languages are too poor to express the best thought, then I say that the
> sooner we are wiped out of existence, the better for us. . . . The charge
> against us is, that we have no initiative. How can we have any if we are
> to devote the precious years of our life to the mastery of a foreign
> tongue? We fail in this attempt also. Was it possible for any speaker
> yesterday and today to impress his audience as was possible for Mr.
> Higginbotham?

His ruminations turn to the holy city he has just traversed, and
his language gradually becomes militant:

. . . In every city there are two divisions, the cantonment and the city proper. The city mostly is a stinking den. But we cannot reproduce the easy-going hamlet life. . . . If even our temples are not models of roominess and cleanliness, what can our self-government be? Shall our temples be abodes of holiness, cleanliness and peace as soon as the English have retired from India, either of their own pleasure or by our compulsion, bag and baggage?

As if this were not militant enough, he now points to those present:

. . . I now introduce you to another scene. His Highness the Maharajah, who presided yesterday over our deliberations, spoke about the poverty of India. Other speakers laid great stress upon it. . . . I compare with the richly bedecked noblemen [on the platform behind him] the millions of the poor. And I feel like saying to these noblemen: "There is no salvation for India unless you strip yourselves of this jewelry and hold it in trust for your countrymen in India." . . . Our salvation can only come through the farmer. Neither the lawyers, nor the doctors, nor the rich landlords are going to secure it.

It is quite possible, even probable, that Gandhi when he made these and similar remarks was not fully aware of what Mrs. Besant later called the "gun-powder" mood of his young audience, "seething with anger" over the internment for the day of some fellow students. But it is equally possible, and in fact probable, that he found himself thinking aloud in response to the very mood of his audience. Eager to capture and reform nationalist youth, he probably could also count on some hidden violence in himself. To make this plausible, we shall have to see this remarkable scene unfold in slower motion.

He began to enlarge on the subject of violent revolutionary acts, no doubt with the intention of disengaging himself from all violence, after he had expressed his own revolutionary spirit. "I myself am an anarchist, but of another type" was his intended trump line, but both the student audience and the leaders present by then were so tense and noisy that he was misunderstood at the decisive moment. He had just referred to the superabundance of detectives stationed in the streets of Benares to protect the Viceroy's life against bomb-throwing anarchists. Nobody would claim that his choice of words was fortunate when he added:

. . . We asked ourselves: "Why this distrust? Is it not better that even Lord Hardinge should die than live a living death?" But a representative of a mighty Sovereign may not. He might find it necessary even to live a living death.[44]

Gandhi later explained that only his sympathy for "one of the noblest of Viceroys, an honoured guest in this sacred city" had made him utter these words; they did, nonetheless, gratuitously counterpoint a "living death" with death by assassination. One can well imagine that a large and tense audience missed the finer points in such a performance, and heard what it wanted to hear or feared to hear when Gandhi said:

If we trust and fear God, we shall have to fear no one, no Maharajahs, not Viceroys, not the detectives, not even King George. I honour the anarchist for his love of the country. I honour him for his bravery in being willing to die for his country; but I ask him: Is killing honourable? . . . I have been told: "Had we not done this, had some people not thrown bombs, we should never have gained what we have got."[45]

It was then that Mrs. Besant exclaimed, "Please stop it." As she explained later, this was an appeal to the chairman to stop Gandhi, but Gandhi thought she meant to shut him up. He interrupted his speech, turned to the chairman, the Maharajah of Darbhanga, and announced that he awaited *his* orders. Many in the audience cried, "Go on," and the chairman, sensing that Gandhi had been misunderstood, asked him "to explain his object." Gandhi did so by expressing the stereotyped hope for an empire "based upon mutual love and mutual trust" but added:

. . . Is it not better that we talk under the shadow of this college than that we should be talking irresponsibly in our homes? . . . I know that there is nothing that the students are not discussing. There is nothing that the students do not know. I am therefore turning the searchlight towards ourselves.

Having regained the right to speak, he also resumed his former tone and turned on yet another group, namely, the "Civilians" present.

. . . Yes, many members of the Indian Civil Service are most decidedly overbearing, they are tyrannical, at times thoughtless. Many other adjectives may be used. . . . But what does that signify? They were gentlemen before they came here, and if they have lost some of their moral fibre, it is a reflection upon ourselves. [Cries of "No."] Just think out for yourselves, if a man who was good yesterday has become bad after having come in contact with me, is he responsible that he has deteriorated or am I?[46]

And then, vastly overestimating the capacity for historical discrimination in his overwrought audience, he began to speak, of all things, of the Boers' rebellion!

At this point a number of princes rose, the chairman left his dais, and the meeting broke up. Gandhi later blamed Mrs. Besant's behavior for the whole denouement, although she attempted to explain that she knew every word would be taken down by a secret service operative and that she had therefore feared for Gandhi's personal safety. She had not misunderstood him, knowing well that "Mr. Gandhi would rather be killed than kill."

It is, of course, remarkable that the founder of Satyagraha should be misunderstood publicly as an anarchist and an advocate of violence. But I believe that those present understood something in this tone and in his choice of words only too well. He was sensitively aware of the fact that his speech followed that of "Mother Besant," the advocate of a strictly constitutional change of India's position within the Empire, and that she was sitting among the resplendent Maharajahs. Maybe, just for once, Gandhi's heart was on the side of the potential young revolutionaries before him, wishing, as he did, to attract their "seething" allegiance (and to attract it away, no doubt, from Tilak) so as to use it for his own ends, namely, the establishment of a new, a nonviolent style of indigenous leadership. But he may have overidentified with them, and some impatience with parental authority may have broken through. At any rate, he dragged every available father-figure into the debate, from "cops" to native princes to King George himself. And indeed, if he was the only one who could do the job which an older generation of leaders had failed to do (as he had clearly implied in *Hind*

*Swaraj*), now was the time to "declare himself": for Gokhale was no more, the "probation" was over.

In his Autobiography Gandhi does not mention Benares—surely his Wittenberg church door. Up to this moment, he had obeyed Gokhale's advice, although the Moniya and the propagandist in him had not failed to tell audience after audience that he was "on probation" by dint of a pledge to Gokhale—not unlike the way in which young Gandhi in England had confided to friends and strangers alike that he was under a vow to his mother. As to Gokhale as a father-figure, we have already noted clear signs of Gandhibhai's ambivalence toward him in South Africa. And, indeed, the theme of sickness as a result of self-neglect continues to the end. In his Autobiography the Mahatma recounts his last meeting with Gokhale and describes how the then very sick old man, who had forced himself to attend a reception in Gandhi's honor, suddenly had one of his by then common fainting spells and was carried away. The Mahatma concludes: "But the fainting fit was to be no common event in my life,"[47] and one should probably italicize the word *my*. Did Gokhale's fainting spells reawake Mohandas's complex feelings toward his sick father whose stature he was to surpass and whose weaknesses and self-indulgences he was so determined to avoid?

Gandhi had heard of Gokhale's death when he was in Shantiniketan, Rabindranath Tagore's sanctuary. Here, too, Gandhi was reverent and yet intent on teaching even the renowned poet a lesson in his own school community. He spoke of Shantiniketan as a shrine of "simplicity, art, and love," but he lost no time in converting it into a "busy hive." He organized the boys into batches to cut vegetables, to clean grain, and to do the sanitary cleaning of the kitchen and its surroundings—all of which the majestic "gurudev" himself let pass in patience (and pass it did, after Gandhi's departure).

Under the immediate impact of the news of Gokhale's death, Gandhi had said to C. F. Andrews in one of his overobedient moods: "I do not suppose there will be any occasion for Satyagraha for five years or so." Later in his Autobiography the

Mahatma cannot report the shock of hearing the news of Go-khale's death without recounting again that even benevolent father Gokhale "used to laugh at some of my ideas . . . and say: 'After you have stayed a year in India, your views will correct themselves.' "[48]

Benares followed Gokhale's death by exactly one year, and it seemed time to pull out all the stops. So if the injunction of his paternal friend had made Gandhi's activist nature fret, we can well imagine how Mother Besant's "Stop it," perceived as it was as a direct command from an older woman, could only aggravate the memory of prolonged frustration. This I see as the emotional background of the fact that Gandhi at Benares did continue to speak ambiguously and was generally understood as supporting anarchist and militant youth. Afterwards his and Annie Besant's mutual recriminations came ludicrously close to resembling a family quarrel, and at least one intelligence agent (the kind of man whom Mrs. Besant meant to protect Gandhi from) reported to Delhi that Mrs. Besant was apparently becoming jealous of the little man in the loincloth. At any rate, if in Benares Gandhi lost his light touch and let loose some of the more sadistic ingredients which turn teasing into taunting, the students were right "with it."

So much about the way Gandhi confronted his friends and adversaries with the calamities which to him added up to the four-fold ruin. We must now include reference to certain issues which Gandhi attempted to explain to all India in a usually less dramatic fashion and often, no doubt, in a kind of mixture of lecture and sermon. Take, for example, the issue of *language*. At the opening of a Jain Students' Library in Surat, he said:

. . . students who deliver speeches in English do not see whether or not the audience can follow what they say. Nor do they consider whether those who understand English will feel interested or bored by their broken, incorrect English. . . . They ought to consider whether the new era will draw closer or recede farther by their prating in a language which their parents do not know, which their brothers and sisters do not know, and their servants, wives, children and kinsfolk cannot follow.[49]

And on another occasion (an all-India Common Script and Common Language Conference in Lucknow) he could call on an all too well-known model:

. . . Gentlemen, you see that the Christian Literature Depot and Bible Society is going all round the world. It scatters its books everywhere. It has them translated into all the languages and then distributes them at the right places. Even to the aborigines and working people in Africa it provides the Bible in their own languages. It spends crores of rupees on this job. They do not simply hold conferences like we do.[50]

But one more quotation will make it quite obvious that it would take at least a whole monograph to settle even the one question of language, or rather to show why it is still not settled today. What counts here is solely the spirit in which Gandhi called on his people to recognize the most vital and potentially most fatal of their problems:

. . . The number of those speaking Hindi is almost 65 million. If we include languages (which) are sisters of Hindi . . . the number is almost 220 million. How then can English which even a hundred thousand Indians cannot speak correctly compete successfully with a language which is so widely used? That to this day we have not even begun conducting our national business in Hindi is because of our cowardice, lack of faith and ignorance of the greatness of the Hindi language . . . The beginning should be made in the Provinces. If there is some difficulty in this, it is for people speaking the Dravidian languages like Tamil . . . Hindi-knowing men who are zealous, brave, full of self-respect and energetic should be sent to Madras and other provinces to teach Hindi without receiving payment.[51]

Another complex issue, that of *caste*, was taken up by Gandhi with utmost honesty and vigor. But a few excerpts will show the complexity of his position, which was at the same time forthright in fighting against prejudice and yet cautious in leaving intact ancient fundaments for which he had no immediate revolutionary alternatives—prejudiced as he was in his moralism and in his fear of the hedonism that might accompany a loosening of traditional strictures. Thus he would defend the traditional prohibition against the consumption of food in intercaste company by claiming that there is, anyway, a tendency to exaggerate the importance of eating.

. . . The process of eating is as unclean as evacuation, the only difference being that, while evacuation ends in a sense of relief, eating, if one's tongue is not held in control, brings discomfort. Just as we attend to evacuation, etc., in private, we should likewise eat and perform other actions common to all animals always in private. . . .[52]

He was, then, not for equality in principle, if this amounted to what he would consider libertinism; he was for self-control. In the case of eating in the

. . . company of a *Bhangi*, there being, from my point of view, greater self-control in doing so, the community should have nothing to do in the matter. Or, if I fail to get a suitable bride from my own community and I am likely, if I remain unmarried, to contract vicious habits, it will, in these circumstances, be an act of self-control on my part to marry a girl of my choice from any community and hence my action will not be a violation of the fundamental principle of the caste system. It would be for me to demonstrate that my purpose in taking such a step in disregard of the general rule was discipline of the flesh, and this would appear from my subsequent conduct. Meanwhile, however, I should not resent being denied the usual privileges that go with membership of a community but ought to continue doing my duty by it.[53]

These are not matters to be judged lightly with sentiments or opinions, least of all those of another time and place. For, when it came right down to it, in spite of all the complexity of his point of view, he would not hesitate, on settling down by the Sabarmati, to commit the totally revolutionary act of admitting an Untouchable family to his ashram. In all issues, then, he took only such exemplary actions as he could initiate with a sure sense that he could and would take care of the consequences. This position is especially clearly expressed in a letter to Esther Faering, dated August 3, 1917, on the readiness of India to turn to Satyagraha:

The pertinent question for you and me is what is our duty as individuals. I have come to this workable decision by myself, "I will not kill anyone for any cause whatsoever, but be killed by him if resistance of his will renders my being killed necessary." I would give similar advice to everybody. But where I know that there is want of will altogether, I

would advise him to exert his will and fight. There is no love where there
is no will. In India there is not only no love but hatred due to emasculation. There is the strongest desire to fight and kill side by side with utter
helplessness. This desire must be satisfied by restoring the capacity for
fighting. Then comes the choice.

Yes, the very act of forgiving and loving shows superiority in the doer.
But that way of putting the proposition begs the question, who can love?
A mouse as mouse cannot love a cat. A mouse cannot be commonly said
to refrain from hurting a cat. You do not love him whom you fear.
Immediately you cease to fear, you are ready for your choice—to strike
or to refrain. To refrain is proof of awakening of the soul in man; to
strike is proof of body-force. The ability to strike must be present
when the power of the soul is demonstrated. This does not mean that we
must be bodily superior to the adversary.[54]

Many of his opinions at the time were necessarily more compelling in their spirit of diagnostic courage than in their prescrip-
tion or prognosis. But Gandhi knew that as a nation's reformer
he had to engage in experiments which involved him and the
nation in action on an ever-larger scale. As he staked out the area
for such action, the center remained in the daily life of the
ashram, while the periphery was to be tested in the systematic
study of such acute grievances as would permit him to involve
well circumscribed segments of India's vast population—one at a
time—in discrete Satyagraha campaigns for limited but representative goals.

#### 4. BREAKTHROUGH

THE NAME that Gandhi gave to his ashram in Ahmedabad appointed it the headquarters of any future campaign:

. . . I wanted to acquaint India with the method I had tried in South
Africa, and I desired to test in India the extent to which its application
might be possible. So my companions and I selected the name "Satyagraha Ashram," as conveying both our goal and our method of service.[55]

It took him, not surprisingly, much less than "five years or so"
to find a fitting scene for his first attempt at a Satyagraha
campaign in India: Bihar and its indigo-growing peasants in the
Himalayan foothills. The place chosen could not be much further away from Ahmedabad and still be in India, for it is close to

the border of Nepal, just south of Mount Everest. Straying equally far (that is, about 800 miles) due north from Ahmedabad, one would be in Kashmir, beyond Shrinagar; or in the south, somewhere near Madras. Thus Ahmedabad was an almost geometrically ideal point of origin and return for a charismatic traveler. If such geographic strategy seems foreign in a man who claimed to be guided solely by his inner voice, one need only remember that later, when the Mahatma would, in a sense, have conquered the whole country, he would select as a site for his "house" a poor town in a poor district in the very center of India, almost equidistant from Delhi and Calcutta, from Kathiawar and from Madras. Then the leaders of the country, in order to see him, would have to converge on the heart of India. But now he had to reach the borders of the country—and of the independence movement: for, as yet

. . . no one knew me in Champaran. The peasants were all ignorant. Champaran, being far up north of the Ganges, and right at the foot of the Himalayas . . . was cut off from the rest of India. The Congress was practically unknown in those parts. Even those who had heard the name of the Congress shrank from joining it or even mentioning it.[56]

His biographers, and even the editor of the *Collected Works*, claim that Gandhi was drawn to the scene of his first skirmish "more or less accidentally." He himself creates a modern parable by claiming a peasant, "ubiquitous Rajkumar," to have been responsible for the whole thing. Rajkumar was simply one of the many small farmers who had suffered under the "tinkathia" system in Bihar, by which the farmers were bound by law to plant "three of every twenty parts" of their best land with indigo, to be delivered at fixed prices to their landlords. This, of course, was only the core of a whole system of grievances; and Rajkumar Shukla, not satisfied with what the remote Congress could do for men like him, pursued Gandhi from Lucknow to Ahmedabad and back to Calcutta before Gandhi agreed to follow him. "One day will be enough," Rajkumar said, and he was right, for Gandhi immediately became fascinated with the problem, and the very hindrances which beset his first attempt to orient himself must have aroused his stubbornness. In the lodging where Shukla took him (the presumptive host was out of town), the servants took Gandhi for a kind of beggar, forbade him to draw water at the well or to use the indoor latrine because his general appearance in no way revealed his caste. Gandhi soon sat down with some of the farmers to ascertain the facts and then turned to the professors and lawyers of the region who, of course, did know of him.

"I shall have little use for your legal knowledge," I said to them. "I want clerical assistance and help in interpretation. It may be necessary to face imprisonment, but, much as I would love you to run that risk, you would go only so far as you feel yourselves capable of going. Even turning yourselves into clerks and giving up your profession for an indefinite period is no small thing. . . . We cannot afford to pay for this work. It should all be done for love and out of a spirit of service."[57]

Thus, in a minor cause on the outskirts of an empire, a number of future national workers were recruited; and one of the local lawyers, who became a "clerk and translator," would thirty years later become India's first President: Rajendra Prasad.

The local government and the planters, not knowing yet whom (and what) they were up against, immediately tried to use local ordinances to make him leave on threat of arrest and imprisonment. In doing so, they set the ideal scene for Gandhi, and he could move into his accustomed role of pleading guilty. Insisting that in his "humble opinion" there was a "difference of opinion" between the local administration and himself, he stated before the court:

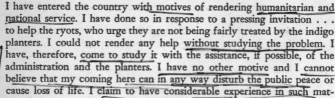

I have entered the country with motives of rendering humanitarian and national service. I have done so in response to a pressing invitation . . . to help the ryots, who urge they are not being fairly treated by the indigo planters. I could not render any help without studying the problem. I have, therefore, come to study it with the assistance, if possible, of the administration and the planters. I have no other motive and I cannot believe that my coming here can in any way disturb the public peace or cause loss of life. I claim to have considerable experience in such matters.[58]

In other words, the invading Satyagrahi puts himself on equal footing with the lawful government and then asks their assistance in getting the facts necessary to proceed against them. And as for their power to detain or expel him:

> It is my firm belief that in the complex constitution under which we are living, the only safe and honourable course for a self-respecting man is, in the circumstances such as face me, to do what I have decided to do, that is, to submit without protest to the penalty of disobedience. I have ventured to make this statement not in any way of extenuation of the penalty to be awarded against me, but to show that I have disregarded the order served upon me, not for want of respect for lawful authority, but in obedience of the higher law of our being—the voice of conscience.[59]

This, the Mahatma later claimed, was his country's first direct object lesson in Civil Disobedience. And the lesson worked:

> A sort of friendliness sprang up between the officials—Collector, Magistrate, Police Superintendent—and myself. I might have legally resisted the notices served on me. Instead I accepted them all, and my conduct towards the officials was correct. They thus saw that I did not want to offend them personally, but that I wanted to offer civil resistance to their orders. In this way they were put at ease, and instead of harassing me they gladly availed themselves of my and my co-workers' co-operation in regulating the crowds. But it was an ocular demonstration to them of the fact that their authority was shaken. The people had for the moment lost all fear of punishment and yielded obedience to the power of love which their new friend exercised.[60]

But, in a way, things came too easily in that not only was the case withdrawn, but full governmental support was promised for the inquiry. In the meantime, Gandhi was ". . . enjoying a kind of solitude. The house is not so bad. There is facility for bathing and so the body is served well enough. As for the self, this helps it grow."[61] And he prepared himself "joyfully" for his arrest, writing to Maganlal:

> Please send my gold medal by registered parcel to the Private Secretary to H. E. the Viceroy, Simla. An order to leave the District has been served upon me and I have refused to obey. It is likely that a warrant of arrest or something like it will be served upon me any moment. . . .

None of us could have imagined that I should be sent to jail in Bihar, a province hallowed by the footsteps of Ramachandra, Bharata, Janaka and Sitaji [all characters in the Ramayana].[62]

To South Africa he reported promptly, if prematurely:

. . . I am recalling the best days of South Africa. And to have them in a place where Rama and Janaka lived! The people are rendering all assistance. We shall soon find our Naidoos and Sorabjis and Imams. I don't know that we shall stumble upon a Cachalia.[63]

Thus does a man forever try to repeat the first fight in which he felt at home! This time, however, no heroes comparable to the already mythological South African Satyagrahis were needed, because the Viceroy intervened; to him, the visitor out in Bihar was by no means an unknown quantity. Thus Champaran became an object lesson in the way in which a local civil disobedience campaign might serve as an opening wedge into *national* issues. "For me now Champaran is my domicile," Gandhi wrote home, and for the next six months he would refer even to his trips back to the home country as traveling "out of Champaran." To this extent any place became his home, where he determined to dig in as a Satyagrahi; and that meant to make a painstakingly detailed and fair study of the facts, to present them in an open and generous way in public meetings, to formulate minimum demands backed up by the threat to take recourse in Satyagraha. This threat, in turn, was always based on the expectation of the support of the poorest among the local population *and* on that of wide publicity throughout India. Thus Gandhi, right at the start, won his most important point, namely, that a man who takes it upon himself to redress a local injustice even in a place remote from his own "home," if he could only prove welcome as a helper to the victims of that injustice, may consider himself a native there, provided only he is willing to accept the suffering thus invited and to play the game with the fairness dictated by a more inclusive identity. The point was sealed when Gandhi was made a full member of an official Inquiry Committee which in October of 1917 issued a unanimous report abolishing the "tinkathia" system. Even if this was something of an empty victory in view of the declining value of indigo on the world market, Gandhi had succeeded in demonstrating, in an area and in an issue of his choosing, the applicability to any part of India of the instrument which he had created in South Africa.

Gandhi immediately proceeded to the further and final phase of any of his campaigns: re-education. He set up a small network of schools for the Bihari peasants' children staffed by volunteers (among them Kasturba) who were imported from many different regions and vocations. This enterprise, too, was of short duration; but the principle remained powerful, beyond Gandhi's own campaigns.

To the local planters, of course, the whole event was and remained something of a ludicrous nightmare, and they used all possible means to slander the Gandhis. And since (being visually inclined) we have in our various chapters paid close attention to the changing styles of clothing characteristic of Gandhi's changes of identity and of occupation, we conclude this chapter with a letter Gandhi wrote to the press in reply to remarks on his appearance made by a Mr. Irwin (whom Gandhi, incidentally, had caught whipping one of his peasants). Gandhi himself justifies our interest in the matter by urging his friends to save any clippings of this letter because it "proved more effective than any number of speeches could have been":

. . . Mr. Irwin's letter suggests that I appear before the ryots in a dress I have temporarily and specially adopted in Champaran to produce an effect. . . . [Actually] my familiarity with the minor amenities of western civilization has taught me to respect my national costume, and it may interest Mr. Irwin to know that the dress I wear in Champaran is the dress I have always worn in India except that for a very short period in India I fell an easy prey in common with the rest of my countrymen to the wearing of semi-European dress in the courts and elsewhere outside Kathiawar. . . . We are committing a national sin in discarding a dress which is best suited to the Indian climate and which, for its simplicity, art and cheapness, is not to be beaten on the face of the earth and which answers hygienic requirements. Had it not been for a false pride and equally false notions of prestige, Englishmen here would long ago have adopted the Indian costume.[64]

CHAPTER
# III

# Companions and Counterplayers

---

## 1. THE SARABHAIS

WHILE Gandhi was still deeply involved in Champaran, he received disquieting news of labor conditions in Ahmedabad. Also, Anasuya Sarabhai had written Gandhi of her increased involvement in textile labor problems and had, apparently, asked him for advice and sanction. On December 21, 1917, Gandhi wrote to Ambalal as follows:

Dear Bhai Ambalalji,

I do not wish to interfere with your business affairs at all. However, I have . . . no option but to write. I think you should satisfy the weavers for the sake of Shrimati Anasuyaben at any rate. There is no reason to believe that, if you satisfy these, you will have others clamouring. Even if that should happen, you can do what you think fit then. Why should not the mill-owners feel happy paying a little more to the workers? How could a brother be the cause of suffering to a sister?—and that, too, a sister like Anasuyaben? I have found that she has a soul which is absolutely pure. It would be nothing strange if you took her word to be law. You are, thus, under a double obligation: to please the workers and earn a sister's blessing. My presumption, too, is doubly serious; in a single letter I have meddled in your business and your family affairs. Do forgive me.
Vandemataram from
Mohandas Gandhi[65]

This letter is only one example of Gandhi's charming and intuitive way of meddling—while denying the wish to meddle—

in the affairs of his friends in general and in their familial relations in particular. Therefore, before attending to those developments which soon would bring Gandhi back to Ahmedabad, this
time to be fatefully caught up in its affairs, I shall enlarge on the
patterns of his friendships with his principal counterplayer and
his main companions in the Event. This must be of special
interest to us today, for these men and women, when they met
Gandhi, were in their twenties and were emerging from a
generation of young Indians who certainly could be called
alienated and, as Indians, were often torn between religious
withdrawal and activist participation. Beyond the immediate
issues, then, we must try to comprehend the particular appeal by
which a man at the beginning of his national career attracts,
selects, and trains his retinue of co-workers—and, indeed, how
he cultivates those whom he recognizes as promising opponents.

We have already heard how Ambalal had entered Gandhi's
life shyly but decisively as the "anonymous gentleman" who
drove up to the ashram gate with a packet of money just when
Gandhi was so short of means that he thought of abandoning the
whole enterprise and moving into the Untouchables' quarters.
Gandhi reports that he had met this man only once before,
which was, as far as I can make out, at a get-together arranged to
discuss the founding of the ashram and held at Ambalal's house
—as were, no doubt, many other meetings of a philanthropic
nature. Ambalal, then in his twenties, had already manifested his
courage in breaking through the prejudices of his time and his
community in a number of ways; and this courage, as hindsight
now verifies, made him a "natural" for his role as one of Gandhi's truest friends in general and one of his most determined
adversaries in the Event. Ambalal had, in fact, founded his own
house and family on a principle of freedom of choice which was
to make significant men and women of his children. Just how
unusual his marriage to Saraladevi in 1913 was can be appreciated only by one who knows the rigidity and occasional cruelty
of Hindu (and Jain) marriage arrangements. For one thing, his
and Saraladevi's families were not of the same caste. But even
more outrageous was the way in which the young man let his

personal preference rather than parental will decide the choice
of his bride. There are several versions of this story; however,
the essence (which I cannot present as anything but a local
myth) seems to be that his family and that of Saraladevi had
arranged long before that he should marry her older sister, who
was reputedly "fairer." But on visiting his future in-laws' home,
Ambalal noticed the younger sister, shy and dark Saraladevi, and
was immediately fascinated by her. Always ready to act upon
strong and "right" feelings, he asked his future father-in-law (a
judge) to allow him to take this sister out for a ride in his carriage, and asked her then and there whether she would consider
marrying him. They went back to the house promised to one
another and the terms were settled. Eventually, driving from
their intercaste wedding to their new home, the couple were
forced to take a secret route in order not to be stoned by the
populace—the first but not the last instance when Ambalal's
independence of action endangered their security. Ambalal continued to consider his wife a complete social equal and—this he
reported with some pride—insisted on taking her along to
parties long before general custom made this acceptable. And he
permitted their children, as soon as they could do so with
pleasure and profit, to participate fully in the family's social life.
As I indicated earlier, his house was always open to traveling
men of politics or of the mind; thus his children became accustomed early to listen to and speak with such regular guests
as Motilal Nehru or Tagore, the Polaks, C. F. Andrews—and
eventually Gandhiji.

On the other hand, the walls around his house were also symbolic of the solicitude he confined to the inside and the exclusiveness he maintained on the outside, protecting both his private
life and his philanthropic decisions. It is, then, an extraordinary
young man who in his late twenties became part of the Event—a
man whom I would consider, all in all, a Renaissance man Indian-
style. For no matter what enemies he may have made and what
his conflicts and contradictions may have added up to, the heart
of his orientation has been a voluntaristic and individualistic
interpretation of *dharma* notwithstanding all priestly predestina-

tion, social convention—and psychological interpretation. But each appropriated freedom is accompanied by its own fateful anxiety; and later, the loss of his oldest son in the flower of his youth seems to have caused in this man a deepening of his concerns.

But what would bring such a man to Gandhi and Gandhi to him? To put it briefly, I think that originally Ambalal offered Gandhi money out of a sense of comradeship with a *manly voluntarist* of a high order and a *maternally concerned* man of universal dimensions. When I asked Ambalal, he suggested that the basis of his and Gandhi's friendship was first of all a common passion for abolishing caste and other inequalities within Indian society, and a joint interest in ending British domination. And then there was the fact that Ambalal's wife shared Gandhi's interests to the point of being fascinated with ashram life—as Ambalal was decidedly not. There is a story that in the early days of primitive ashram life Saraladevi sat next to Gandhi on the ground during a prayer meeting. "You will make your beautiful sari dirty," he said to her smilingly; and she is said to have worn khadi ever since—as have the mill owner's sister and oldest daughter, although none of them ever lived in the ashram.

Gandhi was fond of teasing Ambalal about how much "better a human being" his wife was than he, and Ambalal chuckled about it fondly. This, too, is typical: some men whose friendship with Gandhi survived his initial attempts (and failures) to influence their home lives and private styles remember his humorously vindictive remarks as if by those words they had been knighted; and one has a feeling that Gandhi abidingly respected these men for their capacity to remain counterplayers rather than becoming followers. There was, then, a sense of equality between the two men, notwithstanding the fact that one was to become a mahatma. And, indeed, Gandhi would always pierce with humor any attempt to treat him as a human being of a special kind. "If I would admit that I am a Mahatma, a Great Soul," he would say, "I would also admit that others are small souls. But *small soul* is a self-contradiction!"

I will have more to say later about a common maternal

"complex" in most of the men close to Gandhi. As an *industrialist*, Ambalal's relationship to Gandhi was always most cordial and frank, "man to man," and yet of determined stubbornness when their economic roles conflicted. In advocating a national boycott of English textiles, Gandhi, of course, eventually became an ally of Indian industrialists—until he insisted on their making corresponding sacrifices by keeping the price of Indian goods down once the populace spurned British imports. Ambalal, then, must be considered a counterplayer in whose presence Gandhi might become maternally admonishing or paternally sharp, but who would never sacrifice the pleasure of a man-to-man relationship. Such counterplayers were usually men who might be called—up to a point—political or philosophical Gandhians, but who would never become professional Gandhiites in the sense that they would join Gandhi's daily way of life.

Anasuya's life has been a virginally maternal life, par excellence. Now called the Mother of the Labor Union, she remembers her own mother as very beautiful and very worshipful in her prayers to a mother-goddess. Her mother was only twenty-seven years old when she died, leaving seven-year old Ambalal in the care of ten-year-old Anasuya. Anasuya was already engaged to be married, and when the time of marriage arrived, that is, when she reached puberty, their uncle-guardian refused to renege on the solemn arrangement made by her parents. So she was married to the boy of their choice who was one year older—married with the same mixture of lavish festivity and lonely dread which we described in Gandhi's wedding.

Anasuya, a very intelligent girl, had to leave school because her husband was failing in his studies and no Hindu wife could overtake her husband scholastically. So she sat in a corner listening in on Ambalal's home-tutoring, for she refused for a long time to join her husband in his house (we have seen that Kasturba, too, spent much time in her parents' home). But this could not protect her forever, while a divorce, it was said, would have disgraced the family and the caste. Finally, she told her husband that he was free to do with his life as he wanted, but she would abjure married life forever. When her husband became abusive in the then quite sanctioned manner, Ambalal went to fetch her—again, a most unusual act of social courage. She took care of his household until his marriage and then went to England to study medicine. However, the sight of a calf's head hanging in a butcher shop convinced her that a bloody profession was not for her. (Gandhi, too, we may remember, gave up the idea of becoming a physician because of the bloody aspects of medicine.) Anasuya then transferred her therapeutic ambitions, and her wish to give personal and tangible service, to the study of social work. The ascendance of women in social work was at that time associated with the feminist movement guided most militantly by the suffragettes and most intelligently by the Fabians. If one should be inclined to see in Anasuya a certain shying away from bodily processes (then not uncommon in upper class girls the world over) one would also have to note that she resolutely overcame her reticence when facing filthy quarters, dirty children, uncared-for patients, and all manner of depraved individuals.

On her return to India, she embarked on a course which slowly but surely led to a position antagonistic to that of her brother—who had protected her against her husband and now, even where she meddled in the labor problems of his own industry, was again willing to protect her, in spite of his own right as the head of the family to dictate her life.

Having suffered under the injustice of an unwanted marriage at such an early age, Anasuya decided to work for women's rights, and particularly for those of women laborers whose lot was even worse than that of the men. They earned less and worked harder than the men, for they had to rise at about four o'clock in order to feed their families and tend to their households before going to work, and then they were obliged to cook the evening meal on their return home from work. And there were no buses in those days! Anasuya, as early as March 1914, started a school for workers' children. Two sessions (from 8 to 10 A.M., and from 2 to 6 P.M.) served the children too young to work, and evening classes were organized for those children who themselves worked in the factories. Night classes were also held for adult laborers. Such schooling naturally included instruction in cleanliness and hygiene and supplied direct medical help where needed. The totally unhygienic and immoral conditions of employment, even after the passage by the Delhi government of a universal Factory Act, were blatantly obvious. According to "enlightened" labor laws, no child was to work in a factory before the age of nine, and children between the ages of nine and twelve only half a day, but (quite aside from the inhumanity implicitly sanctioned by such "protective" laws) Anasuya found that many worked in the mills under alternate names during different shifts. The adults (that is, all workers above the age of twelve) at that time worked a "humane" maximum of 12 hours a day, and some warpers were working 36 hours at a stretch with only a few short breaks. Anasuya recalled that their eyes were always bloodshot and that they felt miserable and sick. For a woman of Anasuyaben's character and training, it was impossible, then, to engage in "social work," without becoming a "labor leader" simply out of a maternal concern and outrage which could not overlook the conditions of work and the brutal and occasionally assaultive behavior of the supervisory staff. What upset Anasuya most was to find babies asleep between the machines, breathing air full of dust and cotton fluff. And more than once Anasuya, wishing to complain directly to the government's Factory Inspector, would find him being entertained convivially by one of the mill owners. So before long young Anasuya assumed in earnest the role of "mother" to the workers and concerned herself directly with every aspect of working and living conditions. Her brother, it seems, while "tough" in playing his prescribed role, and "soft" only when the posture sanctioned by his *dharma* was softened by paternal sentiments, fully understood and supported his sister's concerns. She, one concludes, truly was his "alter ego."

When Gandhi settled near Ahmedabad in 1915, it was only natural that he would hear of Anasuya's local fame and that she would come to ask him for advice. Thus she was well known to him before the other witnesses. But it was not until 1917—while

Gandhi was in Champaran—that Anasuya became Ahmedabad's first labor leader.

Knowing a bit of Ambalal's and Anasuya's joint background, we can now appreciate Gandhi's diplomacy at work. Anasuya, we reported, had written to him about the strike and had asked for his blessing, and we now recognize his perfect intuition in appealing to a younger and early motherless brother to mind his older sister. But Ambalal proved an adversary of a superior kind, a man able to apportion for himself what it was his *dharma* to give to his sister, to the company, to the workers—and to a mahatma.

## 2. SHANKERLAL BANKER

DETAILS OF Shankerlal's life history will make apparent how ready he was for Gandhi, who immediately recognized in him a potential Satyagrahi with special practical gifts. Shankerlal was born in 1889 in Bombay, into a conservative and highly religious family—one of a Vaishnava sub-caste of about a hundred families. In his words, "All of us used to worship God every day after our daily bath, and after bowing down we used to repeat his name with a string of beads." His father worked in a major bank, and family circumstances were comfortable. But the little boy had a singular life problem: he had seven older sisters! However, he had been lovingly encouraged by his father—as was not unusual for the only or youngest son—to lord it over the much older girls and to show anger when he could get away with it. Every morning after morning prayers, the father wanted to see his son's face before any other; for if the oldest son is any Hindu father's link to eternity, this one had been long and anxiously awaited. This gave the son a special strength and yet, also, understandably, special conflicts, especially when he saw the effect on the spirit of some of his sisters of the traditional marriage arrangements.

After his father's death, a doctor friend became Shankerlal's guardian. The self-willed boy, ever insistent on pursuing his own course of action, went to (Scotch Presbyterian) Wilson College at 16 and immediately became involved in the "unrest"

which overtook students all over India after that blunder of
blunders, the partition of Bengal in 1905. Tilak, the militant
martyr, became his hero; and while Shankerlal had been deeply
interested in spiritual literature (such as Swami Vivekananda's)
he now drifted away from his family's "idol worship," and his
enthusiasm shifted to politics. Here his story becomes highly
analogous to that of some of our students today:

When Lokamanya Tilak was sentenced to imprisonment for six years,
the students of the college, led by (later Acharya) Kripalani, went on
strike, and began to take an interest in politics and to listen to the
extremists. . . . The partition of Bengal gave rise to the movement for
the boycott of British goods. Students of our college started using Indian
cloth and sugar. . . . But it was difficult to get Indian caps. Students at
that time used to wear caps known as "Bangalore" or "Hungarian" caps
made of felt. They now changed over to caps made with Indian cloth
covering cardboard of Sanitian shapes. . . . They entertained great rev-
erence for Lokamanya Tilak, and sympathized in a way with the more
violent activities.
    Personally I did not feel attracted to this movement as I was inclined
towards constructive work.[66]

    In the context of Indian politics, constructive means not only
non-destructive activity, but restitutive "social work." Through
a co-student, Shankerlal became interested in the "Depressed
Classes Mission," an organization devoted to the "uplift" of the
"backward" classes, especially the Untouchables. He did not
hesitate to visit them in their quarters:

. . . My mother used to dislike my interest in the backward communities. I would tell her of the miserable plight in which these people lived,
and she would say that I could give any amount of money for that kind
of work but that I should refrain from going to the Untouchables'
quarters. But if I insisted on doing so, I should at least take a bath on my
return. I continued to visit the so-called untouchable areas, but in deference to my mother's sentiments I bathed on returning home. . . . My
guardian, in turn, was worried about my studies, but in the examination I
was able to do fairly well. . . .

    His guardian suggested to Shankerlal that he should select
"some suitable line of business" and took him to important

persons in the business world and in the university administration. But Shankerlal was adamant in his interest in social work. One highly placed adviser used the logic of predestination in the effort to dissuade him: "If we improve the condition of the Untouchables, who would clean the latrines?" Another tried foresight and sympathy: "If we give these children more and more education, what will they do after that?" But he added a constructive afterthought: "The condition of these people can improve only if their traditional work like tanning and leather craft can be industrially developed." And this idea fascinated Shankerlal, and set him thinking about ways of preparing himself for such a mission. He returned to Xavier College to study Chemistry, received the M.A. in 1911, went to work in the Tata Institute in Bangalore (working one summer in a leather factory), and finally in March 1914 went to England to study in the Leathersellers' College, where he soon was drawn into the wider currents of Fabian thought. He had, at any rate, tried to find a compromise between his guardian's insistence that he train for a business career and his own determination to serve the underprivileged; and now that some inkling of social thought joined his comprehension of science, and some organizational principles were added to his passion for service, he was much better equipped to find a personal resolution of an Indian conflict between masculine and heroic pursuits and a deep maternal identification. But his need for a new kind of guru remained unfulfilled.

So insistent was this young man on finding his own way that he did not recognize destiny when his path first crossed Gandhi's briefly in 1914, when Gandhi visited England to offer his samaritan services to the British war effort. In fact, Shankerlal was less than impressed: the role of recruiting Indians for the British Ambulance Corps did not appeal to him. And, indeed, he had encountered Gandhi in a late and second-to-the-last flowering of the conflict between his philosophy of Satyagraha and his solicitude for the Empire now endangered from outside, between Gandhi's wish for a large-scale constructive program and what he considered his duty as an Imperial citizen—all undoubtedly expressed in 1914 in a last and unconvincing display of the manners of an English barrister and servant of the Raj.

In March 1915 on returning to Bombay and his mother's bungalow, Shankerlal became acquainted both with a new tenant on the ground floor and with a new ideological orientation. Jamnadas Dwarkadas presided over the Home Rule movement initiated by Mrs. Besant. Shankerlal at first resisted him too, but when he did join him in 1916, at the age of twenty-seven, he immediately proved to be an effective and militant organizer who could muster a mass meeting of 50,000 for the Home Rule League, which had only 1,000 members.

Shankerlal, then, was an efficient organizer for the Home Rule League when, in 1917, Mrs. Besant was arrested. He went to Gandhi, who was then in Bombay, to ask him to speak at a mass meeting of protest. He had seen Gandhi once in England and had been less than impressed with his anglicized dress; now Shankerlal himself was wearing his best English city clothes and was taken aback by Gandhi's peasant attire. He sat down in front of Gandhi and said, "We want you to speak at a mass meeting to free Mother Besant." Gandhi said quietly and firmly, "I cannot do this." Shankerlal cockily interpreted: "I know that some ill-feeling was created by the way in which Mrs. Besant treated you in Benares, but we must remember what she has done for India. *One must forgive!*" Gandhi took this affront with perfect calm and said, "I was not thinking of that, but ask yourself what you want to accomplish to help Mother Besant. To make any progress we must not make speeches and organize mass meetings *but be prepared for mountains of suffering.*" As Shankerlal told me this, it was clear that with those few words Gandhi had touched one chord of Shankerlal's passionate identity conflict, namely, a religious need to empathize without sacrificing masculine capacities. It was then only a matter of time before Shankerlal would change his affiliation—and attire.

During the whole interview, a young woman was with Gandhi: Anasuya Sarabhai. She was under the impression that the forward young man was a Muslim—she even offered him a chair! She was shocked by Shankerlal's behavior; but as Shankerlal was getting up to go, Gandhi (always intent on making a match between people who could serve one another—and him) said to him: "You have a car. Why not drive Anasuya home?" Thus a lifelong friendship began.

There was agreeable surprise in the Home Rule League when Shankerlal conveyed Gandhi's suggestion to start a Satyagraha campaign for Mrs. Besant's release. Anasuyaben volunteered to join the movement and signed the Satyagraha pledge. A branch of the League was formed in Ahmedabad, which, in turn, brought Shankerlal there. He became acquainted with Anasuyaben's labor activities, including her budding warpers' organization. Already knowing the labor situation in Bombay well, Shankerlal was Gandhi's man when the latter came to need comparative data on textile labor in making his decision on whether or not to support the forthcoming weavers' strike.

Needless to say, this also began Shankerlal's indoctrination. He at first resisted giving up English habits and wearing Indian clothes. He also was an occasional meat-eater. One day he received a letter from Gandhi from his Satyagraha camp at Nadiad: "Anasuya has told me that you eat meat and it hurts me to think that you have never told me this. I would gladly have offered you non-vegetarian food in this camp. Am I not your brother to whom you can tell the truth?" One must study a number of Gandhi's recruitments to realize how typical is this teasing, seemingly so casual, and yet always perfectly well-timed. Remember that his admonition to Saraladevi not to get her elegant sari dirty on the ashram grounds resulted in her wearing khadi forever after. Shankerlal never ate "non-vegetarian" again.

And then there was always Gandhi's concern with the relationship of his prospective followers to their parents, or their guardians. At the time, Shankerlal had turned against his mother's ways and had stopped wearing the sacred string of his caste. His mother spoke to Gandhi, who called Shankerlal in and reminded him of the story of the rat and the peacock. The two sons of Lord Shiva, Ganesha—whose means of transport was a rat—and Kartika—who rode a peacock—both claimed a certain special fruit. The god, who had been approached, decided that the fruit would go to the one who circled around the universe fastest. Kartika impulsively mounted his peacock to race around the world. Ganesh quietly bowed to his mother, Parvati, and slowly led his rat around her. He was awarded the fruit. Shankerlal put on the string and was glad he had done so when, a year later, his mother died.

Since Shankerlal combined organizational and business competence with a fervent wish to work for the poorest, Gandhi groomed him to be the secretary of the khadi movement, that is, the re-introduction of the spinning wheel and loom into the villages and towns of India. And he managed to give Shankerlal's mother, shortly before her death, the task of teaching spinning to other women.

Anasuya, in turn, became Shankerlal's link to Labor. So he was there—in the right place and at the right time, with the "right conflicts" and the right interests and talents, when Gandhi decided to make something of the Ahmedabad labor situation.

In the meantime, Gandhi had personally written out and had printed for Shankerlal a brief document which is probably his most succinct statement of Satyagraha up to that time; and one can well understand that such an effort on the part of a new master toward a new son can forge a bond for life. We will quote from this document a few passages which seem to indicate new directions in Satyagraha:

Satyagraha and arms have both been in use from time immemorial. . . . Both these forms of strength are preferable to weakness, to what we know by the rather plain but much apter word "cowardice." Without either, swaraj or genuine popular awakening is impossible. Swaraj achieved otherwise than through resort to one or the other will not be true swaraj. Such swaraj can have no effect on the people. Popular awakening cannot be brought about without strength, without manliness. . . . We can, with the help of satyagraha, win over those young men who have been driven to desperation and anger by what they think to be the tyranny of the Government and utilize their courage and their mettlesome spirit, their capacity for suffering, to strengthen satyagraha.[67]

### 3. MAHADEV

THE prospective chronicler of the Event, Mahadev Desai, had joined Gandhi in Champaran. He was to die, many years later, mourned like a son, when sharing one of the Mahatma's incarcerations. From the first to the last, however, he was always in the habit of noting down immediately what happened to him—a habit to which we owe the only full account of the Event. He, too, was in his twenties when he met Gandhi, and one need only read what Mahadev's friends have said about him then to know how ripe he was for Gandhi's ingathering.[68]

Born in a village in the very language area from which Gandhi's family had come (and sharing his love for their mother tongue), Mahadev had been made to feel by his parents that he was the most precious of their children, for they had lost his three brothers in their infancy. His mother died when he was seven, and his father (who had always lived in restricted circumstances) worried over the little boy's health and future for the rest of his life—and well into the time when Gandhi had become Mahadev's guiding spirit. Not to disappoint his father became, in turn, the central concern of the boy's scrupulous nature. He was extraordinarily studious, and had no interest in extracurricular activities, although in lasting response to his mother, who always "treated him like a prince," he could display a somewhat erratic and often all-too-credulous enthusiasm. Everybody seems to have loved him—except, of course, some of his competitors for Gandhi's affection and literary estate, whose occasional mistrust of the way he rendered Gandhi's utterances I must share: we shall see a questionable example presently.

Mahadev too was married at thirteen, and in his case as in Gandhi's, premature sexual activity seems to have upset his sensitive need for intimacy. Mahadev's crisis came in his youth when he spent some time alone in Bombay. On the night before his law examination, he records, an amorous woman slipped into his bed and was persuaded only with some difficulty that she should save her soul by leaving. The next day, although Mahadev "would have easily passed . . . if he had written what he knew," he suddenly ran out of the examination room, weeping loudly. Not then confiding in anyone, he "fell ill," and left for "some suitable place for a change." This, however, was only the most fateful of a series of similar crises: whenever he traveled without his wife, other women seem to have been attracted to the young man to the point of wishing to exploit his gentle chivalry and tender susceptibility. At any rate, the same danger of seduction is reported to have recurred in the form of at least two Indian and two European women; but he managed to "preserve the purity of his body."

Well, Mahadev did become a most effective worker as translator, pleader, and eventually inspector of cooperative rural societies. He gathered much insight into rural needs and habits, although his employers thought him a bit too eager to expose the moral "weaknesses" of the cooperatives. It was this same eagerness which made him and his friend (and eventual biographer) Narahari Parikh write a letter to Gandhi early in 1917 warning him that compulsory celibacy at the ashram might "give rise to a number of evils." Gandhi probably liked the letter more than the subject matter, for he invited the two young men to the ashram and lost no time in testing and teasing them.

GANDHIJI: What are you doing?
WE: Practicing as pleaders.
GANDHIJI: Have you got the latest *Indian Year Book?* I want to look up something in it.
I: I have one of the last year. I shall, however, procure the latest for you.
GANDHIJI: Is this how you practice? When I used to shave, I used to keep the latest shaving equipment.[69]

Lest this last remark seem un-Gandhian, there is a more than life-size photograph of the Mahatma shaving himself in the very entrance hall to the ashram's library—an incidental fact worth mentioning because it illustrates both Gandhi's lasting concern with his appearance and also the occasionally gay intimacy which characterized his relation to those close to him.

And Mahadev kept in touch with Gandhi. On one occasion he asked his opinion about a letter he had written to a prominent

Englishman. Gandhi not only read and criticized it carefully, but dictated to him what he thought he should have written. Thus, the unsuspecting Mahadev was already in training as a future secretary when the decisive encounter occurred, as it is recorded in the undoubtedly somewhat romanticized account he sent to Parikh, when he was twenty-five years old.

. . . On the morning of 31st August, certain words of Bapuji created in me the mixed feelings of love, dismay and joy. I shall now try to pen in this letter my short talk with him on that day, although it cannot be easily put into words. Bapuji said:

It is not without reason that I have asked you to visit my place every day. I want you to come and stay with me. I have seen your capacity during the last three days. I have found in you just the type of young man for whom I have been searching for the last two years. Will you believe me if I tell you that I have got in you the man I wanted—*the man to whom I can entrust all my work some day and be at ease, and on whom I can rely with confidence?* You have to come to me. Leave the Home Rule League, Shri Jamnadas and everything else. I have spoken like this only to three persons before this, *Mr. Polak, Miss Schlesin,* and *Shri Maganlal.*[70]

Gandhi then told Mahadev how he had enlisted his co-workers in South Africa, determined to make something of them, even though, as he said of Polak, "there was nothing special in him externally." And Gandhi added: "Let us, however, leave aside Maganlal. The intelligence I have found in you I did not see in him. I am confident that you will be useful to me in various ways because of your good qualities."

Such bluntness of personal approach and such free admission of self-interest is, of course "objectified" by the offer of participation in a universal cause; and under the impact of such a multiple appeal the recipient soon flutters like a trapped bird;

I listened to all this with surprise and shyness, without speaking a single word. I interrupted by saying, "I have never shown you anything I have done," to which he answered as follows:

"How do you know? I can judge people in a very short time. I judged Polak within five hours. He read my letter published in a newspaper and wrote me a letter. He then came to see me and I at once saw what he was, and since then he became my man."

What "my man" means is further clarified by the fact that the recruiting leader now tells the aspirant that *he* gave Polak away in marriage—that is, that he did not hesitate (even in South Africa and in the life of a man named Polak) to take over a parental function of singular significance in traditional Indian life. And, indeed, it would always be Gandhi's explicit intention to incorporate a follower's marriage into his orbit—if he could not prevent it. And he assumed without delay prerogatives of the utmost consequence in any new follower's life. Here is more of Mahadev's report of what Gandhi told him about his recruitment of Polak:

. . . I told him plainly, "You are mine and the responsibility to provide for you and your children is mine, not yours. I am getting you married, as I see no objection to your marrying." His marriage was celebrated at my residence. But to revert to the point under discussion. I advise you to give up all thought about the Home Rule League or Jamnadas. Go to Hyderabad. Enjoy yourself for a year or so. Enjoy the pleasures of life to your satisfaction. The moment you start feeling that you are losing yourself, resign from there and come and join me.

If I had not heard similar stories, and if I did not feel constrained to admire their rare clinical logic, I would consider this story somewhat contrived. Gandhi, of course, was quite safe in urging this particular young man to test the world's pleasures "until satiated." For he had already diagnosed the fact that experiences of premature intimacy were jeopardizing the young man's insecure identity, while *Brahmacharya* combined with absolute devotion to service would restore his sense of purpose. Who would doubt that the young man had little intention of engaging in the pursuit of *kama* "for a year or so"? So Mahadev, of course, told him that he was prepared to join him "even at that moment." Gandhi, however, not wanting to seem over-eager, said, "I know that you are prepared but I want you to see a little more of life and enjoy yourself. I would need your knowledge of the Co-operative Movement also. We have to free that department from its defects. Do not be anxious about anything and come back to me after enjoying life for a little longer." Only now do we realize that Gandhi had chosen Hyderabad less because that courtly capital was conducive to *kama*, than because of the well-developed cooperative movement there, knowledge of which could only contribute to Mahadev's usefulness. And whatever libidinal strivings may have been encouraged, their eventual transfer onto the leader (who, in the meantime, will "carry on as well as he can") is clearly demanded: . . . "I do not want you for the ashram school or other work but for me personally.[71] I shall carry on without you for a year or six months while you are away."

Such a total new commitment must raise the question of existing ones, such as a promise to work for Shankerlal which, however, was now easily disposed of. But Mahadev closes his letter with a thought which has oppressed many a new convert:

I have not told my father or anyone else the reasons for changing my decision to join the Home Rule League. It would be foolish to write such things in letters. I would like to read this letter to my father and my wife on a suitable occasion.

This wife, then, would be informed of it all only when it had become irreversible. In a postscript to this long letter, we finally hear of the general mood which made Mahadev so receptive at that moment and so apt to pledge his energies with a total and long-range commitment to the one man who had so unexpectedly "confirmed" him:

PS.: I was sometimes tired of life and regarded it as futile, but now I have developed enough faith in myself to think that life is worth living. Although Bapu told me all these nice things about me and completely embarrassed me, I am unable even now to accept his estimation of me. The only thing certain is that I have never got, nor shall I ever get, such a testimonial in my life. Maybe, I shall be an instrument to achieve something in life for which the world will praise me; but these utterances, emanating from Bapu's heart, shall ever remain with me as my lifelong treasure.

As could be expected, however, Mahadev's father objected to ashram life as too strenuous; and a good Hindu at any rate should be a total disciple only earlier in life—or again *after* having gained "a place of honor in society." His son wrote him,

. . . I am not going to Gandhiji with the ambition of achieving success. I want to live like his shadow, going about with him, receiving training under him, and getting more and more knowledge. I would have considered your objection, if I wanted to be a leader. As to honour, Gandhiji has got it already. Why should I then bother?[72]

A tragi-comic sequence, much to Gandhi's heart, ensued. Mahadev wired Gandhi in Champaran that he and his wife were coming to join him in the indigo campaign. As Parikh reports:

I went to the station to receive them, but they did not turn up. When I returned from the station, Gandhiji showed me another telegram from Mahadev, stating that in spite of his strong desire he could not join Gandhiji, as his father would be greatly grieved if he did so . . . [But] his father could not bear Mahadev's subsequent mental agony. He, therefore, gave him his blessings and permission to join Gandhiji. On the third day we again received a telegram from Mahadev that he was starting, as he had received his father's blessings. When I left for the station, Gandhiji said to me, "How funny it would be if we received another telegram saying that Mahadev was not coming." To this I replied that he was sure to come that day.

And Mahadev did come that day, accompanied by his wife. Since that day right up to his death, he remained with Gandhiji, into whom he merged himself completely.[73]

The merging of shadow and secretary was so complete that none of the other participants in the Event even remember Mahadev's presence there. However, his remark, "Very few except those who attended these meetings know what historic incidents occurred under the babul tree,"[74] seems to attest to his status as a prime witness. The meetings under that tree will occupy us presently. In the meantime, Gandhi wrote to Polak from Ahmedabad: "Mr. Desai . . . has thrown in his lot with me. He is a capable helper and his ambition is to replace you. It is a mighty feat. He is making the attempt."[75] Would Gandhi ever acknowledge that any of his followers—or his sons, for that matter—could do more than make a mighty attempt?

## 4. SONS AND FOLLOWERS

WE CAN now see that the confession with which Gandhi ended his letter to Ambalal—"I have now meddled in your business and in your family affairs"—diagnoses accurately and with his aggressive candor what he is in the habit of doing: he has his own surgical way of severing family bonds with a deft cut, leaving an optimum chance for later healing. In fact, it is my conviction that the rare coincidence of an economic and a familial conflict within the Sarabhai family fascinated him—as a corresponding political and filial conflict in the Nehru family did later. This entanglement between brother and sister may well have been a key factor in inducing him to decide on Ahmedabad for the first Satyagraha—and to fail in it in a specific way.

As we have seen, everything that had made Ahmedabad his city and the ashram his family also made Gujarat the center of his homeland. What he had made of himself, resisting his brother's ambitions and sacrificing his family's hopes for local distinction, was now to be tested for its purity on this very homeground. That here, in Ahmedabad, a young brother and his sister had pitched their *dharmas* against each other in a mutual test—this must have corresponded to some of his own inner conflicts. The very aspect of "a domestic affair," then, had symbolic significance for Gandhi, for in this Satyagraha (as in the following one in Kheda, less than fifty miles from the city) he was to be a prophet in his own country. And if it is proverbially difficult for a prophet to gain a hearing in the land of his origin, a corresponding inner difficulty may make it hard for him to take the measure of his matured stature in a land reminiscent of his childhood dimensions. We have seen young Gandhi's inhibition in speaking up on his early visits to India "out of South Africa." That certainly had now passed. We had reason to connect these early failures with his embarrassment over being and becoming a biological father; and it now seems that at the moment of his full commitment to his own method in his own region some of the old scruples concerning fatherhood and sonhood were re-awakened. We owe to the *Collected Works* a series of intimate letters, culminating in the report of a dream to his son, which will permit us for once to observe a leader fight a life-crisis on two fronts at once: his battle for supremacy in historical actuality and his conflict with the personal past that marks every man as a defined link in the generational chain. As Gandhi put it in a letter to "my child":

Life to me would lose all its interest if I felt that I could not attain perfect love on earth. After all, what matters is that our capacity for loving ever expands.[76]

That an inordinate number of intimate letters are preserved from this period may be partially due to the chronicler Mahadev, who kept the notes he took when Gandhi dictated letters to him. In addition, the editor of Gandhi's *Collected Works*—who must have been a sensitive judge of the changing nature of the available material—notes that at the time of ever more strenuous political contacts, Gandhi's "concern for individual men and women seems, if anything, to grow deeper and more active":[77] it must be emphasized that this concern includes quite prominently his sons and his closest relatives. On the verge of becoming the father of his nation, he did not (as he has been accused of doing) forget his sons, although the way in which he did remember them was not without tragic undertones and consequences. And it is true that in his search for followers, helpers, and worthwhile opponents, he devoted to them all, with almost painful self-awareness, something akin to the care of a father—and a mother.

Before we review some of the letters from the immediate pre-strike period, however, we should remind ourselves of two intensely Indian themes. One is that of fatherhood and sonship widened to include both the avuncular relationship with nephews and nieces and the guru's with his disciples; and the other is the lifelong issue of *Moksha*, of deliverance. We know Gandhi's sons often served as the living reminder of his earlier incontinence; and he now, it seems, had to "cure" his own curse by making them repent their own existence. When Kasturba exclaimed "You want my sons to be holy men before they are men!" she compressed in this one sentence all the tragedy in Gandhi's impatient aspirations: but, as he saw it, India could not wait, and service to India meant immediate sainthood, if of a self-made kind.

Gandhi's greeting on Divali 1917, the Gujarati New Year, to his oldest son Harilal (then thirty years old) is almost formal in its reiteration of his wish that his son, the "seeker after money," may recognize that wealth of character alone is worth worshipping; while for his nephew and chosen son Maganlal, he translated into Gujarati the whole thirteenth chapter of First Corinthians! And one month before the Event, in January 1918, he wrote to his nephew Jamnadas:

If I had been, from the beginning, a poor man with no interest other than in the service of the country, nothing more would have been expected of me. I could then have brought up my children according to my ideals, and they, on their part would have been free, on growing up, to follow a path different from mine. In that case, they would expect from me nothing more than my blessings. I could have claimed this right if I had always been a poor man; if so, I should be able to claim it even now. Parents may change their ideals; when they do, the children should either follow them or gently part company with them. Only if this happens can everyone enjoy swaraj.[78]

To this he added a note to Meva, Jamnadas's wife:

If you have the courage to stay with me by your self, do come. I shall improve your health and you may try to be a daughter to me and so help me to forget the want of one.[79]

On January 31, just before leaving Champaran for Bombay, where he would meet Ambalal and be apprised of the impending lockout in Ahmedabad, he wrote his son Manilal, then twenty-six, who was lonely in South Africa:

I hear from Devibehn that you showed yourself unhappy before Sam at being unmarried. Please do not allow anything to stand in the way of your telling me what you think. You are not my prisoner, but my friend. I shall give you my advice honestly; you may think over what I say and then act as it seems best to you. I should not like you to do anything sinful out of fear of me. I want you not to stand in awe of me or anyone else.

And then, in his almost pathetic inability not to demand the impossible:

See that you don't lose your cheerfulness; and don't indulge in day dreams.[80]

And as the Satyagraha struggle in Ahmedabad became more imminent ("I am handling a most dangerous situation and preparing to go to a still more dangerous") so does his passionate search for sons who would be worthy disciples and for disciples who would be ideal sons. He wrote to Vinoba Bhave, who, indeed, is today considered by many Gandhi's only true heir:

I do not know in what terms to praise you. Your love and your character fascinate me and so also your self-examination. I am not fit to measure your worth. I accept your own estimate and assume the position of father to you. You seem almost to have met a long-felt wish of mine. In my view a father is, in fact, a father only when he has a son who surpasses him in virtue. A real son, likewise, is one who improves on what the father has done; if the father is truthful, firm of mind and compassionate, the son will be all this in a greater measure. This is what you have made yourself. I don't see that you owe your achievement to any effort of mine. Hence, I accept the role you offer to me as a gift of love. I shall strive to be worthy of it; and if ever I become another Hiranyakashipu, oppose me respectfully as Prahlad, who loved God, disobeyed him.[81]

Here, as he sovereignly invites a potentially powerful follower to be his son, even though this might mean that the follower could become a Prahlad resisting his leader to the death, he also can admit that there may be a Demon King in himself.

But to his sister, again, he is cold:

I only pray, if you have any compassion in you, that you come over and live with me and join in me in my work. You will then cease to feel, as you perhaps do at present, that you have no brother and will find not one but many brothers and be a mother to many children. This is true *Vaishnava* dharma. And till you see that it is, we cannot do otherwise then endure separation.[82]

And as the pressure increased ("at the present moment I am trying to deal with imminent passive resistance") his demands on others became more stringent. "Your duty," he wrote to a man who had taken the ashram pledge but had suddenly departed, "lay in honouring it, even if your entire family were to starve in consequence. Only persons of that stamp can mould a nation. Others are just not to be reckoned as men."[83]

The whole extent of his inner turmoil, however, seems to be condensed in a dream. In the middle of February, when he had decided not to return to Bihar, Gandhi wrote to his youngest son, Devadas, "I came here for a day, but it seems I shall have to stay for about a month. If I back out now, thousands will be put to heavy loss. People will yield and be utterly dispirited." Then he told him of a dream which gives us at least an inkling of what we are now ready to perceive "in depth":

I keep thinking of you all the time. I know you have plenty of zeal and can interest yourself in anything. Had you been here, you would have every moment observed the supreme wonder and power of truth. This is all the legacy I can leave for you. As I believe, it is an inexhaustible legacy. For him who knows its worth, it is priceless. Such a one would ask to have or desire no other legacy. I think you have realized its worth and will cherish it with love. I dreamt last night that you betrayed my trust in you, stole currency notes from a safe and changed them. You spent the amount on vices. I came to know about it. I took alarm; felt very miserable. Just then I awoke and saw that it was all a dream. I thanked God. This dream bespeaks my attachment to you. You, of course, want it. You need not fear that it will ever disappear altogether during this present life. I am making a supreme effort to bear equal love to all but, from you I do hope for something more.[84]

This is certainly a short dream, but it nevertheless manages to harbor betrayal, thievery, and vice, as well as alarm and misery. Furthermore, it is clearly related to the childhood memory which, as we have seen, the Mahatma himself made so much of in his Autobiography: his and his brothers' theft for the sake of indulging in the vice of smoking, and the confession which made him a truthful Prahlad and an adolescent Satyagrahi in *his* struggle with *his* father. If Gandhi now writes to his son that the dream bespeaks his paternal love because on awakening he was so glad that the dream was not true, the son may well ask why the father would have dreamed of him in the first place as a vice-ridden betrayer and thief. Together with the somewhat gratuitous reassurance that his paternal love would not disappear "altogether" and the somewhat obscure reference to a "something more" which he demands of his son, the dream can only mean that from his own sons, Gandhi demands the most and expects the worst—that is, he associates his sons with what is worst in himself. That Devadas was Gandhi's youngest son, as Gandhi was *his* father's, and that he was still in his teens, as Gandhi had been at the time of *his* theft, only underlines his identification with his son in the dream. At the very moment, then (so I would conclude), when Gandhi was about to be tested as a prophet of nonviolence in his homeland, the childhood antecedents of this new weapon were reactivated with sufficient strength to make him re-dream that old memory: how he had indulged in vice and had confessed to his stunned father, and how in his way of confessing he had disarmed this violent father with the truth. If this was the youthful antecedent of Satyagraha in his life history, he was now getting ready to test it on a scale vastly greater, thus proving to be a greater leader than his father in both essence and extent. Thus, as he was about to become with a vengeance what his father—the erstwhile passive resister to princely despotism—had been on a smaller scale, he identified himself sufficiently with him to dream of himself as the betrayed father.

It will not seem too far-fetched to those who have studied such matters, and not foreign to some fathers among them, if I add that Gandhi's behavior toward his sons, and certainly the tone of his letters, also constituted an unconscious provocation. Many a reader, Eastern or Western, must have shared my feeling that such letters from our fathers might have brought out only the worst in us, even if only in the form of a most costly and strenuous repression of this worst. And behind such provocation, so the dream seems to confirm, can only be a deep, self-punitive wish to have the sons do to him what he had done to his father, and thus to be, as it were, crucified by them for the aspiration to be a son above all sons, and a father to no son.

Spelled out in these letters in rare clarity, then, is the father-son theme which can be found at critical times in the lives of all

great innovators as an intrinsic part of their inner transformation. This theme can be followed between the lines of Gandhi's
public acts and announcements during the Event itself, and it
will again become tragically manifest at the very end of the
struggle.

CHAPTER

IV

# The Event Retold

THE Ahmedabad Event is usually considered to have been initiated by a meeting between Ambalal and Gandhi in Bombay, on one of Gandhi's lightning trips "out of Champaran." It would make a good beginning for a parable: There was a wealthy man, a powerful mill owner from Ahmedabad, who came to see Gandhiji in Bombay: "Master," he said to him, "do not return to Bihar, come back and take care of Ahmedabad, our city." This would be a counterpart to the parable of Champaran —how Gandhi gave in to the poor peasant who followed him from city to city until Gandhi agreed to go with him to the foothills of the Himalayas. The fact is that Gandhi in those years was testing in his mind, by scientific premeditation, a number of situations, as is obvious (if from nothing else) from a letter he wrote to an informed friend asking for a list of grievances then extant anywhere in India. And as we saw, he had begun carefully to select those whom, in the Autobiography, he called his companions.

Gandhi had kept in touch with conditions in Ahmedabad. He had visited his ashram twice from Champaran, and on one occasion had made a speech on the deplorable state of the city's water supply. In July 1917 he had also sent lengthy memoranda on how to meet the acute danger of a plague epidemic.

Conditions had been desperate.[85] One needs to have seen the slums of Indian cities to imagine the damage an excessively heavy monsoon can do to the crowded clusters of floorless lean-tos, not to speak of the ground around them and the fresh water supply—if any. The monsoon of 1917 was extraordinarily heavy and helped to set in motion the whole chain of causes leading to a plague epidemic. Plague had been endemic in the Bombay Presidency since 1896, but serious plague outbreaks had so far stopped short of Ahmedabad. However, beginning in July of 1917, deaths from plague steadily increased in the city, reaching their peak in the middle of November with 600 new cases and 550 deaths. This percentage of about 10 per cent recovery apparently maintained itself throughout the epidemic. And the municipality was nearly powerless. It could neither provide the clean water needed nor keep out the bad water dreaded: vindictively the clean upper section of the Sabarmati River showed a tendency to "recede from the vicinity of the supply wells," while its polluted section overflowed exactly where drainage pumping was insufficient. "The question," so the municipality declared, "is of expert knowledge." To make matters worse, many of the city's employees left town without leave, along with those who had relatives in the vicinity. The health officers did a heroic job in trying to inoculate the remaining population and to disinfect abandoned premises with crude petroleum, paraffin emulsion, and naphthaline powder. But catastrophes always increase superstition, which in India means a fear of pollution—not by dirty water, mind you, nor by rats or rat-fleas, but by health schemers, who would put public hygiene above caste apartheid.

Only about 30,000 people could be induced to accept inoculation. And the city's infectious diseases hospital had room for exactly twenty-six patients. Ambalal turned over his roomy mansion in Mirzapur to a young physician, a Dr. Tankariwalla, as a plague hospital, with one request: not to spare any amount of money to provide help for anybody who needed it. This was an uphill job as it was; and Ambalal insisted that the hospital be "integrated." Although some special accommodations had to be offered to some high-class Hindus who avoided hospitals in normal times (I almost said "like the plague") and otherwise would have preferred to die by "natural" pollution, Jains as well as Christians were admitted, Banias and Mohammedans, Brahmans and Untouchables. The hospital, it seems, never had more than one hundred patients, but it did accomplish a fifty per cent recovery rate and thus tested the efficacy of some hygienic measures, while isolating at least some of the potentially most dangerous patients.

Besides the two European matrons, nurses imported from Baroda, and some conscientious ward-boys and ambulance workers, Dr. Tankariwalla could unexpectedly count on a "heroic party" of stretcher-bearers from Rajputana. I will tell this story briefly, in honor of those among our young people of today who are engaged in self-chosen restitutional work in the Peace Corps or at home. The "party" consisted of seven young men, educated Hindus of high caste and class. They suddenly appeared in Ahmedabad and asked whether they could help. Directed to the Sarala Devi Hospital, they offered to do the dirtiest and most dangerous work without caste discrimination. They accepted food rations but no money, and when after ten weeks the plague had subsided, they disappeared without giving their names, to Ambalal's intense chagrin.

Schools, colleges, and most public institutions had, of course, been shut down. The mills, however, decided to remain open and to offer a special bonus to the workers not for leaving the city, but for staying. Many of them, it must be added, were loath to leave the city anyway lest their meager possessions be looted in their absence. This, then, is the "plague bonus" which was to become the central issue of the strike that followed.

In the midst of this grim story of polluted water and rat-fleas, of municipal failure and mortal superstition, one finds the civic-mindedness of an Ambalal and the humanity of the stretcher-bearers from Rajputana. But one also finds the following item, characteristic of the isolation, geographic and psychological, of the city's élite circles. During a week in early September, when 400 city dwellers contracted the plague and 350 died, the theater critic of the *Praja Bandhu* also reported an "Allies Tableau" to be presented by a number of ladies to raise money for the British war effort:

The Allies Tableau is bound to be immensely appreciated. The heart of every patriotic person will pulsate with emotions at the scene presented. Each of the Allied Nations will be personified by a young lady. You will see Belgium crushed but dignified—hopeful for the future. You will see Servia trampled upon but undaunted—un-broken in spirit. Of course, you will cheer England and her brave friends—cheer with all your might. But, you are entitled to bring down the roof of the Theatre with your shouts of joy when you see India (personified by a young Parsi lady) marching proudly in the procession of Nations. The other scenes will be equally attractive. There will be a scene episode, which Hindus will specially welcome; the representation of the court of Jehangir and Noorjahan will dazzle you with its grandeur; and you will be conveyed to the historical past of your city by the scene representing King Ahmedshah in his beautiful garden.

In the meantime, a labor dispute had arisen owing to the fact that the five hundred warpers in the textile mills—Brahmans, Banias, and Muslims—just because they were a relatively better-paid élite among the workers and were too well settled in their urban homes to be tempted to flee the city, had not been offered a plague bonus and now demanded a 25 per cent "dearness allowance." Anasuya, from her work among these people, knew that this was a justified demand and (as already recounted) suddenly found herself the leader by acclamation of a small group of organized workers and the mill owners found themselves confronted with a strike threat signed by a Sarabhai! They tore it up contemptuously and requested Ambalal to discipline his rebellious sister. He argued, however, that if his sister had been a brother she would have received half his father's property; why should she be deprived of her rights because she was a woman? "I have no right to prevent her from doing her duty."

It was this situation which Anasuya, frightened by her unexpected role, had written to Gandhi about, asking for his blessing. Paradoxically, however, a very much bigger issue arose when the plague began to subside. The mill owners announced their intention simply to disallow the bonus (up to 75 per cent of their wages) which had been given to the weavers while the plague raged.

At a meeting in Bombay, then, Ambalal took Gandhi aside to tell him of the worsening situation in Ahmedabad—that is, of his and his friends' determination to end the plague bonus—and implored him, in his own and Anasuya's names, to intervene. But Gandhi had already seriously considered making Ahmedabad and all it stood for a testing ground for a full Satyagraha in labor relations. He had had a talk with the owners and the workers in Ahmedabad early in January; and there, no doubt, he had recognized the fact, clearly expressed in the behavior of the workers, that Anasuyaben in her simple, womanly way had already initiated a Satyagraha in the labor movement when she had imposed peacefulness on the striking warpers. He knew that the immediate power which this compassionate sister of one of the bosses had gained over the illiterate workers could hardly be overestimated.

However, as we have seen, Gandhi was preoccupied with his inner ambivalences as well as with the ambiguities of the situation, and he did everything to postpone the moment of action and decision—and this just because he knew that he now needed an occasion to demonstrate his principles "to the death." On February 8, in his very first address to workmen (his little talks to the striking miners in Newcastle were not so much on work conditions as on national injustices), he warned them first to clarify for themselves what demands they could justly make. Even though the owners had offered bonuses up to 80 per cent in plague time, a demand for a 50 or 60 per cent increase in wages would be too easy for them to refuse because neither public nor press would sympathize with it. Only if a just demand could be established would arbitration follow. In the meantime, he said, they could count on Anasuyaben ("she lives only for you") and on him. The fact was that Anasuya was then more intimately known to the workers than he was, wherefore all the early suggestions and announcements were actually made in her name. And the ceaseless moralist could not help adding, from the start, that if they were asking for better earnings, he hoped that they also intended to learn to be clean, to get rid of various addictions (among which was included, no doubt, the "tea habit"), and to see that their children got an education.

In the meantime, Shankerlal reported from Bombay that wages there were already about 25 per cent higher than in Ahmedabad. This, however, the mill owners could easily disavow with the argument that Bombay was a harbor, while Ahmedabad was forced to import coal and export goods by rail.

On February 11, the Collector wrote to Gandhi that the mill owners were planning a lockout and that "I am informed that the mill owners will, if at all, only heed your advice; you are sympathetic to them, and you are the only person who can explain their case to me."[86] Shades of Durban: the only person available! But here the Collector was probably also referring to Gandhi's friendship with Ambalal. And Ambalal was becoming a key figure because the president of the Millowners' Association, Sheth Mangaldas Parekh, wanted nothing to do with lockouts or strikes, was willing to continue the plague bonus in his own mills, and saw no reason to close them. From here on, "the mill owners" meant a majority of adamant agents formed for the occasion into a sub-association under the leadership of Ambalal. All kinds of political and economic issues were, no doubt, involved in the disagreements among the mill owners. Indian mills had made enormous profits while the war was keeping British textiles out of African and Asian harbors accessible to Indian ships; and the thrifty Ahmedabadis had hoarded their profits toward future purchases of British and American machinery unavailable during the war. A reliable labor force, therefore, exploited to the utmost, was the only guarantee that the equipment already installed could continue to supply the demand. And a steady labor force with little absenteeism was, then as later, Ahmedabad's main advantage over the larger industrial centers. So it seemed wise to establish the uses and the limits of arbitration then and there—and with Gandhi's soothing help. According to British secret intelligence, in fact, the wartime shortage of coal and transportation made it quite convenient for the mill owners to close down the mills at this time and to settle issues of power which went far beyond the question of the bonus.

Ambalal's judgment as usual was more complex. As the mill owners' leader, he was determined to play it tough, although he recognized in his sister's success signs of a new consciousness in the working class, and he knew that unionization was unavoidable and desirable. He was glad to have to deal with Gandhi, who, he knew, would keep violence to a minimum, although he really wished the man would stay on the other side of the river and attend to the spiritual and national uplift which Ambalal was so willing to finance. He was quite determined to oppose his sister's economic influence in the community, but he was also glad to see her in the guiding hands of Gandhiji; and, at any rate, he continued to be totally unwilling to disavow or hinder her activities authoritatively. What Ambalal could not accept, however, was the interference of that agitator from Bombay who had lately been staying at his sister's house—on his compound. For him and *his* Gandhian pronouncements Ambalal reserved his most scathing remarks:

The points mentioned by Mr. Banker are based on false assumptions. He assumes that mills are run out of love for humanity and as a matter of philanthropy, that their aim is to raise the condition of the workers to the same level as that of the employers. We beg to say that his approach in this respect is wrong. . . . Workers are employed with this aim [profit] in view, and therefore employment of labour and conditions of employment are determined purely on the basis of supply and demand and from the point of view of their efficiency. . . . Mr. Banker's approach is impossible, unachievable, visionary and utopian.[87]

An arbitration board was established, and it clearly reflected the developing line-up: Ambalal and two mill owners on one side, and for the workers, Gandhi, Shankerlal and Vallabhbhai Patel, an as yet unknown Ahmedabad lawyer. The Collector was "umpire." But to the aroused workers this was just one more maneuver which they did not understand and in which they played no active role. So a few groups in a few mills struck anyway. Gandhi rushed back from Kheda, scolded the workers, apologized to the owners, and wrote to the Secretary of the Mill-owners' Association:

I think the principle of arbitration is of far-reaching consequence and it is not at all desirable that the mill-hands should lose faith in it. . . . Banker has collected figures of what the Bombay mills pay. I shall be obliged if you send me, without delay, a statement of wages paid by the local mills. . . . I am not particularly disposed to favour workers as workers; I am on the side of justice and often this is found to be on their side. Hence the general belief that I am on their side. I can never think of harming the great industry of Ahmedabad.[88]

But it was too late. Most mills closed, and the first phase of the Event, the lockout, started: only those workers who agreed to accept a 20 per cent increase would be invited back, the owners announced. They refused to assist Gandhi in any further "research." He by then had made up his mind that 35 per cent was necessary for the workers, bearable for the industry, a worthy public cause—and midway between 20 per cent and 50 per cent. And, as is shown by the correspondents' column of the *Bombay Chronicle*, the public now did become interested. The *Chronicle*'s Ahmedabad correspondent had most of the facts and figures wrong, but he seemed, at any rate, most agitated about the dissenters among the group of owners:[89]

The chief aim of the dissenters, as can be seen, is not to protect the interest of the labourers, but to have a lion's share by working their mills, giving plague allowance only, and then to settle the question according to the settlement to be arrived at, after the strikes and lock-outs of other mills are over.

A few days later the *Chronicle* noted the fact that the Collector had called on Gandhi at the ashram and that arbitration had been decided on.

The readiness with which the Collector fell in with Mr. Gandhi's idea is also encouraging and it shows that if officials show a genuine desire to cooperate with—and not to patronize—the recognized leaders of the people, considerable good can be done to the commonwealth of the community.[90]

The correspondent concludes by asking whether "anybody could bring forward a scheme to overcome these difficulties?" A few days later, another shareholder warned of the danger that locked out workers would find work elsewhere.

All these letters from Ahmedabad, however, were to be found only on the back pages of the *Chronicle*. The whole matter was not newsworthy, and "Mr. M. K. Gandhi" was considered to be not much more than an admirable do-gooder—way down in South Africa or way out in Bihar.

In the meantime, Gandhi and his co-workers quietly attended to the laborers. Mahadev writes:

> Gandhiji believed in silent work, and took care to prevent coloured reports appearing in the Press about his activities. It is for this reason that those who obtain their information from newspapers do not know anything about the steps Gandhiji took in Champaran to transform the inner life of the people, and the results he achieved; people know only about the enquiry he held there. Similarly in Ahmedabad reports of the speeches made by Gandhiji during the struggle of the mill workers were deliberately not supplied to the newspapers.[91]

Anasuya, Shankerlal, and Gandhi's nephew Chhaganlal, a "veteran" from South Africa, spent every morning and evening visiting the workers' districts, questioning and advising them, sending medical help or suggesting temporary employment, and bringing back to Gandhi daily reports on hardships and rumors, on the readiness to hold out and the sporadic inclination to give up. In the evenings, often until after midnight, Anasuyaben's house would be open to any worker with a special question.

Gandhi, in the meantime, seemed to be ready to create a number of new rituals adapted to the requirements of this particular Satyagraha. For one, over the name of Anasuya, he issued daily leaflets so well printed that they are still clear and clean today in the ashram's folders. Furthermore, every evening Gandhiji would gather the workers around him under the famous babul tree on the banks of the Sabarmati outside the Shahpur Gate.

I wanted to find the tree, of course. But a great flood had washed it away. The Shahpur Gate itself has now been torn down, for it could not funnel the traffic of vehicles and animals which at this point converges to spill out of the inner city, onto the approaches to the river and over the bridge which connects the city with a thriving residential suburb. And where this monumental tree once stood towering over sandbanks, today the worst slum of shacks in Ahmedabad hovers, housing, it is said, members of former "criminal" tribes.

Every afternoon Gandhi would arrive with his co-workers in Anasuya's 1915 Overland roadster, over the only then available bridge down river. They would be awaited by a crowd of workers, rarely numbering less than 5,000, and sometimes closer to 10,000, some having walked two or three miles, now seated to watch the little man in the loincloth speak—for very few could hear him. What he said, they knew, would only enlarge on the content of the leaflets which the few literate workers had read aloud in the various quarters of the city, or in the nearby villages. Rarely, if ever, had any man reached out to them more directly and without any trace of talking down to them. And nowhere before or since has Satyagraha been explained so clearly, in an "object lesson" in installments, printed or spoken, and each one attuned to all the participants in the developing struggle.

If Gandhi quietly insisted on transforming this event into a religious experience, some of the workers were prepared for it. On being locked out, they had solemnly said goodbye to their looms, the Hindus putting coconuts on the machines, the Muslims salaaming them, and both promising to return. And as Gandhi addressed the workers daily, what Shankerlal describes as "an emotion of high order" seemed to prevail—for a while. The police had been prepared for the worst, and armed constables began to patrol all streets, especially when the strikers began to march through the streets shouting, *"Ek tek!"*—"Keep your pledge!"—and improvising songs. After two days, however, the Commissioner was convinced that Gandhi had the situation well in hand. He posted some horse carriages with constables at strategic intersections for another two days and then withdrew the special force altogether.

### First Leaflet

As a condition for his and Anasuya's leadership, Gandhi had demanded of the workers the pledge which they affirmed with their cry. The first leaflet, on February 26, the fifth day of the lockout, certified that the workers' demands were moderate:

After giving full consideration to the interests of both the mill-owners and the workers and to all the other circumstances, [the arbitrators] decided that an increase of 35 per cent was justified and that the workers be advised accordingly. . . . The employers did not express their view on this matter. The workers, whose demand was for a 50 per cent increase, withdrew it and resolved to ask for a 35 per cent increase.[92]

Then followed the Workers' Pledge:

The workers have resolved:

1. that they will not resume work until a 35 per cent increase on the July [1917] wage is secured.

2. that they will not, during the period of the lock-out cause any disturbance or resort to violence or indulge in looting, nor damage any property of the employers or abuse anyone, but will remain peaceful.

How the workers can succeed in their pledge will be discussed in the next leaflet.

If workers have anything to tell me [Anasuyaben] they are welcome to see me at my place at any hour of the day.

Under the babul tree, Gandhi added:

Today is the fifth day of the lock-out. Some of you probably think that everything will be all right after a week or two of suffering. I repeat that, though we may hope that our struggle will end early, we must remain firm, even if that hope is not realized and must not resume work even if we have to die. Workers have no money but they possess a wealth superior to money—they have their hands, their courage and their fear of God. If a time comes when you have to starve, have confidence that we shall eat only after feeding you. We shall not allow you to die of starvation.[98]

Gandhi usually drove back with Anasuya to Ambalal's compound and attended her tea hour. The mill owners' committee, too, met Ambalal in the afternoon, and afterward he often would come over to his sister's house. He had accepted Gandhi's proposition that they should talk over developments every day; and he would, in fact, often drive out to the ashram at noon in order to share a meal with Gandhi and Anasuya. On those occasions Gandhi, not without a chuckle, would insist that Anasuya serve her brother; he delighted in making the "domestic affair" more domestic.

Thanks to Mahadev's note-taking, we have, then, three sets of daily announcements which complement one another: in the morning Gandhi would address the daily prayer meeting at the ashram in his usual intimate and candid manner, after which he would go for his walk (which always also meant animated talk), attend to his correspondence and his visitors, and then "dine" with his co-workers—and on occasion, Ambalal. Sometime during the day or evening he would compose the next day's *leaflet;* and in the afternoon he would be fetched by Anasuya and Shankerlal in her Overland, in order to arrive under the babul tree at five o'clock sharp. I by no means trust Mahadev's notes altogether—there are interesting instances in which Gandhi disavows Mahadev's version of his dictation—but all in all, Gandhi's style emerges clearly. I will use the series of leaflets as a chronological guide, since all other details are necessarily less systematic and less complete.

### Second Leaflet

On the day of the second leaflet (February 27), Gandhi told the prayer meeting:

I feel like repeating to you what the Collector told me yesterday, something which I have not mentioned anywhere else. I think I can say it in the Ashram. The Collector did not mean it as mere formality; he said what he really felt. For the first time in his life, he said, he saw here a struggle between workers and mill-owners conducted with mutual regard. I too don't think I have ever observed as good relations between the parties as here. As you see, Shri Ambalal is on the other side in this struggle but he dined here yesterday. When I told him that he was to do so again today, he understood my meaning. He saw why I wanted him to dine with me and immediately agreed.[94]

In the second leaflet, as promised in the first, Gandhi enlarged on the intrinsic strength with which the workers could back up their pledge:

> If workers have no money however, they have hands and feet with which they can work, and there is no part of the world which can do without workers. Hence, if only he knows it, the worker holds the key to the situation. Wealth is unavailing without him. If he realizes this, he can be sure of success.[95]

This Gandhi followed up with moral admonishments which might be read (or bypassed) as mere homilies, were it not for the universal problem of the inherent lack of discipline to be expected in colonialized peoples and in exploited masses—a lack, which may well lead to impulsive rioting when, for the first time, they recognize their potential strength. If the workers, then, are admonished to be *truthful*, this is not merely a matter of not telling factual lies, but also an exhortation against the spread of rumors by which an undisciplined group can easily become a delusional mob. If they are told to be *courageous*, it is because their previous state of near-slavery always opens them to the dread of total abandonment if they arouse anger in their "masters" to the point of being considered expendable: here, too, panic can release senseless violence—or surrender. At this point, Gandhi introduced a seemingly paradoxical device of Satyagraha:

> At present [the employers] are angry. Also, they suspect that, if the present demands of the workers are granted, they will repeatedly harass them. To remove this suspicion, we should do our utmost to reassure the employers by our behaviour. The first thing to that end is to harbour no grudge against them.[96]

That the workers would not simply laugh at such a suggestion could be attributed to the ingrained respect for *ahimsa*, or to a childish trust in saintly leaders. But here it must be remembered that the vast majority of these workers were Muslims who, as a matter of fact, could easily be aroused to fanatic gestures and impulsive action. Yet Gandhi had recognized in South Africa that mastery over anger is less foreign to those who have learned to express anger in traditional and disciplined ways. Besides, to take active charge of senseless suffering by deliberately choosing to court meaningful suffering can be experienced as an exhilarating mastery over fate within a new ritualization[97] such as Satyagraha:

Happiness follows suffering voluntarily undertaken. It is but suffering for the worker to be denied a wage sufficient to enable him to make both ends meet. Because of our ignorance, however, we endure this and manage to live somehow. Seeking a remedy against this suffering we have told the employers that it is not possible for us to maintain ourselves without the wage increase demanded and that if it is not granted to us and we are not saved from continuous starvation we would rather starve right now.[98]

But it is a large order to convince an illiterate mass of workers of the power of self-suffering, especially if counter-leaflets put out by their employers (none, as far as I know, preserved) make fun of their leaders and the leaders' exhortations, while guaranteeing the stubborn workers and their families only one sure outcome: senseless hunger. So under the babul tree that afternoon Gandhi placed the "domestic affair" in the widest possible context, one which certainly the workers in Ahmedabad had never envisaged:

If you had accepted defeat from the beginning, I would not have come to you, nor would have Anasuyaben; but you decided to put up a fight. The news has spread all over India. In due course, the world will know that Ahmedabad workers have taken a pledge, with God as their witness, that they will not resume work until they have achieved their object. In future, your children will look at this tree and say that their fathers took a solemn pledge under it, with God as their witness. If you do not fulfil that pledge, what will your children think of you? The future of your posterity depends on you.[99]

One can easily see the analogy to the struggle in South Africa in which a few thousand Indians were made to feel that not only Mother India but the very principles of the British Empire depended on them. And Gandhi did not fail to teach the workers a new attention and a new concentration:

> Remember each word in these leaflets and keep the pledge conscientiously. There is no point in knowing them by heart mechanically. Many can repeat parrot-like the Holy Koran or the *Gita:* some can recite both the *Gita* and the Tulsi *Ramayana.* It is not enough, though, that one knows them by heart. If, having learnt them by heart, you put the teaching into practice, rest assured that none can whittle down your 35 per cent even by a quarter per cent.[100]

But even as Gandhi came to feel responsible—now to the death—for a few thousand workers whom he had drawn and tied to himself by recourse to the mighty name which must not be used in vain, he wrote the tenderest letter to his son Ramdas, 20 years old, working with a tailor in Johannesburg:

> I keep worrying about you these days. I detect a note of despondency in your letters. It seems you feel the want of education. You feel, too, that you have not settled down to anything. If only you were with me, I would take you on my lap and comfort you. In the measure in which I fail to make you happy, I think I must be wanting in something. There must be something lacking in my love. Please think of any wrongs I may have done as unintended and forgive me. Children are entitled to much from their parents, being all submission to them. A mistake on the part of the parents will ruin their lives. Our scriptures place parents on a level with God. It is not always that parents in this world are fit to carry such responsibility. Being but earthly, they pass on the legacy to their children and so from generation to generation mere embodiments of selfishness come into this world. Why should you think that you are an unworthy son? If you are so, don't you see that that would prove that I was unworthy? I don't want to be reckoned as unworthy; how could you be so then?
>
> You need not ask my forgiveness. You have given me no reason to be unhappy. I want you to come over to me after your experiments there are over. I shall do my part to see you married. If you want to study, I shall help you. If you but train your body to be as strong as steel, we shall see to the rest. At the moment, we are scattered wide apart. You there, Manilal in Phoenix, Deva in Badharwa, Ba in Bhitiharwa, Harilal in Calcutta, and myself ever on the move from place to place. Maybe, in this separation lies service to the nation and the way to spiritual uplift. Whether that is so or not, let us bear with cheerful mind what has fallen to our lot.[101]

### Third Leaflet

The third leaflet (February 28) takes up the matter of the dignity of *all* work, as against that of any particular line of work especially sanctioned by caste and tradition. This is a basic problem which must be faced sooner or later by every civilization. Luther dealt with it extensively; and, of course, the revolution of peasants and workers in Russia was in full swing at the time of the Ahmedabad lockout. In a civilization in which one's caste position in this life, as well as one's eternal *Karma*, is associated not only with the kind of work one does, but with the kinds of work one must avoid at all cost, it was no small matter to address workmen as follows:

In India, a person in one occupation thinks it below his dignity to follow any other. Besides, some occupations are considered low and degrading in themselves. Both these ideas are wrong. There is no question of inferiority or superiority among occupations which are essential for man's existence. Nor should we be ashamed of taking up an occupation other than the one we are used to. We believe that weaving cloth, breaking stones, sawing or splitting wood or working on a farm are all necessary and honourable occupations. We hope, therefore, that instead of wasting their time in doing nothing, workers will utilize it in some such useful work.[102]

With this came detailed advice: do not waste your time in gambling, sleeping, gossiping, and drinking tea; don't loiter around the mills. What a chance you now have to clean and repair your houses; to read, if you can; to learn a subsidiary skill or hobby—so come and ask us for suggestions. But all of this advice involved taking considerable chances with the very core of the workers' problem: having temporarily lost their jobs, what if they were to lose their identity as workmen altogether? Changing conditions in both America and Russia raise similar questions about the symbolic value attached to ordinary and necessary chores. Might an American immigrant or farmer, or a Russian worker, help his wife with the dishes? In other cultures this may be an issue of sex- or class-defined roles, but in India seeing oneself in the "wrong" work role could, (and in some places still does) arouse a metaphysical shudder: one is not in accord with the drift of the universe. Gandhi, never one to exclude himself from a redefinition, promised, in the fourth leaflet, to define his own duties as a leader.

In the meantime, he did not hesitate to tell the highest British dignitary in the city what he thought *his* duty was. He and Commissioner Pratt had had a talk on the Kheda situation on February 27 and, as was so typical for Gandhi, something in the tone of the conversation continued grating on him. So he sent off an immediate and frank letter worded with the force of a prophet who knew that he would implement the change he predicted:

A new order of things is replacing the old. It can be established peacefully or it must be preceded by some painful disturbances. What it will be lies largely in the hands of civil servants like yourself, more than those of the King's representatives quite at the top. You desire to do good, but you rule not by right of love, but by the force of fear. The sum total of the energy of the civil service represents to the people the British Constitution. You have failed, probably not through any fault of your own, to interpret it to the people as fully as you might have. . . . I presumptuously believe that I can step into the breach and may succeed in stopping harmful disturbances during our passage to the new state of things. . . . I can only do so if I can show the people a better and more expeditious way of righting wrongs. . . . The only dignified and truly loyal and uplifting course for them is to show disapproval by disobeying your orders which they may consider to be unjust, and by knowingly and respectfully suffering the penalty of their breach.[108]

### Fourth Leaflet

The fourth leaflet (March 1) was devoted to the *advisers'* role. As if to avoid false promises, it first stated "what we can not do": for example, support the workers in any wrongdoing, such as making irresponsible demands or committing violence. Furthermore, the leaders can only promote the workers' interest "while safeguarding the employers'."

On the other hand, the workers' interest was defined as including vastly more than the 35 per cent increase to which the leaders commit themselves once again.

We shall show the workers how they may improve their economic condition; we shall strive to raise their moral level; we shall think out and teach them ways and means of living in cleanliness and we shall work for the intellectual improvement of such of them as live in ignorance.[104]

And then a fateful promise:

We shall not ourselves eat or dress without providing food and clothing to such of the workers as are reduced to destitution in the course of the struggle.

Before this statement, Gandhi, with his equal tolerance of the wealthy and the poor, had not shown that he fully comprehended what class differences the workers would perceive in the simple daily fact that while they were beginning to starve, their leaders would arrive in an American-built car after—as far as the workers knew or imagined—a good meal in Anasuya's well-stocked house. For the moment, he would only encourage the workers to come, confront, and censure the advisers "whenever you see us committing mistakes or slackening in our efforts to carry out our pledge."

Yet, as if to counterbalance the emphasis in this leaflet on what the advisers and the employers had yet to learn, Gandhi had written to Ambalal in the morning:

If you succeed, the poor, already suppressed, will be suppressed still more, will be more abject than ever and the impression will have been confirmed that money can subdue everyone. If, despite your efforts, the workers succeed in securing the increase, you and others with you will regard the result as your failure. Can I possibly wish you success in so far as the first result is concerned? Is your desire that the arrogance of money should increase? Or that the workers be reduced to utter submission? Would you be so unkindly disposed to them as to see no success for you in their getting what they are entitled to, may be even a few pice more? Do you not see that in your failure lies your success, that your success is fraught with danger for you?

. . . My success everyone will accept as success. My failure, too, will not harm anyone, it will only prove that the workers were not prepared to go farther than they did. An effort like mine is Satyagraha. Kindly look deep into your heart, listen to the still small voice within and obey it, I pray you. Will you dine with me?[105]

### Fifth Leaflet

The fifth leaflet (March 2) told the workers what the *employers* feared. They were apprehensive of two things, according to Gandhi: that the workers, once their demands had been met, would become overbearing and ever-more demanding; and that the advisers' influence over the workers would become permanent. To the first of these fears, Gandhi countered that the greater danger was that the workers, if continually suppressed, would become more and more vindictive. As to the advisers, he agreed that the employers would never succeed in dividing advisers and workers—least of all by disappointing the workers—but he suggested that *generous* employers could always count on help from the advisers if the workers ever failed in their duty toward the employers.[106]

So far, so good. But here the reassuring tone suddenly gave way to what almost amounted to a curse. Was Gandhi, in his turn, beginning to be apprehensive, lest the employers play a cheating game against his way of pure justice? He concluded the leaflet: "the employers have adopted the Western, or the modern, Satanic notion of justice"—an indictment which lumps the capitalist and the communist conception of a labor dispute together in one devilish, Western, modern trend: class warfare.

### Sixth Leaflet

The first words of the sixth leaflet were "pure justice." And it seems understandable that Gandhi felt the need to explain this concept, which opposes Western ways to native Indian systems of justice:

There was a time in India when servants, passing from father to son, used to serve in the same family for generations. They were regarded and treated as members of the family. They suffered with the employers in their misfortunes and the latter shared the servants' joys and sorrows. In those days India was reputed for a social order free from friction, and this order endured for thousands of years on that basis. Even now this sense of fellow-feeling is not altogether absent in our country. Where such an arrangement exists, there is hardly any need for a third party or an arbitrator. Disputes between a master and a servant are settled between themselves amicably. There was no room in this arrangement for increase or reduction in wages according as the changing needs of the two might dictate.

It is obvious that this (possibly oversimplified) version of the good old *jajman-kamin* system was offered in an attempt to save in a new and industrialized world what traditional values still existed on both sides. The leaflet contained a note of disappointment:

We had confidently hoped that the Jain and *Vaishnava* employers in the capital city of this worthy land of Gujarat would never consider it a victory to beat down the workers or deliberately to give them less than their due.[107]

Those who would ride roughshod over such "feudalism" should remember that Gandhi was an excellent judge of what values had retained their actuality for these ex-peasant workmen, and what kind of actuality was apt to confirm an existing sense of identity—on both sides. For while I believe (and Ambalal has confirmed this) that the mill owners, on the defensive, did not hesitate to use all the tricks in the arsenal of ownership, I am also certain that, even to this day, the older generation of owners would be loath to abandon a certain paternalist role, decried of course by socialists and progressivists. This native feudalism Gandhi contrasted with what was then a popular version of Social Darwinism.

[In] the present war in Europe . . . no means is considered improper for defeating the enemy. Wars must have been fought even in the past, but the vast masses of the people were not involved in them. We would do well not to introduce into India this despicable idea of justice. When workers make a demand merely because they think themselves strong enough to do so, regardless of the employers' condition, they will have succumbed to the modern, Satanic idea of justice. The employers, in refusing to consider the workers' demands, have accepted this Satanic principle of justice maybe unintentionally or in ignorance. The employers ganging up against the workers is like raising an army of elephants against ants. If they had any regard for dharma, the employers would hesitate to oppose the workers. You will never find in ancient India that a situation in which the workers starved was regarded as the employers' opportunity. *That action alone is just which does not harm either party to a dispute.*[108]

I have italicized the last sentence because it is the very soul of any Satyagraha struggle. It is fair to assume that at this point relations between Gandhi and Ambalal became rather strained; for it is almost a rule that powerful opponents, in their stubborn bewilderment over being faced with this new nonviolent kind of struggle, become more ruthless. That this bewilderment induces them to use means not entirely in accord with their traditional and personal values provides a critical moment in any Satyagraha struggle, because it shows up the moral weakness of the powerful.

In the meantime, Gandhi managed to give to the meetings under the babul tree the form of a major ritual which would soon sprout minor ones. The descriptions all agree: A crowd of thousands would wait for hours, then make way for Gandhi and his party. Perfect silence reigned while the day's leaflet was read aloud and while Gandhi discoursed on it. Day by day, more and more outsiders would come to witness the strange ceremonial, with its concluding mass reaffirmation of the original pledge, followed by a friendly contest among various groups who had made up new songs for the occasion. Some of these were doggerel and loudly appreciated; others indicated clearly that a transfer of traditional religious feeling to this new kind of social experience was underway. If, to Gandhi's initial horror, much of the religious sentiment began to focus on him as a charismatic figure, one can only say he should have known better: for this was only the beginning of his inevitable Mahatmaship. At the end of the meeting, as he withdrew with his retinue, the workmen would form small processions to march through town singing the newly improvised songs. The texts of these songs, stripped of the gaiety, the improvisation, and the rhythm of musical intonation, now appear to be banal. Nonetheless, here are some examples from Mahadev's booklet and from Shankerlal's notebook:

Be not afraid for we have a divine helper.

   If we are to die of starvation, let us die but it is proper that we do not give up our resolve.

   May God give great glory and fame to kind-hearted Gandhi.

   And incidentally he has awakened us from the dream of ignorance.

   We believe we have found in him a companion in our loneliness.

   Kindhearted Gandhiji and our sister Anasuya.

   May their names remain before the world till the day of resurrection.

   There probably were other kinds of songs (one would almost hope so) such as good Gandhiites would be loath to note down for posterity. Gandhi alluded to this development toward the end of the strike, indicating that he kept an eye on this new kind of poetry, too. "It is not proper," he once interrupted a gay singer who had received enthusiastic applause

that you ridicule the machines and call them "empty show-cases." These inanimate machines have not done you any harm. You had been getting your wages from these very machines. I must advise our poets that we must not use bitter words; we should not cast aspersions on the employers. It is no use saying that the rich go in motor cars because of us. By saying so we only lose our own self-respect. I might as well say that even the King Emperor George V rules because of us, but saying so does not redound to our credit. We do not prove ourselves good by calling others bad. God above sees who does wrong. He punishes him. Who are we to judge? We merely say that the employers are wrong in not giving us the 35 per cent increase.[109]

   But the issue of the 35 per cent increase, as Gandhi knew only too well, had by now been absorbed in a struggle which had its own momentum. He knew that workmen not inspired or intellectually persuaded by an economic ideology could not accept the stark fact of hunger without some religious conviction. And they *were* hungry. What help some had been receiving from their village relatives or from more fortunate co-workers was beginning to dwindle.

   So far, however, the workers had been discouraged from seeking alternative employment: as long as there was hope that the mill owners would give in early in the game, any action had to be avoided which might make it appear that the workers considered themselves a potentially migratory group rather than an indigenous labor force, an organic part of the textile industry.

It seems quite probable that if the lockout continues for about a fortnight or more, a great many labourers who are at present willing to resume work and accept the allowance with the millowners' group have decided to give, would find means of living at places other than this, and so when the settlement is effected and the weaving sheds commence working, an unusual scarcity of labour is sure to be experienced.[110]

It may have been this threat, together with some wish to support Gandhi's "pure justice," which caused a number of outsiders to offer financial aid to the workers. One of Shankerlal's Bombay friends offered a big sum, and Gandhi had to admit that he had had similar offers from Ahmedabad friends. But he adamantly refused all help, giving the usual combination of ideological and practical reasons: "A struggle supported by public charity is not Satyagraha." Furthermore, the mill owners would be provided with an extraneous and artificial factor in their pending decisions: "All they have to do is calculate how long such support could last." But from here on, alternative employment was suggested, and Gandhi himself set an example by offering some employment at the ashram.

### Seventh Leaflet

Leaflet seven (March 4) starts off surprisingly: "South Africa is a large British Colony." Gandhi was now going to give the workers a historical (or is it mythological) perspective on the dawn of Satyagraha in South Africa. But always intent on connecting a new theme with the actuality of the day, he began with the very last phrase of the South African struggle as an example of "pure justice." So almost perversely he told the striking mill hands about the time Satyagraha was suspended because the European railroad workers had gone on strike:

When the railway strike was launched, a strike involving 20,000 Indian workers had already begun. We were fighting the Government of that country for justice, pure and simple. The weapon our workers employed was satyagraha. They did not wish to spite the Government, nor did they wish it ill. They had no desire to dislodge it. The European workers wanted to exploit the strike of the Indians. Our workers refused to be exploited. They said, "Ours is a satyagraha struggle. We do not desire to harass the Government. We will, therefore, suspend our struggle while you are fighting." Accordingly, they called off the strike.[111]

One may ask in passing where, on that occasion, was the solidarity of the working class, that is, of railroad and industrial workers. But the reader will remember that the laboring class in South Africa, then as now, did not extend such solidarity to "coloured" people, and was, if anything, more violent in its racism than the middle class, which was less endangered by competition from immigrant workers. At any rate, he now presented a new gospel, which fit the workers' semi-religious mood.

### Eighth Leaflet

From leaflet eight (March 5):

Let us on this occasion think of what other persons like ourselves have done. Such a satyagrahi was Hurbatsingh. He was an old man of 75 years. He had gone to South Africa on a five-year contract to work on an agricultural farm on a monthly wage of seven rupees. When the strike of 20,000 Indians, referred to in the last leaflet, commenced, he also joined it. Some strikers were jailed and Hurbatsingh was among them. His companions pleaded with him and said, "It is not for you to plunge into this sea of suffering. Jail is not the place for you. No one can blame you if you do not join such a struggle." Hurbatsingh replied: "When all of you suffer so much for our honour, what shall I do by remaining outside? What does it matter even if I die in jail?" And, verily, Hurbatsingh died in jail and won undying fame. . . . and hundreds of Indians joined his funeral procession.[112]

Nor was this a matter of social class:

Like Hurbatsingh was the Transvaal business man, Ahmed Mahomed Cachalia. By the grace of God he is still alive, and lives in South Africa where he looks after the Indian community and safeguards its honour. During the struggle in which Hurbatsingh sacrificed his life, Cachalia went to prison several times. He allowed his business to be ruined and, although he now lives in poverty, is respected everywhere. He saved his honour, though he had to pay heavily for it.

Nor should age be a dividing factor:

Just as an old labourer and a middle-aged business man of repute stood
by their word and suffered, so also did a girl of seventeen years. Her
name was Valliamah. She also went to jail for the honour of the community during that same struggle. She had been suffering from fever
when she was imprisoned. In jail, the fever became worse. The jailer
advised her to leave the jail, but Valliamah refused and with an unflinching mind completed her term of imprisonment. She died on the fourth or
the fifth day after her release from jail.

Under the babul tree, Gandhiji brought home the moral:

These three sought nothing for themselves. These sisters and brothers of
ours did not have to pay the tax. Cachalia was a big merchant and did
not have to pay it. Hurbatsingh had migrated before the tax was imposed, so he, too, did not have to pay it. The law imposing the tax had
not been brought into force at the place where Valliamah lived. And yet
all these joined the struggle. . . . Your struggle on the other hand is for
your own good. It should therefore be easier for you to remain firm.[118]

And as for a few weeks of hardship:

The trouble was not over within twelve days. The entire struggle lasted
for seven years and during that period hundreds of men lived under
great suspense and anxiety and stuck to their resolve. Twenty thousand
workers lived homeless and without wages for three months Many sold
whatever goods they had. They left their huts, sold their beds and
mattresses and cattle and marched forth. Hundreds of them marched 20
miles a day for several days, each getting only ¾ lb. of flour and an
ounce of sugar. There were Muslims as well as Hindus among them.[114]

That day, a letter to South Africa rejoiced

that Satyagraha "is beginning to have full play in all departments of
life."[115]

But there is some exasperation, too: "Ambalal . . . is the most
stubborn opponent in the strike."

### Ninth Leaflet, Tenth Leaflet

At the conclusion of the ninth leaflet, Gandhi finds it necessary to refer to the employers' tactics as "unworthy," "exaggerated," "twisted."

The tenth leaflet (March 7) had to meet an immediate danger: some workers were trying to alleviate their situation by

borrowing money at exorbitant interest rates. And yet, there was no use denying the need:

It is just about a fortnight since the lock-out commenced, and yet some say that they have no food, others that they cannot even pay rent. . . . Such extreme poverty is a painful thing indeed. But a 35 per cent increase will not by itself cure it. Even if wages were to be doubled, in all likelihood the abject poverty would remain unless other measures were also adopted.

Knowing that without some long-range vision a momentary remedy would seem trivial, he promised help beyond the present emergency—a promise which would be kept:

If, as part of the present struggle, all workers take an oath not to pay such excessive interest, they will have an unbearable burden lifted from them. Nobody should pay interest at a rate higher than twelve per cent. Some may say: "It is all right for the future, but how shall we pay back what we have already borrowed on interest? We have this thing with us for a lifetime now." The best way out of this situation is to start co-operative credit societies of workers.[116]

In the meantime, the mill owners exploited the workers' predicament in their own way. They promised a money reward to any worker who could persuade five other workers to return with him to the mill. Furthermore, they spread rumors that the lockout might be lifted any day, possibly as soon as March 12, for those workers who were willing to accept a 20 per cent increase in wages. Compared with nothing, twenty per cent, of course, now seemed like much, and only a little less than the seemingly unreachable thirty-five. There were additional hints that the extra 15 per cent would be granted soon after the resumption of work or paid to the workers indirectly by a distribution of grains and foodstuffs. The city began to sympathize with such promises, and many considered it laughable that hungry workmen, or for that matter *any* Indian workmen, presumed to know how to take or keep a pledge without the dictatorial presence of a mahatma. And, indeed, Gandhiji knew only too well (and would tell the mill hands at the end of it all) that he, as an expert in vow-taking, had single-handedly lifted the workers' moral aspiration to a level which in the long run could be maintained only by a total change in their condition; while the slightest chance for such a change would be forfeited for a long time to come if the workers' temporary awareness were now to be lost. In the meantime, a rush back to the mills could, of course, be easily started by workmen who had not taken the pledge, including those who had not previously returned to town from the villages.

### Eleventh Leaflet

On March 11, therefore, Gandhi suddenly told the workers (and announced in leaflet eleven) that on the following day the meeting under the babul tree would be held at 7:30 *in the morning*—at the very moment the factory whistles might suddenly announce that the mills were open.

You should also search out the workers from other parts of the country who live as strangers to you and who have hitherto not attended these meetings, and see that they attend them. In these days, when you are facing a temptation, all manner of thoughts will occur to you. It is a miserable thing for a working man to be without a job. The meetings will keep up the patience of all workers who feel so. For those who know their strength, there can be no enforced unemployment.[117]

The decisive moment had obviously arrived. In the early hours of March 12, Gandhiji dictated letters to influential men who had urged him to abandon the struggle in view of the pitiful conditions in the workers' districts. To Sheth Mangaldas, the president of the Millowners' Association, who had not joined the lockout, he wrote: "Why don't you participate in this? It does not become you merely to watch this great struggle unconcernedly."[118]

But it was already too late. The lockout *was* declared ended on March 12, a conclusion which Gandhi turned into a beginning—"Today a new chapter begins." It was initiated by a letter from Ambalal which Gandhi immediately destroyed upon reading without even giving Mahadev a chance to copy it. But from Gandhi's answer (which he likewise forbade Mahadev to preserve in its entirety), it can be seen that Ambalal had complained of unfair pressure on the workers, and yet, matching Gandhiji's "will you dine with me?" and maybe in the expectation that the struggle would end that day, he had invited Gandhiji to *his* home. From memory Mahadev reconstructed these passages of Gandhiji's answer:

I have certainly no desire that a labourer should be forced against his will to keep away from it [the mill]. I am even ready, myself, to escort any worker who says he wants to attend the mill. I am altogether indifferent whether a labourer joins or does not join.

In view of the task you have set me, how can I accept the pleasure of staying with you? I should very much like to see your children. How is that possible at present, though? Let us leave it to the future.[119]

### Twelfth Leaflet

At any rate, there was now a new play of forces: "Today," leaflet twelve announced, "the employers' lock-out is at an end and a workers' strike has commenced."

Gandhiji now played for the highest odds. "The workers," he wrote, "may rise from their present condition" only if they

have no other way to advance themselves except to stand by their oath, and it is our conviction that, if only the employers realize it, their welfare too lies in the workers' keeping their oath. Eventually, even the employers will not gain by taking work from workers who are too weak to keep their oath. A religiously-minded person will never feel happy in forcing a person to break his pledge or associating himself with such an effort. We have, however, no time now to think of the employers' duty. They know it all right. We can only entreat them. But the workers must think seriously what their duty is at this time. Never again will they get an opportunity like the present one.[120]

In view of the immediate danger of losing this possibly irretrievable opportunity, Gandhiji at last consented to what he had vetoed so far, namely, an appeal to the solidarity of Indian workers:

It is possible that the workers from outside Gujarat are not well informed about this struggle. In public work we do not, and do not wish to, make distinctions of Hindu, Muslim, Gujarati, Madrasi, Punjabi, etc. We are all one or wish to be one. We should, therefore, approach these workers with understanding and enlighten them about the struggle and make them see that it is to their advantage, too, to identify themselves with the rest of us.

### Thirteenth Leaflet

At the same time (and he may have waited to inform the wider public until this was firmly established), the identity of the struggle as a Satyagraha could not be compromised; and even as, quite in accord with his practice in South Africa, he had offered to guide any scared strike-breaker personally through a threatening picket line, so he now insisted, in leaflet thirteen, that the strikers should not prevent anybody from entering the mills; they should, in fact, keep away from the mills, and look for opportunities to work elsewhere. But this was too much for the workers. To be locked out is a passive thing, and dignity would demand that one not stand by the gates dramatizing oneself as unwanted. To strike, while a mill is open to willing workers, is an aggressive act, and it is hard to forego the opportunity of dramatizing both one's refusal and the power of denying entrance to strike-breakers. The strikers' songs now became more aggressive, and when Gandhi continued to reprimand them, the movement lost much of its previously pervasive spirit. A second crisis was imminent.

As if to signify also the relative national isolation of this "domestic affair," at this critical moment Annie Besant arrived in town to give two lectures in one day, one on "National Education" and the other on "Swaraj." In the afternoon, Gandhiji chaired the meeting and introduced the speaker with his brand of gallantry: "No matter if she commits hundreds of mistakes, we shall honor her." But the strike was not mentioned. At a reception preceding the evening meeting, however, Gandhi, pointed to Ambalal, and said to Mrs. Besant: "These people have decided to destroy the mill workers." To which Ambalal replied, "and they want to do the same to the mill owners." Mrs. Besant, always willing to take over, immediately wanted to know whether she should ask the authorities to intervene—the very gesture of Benares! But Gandhi declared this to be quite unnecessary: "There is full regard for each other amongst . . . us." Mrs. Besant declared this to be rather unusual.

Nothing is recorded for March 14: maybe Annie Besant's presence in town kept Gandhi busy. His staff, however, visited the workers' quarters as usual, and brought back a general report of disillusionment. When Chhaganlal visited the inhabitants of Jugaldas Chawl, one of the poorest "chawls" (if there can be degrees of poverty under such conditions), he was met with derisive laughter: "What is it to Anasuyaben and Gandhiji? They come and go in their car, they eat elegant food, while we suffer death agonies. To attend meetings does not keep us from starving." And, indeed, on the morning of March 15, when seated under the babul tree, Gandhiji saw only

a thousand dejected faces with disappointment written all over them, instead of five thousand or more, beaming with self-determination.[121]

### Fourteenth Leaflet

A fourteenth leaflet was ready exhorting the workmen again to keep busy:

It behooves us that we maintain ourselves by doing some work. If a worker does not work, he is like sugar which has lost its sweetness. If the sea-water lost its salt, where would we get our salt from? If the worker did not work, the world would come to an end.[122]

And he concluded: "Even if only one person holds out, we shall never forsake him."

But the time for leaflets, and even for those with a biblical ring, was passing. Gandhiji obviously felt that he himself would have to be the one person to hold out and also the one not to forsake himself. He suddenly heard himself say: "I cannot tolerate for a minute that you break your pledge. I shall not take any food, nor use a car till you get 35 per cent increase or all of you die fighting for it."

THE fast, begun on March 15, 1918, was the first of seventeen fasts "to the death" which Gandhi was to undertake throughout his long life. In later years, all of India would hold its breath while the Mahatma fasted, and whole cities would leave their lamps unlit in the evening in order to be near him in the dark.

And since then, many others have followed the Mahatma's example, though their reasons have often been impulsive, vindictive, or faddish. It is, therefore, especially important to understand what motivated Gandhiji's decision in this first instance and why he came to regret it as not quite worthy of his cause. But it should be clear that there cannot really be any "pure" decision to starve oneself to death, for such determination can only emerge from a paradoxical combination of a passionate belief in the absolute vitality of certain living issues and the determination to die for them: thus one "lives up" to a principle by dying for it. A martyr, too, challenges death, but at the end he forces others to act as his executioners. The decision to let oneself die is of a different and admittedly more obscure order.

No doubt, this fast was improvised, but no doubt also, fasting as a last resort must have been considered before by the leading Satyagrahi. To those present at the scene, however, it must have come as a kind of metaphysical shock.

Excitable Muslims provided immediate drama. When Anasuyaben declared that of course she would join Gandhi, many workmen burst into tears and swore right then and there to do likewise, or to kill themselves if she should die. One flamboyant Muslim became the hero and the victim of the excitement, and his name is preserved: Banuma—a weaver who was always immaculately dressed, wore a pink turban, and was proud of his four looms and fond of his two wives. He suddenly bared a big knife and was about to stab himself when Gandhiji himself disarmed him. It is significant of the whole atmosphere of subdued violence which pervades situations of dramatic self-suffering that onlookers thought Banuma with his exposed knife was threatening vengeance to the mill owners—and, indeed, the man never found a job in the mills again. After the first shock had subsided, Gandhi simply forbade Anasuya and others to fast with him: "Leave this to me," he said. "Fasting is *my* business." The public in general did not know yet what fasting was going to mean when undertaken by Gandhi and ignored it as another bit of mystical adventurism.

The Overland now rejected as a symbol of capitalist self-indulgence, Gandhi had to walk back to the ashram, wading ahead of hundreds of workers across the Sabarmati, which in March is reduced to a few rivulets. Among those who followed him there were not a few from the Jugaldas Chawl, for they perceived from the content of Gandhi's vow that their remarks had "caused" his decision. They felt abjectly guilty and swore to keep their pledge and to seek substitute work, if ever so despised. The mill owners, in turn, convened in Ambalal's place. The old guard of mill owners felt a mixture of triumph and apprehension—triumph at having taught Gandhi how it felt to fail, and apprehension that a fanatic like Gandhi might really *mean it*. Some of these Jains have never accepted Gandhi's fasts as anything but a clever last-minute recourse when a bargain failed. Ambalal's feelings, as usual, were more complex. He felt more personally touched, and went out to sit by Gandhiji, who had reclined on his mat to preserve his strength. Ambalal felt angry, too. The fast, as he put it, was a "dirty trick." "Look here," he is said to have told Gandhiji, in essence, "you are changing the very premise of this whole affair. This is between owners and the workers—where does *your life* come in? It is impossible for us to yield to a situation where an outsider teaches the workers to defy us. What if they go on doing it? And why should we accept an arbitrator? We would only lose our prestige." It was probably not on the first but on the second day that he offered to accept the 35 per cent figure if Gandhi would promise to stay out of Ahmedabad labor disputes forever.

At any rate, Ambalal offered to settle for 35 per cent with an emphasis on "*this* time" and "only for *you*," but this was quite unacceptable to Gandhiji. At the same time Ambalal was shrewd enough to sense that if he gave the fast the connotation of a blackmail aimed at making him give in rather than at keeping the workers from giving up, the battle would be half won. He, therefore, insisted that, after all, the mill owners, too, had a gentleman's pledge to keep: 20 per cent and not a pice more.

In the meantime, the workmen came streaming to the ashram, and never was more work accomplished there in a few days. One of the leaflets, it will be recalled, had extolled the dignity of labor as such, and the workers knew or sensed that the "inner advance" which Gandhiji expected of them was the conviction that it is more important to keep a pledge and to suffer than to maintain ancient proprieties or to indulge in ancient avoidances. So now, many came and kept demonstratively busy about the place; and it is reported that the two children of the bourgeoisie, Shankerlal and Anasuya, deprived as they were of fasting with Gandhiji, took to carrying baskets of sand on their heads alongside the workmen in the hot sun.

In the late afternoon of the first day of the fast, Gandhiji waded back to the babul tree, where thousands, starving but newly inspired, awaited him. Gandhiji first assured the men and women from the Jugaldas Chawl that he was not angry with them. On the contrary, he and other would-be servants of India could learn only from the workers' criticism. The central problem was the pledge, and the willingness to beat starvation by doing other kinds of available work:

But what should I do to persuade you to maintain yourselves with manual labour? I can do manual work, I have been doing it, and would do so even now, but I do not get the opportunity for it. I have a number of things to attend to and can, therefore, do some manual work only by way of exercise. Will it behove you to tell me that you have worked on looms, but cannot do other physical labour? . . . When I came to know of your bitter criticism of me, I felt that, if I wanted to keep you to the path of dharma and show you the worth of an oath and the value of labour, I must set a concrete example before you. We are not out to have fun at your cost or to act a play. How can I prove to you that we are prepared to carry out whatever we tell you? . . . I am used to taking such pledges. For fear that people may wrongly imitate me, I would rather not take one at all. But I am dealing with hundreds of thousands of workers. I must, therefore, see that my conscience is clean. I wanted to show you that I was not playing with you.[123]

After this meeting, Gandhiji was persuaded by Anasuya to stay at her house in order to save himself further river-bed crossings and to preserve his strength. The next day, March 16, he apparently stayed there and attended to other irons already in the fire. He wrote a letter to the Governor of Bombay that if his pleas concerning the Kheda situation were ignored, he would advise the peasants "openly" not to pay land revenue. He owed the Governor this information, he added, because he had promised to warn him whenever he was contemplating an "extreme step." And he offered to come and see him immediately, if desired!

### Fifteenth Leaflet

He also wrote out leaflet fifteen, again signed by Anasuya for the sake of consistency, and therefore referring to himself in the third person. He now told the workers of the "taint" on his fast:

It is necessary to understand the motive and significance of Gandhiji's vow to fast. The first thing to remember is that this is not intended to influence the employers. . . . we shall be ridiculed if we accept 35 per cent granted out of pity for Gandhiji. . . . Even if fifty persons resolve to starve themselves to death on the employers' premises, how can the employers, for that reason, give the workers a 35 per cent increase if they have no right to it? If this becomes a common practice for securing rights, it would be impossible to carry on the affairs of society. . . . Gandhiji felt, that if he fasted, he would show through this how much he himself valued a pledge. Moreover, the workers talked of starvation. "Starve but keep your oath" was Gandhiji's message to them. He at any rate must live up to it. That he could do only if he himself was prepared to die fasting. . . . But they must rely on their own strength to fight. They alone can save themselves.[124]

But Gandhiji then became homesick for the ashram and *his* "family," and on March 16 he waded back over to the other side of the river again. There is every reason to believe that he needed the prayer meetings at the ashram as a setting for an honest appraisal of the situation. For during the days of his fast he underwent extreme mood-swings which, at one moment, permitted him to see his fast as a necessary step toward all-Indian leadership, and at another, as a betrayal of Satyagraha itself. As I pointed out at the beginning of this book when I justified my interest in the Event, the intensity of these feelings agreed ill with the tentativeness with which this whole episode is treated in the Autobiography as well as by some biographers. The reason for this treatment, we can now see, is identical with the paradox intrinsic to the Event itself. In trying to use his homeland as a platform from which to ascend to national leadership, he suspected he might have slipped into the muck of Bania bickering.

On March 17, early in the morning, a bit of music apparently intensified his need and willingness to make a confession to his "family"; and here is the heroic version of the Event:

It would make me very unhappy to miss the morning and evening prayers in the Ashram. . . . therefore, although it was Anasuyaben's express wish yesterday that I should stay on there, I insisted on coming over to the ashram. At a time like this, the music here has a very soothing effect on me. This is indeed the best occasion for me to unburden my soul to you. . . .

Then comes an evaluation of the extant leaders of India, similar to the summary appraisal of them in *Hind Swaraj*, and yet, one feels, more passionate; and this time, he refers to Russia, as well:

From the ancient culture of India, I have gleaned a truth which, even if it is mastered by few persons here at the moment, would give these few a mastery over the world. Before telling you of it, however, I should like to say another thing. At present there is only one person in India over whom millions are crazy, for whom millions of our countrymen would lay down their lives. That person is Tilak Maharaj. I often feel that this is a great asset of his, his great treasure. He has written on the inner meaning of the *Gita*. But I have always felt that he has not understood the age-old spirit of India, has not understood her soul and that is the reason why the nation has come to this pass. Deep down in his heart, he would like us all to be what the Europeans are. As Europe stands on top at present, as it seems, that is, to those whose minds are steeped in European notions—he wants India to be in the same position. He underwent six years' internment but only to display a courage of European variety, with the idea that these people who are tyrannizing over us now may learn how, if it came to that, we too could stand such long terms of internment, be it five years or twenty-five. In the prisons of Siberia, many great men of Russia are wasting their whole lives, but these men did not go to prison in obedience to any spiritual promptings. To be thus prodigal of one's life is to expend our highest treasure to no purpose. If Tilakji had undergone the sufferings of internment with a spiritual motive things would not have been as they are and the results of his internment would have been far different. This is what I should like to explain to him. . . . To give him first-hand experience of it I must furnish a living example. Indirectly, I have spoken to him often enough, but should I get an opportunity of providing a direct demonstration I should not miss it, and here is one.

Another such person is Madan Mohan Malaviya. . . . But although he is so holy in his life and so well informed on points of dharma, he has not, it seems to me, properly understood the soul of India in all its grandeur. I am afraid I have said too much. If he were to hear this, Malaviyaji might get angry with me, even think of me as a swollen-headed man. . . . I have this opportunity to provide him, too, with a direct demonstration. I owe it to both to show now what India's soul is. . . .

That a pledge once taken, at my instance, should be so lightly broken and that faith in God should decline means certain annihilation of dharma. . . . for ten thousand mill-hands to break faith with themselves would spell ruin for the nation. It would never again be possible to raise the workers' issues. At every turn they would quote this as an example and say that ten thousand mill-hands endured suffering for twenty days with a man like Gandhi to lead them and still they did not win. . . . Well, then to keep those ten thousand men from falling, I took this step. This was why I took the vow and its impact was electrifying. I had never expected this. The thousands of men present there shed tears from their eyes. They awoke to the reality of their soul, a new consciousness stirred in them and they got strength to stand by their pledge. I was instantly persuaded that dharma had not vanished from India, that people do respond to an appeal to their soul. If Tilak Maharaj and Malaviyaji would but see this, great things could be done in India.[125]

The very same day, Gandhi, with equal candor, gave the un-heroic version of the Event:

. . . [But I am also] aware that [this pledge] carries a taint. It is likely that, because of my vow, the mill-owners may be moved by consideration for me and come to grant the workers' [demand for] thirty-five per cent increase. . . . They would do so out of charity and to that extent this pledge is one which cannot but fill me with shame. I weighed the two things, however, against each other: my sense of shame and the mill-hands' pledge. The balance tilted in favour of the latter and I resolved, for the sake of the mill-hands, to take no thought of my shame. In doing public work, a man must be prepared to put up even with such loss of face.[126]

And indeed, it must have been on that day that Ambalal appeared with a compromise formula. Gandhiji answered by urging him to disregard his fast: it "gives me immense pleasure and need not cause any pain to anyone." He called the formula "foolishness to satisfy our conscience or our pride," and something which in the eyes of the simple-minded workers could only be regarded as "calculated deception." But he felt that he had no choice.

I should, therefore, prefer some other way, if we can find any. *If you want me to accept this, I will, but I won't have you decide the matter in haste.* Let the arbitrator meet us and come to a decision right now, and let us announce the wage fixed by him; that is, 35 per cent on the first day, 20 on the second and, on the third what the arbitrator decides. There is foolishness even in this, but things will be left in no doubt. The wage for the third day should be announced this very day.[127]

It is clear, 35 per cent on the first day was meant to keep the workers from feeling that they had broken their pledge; and twenty per cent on the second was to reassure the owners likewise. But how to guide the workers through the narrow straits between "deceptive foolishness" and "religious adherence to honor?"

### Sixteenth Leaflet

While Gandhi was undergoing both his fast and his agonizing conflict, the sixteenth leaflet was written (and signed) by Shankerlal Banker. His opening sentences speak for the man:

This is the first leaflet I write for you. I wish, therefore, to state at the very outset that my right to advise you is only nominal. I have not done any manual labour. I have not suffered the miseries that workers have to endure, nor can I do anything myself to remove that misery. Therefore I feel hesitant in giving advice on this occasion. But, even though I have done nothing for you in the past, it is my keen desire to do what I can hereafter according to my capacity. I write this with that desire.[128]

Otherwise he reiterated in his own words what had been stated in the other leaflets, emphasizing only the principle of negotiation which he hoped to work for, beyond this strike. And, indeed, he would keep his word.

At the prayer meeting of March 18, a tired, dejected, and ashamed Gandhiji announced the impending "solution." "My weak condition left the mill-owners no freedom," he said, reminding his audience of the simplest principle of justice—

namely, that nobody should be forced to sign his name to anything under duress. They would have met the workers' demands in full, had he insisted, but:

If I had done anything of the kind, I would have felt that I was breaking my fast by swallowing something most repulsive; how could I, who would not take even *amrit* [a drink of the gods, supposed to confer immortality] except at the proper hour, swallow such a thing?[129]

The oral simile may well prepare us for a deeply depressed discourse. He attempted to relieve the pressure with a bit of rough talk: "If an honest man finds himself surrounded on all sides by crooks, he should either turn his back on them or be as they are." But then his mind turned to sacred matters, to the Himalayas, the Vindhya mountains—and to Thoreau, whose poetic oratory he always mistook for a heroic life actually carried through.

When I compare my state with that of these illuminated souls, I am such a mere pigmy that I don't know what to say. To be sure, it is not as if I did not know the measure of my strength. But in the outside world it is esteemed much higher than it ought to be. Every day I discover so much of hypocrisy in the world that many times I feel I just cannot go on being here. At Phoenix, I often told you that, if one day you did not find me in your midst, you should not be surprised. If this feeling comes over me, I will go where you will never be able to seek me out. In that hour, do not feel bewildered, but go on with the tasks on hand as if I were with you all the time.[130]

It is this Gandhi, sad to the bone, who, in the afternoon marched and waded for the last time to the babul tree. To a crowd joyous over the end of the misery—a crowd joined by many prominent Ahmedabadis and by the Commissioner himself—he had only a low-key and cautionary address to offer. The settlement, he said, merely (and he obviously meant "barely") upholds the workers' pledge; but at least it forces the mill owners to accept the principle of arbitration. But, if the report of a local Gujarat newspaper is correct, he added: "I shall succeed in getting 35 per cent from the arbitrator"—a strange way for him to "accept the principle of arbitration." Here is the deal that was made:

On the first day, an increase of 35 per cent will be given in keeping with our pledge; on the second day, we get 20 per cent in keeping with the mill-owners'. From the third day till the date of the arbitrator's award, an increase of 27½ per cent will be paid and subsequently, if the arbitrator decides on 35 per cent, the mill-owners will give us 7½ per cent more and, if he decides on 20 per cent, we shall refund 7½ per cent.[131]

One hates to think of the mechanics of a refund under such conditions, and one joins, for a brief moment, those habitual anti-Banias who shudder derisively at the logic of the formula given on March 19 in the final leaflet:

We have accepted 35 per cent for one day deliberately as the best thing to do in the circumstances. "We will not resume work without securing a 35 per cent increase" may mean one of two things; one, that we will not accept anything less than a 35 per cent increase at any time and, two, that we will resume work with a 35 per cent increase, it being enough even if we get it just for a day.[132]

It is now fully understandable that Gandhiji concluded his speech to the mill hands that day with a remark both dejected and rejecting:

What I have brought for you is enough to fulfil the letter of the pledge, but not its spirit. Spirit does not mean much to us and so we must rest content with the letter.[133]

And then he formulated a warning which would be echoed many a time in later years when Gandhi would come to feel that what the masses at times could do for him, they could not be counted on to do for themselves:

After twenty years' experience, I have come to the conclusion that I am qualified to take a pledge; I see that you are not yet so qualified. Do not, therefore, take an oath without consulting your seniors. If the occasion demands one, come to us, assured that we shall be prepared to die for you, as we are now. But remember that we shall help you only in respect of a pledge you have taken with our concurrence. A pledge taken in error can certainly be ignored. You have yet to learn how and when to take a pledge.[134]

At that, Gandhi broke his fast before the hushed crowd. Other speakers followed. Even the Commissioner, who already was Gandhi's principal opponent in the Kheda situation, congratulated everybody and told the workers that as long as they followed Gandhi Saheb's advice and did what he told them, they

would fare well and secure justice. As he said this he undoubtedly hoped the peasants in Kheda were not listening in. But
then, the Ahmedabad workmen were probably not listening any
more either, because everybody felt that a parade was in order.
Gandhiji, together with Anasuya and Ambalal, was put in a
carriage, which on this occasion may even have been pulled by
the workmen themselves, although Gandhi disliked that kind of
honor. To Anasuya the workmen gave a red silk sari.

When the parade returned to what now had been named the
*Ek-Tek* Tree, the mill owners had carted enormous quantities of
sweets under its generous branches. But this proved to have been
unwise. As if to relieve a situation overloaded with words of
good will, the evening ended in confusion, because the beggars
of Ahmedabad crashed this party of owners and workers and
scrambled for the supply of sweets, much of which was trampled underfoot. This caused an embarrassing tension, for some
outsiders immediately believed that the workmen themselves
were behaving in this undignified way; however, when the intruders were identified as beggars, the honor of labor was restored, and the workers were invited to a more select gathering
on Ambalal's compound, where the salvaged sweets had been
taken. Deeply touched by the mill hands' trust, Gandhiji made
one more speech, at last awakening to the fact that all in all, this
had been a most remarkable struggle:

I have never come across the like of it. I had had experience of many
such conflicts or heard of them but have not known any in which there
was so little ill will or bitterness as in this. I hope you will always
maintain peace in the same way as you did during the strike.[135]

Gandhi concluded that the whole of India had reason to be
proud of the Ahmedabad workers.

The country had, to some extent, taken notice of the fast.
But, as a perusal of the major papers of that day shows, it was
nowhere reported as newsworthy. True, Annie Besant had
wired the mill owners, "Do not sacrifice a great man to a small
cause," probably not endearing herself to them with such a
formulation; and there had been much comment in informed

circles, which called his fast alternately "silly" and "cowardly" or, as Gandhi put it, "still worse." For the sake of these critics as well as that of all those readers who had never heard of the strike or the fast, Gandhi himself sent a lengthy summary of the whole struggle to the leading newspapers in India's largest cities. As I reported at the beginning of this book, this letter was relegated to the Letters-to-the-Editor column on page 12 of the *Bombay Chronicle* of March 27. It certainly invalidates any later attempts, even of the Mahatma himself, to disparage the Event; for he declares: "Perhaps I owe an explanation to the public with regard to my recent fast." And the letter is (for once) a document written, or at least corrected, in Gandhi's English.

I felt that it was a sacred moment for me, my faith was on the anvil, and I had no hesitation to rising and declaring to the men that a breach of their vow so solemnly taken was unendurable by me and that I would not take any food until they had the 35 per cent increase given or until they had fallen. A meeting that was up to now unlike the former meetings, totally unresponsive, woke up as if by magic.[136]

He then describes the ambiguities of his decision but concludes:

Whatever may be the verdict of friends, so far as I can think at present, on given occasions I should not hesitate in future to repeat the humble performance which I have taken the liberty of describing in this communication.[137]

And he ends with the characterization of Ambalal and Anasuya which I quoted at the beginning of this book:

I have not known a struggle fought with so little bitterness and such courtesy on either side. This happy result is principally due to the connections with it of Mr. Ambalal Sarabhai and Anasuyaben.

One can well see, however, that few individuals even among Gandhi's friends at that time were able to recognize the principles of a nonviolent struggle in a "domestic affair" which remained unpopular because of its obvious personal and economic ambiguities. And yet, great movements can begin with small moments, and if Gandhi cannot be said to have made a deep dent in the national affairs of India with this campaign of three weeks, he certainly came one step closer to his people, identifying his name now with the kind of saga which travels by word of mouth and reaches the vast constituency of the Indian masses, who in those days were almost totally untouched by the news which the press saw fit to print. Maybe in historical actuality the most important objective is to make one's encounters matter, whether at the time they seem big or small.

But by the time his letter appeared in the press, a fully recovered Gandhi had already chaired a meeting in Ahmedabad on the situation of indentured labor in the Fiji Islands, had on March 22 inaugurated the Kheda Satyagraha by addressing 5,000 peasants in Nadiad, and had traveled to Delhi to meet the Viceroy's Private Secretary in order to discuss the release of the Ali brothers, two prominent Muslim rebels. This, then, is the difference between a case history and a life-history: patients, great or small, are increasingly debilitated by their inner conflicts, but in historical actuality inner conflict only adds an indispensable momentum to all superhuman effort.

# CHAPTER
# V

# Aftermath

---

## 1. SATYAGRAHI AND SOLDIER

I MUST NOW REPORT an inglorious aftermath. Not that the Event
itself offers a glorious story: casting Ahmedabadis against one
another, it was largely a local show, like a rehearsal before a
provincial audience. This will become especially clear when we
look back on Ahmedabad from the first nation-wide Satyagraha
exactly one year later, on the Ides of March 1919. Then hundreds of thousands of Indians of all regions and religions would
be on the move; the British Empire itself would be the principal
counterplayer and world opinion the awed onlooker. But at least
Ahmedabad will prove to have been a real, a craftsmanlike rehearsal, in spite of a few devastating shortcomings such as earnest
rehearsals bring to light.

The Satyagraha involving peasants in Kheda was already in
preparation while Gandhi led the workers in Ahmedabad. And,
as we saw, only a few days after the fast, with a haste signifying
a long-delayed obligation and probably also a hope of leaving
the ambiguities of Ahmedabad behind him, Gandhi took over in
Kheda. Within these pages, we can treat this new campaign only
as an aftermath of Ahmedabad, for nothing short of a separate
book can do justice to any of Gandhi's campaigns. At the inception of each he suffered what he himself compared to the pains
of childbirth, and at the end of most he was not sure—as he was

never sure with his own children—that he had produced a worthy model of what such an enterprise should and could be. The original issue in Kheda was clear and simple enough: there, too, the monsoon of 1917 had been excessive and had caused widespread crop-failure in a district known for some prosperity in normal times.

The law provided that the payment of land revenue could be postponed or omitted in years when the crop was 25 per cent less than normal, and Gandhi had convinced himself that this was certainly the case in 1917. As president of the Gujarat Sabha, a body established to study and bring to the attention of the government the periodical hardships of the cultivators, he had advised the people of Kheda in January 1918 to suspend payment until the government could study the matter. The government, referring to Gandhi and his friends merely as "outside agitators," refused to accept their assessment of the crop and insisted on the payment of taxes in this "rich and fertile district," especially since they had good reason to attribute some of the rise in prices to grain speculation and war profiteering. The fact was that many of the more prosperous farmers could well afford to pay up, while others decidedly could not, and Gandhi saw in this situation an opportunity for the prosperous and educated to demonstrate their solidarity with the downtrodden and to help them overcome their fear of an officialdom which did not hesitate to confiscate and sell the land and cattle of those in arrears. On March 22, then, the Kheda Satyagraha was inaugurated with a pledge by all to suffer any consequences rather than pay all or part of the revenue and, of course, to do this with nonviolent restraint.

The matter dragged on almost three months, and only on June 6 could Gandhi announce the end of the struggle—an "end without grace" as he put it then and as he repeated in his Autobiography, because "a Satyagraha campaign can be described as worthy only when it leaves the Satyagrahis stronger and more spirited than they are in the beginning."[138] But it is clear that he missed such a spirited outcome not so much in the peasants as in the government. To the peasants the campaign did mark, he was sure, what was always more important than limited gains, namely, "the beginning of an awakening . . . the beginning of their true political education." But the government haughtily "granted" without any generosity in tone or spirit what it could have yielded so easily, namely, that small percentage of the revenue that was to come from the poorest, while it had secured the promise of the much larger amount now freely pledged by the prosperous farmers. Gandhi could not enthuse over this, although the peasants, of course, were delighted to have, for once, expressed themselves and resisted without penalty.

There is every reason to believe that, having demonstrated the feasibility of Satyagraha among both workers and peasants in his native Gujarat, Gandhi was eager for bigger tasks: "We want the rights of Englishmen, and we aspire to be as much partners in the Empire as the Dominions overseas. We look forward to a time when we may aspire to the viceregal office."[139] While he stuck to the local jobs with utmost devotion in detail and spirit, his imagination and his need for action suddenly seem to have been freed for national issues—freed, maybe also, from the last restraints of Gokhale's advice. But as he embarked on nation-wide ambitions, he was once more drawn into that strange complexity of emotions and ideas which had characterized earlier confrontations involving the necessity of fighting the British giant: he first had to offer his help and his succor to the parent body while it was in danger. In this gesture, at first, he did not deny a clearly ulterior motive.

As he wrote to the Viceroy[140] when accepting an invitation to a war conference in Delhi in April, while the Kheda matter was as yet unsettled:

I recognize that, in the hour of its danger, we must give—as we have decided to give—ungrudging and unequivocal support to the Empire, of which we aspire, in the near future, to be partners in the same sense as the Dominions overseas. But it is the simple truth that our response is due to the expectation that our goal will be reached all the more speedily on that account—even as the performance of a duty automatically confers a corresponding right. The people are entitled to believe that the imminent reforms alluded to in your speech will embody the main, general principles of the Congress-League Scheme, and I am sure that it is this faith which has enabled many members of the Conference to tender to the Government their whole-hearted co-operation.

The Congress-League scheme was a proposal for sweeping political reforms passed by both the Indian National Congress and the Muslim League in 1916, with the expectation of preparing self-government for India as an integral part of the Empire "at an early date—in full harmony with the British history and policy." But one cannot read the way Gandhi took hold of this precarious situation without judging him to be emotionally involved in a somewhat irrational manner. His companions as well as his counterplayers wondered at the time what was happening to him, and not a few questioned exactly what to him seem to have been above all doubt, namely, his consistency and his attachment to truth. Gandhi's *Collected Works* again permit us to follow his acute conflicts into their various dimensions—his relationship with friends and sons, as well as with the Viceroy; his mental and physical condition, as well as his speeches and actions. And in all these matters we are now prepared to recognize as typical some tensions and anxieties which haunted his search for the truth throughout his life, from his father's deathbed to his own death.

As Gandhi wrote to the Viceroy: "In fear and trembling I have decided as a matter of duty to join the conference." The Viceroy let him know by dictated letter that he neither understood nor believed in such fear and trembling. "Nor do I," the Viceroy's secretary added, gratuitously. But Gandhi continued to display an attitude half troubled and half challenging, and at the meeting established a precedent by saying in Hindi: "With a full sense of my responsibility, I beg to support the resolution" —the resolution calling for the immediate recruiting of 500,000 Indians for the British army. This was the first time, some say, that an Indian had officially spoken an Indian sentence in the presence of the King-Emperor's representative! But the content showed Gandhi to be an over-eager subject; and he could never obey without going all out in submissive and utopian sentiments:

If I could make my countrymen retrace their steps, I would make them withdraw all the Congress resolutions, and not whisper "Home Rule" or "Responsible Government" during the pendency of the war. I would make India offer all her able-bodied sons as a sacrifice to the Empire at its critical moment; and I know that India by this very act would become the most favoured partner in the Empire and racial distinctions would become a thing of the past.

On the other hand, he did not hesitate to re-interpret his own actions in Champaran and Kheda which, one may be sure, up to then had been of little concern to the Viceroy: "Champaran and Kaira affairs are my direct, definite, and special contribution to the war. Ask me to suspend my activities in that direction, and you ask me to suspend my life."[141] But he began immediately to state his conditions. First he exempted himself from the implications of recruiting in that "I personally will not kill or injure anybody, friend or foe." And then he committed his fellow Satyagrahis—at a price—to what he had exempted himself from: "Relief regarding the Kaira trouble . . . will also enable me to fall back for war purposes upon my co-workers in Kaira and it may enable me to get recruits from the district."[142] But so much did the Mahatma-on-the-rise now assume the posture of a uniformed subject of His Majesty, that he voluntarily submitted his "past record" to the Viceroy's secretary—meaning by his past record his military service!

I was in charge of the Indian Ambulance Corps consisting of 1,100 men during the Boer Campaign and was present at the battles of Colenso, Spionkop and Vaalkranz. I was specially mentioned in General Buller's dispatches. I was in charge of a similar corps of 90 Indians at the time of the Zulu Campaign in 1906, and I was specially thanked by the then Government of Natal. Lastly, I raised the Ambulance Corps in London consisting of nearly 100 students on the outbreak of the present war, and I returned to India in 1915 only because I was suffering from a bad attack of pleurisy brought about while I was undergoing necessary training.[143]

And finally, on that same day, he wrote to the Viceroy's secretary a letter of an almost perversely ingratiating nature:

I would like to do something which Lord Chelmsford would consider to be real war work. I have an idea that if I became your recruiting agent-in-chief, I might rain men on you. Pardon me for the impertinence.

The Viceroy looked pale yesterday. My whole heart went out to him as I watched him listening to the speeches. May God watch over and protect him and you, his faithful and devoted Secretary. I feel you are more than a secretary to him.[144]

The last and gratuitous sentence strengthens the impression that there has been a breakthrough of irrational filial devotion—an impression first created by Gandhi's expressed wish to offer all of India's able-bodied sons as a sacrifice to the Empire. Obviously, in suggesting that he be the endangered Empire's recruiting agent-in-chief, he comes close to presenting himself as the "only one available"; while he seems almost to envy the secretary's opportunity to be more than a secretary to the wan-looking Viceroy—and what else could this mean but a nursing son?

In the meantime, the father-and-son theme has been aggravated in the legitimate sphere of his own family—in fact, a catastrophic turn in Harilal's relation to his father may well have coincided with the personal turn in Gandhi's letter to the Viceroy's secretary. At any rate, the very next day Gandhi wrote a letter to Harilal, with all the abysmal and yet apparently unconscious ambivalence that we have come to take for granted. That Harilal, in turn, was out to get even with his moralistic father is all too clear by now. The letter refers to a con-game by which Harilal seems to have gotten himself and a business partner into legal difficulties. What must interest us are the themes which Gandhi, no doubt unaware of their vindictive impact, develops in his letter. "Everyone acts according to his nature"—a theme which confirms Harilal as a constitutional thief as it dooms him again as the victim of his father's sins. Harilal is then informed that his father has "done something very big in Delhi," a cruel emphasis at a time when the son has done something very petty. But the father does not let the son know what the big deal is—that the son can read in the papers or maybe hear from Mahadev if, indeed, the secretary has time to write to him. Mahadev (the father adds)

*has taken your place*, but the wish that it had been you refuses still to die. I would have died brokenhearted if I had no other sons. Even now, if you wish to be an understanding son *without displacing anyone who has made himself such to me,* your place is assured.[145]

This was on May 1. Two weeks later Gandhi had not as yet received any official encouragement to go ahead with his filial offer to the Empire; the vice-regal secretary had, in fact, sent the whole bewildering correspondence to Lord Willingdon, the Governor of Bombay. In the meantime, Gandhi made a quick trip to Bihar. There, according to an intelligence report sent to the government, the initial enthusiasm of 8,000 listeners in Patna "waned very low as his speech proceeded." Presenting himself as the government's devoted agent and yet also as a leader in Bihar, he advised his audience to raise a republican army and "to go along with him and to wherever the Government directed." A large number of people "quietly slipped away." On May 30, four weeks after his offer, Gandhi wrote to Willingdon's secretary again and was told bluntly that no conditions were acceptable for war work. Upon receiving a sharp retort from Gandhi on June 11, the secretary questioned "the propriety of admitting a contentious political discussion on a resolution expressing loyalty to His Majesty the King-Emperor," reminded Gandhi of his unconditional pledge, and referred to conditional pledges (such as Tilak's) as "only differing from an open refusal to cooperate by its lack of candour."[146] Gandhi swallowed the insult, later demanding from both Annie Besant and Jinnah an "emphatic declaration . . . in favor of unconditional recruiting." In the letter to Jinnah, there is a note of sick humor when he advocates that the Home Rule Leaguers should be told, "seek ye first the Recruiting Office and everything will be added unto you."[147]

This, in essence, is the very message which Gandhi as a recruiting savior now tried to bring to the peasants whom only a few months before he had exhorted to resist the government. So within a month, those same peasants in Kheda whom he had admonished to be nonviolent and gentlemanly even against the most brutal British officials saw the Mahatma come down the road again—this time to beg them to take up arms and become

British soldiers. They were dumbfounded. "We made you great!" they yelled at their leader (as Shankerlal recalls), "we helped you make Satyagraha work!—and see what you ask of us now." They not only refused to come and listen to him; they bluntly denied him transportation and food, so that he failed in his endeavor and eventually collapsed physically and mentally. But it was not only he who had thus lost "the touch": both Vallabhbhai Patel and Indulal Yagnik were listed as his co-operators in Recruiting Leaflet No. 1, which used the appalling logic of all recruiting schemes which sacrifice a given number of men for the common good:

There are 600 villages in Kheda district. Every village has on an average a population of over 1,000. If every village gave at least twenty men, Kheda district would be able to raise an army of 12,000 men. The population of the whole district is seven lakhs and this number will then work out at 1.7 per cent, a rate which is lower than the death rate.[148]

It is clear that by then Gandhi was, in a significant way "out of his mind," too far gone to take anybody's "no" for an answer. Even as he had to write to friend after friend week after week, that "So far I have not a single recruit to my credit," he worked only more desperately, until, indeed, he was "recruiting mad. I do nothing else, think of nothing else, talking of nothing else."[149]

On the very day when he wrote this clear confession of having lost control over himself, Gandhi fell ill with an extremely painful dysentery and high fever; and within a few days he dictated (for he would not be able to write or walk for months) that he was passing through the severest illness of his life. There was what one can only call a subdued fury about this illness, in all its extreme weakness and demonstrative meekness; for it was by no means clear whether he was dying from natural causes or from his refusal to accept any remedies but his own. Only after Ambalal and Saraladevi had come, toward the end of August, with a comfortable car to take him to their mansion, and a month later, on his insistence, to the ashram; and only after he had ceremoniously prepared his dying hour among the faithful ashramites did Anasuya insist on calling a "real" physician. The doctor told Gandhi bluntly that his pulse was entirely normal, and that he was suffering from a "nervous breakdown," attributable—as were all nervous breakdowns in those days—to exhaustion. This diagnosis was candidly admitted by the Mahatma himself, although even today the official *Collected Works* prefers to say that he was "at death's door." But what interests us today is not whether he really was or only imagined himself to be deathly ill. The question is what caused this man at that historical moment to become the living and suffering center of a conflict between two alternatives which had always existed in men's minds: seeking glory and immortality through killing and being killed, in the heroic defense of a territory or world-image deemed in mortal danger—and saving one's soul at the risk of losing one's life in extending even to the enemy the faith of human love. As Gandhi now noticed with horror and contempt, not one of his Satyagrahis refused to go to war because of a reluctance to kill: clearly, they simply did not wish to die.

And before long Gandhi uttered the fateful words:

> What we have taken as dharma is not dharma. We commit violence on a large scale in the name of non-violence. Fearing to shed blood, we torment people every day and dry up their blood. *A Bania can never practise non-violence.*[150]

One is in awe of such a sudden insight, especially if one has just tried to understand why the prophet *had* to make himself heard in his own country. Must he also learn what may be wrong with his message? Gandhi now took a new look at men who are different from Banias—Englishmen, Maharashtrians, Kshatriyas—and recognized something in his own nature and background which might make the inclination toward Satyagraha a very relative virtue. As he wrote to C. F. Andrews:

> When friends told me here that passive resistance was taken up by the people as a weapon of the weak, I laughed at the libel, as I called it then. But they were right and I was wrong. With me alone and a few other co-workers it came out of our strength and was described as satyagraha, but with the majority it was purely and simply passive resistance that they resorted to, because they were too weak to undertake methods of violence. This discovery was forced on me repeatedly in Kaira.[151]

Once he saw this, he recognized it "in depth." *Ahimsa*, he realized, had not been invented by meek or defenseless people, even as in Western civilization Puritanism was the way of life not of "repressed" people, but of essentially lusty ones: "*Ahimsa* was preached to man when he was in full vigour of life and able to look his adversaries straight in the face." It is touching to hear Gandhi, once he had let himself feel the appeal of the warrior's values, indulge in such racy thoughts as this outbreak against doctors when writing to a patient who had asked his advice:

But you can expect nothing but licensed murders from that most empirical of professions. Whenever I hear of your illness, I feel like shooting some doctor or other but my ahimsa comes in the way.[152]

Or, taking his clue from the daily lusty outcries of the washermen by the river, he would accept at least one of the instinctual bases of all aggression: "When washing clothes, we strike them but feel happy doing so because we know that this makes them clean."[153] One suspects, in fact, that Gandhi could come closest to an emotional acknowledgement of violence by way of the idea that one must violently rid oneself of what is hopelessly impure. He wrote to Devadas in the same week that his dislike of dirt was increasing, not diminishing. And the same impatience with the depraved and the cowardly—or with the *negative identity* of the merely defenseless—can be seen in the words spoken earlier at the very inauguration of his recruitment campaign on June 21 in Nadiad—a meeting attended by a thousand people:

It is essential that the country should come to be entrusted with her defense, that she should become capable of defending her people. We shall not be fit for swaraj till we have acquired the capacity to defend ourselves. That India should always have to depend on the British for her defense—this is her helplessness. To remove this is a sacred duty which we should first attend to.[154]

From this emotional base line, then, Gandhi began to see and spread the truth as he then felt it.

With this cowardly fear in us, how can we be the equals of the British? If I see a *Dhed* [Untouchable] and ask him to sit by my side and offer him something to eat, he will shake with fear. He will be my equal only when he feels sufficiently strong in himself to have no fear of me. To describe him as my equal (when he lacks such strength) is like adding insult to injury.

He comes to the conclusion that the problem of untouchability which pervaded India repeated itself on the level of the Empire, with all of India in the role of the Untouchables. "Besides," he added with the kind of candor which is both insightful and foolhardy, unless one is willing to stake everything on faith,

we shall learn military discipline as we help the Empire, gain military experience and acquire the strength to defend ourselves. With that strength, we may even fight the Empire, should it play foul with us.

And, in answer to Esther Faering's anxious questioning (typical for his friends' concern over his lack of consistency), he stated the case from the Satyagrahi's point of view:

What am I to advise a man to do who wants to kill but is unable owing to his being maimed? Before I can make him feel the virtue of not killing, I must restore to him the arm he has lost. . . . A nation that is unfit to fight cannot from experience prove the virtue of not fighting. I do not infer from this that India must fight. But I do say that India must know how to fight.[155]

I realize that I am quoting more than good pages of type can stand or a willing reader endure: but no paraphrasing could convey the superb clarity of Gandhi's new and surprising insights—insights indispensable in the history of militant non-violence:

I have come to see, what I did not so clearly before, that there is non-violence in violence. This is the big change which has come about. I had not fully realized the duty of restraining a drunkard from doing evil, of killing a dog in agony or one infected with rabies. In all these instances, violence is in fact non-violence. Violence is a function of the body. *Brahmacharya* consists in refraining from sexual indulgence, but we do not bring up our children to be impotent. They will have observed *brahmacharya* only if though possessed of the highest virility they can master the physical urge. In the same way, our offspring must be strong in physique. If they cannot completely renounce the urge to violence, we may permit them to commit violence, to use their strength to fight and thus make them non-violent. Non-violence was taught by a Kshatriya to a Kshatriya.[156]

*fit for being*

And to C. F. Andrews he conveyed that "War will be always with us. There seems to be no possibility of the whole human nature becoming transformed."[157]

And yet, this was written not only in a pre-atomic but also in a post-Darwinian era and therefore must be put into perspective, as I shall try to do in conclusion. More normative is the insight that man also fights for the territory he has staked out for himself, his place on earth, and his progeny,

> *Moksha* and ahimsa (are) for individuals to attain. Full practice of ahimsa is inconsistent with possession of wealth, land or rearing of children. There is real ahimsa in defending my wife and children even at the risk of striking down the wrongdoer. It is perfect ahimsa not to strike him but intervene to receive his blows.[158]

If this insight helped Gandhi see his own role more clearly, it also clarified for him his place in Indian culture—a culture which had cultivated martial virtues only in defined military castes and tribes. In a caste system, those "professionals" whose *dharma* and training found a wholeness in the discipline and in the ethics of organized warfare could protect those wider sections of the community who devoted themselves to the peaceable "maintenance of the world"—a world which could therefore be all the more sensual and indulgent. But in a nation of equal citizens not willing to leave their defense to a foreign power, the function of the various *dharmas* would have to be distributed differently; and the chances of a popular Satyagraha would be only as strong as the fearlessness of a representative section, not an élitist selection, of the citizenry.

We in the West have experienced, I believe, an analogous problem in the dispersed descendants of the Jewish nation, who became over-specialized in mercantile and intellectual pursuits, and, for centuries, had to leave their own defense to the warriors of the host countries, who often turned in sadistic disgust against those who could not or would not defend themselves. The mere suspicion that the Jews—who had let their God demand a covenant in the form of the foreskins of their maleness—would not fight because they could not fight, has, no doubt, been a strong factor in popular anti-semitism, which reached rock-

bottom when a strutting and vain breed of military criminals
took over a defeated nation in desperate fear for its own skin. In
view of the values which the Jews of the diaspora have come to
stand for, the belated proof that Jews *could* fight a national war,
may impress many as an historical anachronism. And, indeed, the
triumph of the Israeli soldiery is markedly subdued, balanced by
a certain sadness over the necessity to re-enter historical actuality by way of military methods not invented by Jews, and
yet superbly used by them. I would go further: is it not possible
that such historical proof of a military potential will make
peace-loving Jews everywhere better potential Satyagrahis?
And is it not also obvious that the advocates of Black Power
anywhere incorporate in its tenets, more or less fanatically, the
assumption that only the experience of disciplined rage provides the basis for true self-control? And they (as well as their
nonviolent brethren) find support in this aspect of Gandhi's
message:

It is a difficult thing to teach them to defend themselves and yet not be
overbearing. Till now, we used to teach them not to fight back if anyone
beat them. Can we go on doing so now? What will be the effect of such
teaching on a child? Will he, in his youth, be a forgiving or a timid man?
My powers of thinking fail me. Use yours. This new aspect of nonviolence which has revealed itself to me has enmeshed me in no end of
problems. I have not found one master-key for all the riddles, but it must
be found. Shall we teach our boys to return two blows for one, or
tolerate a blow from anyone weaker than themselves but to fight back,
should a stronger one attack them, and take the beating that might
follow? What should one do if assaulted by a Goverment official? Should
the boy submit to the beating at the moment and then come to us for
advice, or should he do what might seem best in the circumstances and
take the consequences? These are the problems which face us if we give
up the royal road of turning the other cheek. . . . One cannot climb the
Himalayas in a straight line. Can it be that, in like fashion, the path of
non-violence, too, is difficult? May God protect us, may He indeed.[159]

By the same token, it may be disastrous for any peace movement to indulge in contemptuous attacks on (or neglect of)
those men who are as yet obeying a military oath and are honoring the duty it stands for. And, indeed, the volume of the *Col-*

*lected Works* which contains Gandhi's letters, speeches, and notes of this period ends on an ominous and prophetic note: once it was clear that the virtues of disciplined violence could not be bypassed, then the future of a people like the Indians, the majority of whom had not learned to assume the identities based on organized warfare, would always be in danger of erupting into disorganized violence—or undisciplined nonviolence:

Today I find that everybody is desirous of killing but most are afraid of doing so or powerless to do so. Whatever is to be the result I feel certain that the power must be restored to India. The result may be carnage. Then India must go through it. Today's condition is intolerable.[180]

Whether or not the Mahatma ever integrated these insights with his basic beliefs, he has not ceased to amuse the intellectuals and the politicians, who demand that he be "consistent" in his utterances. But as we saw and will see again, such truth, to him, would have to be revealed in action and in conflict, not in textbooks. And in the long run, the martial Pathans, the only kind of Indians ever to attack him bodily (until the assassin struck) were to be the very people who would help him clarify this issue, when in the 1930's they accomplished the nonviolent occupation of Peshawar and the moral disarmament of some of the Empire's élite troops. Otherwise, Gandhi's consistency was always in the continuation of "the experiment": if he ruined many a seemingly perfect opportunity on the way, he also turned some totally hopeless situations into unheard-of successes. Within a few months, hardly recovered (or maybe recovering thereby), he was to spring into nationwide action, give masses of his countrymen a new kind of collective experience, namely, triumph by non-cooperation. Then again, he would face the danger of disorganized violence in a people ready neither for violence nor for nonviolence. In the meantime, the utterances of this period show how uninformed are the casual criticisms with which even some of the best educated among us declare Gandhi to be so one-sided and visionary as to be irrelevant; or to have been unable to foresee the riots which, indeed, eventually scarred the face of independent India. What, they ask, would he have done about or against the invasion of the Chinese hordes? Well, he *did* foresee disorganized violence in India and elsewhere; and as to the Chinese, nobody can know what a man of such complexity *would* have said or done.

But it is equally important to acknowledge that he did not envisage a possible triumph of Satyagraha on a national or international scale with a naive "peace of mind," or, indeed, without severe symptoms of inner conflict. To deny this by declaring him only physically exhausted as his adherents do would seem to do an injustice to the stature of the man. He himself does not mind reporting as a "nervous breakdown" what others make out to be a physical crisis followed by recovery. All that it was, too; but is it not high time to do away with the categorical constructs of purely physical, mental, or spiritual disturbance when we speak of the inner struggles of one of the wholest of men and one of the most miraculously energetic—most energetic, in fact, when inspired by the very momentum of recovery from temporary self-doubt and inactivation?

## 2. PATIENT AND MAHATMA

GOING BACK once more to August 1918, let us retrace, then, Gandhi's subjective view of his illness before we sketch his recovery. It must interest a clinician that Gandhi in all his preoccupation with hygiene could be as obstinate and as foolish as any patient—or, indeed, as many a physician—in the conviction of being in the possession of a medical formula for himself.

Today I am too weak to get up or walk. I have almost to crawl to reach the lavatory and I have such griping pain there that I feel like screaming. Though in such pain, I am very happy indeed. I am getting a vivid idea of what well-deserved, immediate punishment can be. I am sure my pain will subside at a quarter to six. . . . I shall be my normal self in three or four days.[161]

As fate would have it, he received, at this moment of physical debility, the decision handed down by the arbitrator, Professor Dhruva, in the Ahmedabad wage-dispute. It was, of course, 35 per cent—and Gandhi spends a few lines acknowledging it: "I have read your reward. The workers were waiting for it as people do for the rains and now they will have peace. I, too, was awaiting it. Although they have been getting 35 per cent [anyway] I believed your award would greatly strengthen their position."[162] This acknowledgment, however, almost disappears between two long paragraphs devoted to the diagnosis of his illness. The first begins with the sentence "Here is an exact description of what I have been through," the second with "I must tell you the cause of my ailment." One must remember here Gandhi's continuing passion for nursing. Only a few days before the outbreak of his illness he had written to another patient, C. F. Andrews:

If you cannot have a nurse like me, who would make love to you but at the same time enforce strict obedience to doctor's orders, you need a wife who would see that you had your food properly served, you never went out without an abdominal bandage and who would not allow you to overworry yourself about bad news of the sickness of relatives. But marriage is probably too late. And not being able to nurse you myself I can only fret.[163]

Such a man cannot easily admit that he may not understand what ails him, and so, for weeks and months, he must repeat his nosological formula with the same clinical righteousness. As is already clear, however, the correctness of his self-diagnosis is based on a moral-medical nosology and suggests a moral cure for the medical problem: the dysentery is a punishment, and the cure is the full recognition and joyful acceptance of it. But, as one often wonders in the case of an ailing moralist, a punishment for whom? One must recognize here also that a sick man (or woman) is never alone in India. Can one fathom what ambivalent punishment Gandhi inflicted on Kasturba by making *her* fret while he was racked with unbearable pains and became totally incapacitated by weakness? And he had clearly blamed her for the illness and even the immorality of falling ill; a decade later he would remember the details in his Autobiography:

There was some festival that day, and although I had told Kasturbai that I should have nothing for my midday meal, she tempted me and I succumbed. As I was under a vow of taking no milk or milk products, she had specially prepared for me a sweet wheaten porridge with oil added to it instead of *ghi*. She had reserved too a bowlful of *mung* for me. I was fond of these things, and I readily took them, hoping that without coming to grief I should eat just enough to please Kasturbai and to satisfy my palate. But the devil had been only waiting for an opportunity. Instead of eating very little I had my fill of the meal. This was sufficient invitation to the angel of death. Within an hour the dysentery appeared in acute form.[164]

It had been Kasturba, then, who had tempted his palate, his palate had invited the devil, and the devil had opened the door to the Angel of Death. Kasturba could hardly be expected to look happy, but Gandhi described her looks, too, with an ambivalent twist:

I simply cannot bear to look at Ba's face. The expression is often like that on the face of a meek cow and gives one the feeling, as a cow occasionally does, that in her own dumb manner she was saying something. I see, too, that there is selfishness in this suffering of hers; even so, her gentleness overpowers me and I feel inclined to relax in all matters in which I possibly may.[165]

All this time, however, Kasturba's "dumb" mind was working furiously in the name of all the milk-giving creatures of this earth and alas, she would before long find the very solution which defeats the great man's suicidal vow.

In the meantime, however, his righteous combination of diagnostic formula and moral posture permitted the patient to maintain a rectitude which must have been all the more upsetting (for they could not admit how infuriating it was) to those who saw him so utterly wretched. "My mind," he would say and dictate again and again, "my mind is at peace," and, looking back on weeks of pain and weakness, "my mind has never been disturbed." The self-centeredness in these announcements comes once more to the fore in a letter to Harilal, at about the halfway mark of the illness. To add to all his troubles, Harilal's wife had died, and foremost in his and his family's mind was the question of what to do with the children. But his father can only praise his own kind of inner peace:

The only thing that pleases me is to be ever occupied with activity of the utmost purity. It is no exaggeration to say that I experience wave after wave of joy from the practice of self-restraint which such work requires. One will find true happiness in the measure that one understands this and lives accordingly. If this calamity puts you in a frame of mind in which such happiness will be yours, we may even regard it as welcome.[166]

But then, something "gives." And it is in a letter to the same son, Harilal,[167] that a month later the father can for once admit to despair:

One cannot pray to God for help in a spirit of pride but only if one confesses oneself as helpless. . . . As I lie in bed . . . I am filled with shame by the unworthiness of my mind. Many a time I fall into despair because of the attention my body craves and wish that it should perish. From my condition, I can very well judge that of others. I shall give you the full benefit of my experience; you may accept what you can.

And he urges him to come, adding

If you cannot give vent to your feelings before me, before whom else can you do so? I shall be a true friend to you. What would it matter if there should be any difference of opinion between us about any scheme of yours? We shall have a quiet talk. The final decision will rest with you.

Here, one can see Satyagraha at work domestically, as it were; and, indeed, Professor Swaminathan, the editor of the *Collected Works*, suggests significantly that this illness also taught the Mahatma how to practice Satyagraha toward his own body as "an autonomous entity." Is it only when he learns some non-violence toward his own body that the Mahatma can be nonviolent toward the son, the resented offspring of that often despised "autonomous entity"? Be that as it may; in passing we should note that even a great man may be only as great as the degree of despair that he can allow to himself—and admit to a few others.

And now we come, again, to this strangely ambivalent man's most ambiguous defense and weapon against himself: his vows. By "again" I mean that we have followed him as a youth through a period in a foreign country, when a triple vow had to serve him (to stretch a metaphor somewhat) as a spiritual navel cord, providing maternal strength and yet also hindering his full autonomy. Later again he had to save the essence of his Vaishnavite commitment by a vow: he would not drink milk, because of the cruelties inflicted on cows in order to extract the last drop of milk from them. As he wrote during his illness to a pleading medical friend:

> The milk problem with me is not quite so simple as you have stated it. It is not regard for the calf that in my illness prevents me from taking milk, but I have taken a definite *vow* not to take milk or its products even in illness and I feel that it is better to die than to break a vow knowingly and deliberately taken. Every consequence that I am taking today was before me when I took the vow.[168]

But now the maternal woman with the "dumb" cow eyes had a moment of feminine genius. Around the turn of the year 1919 Gandhi was transferred to a hospital in Bombay for an operation on his painful boils—a symptom that had plagued his father. Either the worried surgeon asked him what really was the nature of his vow, or Kasturba suddenly blurted out this question in the surgeon's presence. At any rate, she added that to her knowledge he had never sworn not to drink *goat*'s milk; and he immediately saw the chance to please everybody and yet to remain true to his vow, for, indeed, goats had not crossed his mind when he had taken the vow. He hesitated, and his explanation reveals again the will to power which, all along, had been the more or less conscious counterpart of his self-abnegation:

> My conscience does not, for a single moment, cease asking me, "Why all this labour?" "What would you do with life?" "What is it you would so much exert yourself to reform?" When I think of the plight of Germany's Kaiser, I feel as if a great Being were playing with us as we play with cowries.[169]

But after 24 hours he took some goat's milk, and soon two goats were kept busy being gently milked under his fatherly eye. His young disciples wondered why he could not just as well scrap a vow altogether, and his "dear child" Esther wondered, in her Lutheran simplicity, whether God would mind the abandonment of such a vow more than He would resent being made a partner to it in the first place. But the Mahatma continued to feel righteous in drinking his goat milk and keeping his vow, too— except that now two entirely new and previously unthinkable words appeared in conjunction with "vow," namely, "liberal" and "interpretation." He would even go so far, he wrote,

as to maintain that the fact of big loopholes having been left in both my vows is evidence of their utter sincerity. . . . In regard to the vow concerning milk, the goat has proved a mother to me. There are many instances in our scriptures of vows having been kept, though interpreted in a restricted sense. I understand the significance of these instances better now.[170]

The relief from the vow, together with an immediate improvement of his local and general condition, seems to have aroused in Gandhi an almost manic mirth. He had already referred to his four-legged friend as "Mother Goat." He now bestowed the name "Brother Milk" on a naturopathic healer whom all along he had tolerated as an advisor because he was a "crank like me." He again made fun of the "snappy temper" that was soon fully restored to victorious Ba. And he wrote a lovely letter to Harilal, describing how he was playing mother to his orphaned children and how they were playing around and on his bed. He added: "The scene reminds me of your childhood."

On February 24, 1919, almost on the anniversary of the Ahmedabad campaign, Gandhi composed a new Satyagraha pledge. It was made against a law that (like the law which had committed him to resistance in South Africa) was to be known by the name "Black Act"; and again he claimed to have learned of it accidentally "by the papers." This was the Indian Government's anti-sedition law, the Rowlatt Act, which summarily disposed of the civil rights of convicted and suspected rebels. The pledge was signed by a few Ahmedabadi friends who happened to be around (Vallabhbhai Patel and Anasuya among them) and was sent, as usual, to the major papers. Shankerlal Banker, the Mahatma records, "took up the agitation in right earnest, and for the first time I got an idea of his wonderful capacity for organization and sustained work."[171] And the pledge, to their joint surprise, *struck the religious imagination of an angry people*," as the Mahatma later wrote to Lord Montagu. Gandhi now recovered rapidly. But he would retain for years an incapacity to address mass meetings standing. As he had done years before, he complained—in terms reminiscent of Arjuna's panic—of a heavy throbbing of his whole frame. Nevertheless, two weeks later, Gandhi was on his way to Madras to gain the support of his Madrasi friends as well; and there he conceived—he says, in a half-dream—of a nationwide demonstration with which the Gandhian era in Indian history can be said to have begun in earnest.

One evening, having discussed the proposed act with his friend and host, the Madrasi Rajagopalachari (once prominent as a leader of Congress) Gandhi fell asleep with indignant thoughts: and waking up somewhat earlier than usual (which must have been early, indeed) "in a twilight condition between sleep and consciousness" the idea "broke upon me . . . as if in a dream" that the whole country should observe a *hartal* (that is, a closing down of all places of business and work) and "observe the day as one of fasting and prayer."[172] The date was first fixed for March 30 but was subsequently changed to April 6. This was not duly registered in Delhi, which fasted and demonstrated on March 30, not without bloody incidents that could have served as warning for what was to follow elsewhere. It speaks for Gandhi's sudden power that he could wire a pontifical dispensation to the effect that "it will be unnecessary for Delhi to fast again next Sunday." That day, however, was called Black Sunday all over India, and the Mahatma later mused:

But who knows how it all came about? The whole of India from one end to the other, towns as well as villages, observed a complete *hartal* on that day. It was a most wonderful spectacle.[173]

As dreamlike as all this sounds in the Autobiography, the basic strategy of Satyagraha established in Ahmedabad was now unfolded on a national scale. There was, again, *a pledge:*

Being conscientiously of opinion that the Bill known as the Indian Criminal Law Amendment Bill No. 1 of 1919 and the Criminal Law Emergency Powers Bill No. 2 of 1919 are unjust, subversive of the principles of liberty and justice, and destructive of the elementary rights of an individual on which the safety of India as a whole and the State itself is based, we solemnly affirm that in the event of these Bills becom-

ing law and until they are withdrawn, we shall refuse civilly to obey
these laws and such other laws as the committee to be hereafter appointed may think fit and we further affirm that in the struggle we will
faithfully follow truth and refrain from violence to life, person or
property.[174]                    / & cowardice

The selection and preparation of the Satyagrahis had to depend
on religious conscience and tradition: those who were to engage
in civil disobedience proper had to give the assurance that they
had purified themselves by a 24-hour fast. A clear *ultimatum*
was sent to the Viceroy; it was to go into effect if and when the
bill became law. The *civil action* planned and taken was circumscribed as a closing of all shops—an event which in countries like
India changes the character of daily life in that it brings to a halt
the social life pulsating in and around and between small stores,
markets, stands, and peddlers' wagons. And Sunday, it must be
remembered, was not a normal closing day for either Hindus or
Muslims. The *hartal* was to announce a future disobedience to
the Rowlatt Bill only; but an action committee had the power to
select other and minor laws to be disobeyed immediately, such as
the salt tax law and, most of all, ordinances against proscribed
literature. A newspaper called *Satyagrahi* was to be published
by Gandhi and Banker without a license. Books were to be sold
illicitly on street corners; they included the life of Kemal Pasha,
Gandhi's adaptation of Ruskin's *Unto This Last*, as well as *The
Story of a Satyagrahi* (Gandhi's paraphrase of Plato's *Death of
Socrates*), and extensive extracts from *The Duty of Civil Disobedience* by one Henry Thoreau, "school master of Massachusetts."[175]

The Mahatma—now so named on leaflets cleared by him—
took part in the Bombay demonstration, and the *Bombay Chronicle* expressed no further doubt as to what he was going to gain
by getting involved:

Long before the sun had risen, the Back Bay foreshore was humming
and throbbing with life, for it was full of people. From an early hour in
the morning, people had come to Chowpatty to bathe in the sea. . . . It
was a Black Sunday, and the day's programme had to begin with a
purifying sea bath. . . . Mr. M. K. Gandhi was one of the first arrivals at

Chowpatty with several volunteers, and by 6:30 A.M., or earlier he had taken his seat on one of the stone benches with about a hundred satyagrahis around him. . . . As the day advanced people kept pouring in on the seashore. Every new arrival took his bath in the sea first and then came and sat round Mr. Gandhi. In this manner the crowd swelled and swelled until it became one huge mass of people. Mr. Gandhi, as the time for the meeting on Chowpatty sands neared, moved in that direction, where he was shortly joined by Mrs. Sarojini Naidu, Mr. Jamnadas Dwarkadas, Mr. Horniman and others. There were also about twenty-five ladies. It was a splendid sight at this time, for the whole Sandhurst Bridge swarmed with people and there must have been approximately one and a half lakhs [150,000] of people. . . . All communities were represented there—Mohamedans, Hindus, Parsis, etc., and one Englishman.[176]

The Mahatma's speech started with the declaration that he wanted to say as little as possible on "this occasion, which is perhaps the most solemn of our lives for most of us . . . and could be made more eloquent if we could do away with speeches." Yet, his talk was lengthy and defensive. For the accident of Delhi's premature demonstration (whether it had been due to sloppy communication or to some design on the part of the Delhi city bosses) had demonstrated the fact that even if the Mahatma could restrain the now large core of his followers, he could not restrain the mob on the fringes or the panicky harshness of the authorities in the face of an unfathomable mass-spirit. The Mahatma's suggestion that the governmental authority should endeavor to regulate the masses through their natural leaders, rather than "overawing" the people by displaying Gurkhas with pointed rifles and naked knives, was the kind of obvious demand which few in power ever understand.

More colloquially the Mahatma took the time, sitting there on one of the stone benches, to tell the crowd about the Police Superintendent in Durban who in 1897 alone with a dozen constables had dispersed peacefully (and guilefully) a crowd of 6,000 Europeans determined to lynch "one who, I believe, had given no cause for it." But he soon diverted his criticism from the Delhi police to his followers, who had noisily protested the arrest of the first Satyagrahis.

It is arrest and imprisonment that we seek by civil disobedience. It therefore ill becomes us to resent either. And it was wrong not to disperse. In this movement, it is open to satyagrahis to disobey only those laws which are selected for the purpose by the committee contemplated in the Pledge. When we have acquired habits of discipline, self-control, qualities of leadership and obedience, we shall be better able to offer collective civil disobedience, but until we have developed these qualities, I have advised that we should select for disobedience only such laws as can be disobeyed by individuals. . . . And then when we have reached the necessary standard of knowledge and discipline, we shall find that machine-guns and all other weapons, even the plague of aeroplanes, will cease to afflict us.[177]

Some resolutions were passed by acclamation, among them

a simple prayer to the Secretary of State for India that he will be pleased to advise His Majesty the King-Emperor to disallow the Revolutionary and Anarchical Crimes Act and an equally simple prayer to H. E. the Viceroy that he will be pleased to withdraw Rowlatt Bill No. 1.

Then a procession was formed to proceed to the Madhav Baug Temple for prayer. The volunteers had to form a cordon around the leaders (this being the first but not the last occasion on which the Mahatma was in danger of being lovingly crushed to death), and the enormous mass began moving slowly from the seashore to the temple compound. There, the Mahatma offered prayers and requested the crowd to disperse quietly— which they did. On the evening of that day, an army of volunteers began to sell forbidden literature on the streets; the Mahatma himself later proudly remembered having peddled one of his own books for fifty rupees. We can discern once more a trace of Moniya in the letter Gandhi sent to the Police Commissioner:

Laburnum Road, Gamdevi, Bombay

Dear Mr. Griffith,                                        April 7, 1919
    May I send you a copy of the unregistered newspaper issued today by me as its Editor?

Yours sincerely,<br>M. K. Gandhi[178]

But then, Gandhi had as yet every reason to rejoice: initial reports of violence in Calcutta were disavowed in a wire which reported instead that all shops and markets had closed down on

Satyagraha Sunday, and that a crowd of 200,000 had demonstrated and dispersed peacefully—with only a few minor incidents.

On April 8, however, Gandhi left for Delhi and the Punjab, and a crescendo of disturbances ensued. His mission was one of peace, but the authorities felt sufficiently provoked to arrest him before he reached Delhi and to force him to return to Bombay, where he would be freed if he promised to remain in the Presidency. Not yet aware of the possible consequences, he was, as usual, delighted to be arrested. He never felt happy in making life harder for others unless he could put in a demonstration of self-suffering. On the train back to Bombay and under custody, he wrote to Esther Faering:

I am perhaps the happiest man on earth today. I have during these two months experienced boundless love. And now I find myself arrested although I bear no ill will to anybody and although I am the one man who can today preserve the peace in India as no other man can. My imprisonment therefore will show the wrongdoer in his nakedness. And he can do me no harm for my spirit remains calm and unruffled.[179]

The phrase "I am the one man who . . ." suggests more strongly than ever the politician-savior's *hybris*, for which he would again pay dearly. For the very news of his arrest caused widespread disturbances; and, more specifically, the (false) rumor of Anasuya's arrest caused the workers in Ahmedabad to riot.

This the Mahatma did not know as yet. He did, in fact, expect it so little that on visiting the Police Commissioner on his arrival in Bombay, he as much as vouched for the Ahmedabadis. The Commissioner, already in the possession of initial reports, tried to warn him that the police officers were in a better position than was the Mahatma to judge the effect of his teaching on the people. "They will follow their natural instinct," he said. Gandhi proudly replied that he would be surprised as well as pained if there were disturbances, of all places, in Ahmedabad. But there were; and Gandhi rushed back to his home town only to find it in the grip of martial law. A British officer (off duty) had been brutally murdered, and the population had indulged in "mad incendiarism," which, one way or another, resulted in the death of nearly fifty people, mostly Indians. Gandhi asked for permission to hold a mass meeting at the ashram, where he took even the guilt of the fringe mob upon himself:

Now, instead of going to Delhi, it remains to me to offer satyagraha against our people, and as it is my determination to offer satyagraha even unto death for securing the withdrawal of the Rowlatt legislation, I think the occasion has arrived when I should offer satyagraha against ourselves for the violence that has occurred. And I shall do so at the sacrifice of my body, so long as we do not keep perfect peace and cease from violence to person and property.[180]

He started a three-day fast and asked every Ahmedabadi to contribute to a fund for the families of the Englishmen who had been killed or wounded. There were no more disturbances, but Gandhi, now in possession of similar news from elsewhere, made up his mind to suspend the whole campaign "temporarily." He did so on April 19, 1919. He still was rightly convinced that violence had erupted not as a direct result of disciplined Satyagraha but because of the collision of nervous police and fringe mobs. Yet he acknowledged that the Satyagraha movement needed a harder and more disciplined core of expert volunteers: his, he said, had been a "Himalayan miscalculation."

*Was* the campaign, then, a "failure," and *did* the "initiative pass to the opposition" as should never, never happen to the leader of a Satyagraha? Not, I would think, from a long-range point of view. By his very suspension the Mahatma kept the initiative and demonstrated his ability first to mobilize and then to call a halt to a national movement of unprecedented grandeur. In contrast, the government, in displaying nervous as well as naked force, lost face in an irretrievable way and helped to precipitate the eventual fate of colonialism in India. And as the  central problem of an age is often highlighted quite unintentionally by a zealot creating an "ism" that will live in infamy (as did Senator Joseph P. McCarthy in our time), there suddenly appeared "Dyerism" on the scene in the person of a British brigadier general. In ten minutes of tensest history, he established a model for cold military murder which would show up colonialism at its most brutal.

On April 13, 1919, General Dyer had forbidden the citizens of Amritsar, the Sikh holy city in the Punjab, to gather in public assembly. A few thousand, many without knowledge of the ordinance, had gathered unarmed, as previously planned, in the ruins of a public garden named Jallianwalla Bagh, which was surrounded by high walls permitting access and exit only through a few narrow gates. The general had ordered his men to fire on "the mob." All of this is well known as the "Massacre of Jallianwalla Bagh." But the word *massacre* suggests the hot carnage of a multitude by a rampant soldiery or mob. It does not convey the cold-bloodedness of this event, which was rather in the nature of mechanized slaughter. The soldiers stood on somewhat higher ground only 150 yards from the first row of an entirely unarmed mass of over 10,000 people crowded into one corner of the walled-in grounds. Twenty-five of the general's soldiers were equipped with rifles; the general ordered them to start shooting without warning, and the men fired 1600 shots in ten minutes, killing 379 persons and wounding 1,137. Thus, they wasted less than one tenth of their shots in this shooting gallery.

I present these well-known details because one must try to envisage what has become of man as a military, or maybe one should say a *policing mind*, in the possession of mechanized weapons. Not that one could entertain the idea of a society altogether without police or should indulge in treating policemen as a separate species, like henchmen. They are only the willing puppets serving an overwhelming propensity of human nature, namely, brutal righteousness. I cannot make this point any stronger than by reminding the reader that, in my open letter to the Mahatma, I had reason to accuse him, too, of implicit violence in his policing and sentencing of the bathing children in South Africa. For we all have become obedient to the policing mind; and once we have learned to reduce "the other"—*any* living human being in the wrong place, the wrong category, or the wrong uniform—to a dirty speck in our moral vision, and potentially a mere target in the sight of our (or our soldiery's) gun, we are on the way to violating man's essence, if not his very life.

What, then, could the Bombay police chief have meant by the "instinct" of the masses? And what kind of instinctual aberration explains the policing mind that massacres with righteousness as well as with accuracy? That we must discuss in the conclusion of this book. In the meantime, we may say that to have faced mankind with nonviolence as the alternative to these aberrations marks the Mahatma's deed in 1919. In a period when proud statesmen could speak of a "war to end war"; when the super-policemen of Versailles could bathe in the glory of a peace that would make "the world safe for democracy"; when the revolutionaries in Russia could entertain the belief that terror could initiate an eventual "withering away of the State"—during that same period, one man in India confronted the world with the strong suggestion that a new political instrument, endowed with a new kind of religious fervor, may yet provide man with a choice.

A PERUSAL of the Indian and overseas press of the years 1918 and 1919 provides a fascinating spectacle of the way in which Gandhi's name, now increasingly synonymous with "the Mahatma," came to the attention of a charisma-hungry world; but this would be a subject for a separate book. Maybe most prophetic was Gilbert Murray's reference, in the *Hibbert Journal* of London in July 1918, to "a battle between a soul and a government." Gandhi, he predicted, would be "a dangerous and uncomfortable enemy, because his body, which you can always conquer, gives you so little purchase upon his soul."

In the 1918 Delhi session of the Indian National Congress, the President, Pandit Malaviya, had lauded an imposing list of scientists, poets, lawyers, judges, patriots, and public men, before he added "and a servant of humanity like Mr. M. K. Gandhi and soldiers who have rendered a good account of themselves in all the theatres of war."[181] When a year later the then president of Congress, the elder Nehru, first referred to

Gandhi as "Mahatmaji,"[182] he only made official the fact that Gandhi and his movement had sunk deep and lasting roots into the Indian masses. In 1920, finally, the Mahatma assumed political leadership. Up to then he had almost mockingly insisted on declaring himself a professional political expert only in certain subsidiary jobs like collecting money and drafting resolutions; but now Congress gave him a mandate to revise the whole organization, from setting up party cells in the villages to redefining the functions of the grand committees. For he was now truly the "only one available" for the political job of anchoring the independence movement in the spirit of the Indian masses. And he could now live and function as a whole man: spiritual leader as well as astute lawyer and crafty politician, and this not in search of the insignia of power, but of a position above all defined jobs—a position which would permit him to combine *caritas* with "rationally effective political behavior."[183]

# PART FOUR

# The Leverage of Truth

# CHAPTER

# I

# Homo Religiosus

AT THE TIME OF the Ahmedabad strike, Gandhi was forty-eight years old: middle-aged Mahatma, indeed. That the very next year he emerged as the father of his country only lends greater importance to the fact that the middle span of life is under the dominance of the universal human need and strength which I have come to subsume under the term *generativity*. I have said that in this stage a man and a woman must have defined for themselves what and whom they have come to care for, what they care to do well, and how they plan to take care of what they have started and created. But it is clear that the great leader creates for himself and for many others new choices and new cares. These he derives from a mighty drivenness, an intense and yet flexible energy, a shocking originality, and a capacity to impose on his time what most concerns him—which he does so convincingly that his time believes this concern to have ema-nated "naturally" from ripe necessities. And historians must agree, for they are able only to study the confluences in what has come to pass and to be recorded—unless, of course, they come to the conclusion (and not a few have done so) that India, if not much better, would certainly not be much worse off if the man had never lived. And, indeed, compared with the charis-matic men of his time, Gandhi and his "inner voice" may seem more moodily personal, more mystically religious, and more formless in ideology than any of them. There is nothing more consistent in the views of Gandhi's critics than the accusation of inconsistency: at one time he is accused of sounding like a socialist, and at another a dreamy conservative; or, again, a pacifist and a frantic militarist; a nationalist, and a "communalist"; an anarchist and a devotee of tradition; a Western activist, and an Eastern mysticist; a total religionist and yet so liberal that he could say he saw God even in the atheist's atheism. Did this polymorphous man have a firm center?

If, for the sake of the game, I should give his unique presence a name that would suit my views, I would call him a *religious actualist*. In my clinical ruminations I have found it necessary to split what we mean by "real" into that which can be known because it is demonstrably correct (factual reality) and that which feels effectively true in action (actuality).[1] Gandhi absorbed from Indian culture a conception of truth (*sat*) which he attempted to make actual in all compartments of human life and along all the stages which make up its course. I will in the next section make the most of the claim that the Mahatma (in spite of his enmity toward all erotism) was a mighty good bodily specimen—as is attested in motion pictures which show him to be so much more agile and of one piece than most men seem to be.

At the same time, he was as actual an Indian as can be imagined, aware that the great majority of his country's massive population was held together only by an ancient culture which, even if disintegrating, was all there was for India to rely on in the face of irreversible modernization. As an Indian, he had been born a Bania, and it was as a Bania and a Gujarati that he entered on the fateful path toward an all-Indian Mahatmaship. But while he learned to utilize craftily what was his first professional identity, namely, that of a barrister English style, and while he then became a powerful politician Indian style, he also strove to grasp the "business" of religious men, namely, to keep his eyes trained upon the all-embracing circumstance that each of us exists with a unique consciousness and a responsibility of his own which makes him at the same time zero and everything, a center of absolute silence, and the vortex of apocalpytic participation. A man who looks through the historical parade of cultures and civilizations, styles, and isms which provide most of us with a glorious and yet miserably fragile sense of immortal identity, defined status, and collective grandeur faces the central truth of our nothingness—and, *mirabile dictu*, gains power from it.

Gandhi's actualism, then, first of all consisted in his knowledge of, and his ability to gain strength from, the fact that nothing is more powerful in the world than conscious nothingness if it is paired with the gift of giving and accepting actuality. It is not for me to say what this power *is*; yet obviously it demands the keenest of minds and a most experienced heart, for otherwise it would be crushed between megalomania and self-destruction. As for the rest of mankind, I have an inkling that our response to such a man rests on the need of all men to find a few who plausibly take upon themselves—and seem to give meaning to—what others must deny at all times but cannot really forget for a moment. Freud, in one of his "economic" moods, might well have said that, psychologically speaking, such men save others not so much from their sins (this Freud would not have claimed to know), but from the fantastic effort *not* to see the most obvious of all facts: that life is bounded by not-life.[2]

Indian culture has (as have all others) made out of this special mission of saintly men a universal and often utterly corrupt institution, and Gandhi was well aware of the fact that the Mahatmaship could type him to the point of in-actuality. He considered it all the more incumbent upon himself to make his spiritual power work in political realities—for which he brought along both a specific giftedness and, as we saw, favorable identifications. I think the man was right who said that Gandhi, when he listened to his inner voice, heard the clamor of the people. It may be just this alliance of inner voice and voice of mankind which must make such a man at times insensitive to those closest to him by familial bond.

Swaraj in the sense of home-rule *and* self-rule was Gandhi's "way": if the power of actuality—as we now may add—is the mutual maximization of greater and higher unity among men, then each must begin to become actual by combining what is given in his individual development and in his historical time. Gandhi, I think, would make his own those pronouncements of Luther which I once singled out as the essence of religious actualism: *Quotidianus Christi adventus*—Christ comes today; *via dei est qua nos ambulare facit*—God's way is what makes us move; *semper oportit nasci, novari, generari*—we must always be reborn, renewed, regenerated; *proficere est nihil aliud nisi semper incipere*—to do enough means nothing else than always to begin again. Thus, out of the acceptance of nothingness emerges what can be the most central and inclusive, timeless and actual, conscious and active position in the human universe. We have seen that Gandhi was never too proud to find universal meaning in petty circumstances, for he knew that one must build on the values of one's childhood as long as they are revalidated by experience, until one perceives a wider truth which may make them relative or obsolete. Thus Gandhi could be and remain a Jain—a religion which, of course, provides ritual choices in a multiplicity of images and values—and yet could also absorb some of the essence of other, all other, religions. By the same token, he could live in symbiosis with the technology of his time and yet comprehend and exploit the fact that some such symbolic and pragmatic item as the spinning wheel could dramatically activate in hundreds of thousands of localities what was at the time not at all ready for industrialization.

Here, as in many other aspects of his life, the appearance of inconsistency is only a function of the critics' confusion in regard to elusive ends and self-fulfilling means. For it is in the daily means that *dharma*, practicality, and ethics coincide, wherefore the devotee of the hum of the charkha is not necessarily further removed from actuality than is he who feels vitalized by the clang of industrial activity. If each worker continues with full attention to the mood and the style of his activity, and as long as this activity lifts him above otherwise fallow or regressive potentials, he adheres to the Gandhian dictum that means are "ends-in-the-making" or "ends in process."[3] A "true" man, then, will not remain fixated on either means or ends for their own sake. He will not permit himself or others to use foul means with the illusory justification that their continuance "for a little while longer" will end in a utopian future when the truth will at last become the universal means—whereupon the world will forever after be free for democracy, or free for communism, or free for the stateless society, or whatever. What is true now will, if not attended to, never be true again; and what is untrue now will never, by any trick, become true later. Therefore I would interpret, and interpret with humility, the truth-force of the religious actualist thus: to be ready to die for what is true now means to grasp the only chance to have lived fully.

The religious actualist, however, inevitably becomes a religious innovator, for his very passion and power will make him want to make actual for others what actualizes him. This means to create or recreate institutions, and it can mean the attempt to institutionalize nothingness. The Hindu concept of the life cycle, as we saw, allots a time for the learning of eternal concerns in youth, and for the experience of near-nothingness at the end of life, while it reserves for the middle of life a time dedicated to the "maintenance of the world," that is, a time for the most intense actualization of erotic, procreative, and communal bonds: in this period of life, adult man *must* forget death for the sake of the newborn individual and the coming generations. But the middle-aged do need all the more the occasional man who can afford to remember, and they will travel regularly and far to partake of his elusive power. We have seen how deeply Gandhi at times minded having to become a householder, for without his becoming committed to a normal course of life by child marriage, he might well have been a monastic saint instead of what he became: politician and reformer with an honorary sainthood. For the true saints are those who transfer the state of householdership to the house of God, becoming father and mother, brother and sister, son and daughter, to all creation, rather than to their own issue. But they do this in established "orders," and they create or partake in rituals which will envelop and give peace to those who must live in transitory reality.

Actuality, however, is by no means a mere denial of nothingness. As I indicated when discussing the Hindu life cycle, actuality is complementary to nothingness and, therefore, deeply and unavoidably endowed with the instinctual energy and the elemental concern of generativity. Thus, men and women in middle age are "assigned" by instinct and custom a time to forget death so that they may maintain the life of their own kind. Here is the origin of one kind of "greatness," the greatness of founding fathers who stake out a territory and sanction its conquest; the greatness of leaders who sanction the killing of those led by other kinds of leaders; and the greatness of young heroes who get killed in so killing. Here also is the origin of all those mutual differentiations into dogmas and isms which combine larger and larger human communities in power spheres providing more inclusive identities. But alas, each such consolidation lives off its exclusiveness and becomes a new example of a *pseudo species*.

Religious presence, however (while often allied with temporal power) has an affinity to the experience of women, who in their hereness and practical religiosity weave together in the chores of daily life what really "maintains the world," and who—while heroes court death—can experience death as an intrinsic part of a boundless and boundlessly recreative life.

Inept as all such talk is, it may at least suggest a fair approach to what is most problematic in Gandhi. To be ascetic in the sense of Hindu *Brahmacharya* is not just a matter of not being active sexually or of cutting off one's masculinity; it is a matter of stepping outside of the daily consolidation and maintenance of what the two sexes create and take care of together, united in an illusion made inescapably and brilliantly real by each child.

But the middle-aged leader is also burdened and burdens others with cares more profound and more tragic than is the usual lot. His idiosyncratic choices may come to create concerns greater than he and his followers can really promise to take care of in their lifetimes. For he must sanction the initiative of a committed following and an irreversibly united multitude: but who will sanction him, the sanctioner, and all that he has generated, originated, promised, at a time of life already more than half lived and yet already totally committed? Thus men like St. Augustine, Gandhi, and Freud write their great introspective works—*The Confessions, My Experiments with Truth, The Interpretation of Dreams*—in middle age and at the threshold of lonely greatness.

We have traced in Gandhi's life the father-son theme—which these men and others like them pursue with almost monotonous guiltiness in their diaries, autobiographies, and self-analyses. We saw this theme erupt like a play within a play in the letter in which the middle-aged Gandhi tells his son of a dream in which the son had done to him what he once had done to *his* ailing father. And we saw it again in the middle-aged man's filial surrender to the "pale" Viceroy. No doubt, both in relation to his sons and to the few men who *could* represent a father to him in his mature years, the Mahatma was highly ambivalent. But such ambivalence is not merely an expression of a sense of guilt telling grown-up Oedipus "I told you so"; in the case of a charismatic leader (as, indeed, in that of King Oedipus) it belongs intrinsically to the ceremonial role held by him who is forced by fate to usurp a position imposed on him, more or less against his will, by the charisma-hungry masses. Here it will not do to treat the data as if they had emerged from the treatment history of a patient significantly inhibited in his perception of the real and in his participation in the actual. We must see what is symptomatic of a "great" man's conflicts in the context of their actuality in the historical period which chooses to crown and to crucify him. And with all his mood-swings and confessions, Mahatma Gandhi could, for a moment in history, make his inner voice consonant with the trend of human history and—we shall come to that—evolution.

Who could deny then that Gandhi was "a man"? However, he was an Indian man engaged in politics but aspiring to saintliness. We were able to follow the infantile and juvenile antecedents of a deep conflict between phallicism and saintliness, and between paternal power and maternal care. But just because Gandhi was so free in providing us with conflictful memories as well as with confessions of "unmanly" aspirations, we must be sparing with our interpretations; for in his revealed life the abnormal and the supernormal vie with such disarming frankness that whatever we could diagnose as his neurosis simply becomes part of his personal *swaraj*, the home ground of his being—and a man must build on that.

I would add that in such a man, and especially in an innovator, much phallic maleness seems to be absorbed in the decisive wielding of influence—and in a certain locomotor drivenness. He must always be on the move, and he must be moving others along, an often excessive need which is only counterpointed, but never diminished, by a corresponding need to be moved by a higher inspiration—*qua mulier in conceptu* (like a woman in the act of conception), as Luther said unhesitatingly. To conceive, obviously, is the all-inclusive word for such moods and periods.

But I wonder whether there has ever been another political leader who almost prided himself on being half man and half woman, and who so blatantly aspired to be more motherly than women born to the job, as Gandhi did. This, too, resulted from a confluence of a deeply personal need and a national trend, for a primitive mother religion is probably the deepest, the most pervasive, and the most unifying stratum of Indian religiosity. Gandhi was able, in deep sorrow, to have engraved on a stone dedicated to the memory of Maganlal that the latter's death had "widowed" him; and Shankerlal did not mind telling Gandhi, who in jail had made him pray at dawn and spin for hours in the daytime: "The worst mother-in-law could not be as tough with her daughter-in-law as you are with me." Gandhi would answer (proving Shankerlal's point): "You will appreciate it later." But the feminine imagery seems to have come naturally. There has been much talk, of course, of Gandhi's love of home spinning, which—no matter what it had been in days past and was to be in the days of national khadi—was traditionally women's work. All such talk, however, would be countered by Gandhi with the simple admission that yes, he aspired to be half a woman, even as he had countered Churchill's slurring remark about the naked fakir with the assertion that yes, he wanted to be as naked as possible. He undoubtedly saw a kind of sublimated maternalism as part of the positive identity of a whole man, and certainly of a *homo religiosus*. But by then all overt phallicism had become an expendable, if not a detestable matter to him. Most men, of course, consider it not only unnecessary, but in a way, indecent, and even irreverent, to disavow a god-given organ of such singular potentials; and they remain deeply suspicious of a sick element in such sexual self-disarmament. And needless to say, the suspicion of psychological self-castration becomes easily linked with the age-old male propensity for considering the renunciation of armament an abandonment of malehood. Here, too, Gandhi may have been prophetic; for in a mechanized future the relative devaluation of the martial model of masculinity may well lead to a freer mutual identification of the two sexes.

THIS is a clinician's book, and for the sake of speculating on the eventual fate of Gandhi's maternalism and, indeed, bisexuality, I must now briefly mention that item from his very last years which is often and eagerly referred to in conversational gossip, East or West, and usually with a slur such as "You know, of course, that Gandhi had naked girls sleep with him when he was an old man."[4] The most authoritative account of the events leading to this story is given in Nirmal Bose's *My Days with Gandhi*,[5] and I have had an opportunity to discuss the matter with him. Considering the personages involved, however, I doubt that the story will ever be fully told.

As far as I can make out, two circumstances are condensed in the story. For one, on her deathbed, Kasturba had asked her husband to take her place as a mother to an orphaned young relative named Manu; and he had taken this role rather seriously, being concerned, for example, with the girl's physical development, and having her sleep on a mat at the foot-end of his own mat and later, on occasion, "in his bed"—whatever that designa-

tion may mean in sleeping arrangements which include neither
bedsteads nor doors. The marked maternalism governing this
relationship was later acknowledged in the very title of the
young woman's memoir: *Bapu, My Mother*.[6]

This young girl, however, does not seem to have been the
central figure in the major crisis which caused such unrest
among Gandhi's friends. This occurred in the very last phase of
Gandhi's life when the Mahatma was 77 and 78 years old, and
when in Lear-like desperation he wandered among the storms
and ruins of communal riots which seemed to mark an end of
any hope of a unified India. At night he at times suffered from
severe attacks of shivering; and he would ask some of his middle-
aged women helpers to "cradle" him between them for bodily
warmth. This some suspicious companions thought to go beyond fatherly or motherly innocence; and, in fact, some of his
best friends parted ways with him when Gandhi made things
immeasurably worse by claiming publicly that by having (sometimes naked) women near him at night he was testing his ability
*not* to become aroused. This implied, of course, proving to
himself by implication that he *could* be. This explanation is
based on a deeply Indian preconception concerning seminal continence and mental potency. And, indeed, "If I can master this,"
the Mahatma is said to have remarked, "I can still beat Jinnah"—
that is, prevent the partition of India. All this confounded the
question as to whether the whole arrangement expressed a senile
and eccentric self-testing, a belated need for younger women,
or, indeed, a regression to an infantile need for motherly
warmth. It could well have been all of these.

My comparison with Lear indicates how I, for one, would
study such a story: as one of old age despair, characterized, of
course, by the conflicts life had not settled. Lear, a widower, also
wanted to be reassured (and reassured excessively, as his youngest child told him) that his daughters loved and honored him:
thus did the king try to secure his immortality as a father and a
king. As for an old man's need for warmth, one may think of
another king who "was old and stricken in years" and who,
although covered at night with many clothes, "gat no heat."

So they sought for a fair damsel throughout all the coasts of Israel, and found Ab-i-shag a Shu-nam-mite, and brought her to the king.

And the damsel was very fair, and cherished the king, and ministered to him: but the king knew her not.                          I Kings I:3, 4

The method employed here even has a name: shunamitism; and it is said to have been also cultivated, long before King David, by the kings of northern India.[7] Gandhi, however, was not a king; and it was not enough for him to say that he knew these women not. His denial was not enough for him, because he apparently had to prove, to the last, that he was master of all his impulse life, and it was not enough for others who insisted to the bitter end that he prove, or forfeit, what *they* called sainthood.

The whole episode, as Bose brilliantly recognized at the time, points to a persistent importance in Gandhi's life of the theme of motherhood, both in the sense of a need to be a perfect and pure mother, and in the sense of a much less acknowledged need to be held and reassured, especially at the time of his finite loneliness. In this last crisis the Mahatma appears to have been almost anxiously eager to know what those who had studied the "philosophy" of that doctor in Vienna might say about him,[8] although he probably could do little with the interpretation offered by one of his friends, namely that his shivering was an orgasm-equivalent. Bose's main objection to the whole episode was well-taken: the women had too little choice either in being involved or in having their actions publicized, and the general tension was setting them against one another.

As to the Mahatma's public private life, all we can say is that here was a man who both lived and wondered aloud, and with equal intensity and depth, about a multiformity of inclinations which other men hide and bury in strenuous consistency. At the end, great confusion can be a mark of greatness, too, especially if it results from the inescapable conflicts of existence. Gandhi, one may conclude from all the parental themes we have recounted, had wanted to purify his relationship to his father by nursing and mothering him; and he had wanted to be an immaculate mother. But when, at the end, he was defeated in his aspiration to be the founding father of a united India, he may well have needed maternal solace himself.

BUT how about the Mahatma's followers? As I have indicated, he skillfully selected them for particular kinds of functions, often diagnosing with psychological acuity the identity conflicts of our witnesses, who met him in the rebellious days of their twenties and were attracted to him to the point that their lives fused, in variable degree, with his. The degree, I would judge, often depended on their willingness to sacrifice sexual and social freedom to the communal rules of the ashram. Those who escaped such commitment can now discuss the Mahatma more freely than those who did not, but they often do so in order to rationalize their escape; the real "inmates" almost never express ambivalence, although Gandhi himself was wont to recognize it teasingly. But surely, the reader will surmise, they must have told me, directly or indirectly, about the emotional and irrational concomitants of such discipleship. And it is true that the psychoanalyst in me was not so subdued by the amateur historian that I was without curiosity about the motivational patterns these men and women may have shared. But here the question arises whether one has a right, methodologically and ethically, to lay bare data pointing to the unconscious motivations of trusting informants who have tried to be of help in the reconstruction of an historical event. A number of informants shared with my witnesses a certain propensity to tell me of memories, dreams, and daydreams that haunted them. Such data would be offered during a drive through such traffic as nearly incapacitated my "third ear," or during meals when I could and would not reach for writing paper, and sometimes as confidences offered, in my presence, to my wife. Whether on my part a certain professional propensity for attracting confidences was involved here, I could not know; but I am reasonably sure that such data emerged in a mood of re-evoking the Mahatma's image, which, in turn, awakened memories of more complex emotional involvements. Varied as these moments were, it soon became clear that they fell into two groups of themes. The first was *a deep hurt* which the informant had inflicted on one of his parents or some guardian (uncle or aunt) in such a way that the memory had become a kind of curse; and we have seen how determinedly Gandhi helped some of his early followers to sever already frayed bonds. The second category is an obsessively intense wish *to take care* of abandoned people or animals, paired with a strong sense of identification with all fatherless and motherless creatures who have strayed too far from home.

All this "accidental" material combined with other data available to me in creating a certain conviction that all these informants harbor a sense (maybe unconscious, maybe un-verbalized) of having vastly outdistanced their childhood loyalties, and with these, their personal *dharma*, by serving a man who had the power to impose his *dharma* on his contemporaries—a very special kind of guru who would make radical and total use of an age-old emotional (and once well institutionalized) necessity for finding a second, spiritual father. And I would think that the inner conflicts which lead a young person to such an unconventional leader, and to acceptance of him, come to include a deep ambivalence toward that leader. As we saw, Gandhi sought out his followers with a determination tempered only with diplomatic reserve, and he did not hesitate, as it were, to take over the spiritual parentage of these young people. Gandhi, of course, always wanted to be sure that an applicant could be expected to do some essential thing really well, but he also demanded a potential of total devotion in his future followers. From a man with high academic qualifications, for example, he demanded to know only whether he would be willing "to become a scavenger." Scavenging included what in America we subsume under the word "dirty work," but it also literally meant cleaning latrines. In the name of truth and in the service of India, however, they had to accept what was his own family's plight, namely, that he belonged to all—and to none.

These young people, then, highly gifted in a variety of ways, seem to have been united in one personality "trait," namely, an early and anxious concern for the abandoned and persecuted, at

first within their families, and later in a widening circle of intensified concern. At the same time, they were loyal rebels: loyal in
their sorrow, determined in their rebellion. All this they offered
Gandhi, displaying a wish to serve, which was determined as much
by personality as by tradition. Gandhi's capacity both to arouse
and to squelch ambivalence must have been formidable; but he
put these men and women to work, giving direction to their
capacity to care, and multiplying miraculously both their practical gifts and their sense of participation.

Followers, too, deserve a formula such as was suggested in
Part I for the recorder or reviewer of history or life history.
Whatever motivation or conflict followers may have in common
as they join a leader[9] and are joined together by him has to be
studied in all the complementarity of

1. their personal lives, that is
   a. the moment when they met the leader, their state of
      mind, and their stage of life;
   b. the place of that moment in their life history, especially
      in lifelong themes transferred to the leader;
2. their communities, insofar as these are relevant to their
   search for an identity by participation, that is
   a. their generation's search for leadership
   b. traditional and evolving patterns of followership.

As to the last point, Gandhi, as we saw, was a master not only in
the selection and acquisition of co-workers, but also in assigning
them to or using them in all manner of different tasks and ways
of life—from the position of elected sons and daughters in his
ascetic settlement to that of revolutionary organizers all over
India and of aspirants for highest political power, including the
prime ministership, for which he "needed a boy from Harrow."

But any explanation, psychoanalytic or other, of how followers became singly what they proved to be together, is
relative to—well, to the historical moment. The first Satyagrahi
was, of course, unique in the manner of his ascendance and
comparable only with equally unique individuals. His followers,
however, were characterized primarily by the fact of having

found this particular unique man among their contemporaries at a crucial moment in their own lives as well as in history—and of having been selected by him. My data (unless the data should prove to be "typically Indian") may offer a fleeting glance into the mutual assimilation of motives which might take place in a self-chosen group making history together.

# CHAPTER

# II

# The Instrument

## 1. TACTICS

WE HAVE REPORTED Gandhi's saying that God appears to you not in person but in action. But this also means that the full measure of a man—and that includes his unconscious motivation—can never be comprehended in isolation from his most creative action. What, then, is the essence of the social tools which Gandhi created?

Here I will roughly follow Joan Bondurant's indispensable treatment in her *Conquest of Violence*, which analyzes six Satyagraha campaigns in a fashion both scholarly and compassionate. If I do not fully accept either her discourse or her conclusions, it is, I believe, because she writes as a political scientist, whereas I must come to some psychological conclusions. Neither of us (she would agree) can hope to do more than approximate the meaning which Satyagraha had for its originator, his first followers, and the Indian masses. And both of us must restate these meanings in the terms of our disciplines and our days in the West: the truth (Gandhi would tell either of us) can only be revealed in the kind of appraisal which is *our* action. Satyagraha purports to be a strategy which depends, every minute, on the unmistakable experience of something as evasive as "the truth." I have tried to trace what truth had come to mean to Gandhi, throughout his development, in order to fathom what it may have meant to him in a given action; and even then the interpretation of his meaning was bound by our own imagery and terminology. If this seems too elusive even to attempt to formulate, I will ask the reader in how many connotations he has used the term "reality" throughout his life, or "virtue," or "health," not to speak of "identity"—all terms which serve to characterize the essence of a man's being and action.

*Sat*, we are told, means "it is." We can come closer to "what 'is' " only by asking further: in comparison with what, where, and when? In comparison with what might have been or what should be, or with what only seems to be or is only felt to be? Thus "what is" is obviously relative to any era's world-image, and to the methodologies which determine what questions are considered important and are asked relevantly. Yet, for each individual, "what is" will also depend on his personal way of facing being in all its relativity—relative to an absolute Being who alone is truth, or relative to non-being, or relative to becoming. Gandhi commits himself only to "the relative truth as I have conceived it," but he also clings firmly to the dictum that only insofar as we can commit ourselves on selected occasions "to the death" to the test of such truth in action—only to that extent can we be true to ourselves and to others, that is, to a joint humanity. This seems to call for an altogether rare mixture of detachment and commitment, and for an almost mystical conflux of inner voice and historical actuality. And in spite of the fact that it opens up wide every opportunity for self-deceit and the misuse of others, Gandhi, "in all modesty," considered it his mission to lead his contemporaries into "experimental" action. As he wrote to C. F. Andrews:

I have taken up things as they have come to me and always in trembling and fear. I did not work out the possibilities in Champaran, Kheda or Ahmedabad nor yet when I made an unconditional offer of service in 1914. I fancy that I followed His will and no other and He will lead me "amid the encircling gloom."[10]

Yet there is no reason to question the fact that the sudden conviction that the moment of truth *had* arrived always came upon him as if from a voice which had spoken before he had quite listened. Gandhi often spoke of his inner voice, which would speak unexpectedly in the preparedness of silence—but then with irreversible firmness and an irresistible demand for commitment. And, indeed, even Nietzsche, certainly the Mahatma's philosophical opposite, claimed that truth always approached "on the feet of doves." That is, the moment of truth is suddenly there—unannounced and pervasive in its stillness. But it comes only to him who has lived with facts and figures in such a way that he is always ready for a sudden synthesis and will not, from sheer surprise and fear, startle truth away. But acting upon the inner voice means to involve others on the assumption that they, too, are ready—and when Gandhi listened to his inner voice, he often thought he heard what the masses were ready to listen to. That, of course, is the secret of all charismatic leadership, but how could he know it was "the truth"? Gandhi's answer would be: Only the readiness to suffer would tell.

Truthful action, for Gandhi, was governed by the readiness to get hurt and yet not to hurt—action governed by the principle of *ahimsa*. According to Bondurant "the only dogma in the Gandhian philosophy centers here: that the only test of truth is action based on the refusal to do harm."[11] With all respect for the traditional translation of *ahimsa*, I think Gandhi implied in it, besides a refusal not to do physical harm, a determination not to violate another person's essence. For even where one may not be able to avoid harming or hurting, forcing or demeaning another whenever one must coerce him, one should try even in doing so, not to violate his essence, for such violence can only evoke counter-violence, which may end in a kind of truce, but not in truth. For *ahimsa* as acted upon by Gandhi not only means not to hurt another, it means to respect the truth in him. Gandhi reminds us that, since we can not possibly know the absolute truth, we are "therefore not competent to punish"—a most essential reminder, since man when tempted to violence always parades as another's policeman, convincing himself that whatever he is doing to another, that other "has it coming to him." Whoever acts on such righteousness, however, implicates himself in a mixture of pride and guilt which undermines his position psychologically and ethically. Against this typical cycle, Gandhi claimed that only the voluntary acceptance of self-suffering can reveal the truth latent in a conflict—and in the opponent.

A few years ago I had occasion to talk on medical ethics to a graduating class of young doctors and found myself trying to reinterpret the Golden Rule in the light of what we have learned in clinical work, that is, in the encounter of two individuals as "unequal" as a therapist and a patient.[12]

I suggested that (ethically speaking) a man should act in such a way that he actualizes both in himself and in the other such forces as are ready for a heightened mutuality. Nothing I have read or heard since has dissuaded me from the conviction that one may interpret Gandhi's truth in these terms. In fact, Gandhi made a similar assumption when he viewed Satyagraha as a bridge between the ethics of family life and that of communities and nations.

Bondurant concludes that the "effect" of Gandhi's formulation was "to transform the absolute truth of the philosophical *Sat* to the relative truth of ethic principle capable of being tested by a means combining non-violent action with self-suffering."[13] The truth in any given encounter is linked with the developmental stage of the individual and the historical situation of his group: together, they help to determine the *actuality*, i.e., the potential for unifying action at a given moment. What Bondurant calls "veracity," then, must have actuality as well as reality in it, that is, it depends on acting passionately as well as on thinking straight; and acting passionately would include acting upon and being guided by what is most genuine in the other. Truth in Gandhi's sense points to the next step in man's realization of man as one all-human species, and thus to our only chance to transcend what we are.

I have attempted to sketch the whole configuration of actualities which led to Gandhi's choice of Ahmedabad as the setting for the Event: the compulsion coming from the Mahatma's individual past and from his cultural tradition as well as from the situational attraction as presented by Ambalal and Anasuya. Gandhi later had reason to repudiate this beginning, but not because any other place on earth would have been more suitable; for origins are inescapable. As to the reality of the situation, Gandhi always made his inner voice "hold its breath" for a while in order to give him time to study the facts; but the sum of the facts consisted not only of the statistics which proved the textile workers right, it also included the over-all political and economic situation which governs public opinion. The goal, in Ahmedabad, was 35 per cent—an increase considerable enough to be of help to the workers, moderate enough to be borne by the industry and to be tolerated by the public, and enough of a compromise to be symbolic. The objective was eventually reached. But it probably could have been reached with less spectacular means, sealed with no more than an announcement on the factory's bulletin board, and a notice in the local press. But the wider objective was that of establishing a method which would prove applicable to other social and national settings, even as in the local milieu it was to improve permanently the relation of each participant to himself (honor), to all others (cooperation), and to a common God (truth). All this, then, depended on stringent conditions which Bondurant summarizes under *rules*, a *code of conduct*, and certain orderly *steps*. Here I must select a few combinations.

As we saw, the essential preliminary steps in any of Gandhi's campaigns were an objective investigation of facts, followed by a sincere attempt at *arbitration*. Satyagraha must appear to be a last resort in an unbearable situation which allows for no other solution and is representative enough to merit a commitment of unlimited self-suffering. It, therefore, calls for a thorough *preparation* of all would-be participants, so that they may know the grievances as factually true and join in the conclusion that the agreed-upon goal is both just and attainable. But they must also be sure of being on the side of a truth which transcends all facts and is the true rationale for Satyagraha. Gandhi's helpers had to be convinced of all the basic propositions, and sufficiently so that they could promise to abide by the nonviolent code. In Ahmedabad, Gandhi was sure that not only the local mill workers, but workers anywhere in the world should refuse to accept conditions such as were then acute, even as he was sure that a man in Ambalal's position should not be permitted (because he should not permit himself) to insist on the defeat of the workers. But he also "picked" Ambalal because, in all his intransigence, Ambalal knew that Gandhi was right, and he respected his sister for standing up for reform—against him, her brother.

But to continue in a more general vein: in any campaign the widest *publicity* or (if one wishes) agitation was necessary in order to induce the public either to intervene in advance, or to provide public pressure in support of the action to be taken. That action, in fact, had to be *announced* in all detail in advance, with a clear *ultimatum* binding to all, and yet permitting the resumption of arbitration at any stage of the enfolding action—an arbitration, that is, conducive to face-saving all around. Therefore, an *action committee* created for this purpose would select such *forms of non-cooperation*—strike, boycott, civil disobedience—as would seem fitting as the *minimum force necessary to reach a defined goal:* no quick triumph would be permitted to spread the issue beyond this goal, nor any defeat to narrow it. The quality of such fitness, however, would vastly transcend the question of mere feasibility: for it would encompass *issues* which were at the same time central to the *practical* life of the community and *symbolic* for its future—as was for example, the land around a peasant's homestead in Champaran, or the right of Untouchables in a given locality to pass over a temple road on the way to work, or the right of all Indians to take from their sea, without paying taxes to a colonial government, the salt necessary to make their food palatable and their bodies resistant in the heat of their subcontinent.

We can see from this once-revolutionary list how the choice of issues in Gandhi's India has changed the legal conscience of mankind in regard to grievances and rights now taken for granted in many parts of the world. As to the rules for the resisters, they must *rely on themselves,* for both their suffering and their triumph must be their own; for this reason Gandhiji forbade his striking workers to accept outside support. The movement must *keep the initiative,* which includes the willing-

ness to atone for miscalculations as well as the readiness to adapt
to changes in the opponent, and to readjust both the strategy
and (as far as they were negotiable) the goals of the campaign.
And in all of this, the resister must be consistently *willing to
persuade* and to enlighten, even as he remains ready *to be
persuaded* and enlightened. He will, then, not insist on obsolete
precedent or rigid principle, but will be guided by what under
changing conditions will continue or come to feel true to him
and his comrades, that is, will become *truer through action*.

Such truth, however, could not depend on individual impressions and decisions. It could reveal itself only as long as the
resisters' actions remained co-ordinated and were guided by a
code which was as firm as it was flexible enough to perceive
changes—and to obey changing commands. The leader would
have to be able to count on a discipline based on the Satyagrahi's
commitment to suffer the opponent's anger without getting
angry and yet also without ever submitting to any violent
coercion by anyone; to remain so attuned to the opponent's
position that he would be ready, on the leader's command, even
to come to the opponent's help in any unforeseen situation
which might rob him of his freedom to remain a counterplayer
on the terms agreed upon; and to remain, in principle, so law-
abiding that he would refuse co-operation with the law or law-
enforcing agencies *only* in the chosen and defined issues. Within
these limits, he would accept and even demand those penalties
which by his chosen action he had willingly invoked against
himself.

And then, there is the leader's self-chosen suffering, which is
strictly "his business," as Gandhi would say with his mild-
mannered rudeness. For there must be a leader, and, in fact, a
predetermined succession of leaders, so that the leader himself
can be free to invite on himself any suffering, including death,
rather than hide behind the pretext that he was not expendable.
As we saw, in the first national Satyagraha, Gandhi's arrest
turned out to be *the* critical factor, even as the Ahmedabad
Satyagraha floundered over the critical issue of Gandhi's decision to fast. For once the leader decides on a "true" course, he

must have the freedom to restrain as well as to command, to withdraw as well as to lead and, if this freedom should be denied him by his followers, to declare a Satyagraha against them. If such singular power produces a shudder in the reader of today —indoctrinated as he is against "dictators"—it must not be forgotten that we are now speaking of the post-First World War years when a new kind of charismatic leadership would emerge, in nation after nation, filling the void left by collapsing monarchies, feudalisms, and patriarchies, with the mystic unity of the Leader and the Masses. And such was the interplay of the private and the public, the neurotic and the charismatic, during the period when these sons of the people assumed such a mystic authority, that we must recognize even that most personal of Gandhi's decisions, namely, his *fast*, as part of an "Indian leadership Indian style."

Fasting, we may consider in passing, is an age-old ritual act which can serve so many motivations and exigencies that it can be as corrupt as it can be sublime. As recently as January 1967, Pyarelal found it necessary to reassert in the Indian press the rules Gandhi had laid down for public fasting in a public issue. And Pyarelal concludes that fasting

cannot be resorted to against those who regard us as their enemy, or on whose love we have not established a claim by dint of selfless service; it cannot be resorted to by a person who has not identified himself with, or worked for the cause he is fasting for; it cannot be used for gaining a material selfish end, or to change the honestly held opinion of another or in support of an issue that is not clear, feasible and demonstrably just. . . . To be legitimate, a fast should be capable of response.[14]

Gandhi, at one time, urged any individual or authority that was "fasted against" and which considered the fast to be blackmail "to refuse to yield to it, even though the refusal may result in the death of the fasting person." Obviously, only such an attitude would do honor to him who thus offers his own life. On the other hand, Gandhi insisted that the fasting person must be prepared to the end to discover or to be convinced of a flaw in his position. The Indian writer Raja Rao told me on a walk how a friend of his had written to Gandhi that he was going to fast in order to underline certain demands. Gandhi wrote back suggesting that the friend write down ten demands worthy of a fast and Gandhi would initial the list without reading it. The friend pondered the matter and thought of other ways to protest!

Everything that has been said here, however, should make us very cautious in referring to the outcome of a sincere fast or to any part of a genuine Satyagraha campaign as a "failure." For as we saw in the national *hartal* of 1919, the choice of withdrawal or suspension may be the only way in which the leader can keep the spiritual initiative and thus save the instrument—dented but not broken—for another day. In this sense, the Ahmedabad mill owners' yielding was not a "capitulation"; for in an ideal Satyagraha campaign both sides will have had a chance to make the outcome a mutually beneficial one—as was the case even with the Bania deal in Ahmedabad. And, of course, new principles far beyond any circumscribed "success" or "failure" are being forced on the imagination of a wider audience in any Satyagraha worthy of the name. At any rate, even today, the surviving mill owners are far from registering a sense of having given in. "*We* forced him to fast," one said; and another: "We were ready to grant that much, anyway"; while all agree that the Event radically changed labor relations in Ahmedabad and in India.

This brings us to a final item in the inventory of Satyagraha which, at least locally, is most far-reaching: it is what in Gandhian terminology is called the "constructive program." In Champaran, the failure most keenly felt by Gandhi (and this, I believe, *was* a failure in the sense of a lack of essential completion) was the absence of any lasting impact on the everyday lives of the people of Bihar. In Ahmedabad, as we saw, Gandhi insisted, in the very days of the strike, on consolidating the gains of labor initiated by Anasuya and subsequently sustained in many significant ways by Ambalal and the other mill owners— gains in the general concept of work as a dignifying activity in itself; in the solidarity of all the laborers, in factory conditions, and in the welfare of the worker population.

In conclusion, I shall describe the practical consequences of the strike in Ahmedabad. The gains were institutionalized in an industry-wide Board of Arbitrators—the first members being Mangaldas Girardhas (then president of the Association, who had never wavered in his willingness to continue the plague bonus) and Gandhiji. Also, the Ahmedabad Textile Labor Association was founded—an organization given first rank in most nonpolitical treatises dealing with the Labor Movement in India. At the time of my first visit to Ahmedabad, the bustling activity of the T.L.A. provided by far the most vivid and most sustained "echo" of Gandhi's presence. The specific gains of labor relations, of course, seem barely to rise above the very minimum of what the post-industrial West would consider decent working and living conditions; and, indeed, some of the items brought up for arbitration in the years after the strike would hardly seem worthy of the attention of such powerful men—in any country, that is, other than India. But the critical point is that a great mill owner and a mahatma *would* discuss, say, toilet facilities, and follow up on it; that they *had* the joint authority to force the mill owners to make ever-so-grudging concessions; and that they *could* induce the mill workers to maintain discipline and to be restrained in their demands; while, in cases of insoluble discord, they *were* in a position to call on the best minds of the country to arbitrate. At any rate, it would be impossible to overrate the changes the post-strike days brought in regard to the concepts of work and collaboration. On one occasion, Anasuya told us, the Muslim workers stayed away from work on five consecutive days so that they could go to the station and greet a Muslim delegation which kept postponing arrival from day to day. Gandhi insisted that these workers work two extra days a month in order to make up for the sixty hours lost. They did. Anasuya went on to say that the workers would not have such discipline today, with Gandhiji gone. But when I asked whether they would even think of going to the station for five consecutive days today, she agreed that they (and the Association) had learned to respect their jobs too much for that.

In 1925 the membership of the T.L.A. had risen to 14,000; in

1959 it was 100,000, and as late as February 1967 the Indian newspaper *The Statesman* reported on the Ahmedabad Association as follows:

A Textile worker in Ahmedabad today is the highest paid among his colleagues elsewhere in the country. He was getting about 20% less wages than that prevailing in Bombay in 1920 when the Textile Labour Association came into being. But today his is 10% more.

This, the TLA leaders claim, is entirely attributable to the long spell of industrial peace in Ahmedabad, which, in its turn is the result of its general adherence to the principle of arbitration in settling labour disputes. In this respect, the TLA can certainly claim to be the pace-setter.

With its Rs 12-lakh [1,200,000 rupees] annual budget; a highly efficient secretariat to assist workers in their day-to-day grievances about service conditions; a bank the working capital of which rose to over Rs 5.3 crores [53,000,000 rupees] in 1963 from a mere Rs 31 lakhs [3,100,000 rupees] 15 years ago; a 200-strong paid cadre mainly to be among the workers in the mills and to act as liaison between them and the employer; and with over 100 cooperative societies run under its aegis, the Association has today an outfit easily comparable to the very best evolved by a trade union in a Western country.[15]

But the Association also became a school for national leaders, as we saw in the case of Shankerlal Banker (later the national chief of the khadi movement, in Gulzarilal Nanda (later Home Minister and acting Prime Minister), and even in the old firebrand Indulal Yagnik, who became the most vociferous opponent of the remnants of "feudalism" which he and many others claim still dominates Ahmedabad's labor peace. Others could be named; but we are concerned here only with one period and one Event, and with the instrument then tried and perfected.

THIS may be the place to come back to the question of why the Mahatma reported the strike the way he did in his Autobiography; and, more particularly, why he interrupted his report of the strike with an account of the snakes which infested the ashram grounds and yet refrained from harming anybody when treated with respectful *ahimsa*. If one cared to be a "busybody" of the psychoanalytic kind, one could make the most of the thematic sequence of these chapters. In the first of the three installments, Gandhi and his followers are shown to be up against recalcitrant mill owners; in the second, against poisonous snakes; and in the third, against mill owners again. Do snakes, then, "stand for" mill owners? This could suggest to a clinician a breakthrough of Gandhi's anger against the mill owners—an anger which he had expressly forbidden to himself as well as to the striking and starving workmen. If one can win over poisonous snakes by love and nonviolence, the hidden thought might be, one can reach the hearts of industrialists too. Or the suggestion might be that it would be more profitable to be kind to poisonous snakes than to industrialists—and here we remember that another Man of Peace, also using an analogy from the bestiary, once mused that big lazy camels might squeeze through where a rich man could not or would not.

If so, the interruption would only underscore the most obvious explanation for the Mahatma's treatment of the Ahmedabad incident, namely, mixed and conflicting feelings toward the mill owners and particularly toward Ambalal. Unnecessary to say, Indian Labour, insofar as it later followed (or talked) the line of Lenin, has considered Gandhi's relation to the mill owners utterly suspect and has never ceased to consider the Ahmedabad brand of labor peace "feudal" and "reactionary." In this they have had the quiet support of those mill owners who believe and admit that they, in fact, used Gandhi for their own purposes at the time and have used his memory ever since. For the Mahatma, however, this was not a matter of ideological propaganda or, indeed, economic interest. For if Satyagraha had in it the stuff to rival Lenin's liberation of labor, then the sole criterion for its success or failure was its inner purity. And this to the Mahatma always centered in the immediate situation and in his relation to concretely present men. Ambalal had supported Gandhi during the most critical period of the young ashram's existence. On this score alone Gandhi's wavering in his fast could be seen as unworthy of the leading Satyagrahi, and unworthy of the goal of *Moksha*.

The Autobiography, however, by its very division of chapters, betrays a conflict on another score. By the time Gandhi came to write the "columns" relating to the strike (rather late, in the 146th installment of a total of 167), he had taken Ambalal's side in an issue reaching into the depth and width of the historical necessity of anchoring Satyagraha in the *ahimsa* of Hinduism. In 1926 Ambalal, as he described it to me, had noticed from the window of his office in one of his mills that the workmen and their wives did not dare to sit by a well which had been a favorite luncheon spot and that the women would approach the well only armed with sticks. On inquiry he learned that an increasing number of ferocious-looking dogs were loose in the area around the mill, some looking clearly rabid. The municipality of Ahmedabad had apparently decided to dispose of its canine problems without breaking the injunction against the killing of animals by catching all stray dogs and letting them loose outside the city limits. Some workers—as is the wont of people who do not have enough to eat themselves—threw food to the emaciated animals, a sign for dozens of the creatures to converge on the well. Ambalal gave the municipality a week to round up the dogs and then requested the police to kill them. Considering arsenic cruel, they shot them. The cadavers were then loaded on carts which (for whatever reason) were pulled right through the old town—and this on a holiday. The Hindu populace was stunned, and many stores immediately closed in protest according to the ancient pattern of *hartal*—a storekeepers' strike. Ambalal's life was in danger.

Gandhi, however, immediately spoke up for him in *Young India*, a fact which aroused such a flood of correspondence that he had to defend himself in five successive issues. As always his defense was both practical and spiritual. In one Ahmedabad hospital more than a thousand cases of hydrophobia had been treated in the year 1925 and almost a thousand thus far in 1926. "In our ignorance," he wrote, "we must kill rabid dogs even as we might have to kill a man found in the act of killing people." As often, he seemed to contradict contradictions by adding new ones, but he concluded prophetically:

They had attributed to me nonviolence as they understand it. Now they find me acting in a contrary manner and are angry with me. . . . I appreciate the motive behind it. I must try to reason with them patiently . . . it is a sin to feed stray dogs. It is a false sense of compassion. It is an insult to a starving dog to throw a crumb at him. Roving dogs do not indicate the civilization or compassion of the society; they betray on the contrary the ignorance and lethargy of its members. The lower animals are our brethren. I include among them the lion and the tiger. We do not know how to live with these carnivorous beasts and poisonous reptiles because of our ignorance. When man learns better, he will learn to befriend even these. Today he does not even know how to befriend a man of a different religion or from a different country.[16]

This new and highly controversial linkage of Gandhi's and Ambalal's names, then, complicated an issue calling for auto-biographic clarification as one of his "experiments with truth," which appears to be the reason for the remarkable fact that Gandhi separates the introduction of the strike and the story of its conclusion with the installment on the ashram. This install-ment does have a moral—Gandhi's lengthy protestation that in his ashrams there had never been any "loss of life occasioned by snake bite." This fact has since been confirmed by both residents and visitors. An old member of the ashram showed me the spot where, he said, Vinoba Bhave once sat when a big poisonous snake crawled under his clothes. He neither moved nor called out but patiently waited for a helper, who calmly folded up Vinoba's clothes and carried the whole bundle to the river. Now the difference between dogs insane with rabies and reptiles essen-tially minding their own business is not to be minimized; this, too, will be a subject indispensable to our more general conclu-sions. Here we are interested only in the fact that Gandhi, while telling the story of the strike, found it necessary to reiterate that his basic position on the killing of animals had remained intact.

## 2. RITUAL

I HAVE now attempted to summarize some spiritual properties and some practical steps essential to the leverage of Satyagraha. There remain two fundamental doubts nagging not only incur-able cynics but also many sympathizers, East and West: if the psychic energy needed for such an instrument is dependent on *Brahmacharya*—and Gandhi seemed to insist at least for himself and his immediate followers that it was—how manageable is this truth in the instinctual life of more ordinary men, and how alien to ordinary man's "instinctive" aggressiveness? In one word: how *natural* is it?

In line with his religious heritage, Gandhi could not tolerate any deliberate harm to animals. Intellectually, however, he was a popular kind of Darwinian, with all the ambivalence contained in the very terminology which makes man a "descendant" from creatures whom he considers far beneath him in instinctual restraint. When on the occasion of his visit to London he was asked to say a word to the American people, Gandhi said in a radio address: "Hitherto, nations have fought in the manner of the brute." This manner he specified as "wreaking vengeance," and he pronounced it "the law that governs brute creation . . . inconsistent with human dignity."[17] Now, in view of what we have learned about animals or men since then, we can not continue to assert that man without self-control is "no better than a brute," unless the implication is that—measured by the code of organisms—he is much, much worse. Yet, it must be remembered that only in the post-Darwinian period has mankind even begun to confront the shocking intelligence that he may be merely some special kind of mammal.

To absorb that shock has been the task of the century after Darwin; and so it comes about that Gandhi's contemporary, Freud, who loved proud dogs for their honesty in love and hate, and who advocated an insightful acceptance of sexuality, would say in turn: "Conflicts of interest between man and man are resolved, in principle, by the recourse to violence. It is the same in the animal kingdom, from which man cannot claim exclusion."[18] Freud thus comes to the grim conclusion that in man "the slaughter of a foe gratifies an instinctive craving." But when he assents to the old dictum that *homo* is *hominis lupus*, one may at least wonder whether he means that man is to man what wolf is to man or what wolf is to wolf.

At any rate, it can not be denied that such post-Darwinism represents the lowest common denominator in the thinking of the two men who invented two corresponding methods of dealing with our instinctuality in a nonviolent manner. It is a striking example of the boundness of even the greatest men in the imagery of their time.

Konrad Lorenz's book *On Aggression*[19] is probably the best known summary of intraspecies aggression in some of the higher animals. There is, of course, an endless display of skillful violence on the part of animals who go hunting, who set out to settle territorial competition, or who feel cornered by a superior enemy. Obviously, to aggress in the sense of *ad-gredere* and to defend in that of *de-fence* must be instinctive in any creature that occupies or moves in space in unison with his own kind and in both symbiotic and antagonistic relation to other kinds.

The question is: when and where does "natural" aggression become raving violence, and the instinctive technique of killing become senseless murder? The inhabitants of an Indian jungle live face to face with "beasts" in their domain; but even they consider an occasional "killer" among tigers something of an outlaw or a deviant, a creature whom one cannot come to terms with, and who, therefore, must be singled out and hunted down. A normal lion, however, when ready for the kill (and he kills only when hungry) shows no signs of anger or rage: he is "doing his job"—or so he appears to be when his physiognomy can be studied in the wilds through long-range lenses. Nor is there any pervasive tendency for mass annihilation in nature's book—except, apparently, in rodents such as rats, under particular conditions. Wolves on the chase (Dante's *bestia senza pace*) do not decimate healthy herds but pick out the stragglers who fall behind. Among themselves, they are capable of devoted friendship; and it is reported that when two wolves happen to get into a fight, there comes a moment when the one that begins to weaken bares his unprotected neck to his opponent, who, in turn, is instinctively inhibited from taking advantage of this now "nonviolent" situation.

A more ritual elaboration of such *instinctive pacific behavior* appears in the antler tournament among the Damstags. The tournament begins with a parade *à deux*: the stags trot alongside one another, whipping their antlers up and down. Then, suddenly, they stop in their tracks as if on command, swerve toward each other at a right angle, lower their heads until the antlers almost reach the ground, and crack them against each other. If it should happen that one of the combatants swerves earlier than the other, thus endangering the completely unprotected flank of his rival with the powerful swing of his sharp and heavy equipment, he instantly puts a brake on his premature turn, accelerates his trot, and continues the parallel parade. When both are ready, however, there ensues a full mutual confrontation and a powerful but harmless wrestling. The victor is the one who can hold out the longest, while the loser concedes the tournament by a ritualized disengagement which normally stops the attack of the victor. Lorenz suggests that there are untold numbers of analogous rituals of pacification among the higher animals; but he also points out (most importantly for us) that de-ritualization at any point results in violence to the death. Skeletons of stags whose antlers are entwined in death have been found; but they are victims of an instinctive ritual that failed.

We owe such observations not only to new techniques of extending our photographic vision into animal territory, but also to a new willingness on the part of observers to let some animals dwell in their own living space[20] or to enter into the animal's domain with not more than reasonable safeguards—reasonable in the sense that the animal under observation could not mistake such presence for anything but a nonviolent approach. An ethologist of this kind, however, has given up more than just excessive fear. He has accepted a measure of joint universe with the animal beyond all question of man's descent or ascent—not to speak of human condescension—and thus has let it become clear that some of the aggressive or fearful behavior ascribed to animals is a response to man's prejudices, projections, and apprehensions. We learn from such observation that "aggressive" behavior is elicited and stopped, displaced, or replaced under given *conditions*. For, as Lorenz says so characteristically, "*Jawohl, ein Trieb kann angetrieben werden*": "Yes, indeed, a drive can be driven, an instinct instigated"—that is, by compelling circumstances. And by the same token, a drive can also remain latent and yet at a moment's provocation impel competent action. This, one would think, should make it unnecessary to apply to animal aggression (as I fear, Lorenz has done) the model of a Freudian instinct, which is essentially derived from sexuality—itself in man a much more ubiquitous, pervasive, and spontaneous drive than in animals.

"INSTINCT" has become an embarrassing term. Biologists are about to discard it and yet in psychoanalysis it is not expendable. When one uses it with too much of a biological connotation one is apt to imply what one did not mean to say. There is something instinctive and something instinctual about aggression, but one would hesitate to call aggression an "instinct." If one abandons the term altogether, however, one neglects the energetic and the driven aspect of man's behavior. Here is the crux of the matter: Freud's *Trieb* is something between the English "drive" and "instinct." In comparing the statements of animal psychologists with those of psychoanalysts, it is always useful to ask whether "instinct" is meant to convey something *instinctive* (an inborn pattern of adaptive competence), or something *instinctual* (a quantity of drive or drivenness, whether adaptive or not).[21]

If for comparative purposes we retain the term "instinct," it becomes clear that the aggressive acts as well as the pacific maneuvers of animals are *instinctive*—that is, pre-formed action patterns which under certain conditions can call on some ready drive energy for instantaneous, vigorous, and skillful release. This makes it quite unnecessary for the animal either to be unduly aroused or to inhibit himself in any individual or "moral" fashion. For the ritualization assures a pre-selection of opponents of nearly equal strength. Such opponents will be equally endowed with the capacity for the clocklike display of a whole set of scheduled and reciprocal reactions, and they will be equally ready for the assumption of either of the terminal roles (what *we* would call victor or vanquished) convincingly and effectively. Much of animal aggression is already thus "ritualized," as Julian Huxley was the first to put it. I have never been able to watch the angry-sounding seagulls, for example, without thinking that they would long since have burned up from emotion were not their behavior an instinctive "convention," invested with relatively small doses of the available drive and emotion—unless an "accident" happens. One can well see in such ritualization, as Konrad Lorenz does, an evolutionary antecedent of man's inborn propensity for a moral inhibition that prevents undue violence; and one could well (and I will) go further and see in Gandhi's Satyagraha the suggestion of a pacific confrontation that may be grounded not only in man's religiosity but also in instinctive patterns already common among some "brutes."

Yet, from everything we have said, it must be clear that for man this is by no means a simple return to nature. Rather it is an instance of man's capacity to let inspiration, insight, and conviction "cure" his instinctual complexity and to reinstate on a human level what in the animal is so innocently and yet so fatefully given. This is why Freud could say that the animal perishes when his environment changes too fast and too radically for his instinctive adaptation, while man, the great creator of his own environment, *"geht an seinen Trieben zugrunde"*—perishes from senseless instinctual needs. Thus man can eat, drink, and smoke, work and "love," curse, moralize, and sacrifice himself to death. For man's instinctual forces are never completely bound in adaptive or reasonable patterns; some are repressed, displaced, perverted, and often return from repression to arouse strictly human kinds of anxiety and rage. Here it must be conceded that even Gandhi's fanatic attempts to simplify his tastes, however moralistic in their scrupulosity, do contain a truth which was, at the same time, made accessible to insight by Freud. If the nutritional instinct, for example, guides the animal in finding and devouring an adequate amount of the right kind of food, this is very different from the oral-incorporative instinctuality which may make man spend a greater portion of his resources on alcohol and soda pop, on tobacco and coffee, than on the schooling of his children.

Thus, Gandhi's awareness of unfunctional drives in man and the necessity somehow to free himself from them—this awareness is essential to man's future. The question is What we will do with this awareness: reassert old moralisms, which, as Gandhi demonstrated in his own life, have a tendency to become as excessive as the drives they are meant to hold in check; or strive for a new ethics, based on new insights? At any rate, Freud could have meant to blame only an "*instinctual*" craving (even if he is translated as having blamed an "instinctive" one) for man's pleasure in torturing and killing an enemy. On the way, however, we must face once more how far civilized man may have sunk in some respects below the animal and probably also below his early human ancestors: for it is civilized man, morality and all, who is, or has become, in Loren Eiseley's terrible phrase, the lethal element in the universe. The question, then, is whether violence of the total kind, that is, characterized by irrational rage, wild riot, or systematic extermination, can be traced to our animal nature at all—or, for that matter, to our primitive forebears.

The motion picture *Dead Birds* shows with great esthetic skill how two tribes discovered only in this century in the New Guinea highlands indulge in regular, ritualized, and dramatized warfare, facing each other across an appointed battlefield in impressive warriors' plumage, advancing boisterously and retreating loudly in alternation. These tribes have many sinister rituals; their blatantly phallic bragging and their mutilation of female fingers can arouse nausea as well as awe. But with all such martial obsession, there is no attempt at annihilation, suppression, or enslavement; and while shouted contempt is part of the bragging display, these tribes must have maintained, for decades or centuries, a *convention of warfare*, in which the enemy can be trusted to abide by a certain ritualization which sacrifices to the martial ethos only a minimum number of individuals on either side. Here the existence of a cultural arrangement somewhere between the instinctual and the instinctive and somewhere also between tribal self-insistence and an intertribal league may well be assumed. Such warfare seems to typify a human potential; and if it can be said that "ritualization" in animals helps the participants to clarify *situational ambiguities* and to restore instinctive trust, the burden of human ritualization may well be the restoration of peace by the periodical settlement of *ambivalences* arising from man's division into pseudo-species.

Although Gandhi may indeed have sensed something of the ritual potential of *traditional warfare* when he perceived the necessity to transfer some of the discipline of soldierdom to militant nonviolence, it must be granted that it made little sense to send tens of thousands of Indians into the mechanized slaughter of the First World War, and to expect them there, of all places, to learn the bravery and chivalry necessary for Satyagraha.

For this we have learned since and are now fighting out with one another and within ourselves: even if human warfare has always included an element of uniformed ritual by which heroes were sacrificed to the survival and the immortality of idealized communal bodies, man's technological evolution has vastly outdistanced what adaptive value wars may once have had. Today we know that all this has evolved together and must be studied together: social identity and the hatred of "otherness," morality and righteous violence, inventiveness and mass murder. From the arrow released by hand to the warhead sent by intercontinental missile, man, the skillful and righteous attacker, has been transformed into a technician who can view his opponent as a mere target in a gunsight or on a map, or a statistic in a genocidal death sentence.

In 1954, Pyarelal related in *The Statesman* how a few hours before the end Gandhi was asked by a foreign journalist, "How would you meet the atom bomb . . . with nonviolence?" He answered, "I will not go underground, I will not go into shelter. I will come out in the open and let the pilot see I have not a trace of evil against him. The pilot will not see our faces from his great height, I know. But that longing in our hearts—that he will not come to harm—would reach up to him and his eyes would be opened." Utter foolishness? Maybe; and yet, perhaps, true for its very absurdity. For Gandhi's answer only dramatizes a basic nonviolent attitude which, while it must admittedly find new methods in an electronic and nuclear age, nevertheless remains a human alternative, enacted and demonstrated by the Mahatma as feasible in *his* times and circumstances. And as for the times ahead, has not the same technology which has given to man the means to incinerate himself also provided him with the techniques of facing his own kind over unlimited distances? And has he not, at the same time, also gained new introspective means to face himself and thus all others in himself, and himself in others?

If we add that man must learn to face himself as he faces all others, we imply that so far in history he has made every effort *not* to see that mankind is one species. If in this connection I have spoken of man's "pseudo-species" mentality, this concept intrigued Konrad Lorenz sufficiently to ascribe to me the term "pseudo-speciation," which I gladly appropriate. But what, stated once more, does it mean?

The term denotes the fact that while man is obviously one species, he appears and continues on the scene split up into groups (from tribes to nations, from castes to classes, from religions to ideologies) which provide their members with a firm sense of distinct and superior identity—and immortality. This demands, however, that each group must invent for itself a place and a moment in the very centre of the universe where and when an especially provident deity caused it to be created superior to all others, the mere mortals.[22]

One could go far back into prehistory and envisage man, the most naked and least identifiable animal by natural markings, and lacking, for all his self-consciousness, the identity of a species. He could adorn himself flamboyantly with feathers, pelts, and paints, and elevate his own kind into a mythological species, called by whatever word he had for "*the* people." At its friendliest, "pseudo" means only that something is made to appear to be what it is not; and, indeed, in the name of his pseudo-species man could endow himself and his universe with tools and weapons, roles and rules, with legends, myths, and rituals, which would bind his group together and give to its existence such super-individual significance as inspires loyalty, heroism, and poetry. One may assume that some tribes and cultures have for long periods peacefully cultivated just such an existence. What renders this "natural" process a potential malignancy of universal dimensions, however, is the fact that in times of threatening change and sudden upheaval the idea of being the foremost species must be reinforced by a fanatic fear and hate of other pseudo-species. That these others, therefore, must be annihilated or kept "in their places" by periodical warfare or conquest, by stringent legislation or local custom—that becomes a periodical and often reciprocal obsession of man.

At its unfriendliest, then, "pseudo" means that somebody is trying with all the semi-sincerity of propaganda to put something over on himself as well as on others; and I am afraid that I mean to convey just that. This "pseudo" aspect of man's collective identities can become dominant under the impact of historical and economic displacements, which make a group's self-idealization both more defensive and more exclusive. This process is so fundamental to man that, as modern history shows, the pseudo-species mentality refuses to yield even to gains in knowledge and experience acquired through progress. Even most "advanced" nations can harbor, and, in fact, make fanatically explicit, a mystical adherence to the mentality of the pseudo-species. The total victory of this mentality in an enlightened modern nation was exemplified in Hitler's Germany.

The most frightening aspect of pseudo-speciation, however, is the fact that a "species" which has come under the dominance of another is apt to incorporate the derisive opinion of the dominant "species" into its own self-estimation, that is, it permits itself to become infantilized, storing up within and against itself a rage which it dare not vent against the oppressor and, indeed, often dares not feel. This can become a curse from generation to generation, leading at first to occasional violence among the oppressed themselves until, at last, all the latent rage can rush into riotous manifestation at a moment when historical circumstances seem to invite and to sanction an explosion. It should not surprise us that such riotousness can be childishly gay even as it is carelessly destructive: for the oppressed have stood their oppression only by cultivating a defensive childlikeness and childishness in their individual lives and a fragmented primitivity in their cultural heritage. It stands to reason, then, that where an emphasis on the pseudo-species prevails—as in much of colonial history—the development of every participant individual is endangered by various combinations of guilt and rage which prevent true development, even where knowledge and expertise abound.

History provides, however, a way by which the pseudo-species mentality of warring groups can become disarmed, as it were, within a *wider identity*. This can come about by territorial unification: the *Pax Romana* embraced races, nations, and classes. Technological advances in universal "traffic," too, unite: seafaring, mechanized locomotion, and wireless communication each has helped to spread changes eventually contained in a sense of widening identity which helps to overcome economic fear, the anxiety of culture change, and the dread of a spiritual vacuum.[28]

We have seen in Gandhi's development the strong attraction of one of those more inclusive identities: that of an enlightened citizen of the British Empire. In proving himself willing neither to abandon vital ties to his native tradition nor to sacrifice lightly a Western education which eventually contributed to his ability to help defeat British hegemony—in all of these seeming contradictions Gandhi showed himself on intimate terms with the actualities of his era. For in all parts of the world, the struggle now is for the *anticipatory development of more inclusive identities*.

I submit, then, that Gandhi, in his immense intuition for historical actuality and his capacity to assume leadership in "truth in action," may have created a ritualization through which men, equipped with both realism and spiritual strength, can face each other with a mutual confidence analogous to the instinctive safety built into the animals' pacific rituals.

Instead of indulging in further speculation, however, let me come back to the concrete Event studied and sketch certain convergences of the Event and the patterns of pacific ritualization just described. In Ahmedabad, as on other occasions, Gandhi, far from waiting to be attacked so he could "resist passively" moved right in on his opponent by announcing what the grievance was and what action he intended to take: *engagement at close range* is of the essence in his approach. Thus, he gave his opponent the maximum opportunity for an informed response, even as he had based his demands on a thorough investigation of the facts. He told the workers not to demand more than what was fair and right but also to be prepared to *die* rather than demand less. He also saw to it that the issue was joined as one *among equals*. He explained that the mill owners' assets (money and equipment) and the workers' assets (capacity to work) depended on each other, and, therefore, were *equivalent* in economic power and dignity. In other words, they shared an inclusive identity, they were—so to say—of one species.

In this sense, he would not permit either side to undermine the other; even as the mill owners became virulent and threatening he forbade his workers to use counter-threats. He exacted from these starving people a pledge that they would abstain from any destruction, even of the opponent's good name. He thus not only avoided physical harm to machines or men (remember that the police appeared unarmed from the third day of the strike on) but also refused to let moralistic condemnation arouse anger in the opponent—and guilt feelings in the accuser.

He refused, then, to permit that cumulative aggravation of *bad conscience, negative identity*, and *hypocritical moralism* which characterizes the division of men into pseudo-species. In fact, he conceded to the mill owners that their errors were based only on a misunderstanding of their and their workers' obligations and functions, and he appealed to their "better selves." In thus demonstrating perfect trust in them, he was willing to proceed with daily improvisations leading to an interplay in which clues from the opponent determined the next step, although he was never willing to exploit any sudden appearance of weakness on the part of his opponent. The *acceptance of suffering*, and, in fact, of death, which is so basic to his "truth force," constitutes an *active choice without submission* to anyone: it includes the acceptance of punishment which one knew one courted. All of this is at once a declaration of non-intent to harm others, and (here the parallel to Konrad Lorenz's stags is most striking) an expression of a faith in the opponent's inability to persist in harming others beyond a certain point, provided, of course, that the opponent is convinced that he is not only not in mortal danger of losing either identity or rightful power, but may, in fact, acquire a more inclusive identity and a more permanent share of power.

Such faith, if disappointed, could cause the loss of everything—power, face, life—but the Satyagrahi would, in principle, choose death rather than a continuation of that chain of negotiated compromises which always eventually turn out to be the cause of future strife and murder. All this was imbedded in a style of presence and of attention. The mood of the Event was, above all, pervaded by a spirit of *giving the opponent the courage to change* even as the challenger remained ready to change with the events. At such periods of his life Gandhi possessed a Franciscan gaiety and a capacity to reduce situations to their bare essentials, thus helping others both to discard costly defenses and denials and to realize hidden potentials of good will and energetic deed.

This, I submit, actualizes something in man which for all its many abortive applications has nevertheless provided the spiritual and tactical rationale for a *revolutionary* kind of human ritualization which, in fact, may derive some of its obvious strength from an *evolutionary* potential, namely, the one so dramatically illustrated by the pacific rituals of animals. Here I am claiming something hopelessly complex and yet as simple as all the best things in life: for, indeed, only faith gives back to man the dignity of nature.

Gandhi's instrument itself, once innovated by one of the rarest of men under specific cultural and historical conditions, now exists in the images, impulses, and ritualizations of many who have become aware of it by what we may call "ritual-diffusion." It now calls for leaders who will re-innovate it elsewhere, sharing, no doubt, some of the personal or historical motivation of the first leader, the first followers, and those first led, but recombining this motivation with totally new elements.

For if the instrument once was "the truth," it can and must become actual in entirely different settings, in which the necessary toolmaking may be based on a different and yet analogous tradition, and where the toolmakers come from different vocations and yet share converging goals. If truth is actuality, it can never consist of the mere repetition of ritualized acts or stances. It calls for reconstitution by a new combination of universal verities and social disciplines.[24]

### 3. INSIGHT

IN RETURNING once more to the correspondences between the method of Satyagraha and that of psychoanalytic insight, it is interesting to note that after World War I the Mahatma could be very sure that he was offering a political alternative to what he felt was Wilson's hypocritical peace moves in Versailles, while Freud (as we now know from his introduction to a book on Wilson allegedly co-authored by him and William C. Bullitt[25]) was equally aroused and equally certain that his method of psychological analysis was needed to show up a man like Wilson as a moralist of a deeply neurotic bent. Together, then, these men saw in Wilson, who for a brief moment in history had become the embodiment of lasting peace, the symbol instead of man's deep hypocrisy as expressed in that combination of contradictory attitudes which we must concede has proven to be the greatest danger to peace: the ceaseless perfection of armament paired with that righteous and fanatic kind of moralism which ever again can pivot from peace to war.

As Gandhi wrote to C. F. Andrews in 1919:

The message of the West . . . is succinctly put by President Wilson in his speech delivered to the Peace Conference at the time of introducing the League of Nations Covenant: "Armed force is in the background in this programme, but it is in the background, and if the moral force of the world will not suffice, physical force of the world shall."[26]

But the Freudian movement was not alone in emphasizing therapeutic persuasion as a cure of man's aberrations. The period here under consideration saw the development of a systematic

concern with "the minds of men" as strategic for both peace and
war, adaptation and revolution. Thought-therapy as a means
of curing the minds of men from political fixations and regres-
sions has become familiar in Chinese thought reform. But it
came as something of a shock when Khrushchev ascribed to
another one of Gandhi's contemporaries these words:

As a special duty of the Control Commission there is recommended a
deep, individualized relationship with, and sometimes even a type of
therapy for, the representatives of the so-called opposition—those who
have experienced a psychological crisis because of failure in their Soviet
or party career. An effort should be made to quiet them, to explain the
matter to them in a way used among comrades, to find for them (avoiding the method of issuing orders) a task for which they are psychologically fitted.[27]

This, so Khrushchev claimed, was said by Lenin in 1920.
Wherever it comes from, it is a remarkable formulation of
therapeutic persuasion as a counterpoint to political terror.
Among more recent revolutionaries, at least in Dr. Guevara's
life, there seems to have been some intrinsic conflict between the
passion to cure and the conviction that one must kill. That
killing, in fact, may be a necessary self-cure for colonialized
people was Dr. Frantz Fanon's conviction and message, which
he carefully documented with psychiatric histories of torturers
as well as with those of tortured men. An implicit therapeutic
intent, then, seems to be a common denominator in theories and
ideologies of action which, on the level of deeds, seem to exclude
each other totally. What they nevertheless have in common is
the intuition that violence against the adversary and violence
against the self are inseparable; what divides them is the program
of dealing with either.

Gandhi's way, as we have seen, is that of a double conversion:
the hateful person, by containing his egotistic hate and by
learning to love the opponent as human, will confront the
opponent with an enveloping technique that will force, or rather
permit, him to regain his latent capacity to trust and to love. In
all these and other varieties of confrontation, the emphasis is
not so much (or not entirely) on the power to be gained as on

the cure of an unbearable inner condition. Some of the revolutionaries of today share with Gandhi the readiness to suffer and to die in the pursuit of their conviction that there are ills in the human condition which an insightful person must not tolerate. Gandhi could sympathize with proud and violent youth; but he believed that violence breeds violence from generation to generation and that only the combined insight and discipline of Satyagraha can really disarm man, or rather, give him a power stronger than all arms.

Important new insights often arise when men and women of imagination accept responsibility for a class of men previously bracketed, judged, and diagnosed as doomed to inferiority: the history of psychiatry and its influence on civilization also began with the insight gained by thoughtful practitioners that certain classes of mental patients were unjustly treated by others, including doctors, as though they were possessed by evil or doomed genetically—were a separate species, as it were. Clinical confrontation, too, revealed how the untruthfulness inherent in man's propensity for pseudo-speciation does violence to man.

I therefore will come back to the fact which provided one rationale for this book, namely, that Freud, when he listened to the "free associations" of his confused and yet intelligent and searching patients, heard *himself* and heard *man* in and through their revelations. In noticing the similarity of their imaginative productions to his own dreams, and of both to themes of mythology and literature, he really was "tapping" for clinical purposes a need to verbalize and to confess certain wishes and imaginings which are, in principle, universal themes but come to awareness and verbalization only under a variety of special conditions: from the dreams of the sleep state to daydreams and the content of creative production; from the ravings of insanity to artificially induced "consciousness expansion," and from impulsive confessions to systematic self-revelation in autobiographies. Both religion and politics have made rituals out of man's basic need to confess the past in order to purge it, while psychoanalysis has clarified the way in which many kinds of imaginative productions are also confessions. But psychoanalysis has done more than lay bare such productions; it has created a controlled situation for studying their emergence.

At the end of this discussion it should not come as a shocking conclusion that historicizing *as such* appears to be a process by which man recapitulates the past in order to render— or even surrender—it to the judgment of the future: an adaptive process. Psychoanalysis, then, may well become operative in curing the historical process of some of its built-in impediments and in providing the conscious insights which are unconsciously sought in all manner of indirect self-revelations. I mean to say here that man by understanding the way he historicizes may yet overcome certain stereotyped ways in which history repeats itself—ways which man can no longer afford.

Gandhi's and Freud's methods converge more clearly if I repeat: in both encounters only the militant probing of a vital issue by a nonviolent confrontation can bring to light what insight is ready on both sides. Such probing must be decided on only after careful study, but then the developing encounter must be permitted to show, step by step, what the power of truth may reveal and enact. At the end only a development which transforms both partners in such an encounter is truth in action; and such transformation is possible only where man learns to be nonviolent toward himself as well as toward others. Finally, the truth of Satyagraha and the "reality" of psychoanalysis come somewhat nearer to each other if it is assumed that man's "reality testing" includes an attempt not only to think clearly but also to enter into an optimum of mutual activation with others. But this calls for a combination of clear insight into our central motivations and pervasive faith in the brotherhood of man.

Seen from this vantage point, psychoanalysis offers a method of intervening nonviolently between our overbearing conscience and our raging affects, thus forcing our moral and our "animal" natures to enter into respectful reconciliation.

When I began this book, I did not expect to rediscover psychoanalysis in terms of truth, self-suffering, and nonviolence. But now that I have done so, I see better what I hope the reader has come to see with me, namely, that I felt attracted to the

Ahmedabad Event not only because I had learned to know the scene and not only because it was time for me to write about the responsibilities of middle age, but also because I sensed an affinity between Gandhi's truth and the insights of modern psychology. That truth, and these insights, are the legacy of the first part of this century to its remainder. A concrete event has served to illustrate their origins in all the complexity of historical actuality. I did not undertake to do and could not do more than that. But as we historicize more consciously, we also assume some of the burden of tradition. Even one past event, seen in the light of a new awareness, must make it apparent that man denies and abandons the visions and the disciplines he has already acquired only at the risk of historical and personal regression.

# EPILOGUE

## March to the Sea

_____

In 1930, AGAIN in the fateful month of March, the Mahatma started a new campaign. He was now leaving Ahmedabad for good, vowing not to return before India had become fully independent. The departure was one of the most dramatic and inspired in history, and a brief account of it is a fitting conclusion to this book—for almost all the men and women, and some of the (then) children who became my friends in Ahmedabad were there the night of March 11. It was the night before the great trek, 200 miles down to the Arabian Sea, where the Mahatma would collect some grains of salt from India's ocean.

The 1920's had provided Gandhi with time for different seasons: a year of undisputed leadership of Congress and the nation, and two years in jail; the "silent year" and the years of autobiographic introspection; another year of despair and illness, and years of inner rebuilding and ambulatory reforming, from village to village.

Now the Mahatma felt ready to stake everything once more on a national Satyagraha—the Salt Satyagraha. For the Salt Act was to be the eminently practical and highly symbolic focus of this campaign of civil disobedience. It netted the English only £25 million out of the eight hundred million pounds yearly collected from India. But these revenues were drawn, literally, from the sweat of the poorest and from a commodity lavishly available to all along the thousands of miles of Indian seashore. One little town, Dandi, near Jalalpur on the entrance to the Gulf of Cambay, would be the scene for the gesture of freedom —and the bloodiest reprisals.

Again, a letter had been sent to the Viceroy: "Dear Friend. . . ." But this time there had been no equivocation: "I hold the British rule to be a curse." Yet: "I do not intend harm to a single Englishman or to any legitimate interest he may have in India." He had pleaded with the Viceroy "on bended knee" to work for the repeal of the Salt Act, reminding the Emperor's representative with his usual militancy *ad hominem* that his salary was five thousand times that of India's average income. He had concluded:

My ambition is no less than to convert the British people through non-violence, and thus make them see the wrong they have done to India. I do not seek to harm your people. I want to serve them even as I want to serve my own. . . .[1]

But His Excellency had only let him know through his secretary that he "regretted to learn," etc.

The evening of March 11, Gandhiji had held his last prayer meeting. To thousands he had announced:

In all probability this will be my last speech to you. Even if the Government allows me to march tomorrow morning, this will be my last speech on the sacred banks of the Sabarmati. Possibly these may be the last words of my life here.

I have already told you yesterday what I had to say. Today I shall confine myself to what you should do after my companions and I are arrested. The programme of the march to Jalalpur must be fulfilled as originally settled. The enlistment of volunteers for this purpose should be confined to Gujarat. From what I have seen and heard during the last fortnight, I am inclined to believe that the stream of civil resisters will flow unbroken.

But let there be not a semblance of breach of peace even after all of us have been arrested. We have resolved to utilize all our resources in the pursuit of an exclusively non-violent struggle. Let no one commit a wrong in anger. This is my hope and prayer. I wish these words of mine reached every nook and corner of the land.[2]

This time he could speak with more realistic assurance and less vainglorious hope. For this time there was an army at his command. This army even had a uniform, if one denoting poverty and humility: it was made of khadi, showed no rank, and was topped by the Gandhi cap, a facsimile of the jail prisoners' headgear. Gandhi was the leader; but other commanders were posted all over the land: Vallabhbhai Patel would stay in Ahmedabad, Rajagopolachari in Madras, Sen Gupta in Calcutta—and Nehru in Allahabad: "Let nobody assume that after I am arrested there will be no one left to guide you. It is not I, but Pandit Jawaharlal who is your guide. He has the capacity to lead."

Whatever other measures of civil disobedience were indicated in various regions would be decided by responsible subleaders. Gandhi concentrated on the main issue:

Wherever possible, civil disobedience of Salt laws should be started. These laws can be violated in three ways. It is an offence to manufacture salt wherever there are facilities for doing so. The possession and sale of contraband salt (which includes natural salt or salt earth) is also an offence. The purchasers of such salt will be equally guilty. To carry away the natural salt deposits on the sea-shore is likewise a violation of law. So is the hawking of such salt. In short, you may choose any one or all of these devices to break the salt monopoly.[3]

This time, a vast group of well-trained Satyagrahis were available, well trained in controlling as well as in propagandizing large crowds. They all were held together not only by a joint pledge but also (at least in Gandhi's vicinity) by the rules of the ashram-in-motion which included the "three essentials": prayer, spinning, and writing a diary.[4]

And such discipline was to be sorely needed; for this time, the tangible opponent was to be the army as well as the police—mostly Indians in uniform, then, who were both goaded on by their contemptuous officers and themselves irritated to the extreme by the seemingly mocking challenge of wave after wave of unarmed and yet militant civilians.

Among the many well-wishers stretched out on the grounds during the night (for the month of March can be pleasant in

Western India, not yet too dry and not yet drenched by the monsoon) was the mill owner's wife Saraladevi ("my blood-sister") and her oldest children, daughter Mridula, then 17, who was to become one of Gandhi's dearest if always totally straightforward followers; Gautam, then only 12, who was to become Ambalal's successor; and Vikram, now in charge of India's nuclear development.

But alas, this time there was also the press, from all over India and from "the world." And then, not having been arrested as had been expected ("the government is puzzled and perplexed") Gandhi, in the morning, led his seventy-eight men and women out the gate of the ashram and down the road to Dandi. Among them were Anasuya, and Pyarelal, then a long-time secretary. Shankerlal, the organizer, had been sent ahead to select and prepare the places where the marchers would stop to eat and spin, pray and sleep. The Mahatma was then over sixty, but twelve miles a day for twenty-four days was "child's play." And, indeed, as the documentary films of the day attest, there was a certain gaiety about this pilgrimage through the festooned villages and along roads which the peasants had sprinkled against dust and bedecked with leaves against stones. And at the end, the Mahatma picked up some salt (which, in true Bania fashion, later was sold to the highest bidder nearby and netted 1,600 rupees)—a signal to do likewise for thousands all over the sub-continent who happened to be near the ocean. The raw material was brought inland to be prepared in pans on rooftops and then to be peddled—mostly "pretty awful stuff," as Nehru hardly had time to observe before he was arrested, one of the first of more than fifty thousand to be jailed. But except for some disturbances in Bengal, there was no violence to speak of in any part of India.

The very absence of violence, however, again aroused the police to pointed viciousness. The report of a British journalist, Webb Miller, has become the classical account of Satyagraha on the front line. Under the leadership of Sarojini Naidu and Manilal Gandhi (Devadas and Ramdas had already been arrested), 2,500 volunteers "attacked" the Dharasana Salt Works not far from Dandi.

In complete silence the Gandhi men drew up and halted a hundred yards from the stockade. A picked column advanced from the crowd, waded the ditches, and approached the barbed-wire stockade. . . . Suddenly at a word of command, scores of native policemen rushed upon the advancing marchers and rained blows on their heads with their steel-shod lathis. Not one of the marchers even raised an arm to fend off the blows. They went down like ten-pins. From where I stood I heard the sickening whack of the clubs on unprotected skulls. The waiting crowd of marchers groaned and sucked in their breath in sympathetic pain at every blow. Those struck down fell sprawling, unconscious or writhing with fractured skulls or broken shoulders. . . . The survivors, without breaking ranks, silently and doggedly marched on until struck down.

They marched steadily, with heads up, without the encouragement of music or cheering or any possibility that they might escape serious injury or death. The police rushed out and methodically and mechanically beat down the second column. There was no fight, no struggle; the marchers simply walked forward till struck down. . . .[5]

After that, the men in uniform, feeling defenseless in all their superior equipment, could think of doing only what seems to "come naturally" to uniformed men in similar situations: if they did not succeed in bashing in the volunteers' skulls, they kicked and stabbed them in the testicles. "Hour after hour stretcher-bearers carried back a stream of inert, bleeding bodies."[6]

What had the Satyagrahis accomplished? They did not take the Works; nor was the Salt Act formally abolished in its entirety. But this, the world began to realize, was not the point. The Salt Satyagraha had demonstrated to the world the nearly flawless use of a new instrument of peaceful militancy. May it only be added that after another stay in jail, Gandhi met the Viceroy for the famous Tea Party to which I have referred. After some compromises all around, Gandhi was invited to talks with the Viceroy. Churchill scoffed at the "seditious fakir, striding half-naked up the steps of the Viceroy's palace, to negotiate with the representative of the King-Emperor." But the Viceroy, Lord Irwin, has described the meeting as "the most dramatic

personal encounter between a Viceroy and an Indian leader."
When Gandhi was handed a cup of tea, he poured a bit of salt
(tax-free) into it out of a small paper bag hidden in his shawl and
remarked smilingly, "to remind us of the famous Boston Tea
Party." Moniya and the Empire! The following year he would
go to England for a Round Table Conference, the sole representative of Congress and a world leader now immensely popular
even with the English masses. What followed in the Mahatma's
and in India's life is well documented.[7]

In May 1930 Tagore wrote triumphantly to the *Manchester
Guardian* that Europe had now lost her moral prestige in Asia.
Weak Asia, he said, praising the Mahatma, "could now afford to
look down on Europe where before she looked up." Gandhi, as I
read him, might have said it differently: Asia could now look
Europe in the eye—not more, not less, not up to, not down on.
Where man can and will do that, there, sooner or later, will be
mutual recognition.

# NOTES

# Notes

## PROLOGUE: ECHOES OF AN EVENT

1. Joan Erikson, in *Mata Ni Pachedi, The Temple Cloth of the Mother Goddess*, Ahmedabad: National Design Institute, 1968.
2. *The Great Trial* (Being A Report of Mahatma Gandhi's Trial), with an Introduction by Mazharul Haque, Ahmedabad: Navajivan, 1965, pp. 32–34. (A reprint of the report published in Patna in 1922.)
3. He has now done so, in Gujarati (Ahmedabad: Navajivan, 1967).
4. See Romain Rolland, *Mahatma Gandhi*, Catherine D. Groth, trans., New York: The Century Co., 1924, pp. 3–5.
5. He is now the Vice-Chancellor of Gujarat University.
6. For a psychosocial conception of the human life cycle, see Erik H. Erikson, *Childhood and Society*, Second Edition, New York: Norton, 1963, pp. 247–274.
7. P. V. Kane, *History of Dharmasastra*, Poona: Bhandarkar Oriental Research Institute, 1941, Vol. II, Part 1, p. 188. See Sudhir Kakar, "The Human Life Cycle: The Traditional Hindu View and the Psychology of Erik H. Erikson," *Philosophy East and West*, XVIII, No. 3, July 1968, 127–136.
8. *The Mahabharata*, Volume XII (Shanti Parva), M. N. Dutt, trans., Calcutta: R. M. Sircar, 1902, p. 186.
9. *The Bhagavad Gita*, Discourse III, 35. See the translation by Franklin Edgerton, 2 vols., Cambridge, Mass.: Harvard University Press, 1952, I, 39.
10. Cited in P. N. Prabhu, *Hindu Social Organization, A Study in Socio-Psychological and Ideological Foundations*, Fourth Edition, Bombay: Popular Prakashan, 1963, p. 73.
11. Erik H. Erikson, *Identity: Youth and Crisis*, New York: Norton, 1968, pp. 221–224, "A Communality of Egos."
12. *The Laws of Manu*, G. Buhler, trans., Vol. XXV in *The Sacred Books of the East*, F. Max Muller, ed., Oxford: Clarendon Press, 1886, p. 335.
13. Adapted from *The Laws of Manu*, p. 70.
14. See *Childhood and Society*, pp. 65, 269–274.
15. Mahadev Desai, *A Righteous Struggle*, Ahmedabad: Navajivan, 1951.

16. M. K. Gandhi, *An Autobiography or The Story of My Experiments with Truth*, translated from the original in Gujarati by Mahadev Desai, Ahmedabad: Navajivan, 1927, p. 291. (Hereafter cited as *Autobiography*.)

17. *Ibid.*, p. 314.

18. *Ibid.*, pp. 316, 317.

19. *Ibid.*, p. 316.

20. *Ibid.*, p. 317.

21. *The London Times*, April 8, 1918.

22. *The Bombay Chronicle*, February 28, 1918.

23. Idem.

24. Weekly Reports of the Director, Criminal Intelligence, for the Month of February 1918, Home Department, *Political Proceedings*. National Archives, New Delhi.

25. *Mahadevbhaini Diary*, Narhari Parikh, ed., Ahmedabad: Navajivan, 1950. Volume IV.

26. This letter has since been published in the Indian Government's chronological publication, still in process, of Gandhi's writings, where it is attributed to the Allahabad *Leader* with a note that the letter was evidently issued generally to the press. See *The Collected Works of Mahatma Gandhi*, Delhi: Government of India, Ministry of Information and Broadcasting, The Publications Division, 1958 and following, XIV, 283–286. (Hereafter cited as *CWMG*.)

27. *Ibid.*, p. 283.

28. *Ibid.*, p. 285.

## PART ONE: THE INQUIRY

1. Cited in B. R. Nanda, *Mahatma Gandhi, A Biography*, Boston: Beacon Press, 1958, p. 234.

2. Quoted in Louis Fischer, *The Life of Mahatma Gandhi*, New York: Harper & Brothers, 1950, p. 223.

3. Gandhi, *Autobiography*, p. 371.

4. *Ibid.*, p. xiii.

5. *CWMG*, XIV, 286.

6. Gandhi, *Autobiography*, p. 333.

7. *Ibid.*, p. 293.

8. Heinrich Zimmer, *Philosophies of India*, New York: Meridian Books, Inc., 1956, pp. 152, 153.

9. *Praja Bandhu*, March 17, 1918.

10. *CWMG*, XIII, 345.

11. *Ibid.*, XIV, 8–36, 48–72.

12. Pyarelal, *Mahatma Gandhi*, Volume I, *The Early Phase*, Ahmedabad: Navajivan, 1965.

13. Pyarelal, *Mahatma Gandhi, The Last Phase*, 2 vols., Ahmedabad: Navajivan, 1956, 1958.

14. Pyarelal, *Mahatma Gandhi, The Early Phase*, p. 209.

15. Gandhi, *Autobiography*, p. 45.

## PART TWO: THE PAST

1. B. R. Nanda, *Mahatma Gandhi, A Biography*, pp. 22, 23.

2. Gandhi, *Autobiography*, p. xvi.

3. *Ibid.*, p. 18.

4. Nanda, *Mahatma Gandhi, A Biography*, p. 18.
5. Pyarelal, *Mahatma Gandhi, The Early Phase*, pp. 192, 193.
6. *Ibid.*, p. 193.
7. *Ibid.*, p. 195.
8. *Ibid.*, p. 198.
9. Gandhi, *Autobiography*, p. 4.
10. Pyarelal, *Mahatma Gandhi, The Early Phase*, p. 201.
11. *Ibid.*, p. 195.
12. Gandhi, *Autobiography*, p. 8.
13. *Ibid.*, p. 11.
14. *Ibid.*, p. 5.
15. Pyarelal, *Mahatma Gandhi, The Early Phase*, p. 207. Cf. Louis Fischer, *The Life of Mahatma Gandhi*, p. 92. In Fischer's version, the last sentence reads: "Of amusement after I was twelve, I had little or none."
16. Gandhi, *Autobiography*, p. 6.
17. *Ibid.*, p. 10.
18. Pyarelal, *Mahatma Gandhi, The Early Phase*, p. 212.
19. Gandhi, *Autobiography*, pp. 20, 21. Italics mine.
20. *The Journals of Søren Kierkegaard, A Selection* edited and translated by Alexander Dru, London: Oxford University Press, 1938, p. 132.
21. *The Autobiography of Eleanor Roosevelt*, New York: Harper & Bros., 1958, pp. 9, 10, 13.
22. Joan Erikson, "Nothing to Fear: Notes on the Life of Eleanor Roosevelt," *The Woman in America*, Robert J. Lifton, ed., Boston: Beacon Press, 1967, pp. 267–287.
23. Gandhi, *Autobiography*, p. 22.
24. Translated by Leo O. Lee for my seminar "History and Life History" at Harvard, from *Lu Hsun ch'uan-chi* (Complete Works of Lu Hsun), Peking: 1956, Vol. II, pp. 261, 262.
25. Pyarelal, *Mahatma Gandhi, The Early Phase*, pp. 207, 208.
26. Gandhi, *Autobiography*, p. 17.
27. "From the London Diary," *CWMG*, I, 6. Italics mine.
28. *Ibid.*, p. 5.
29. *Ibid.*, p. 3.
30. Gandhi, *Autobiography*, p. 14.
31. See the press release in *Harijan*, June 27, 1948.
32. Reprinted from *The Vegetarian*, June 20, 1891, in *CWMG*, I, 62.
33. *CWMG*, I, 22–24.
34. Pyarelal, *Mahatma Gandhi, The Early Phase*, p. 269.
35. Reprinted from *The Vegetarian*, June 13, 1891, in *CWMG*, I, 53.
36. Gandhi, *Autobiography*, p. 56.
37. Stephen Winsten, *Salt and His Circle*, London: Hutchinson & Co., 1951, p. 32. Quoted in Pyarelal, *Mahatma Gandhi, The Early Phase*, p. 246.
38. Gandhi, *Autobiography*, p. 46.
39. Pyarelal, *Mahatma Gandhi, The Early Phase*, pp. 263, 264.
40. Reprinted from *The Vegetarian*, Feb. 28, 1891, in *CWMG*, I, 30, 31.
41. Reprinted from *The Vegetarian*, Feb. 7, 1891; Feb. 21, 1891; in *CWMG*, I, 24, 25, 29, 30.
42. Gandhi, *Autobiography*, pp. 63–65.
43. *Ibid.*, p. 63.
44. *Ibid.*, p. 74.
45. *The Gospel of Selfless Action or The Gita According to Gandhi*, translation of the original in Gujarati, with an additional introduction and commentary by Mahadev Desai, Ahmedabad: Navajivan, 1946, p. 143.

46. Gandhi, *Autobiography*, p. 68.
47. *Ibid.*, pp. 83, 84.
48. *Ibid.*, p. 81.
49. *Ibid.*, p. 90.
50. *Ibid.*, p. 96.
51. *Ibid.*, p. 90.
52. *CWMG*, I, 106.
53. Quoted from the *Natal Mercury* in Pyarelal, *Mahatma Gandhi, The Early Phase*, p. 413.
54. Letter from Colonial Secretary to Governor of Natal. Quoted in Pyarelal, *Mahatma Gandhi, The Early Phase*, p. 578.
55. Quoted in Pyarelal, *Mahatma Gandhi, The Early Phase*, p. 600.
56. Natal Indian Memorial to Joseph Chamberlain, May 22, 1896. Quoted *ibid.*, p. 611.
57. Pyarelal, *Mahatma Gandhi, The Early Phase*, p. 491.
58. For my discussion of this point in theoretical context, see also *Identity: Youth and Crisis*, New York: Norton, 1968, Chapter III ("The Life Cycle: Epigenesis of Identity").
59. *Young India*, January 21, 1926, p. 30. Quoted in Pyarelal, *Mahatma Gandhi, The Early Phase*, p. 277.
60. Gandhi, *Autobiography*, pp. 110 ff.
61. M. K. Gandhi, *Satyagraha in South Africa*, Ahmedabad: Navajivan, 1928, p. 40.
62. *Ibid.*, pp. 15–17.
63. *Ibid.*, p. 73.
64. Stanley A. Wolpert, *Tilak and Gokhale: Revolution and Reform in The Making of Modern India*, Berkeley: University of California Press, 1962, p. 1.
65. Gokhale's Presidential Address before the 14th Annual Meeting of the Students' Brotherhood, October 9, 1909. Quoted *ibid.*, p. 239.
66. Wolpert, p. 25.
67. Gandhi, *Autobiography*, p. 163.
68. *Ibid.*, p. 165.
69. *Ibid.*, p. 167.
70. *Ibid.*, p. 168.
71. *Ibid.*, p. 174.
72. *Ibid.*, p. 182.
73. Gandhi, *Satyagraha in South Africa*, pp. 90, 91.
74. *Ibid.*, pp. 97, 98.
75. Gandhi, *Autobiography*, p. 148.
76. *Ibid.*, p. 150.
77. Gandhi, *Satyagraha in South Africa*, p. 99.
78. *Ibid.*, p. 106.
79. Quoted in Louis Fischer, *The Life of Mahatma Gandhi*, pp. 88, 89.
80. Gandhi, *Satyagraha in South Africa*, p. 133.
81. *Ibid.*, pp. 137 ff.
82. *Ibid.*, p. 149.
83. *Ibid.*, p. 153.
84. *Ibid.*, p. 164.
85. *Ibid.*, p. 167.
86. This is perhaps most impressively illustrated in Louis Fischer's mixed metaphor, according to which Gandhi, before he "sat in the saddle of the Congress" was the "burr under it." *Op. cit.*, p. 133.
87. Gandhi, *Satyagraha in South Africa*, p. 248.

88. *Ibid.*, p. 273.
89. *Ibid.*, pp. 206, 209.
90. *Ibid.*, p. 218.
91. *Idem.*
92. 1968: On a recent trip to South Africa, I had an opportunity to remind the students of Capetown University of the South African export, Satyagraha ("Insight and Freedom," the Ninth T. B. Davie Memorial Lecture, University of Capetown, 1968). Some friends helped me to find Tolstoy Farm near Johannesburg only with some difficulty; certainly nobody in the vicinity had heard of Gandhi. The main building seems to be occupied by an Africaaner farmer's family. As to Kallenbach, a person of that name could affirm on the telephone only that there had once been a "wealthy eccentric" in the family.
93. Gandhi, *Satyagraha in South Africa*, p. 280.
94. *Ibid.*, p. 293.
95. *Ibid.*, pp. 297, 298.
96. *Ibid.*, p. 308.
97. *Ibid.*, p. 309.
98. *Ibid.*, pp. 336, 337.
99. Letter to J. B. Petit, Secretary of the South African Indian Fund, dated June [16], 1915, in *CWMG*, XIII, 110.
100. M. K. Gandhi, *Hind Swaraj*, originally written in Gujarati and published, in installments, in *Indian Opinion* in 1909. Reprinted in *CWMG*, X, 6–68.
101. *Ibid.*, pp. 10, 11.
102. *Ibid.*, p. 40.
103. *Ibid.*, p. 15.
104. *Ibid.*, p. 37.
105. *Ibid.*, pp. 16, 17. In his preface to the Indian edition of *Indian Home Rule* (Madras: Ganesh & Co., 1919), Gandhi admits that "there is only one word I would alter in accordance with a promise made to an English lady friend." This refers to the "indelicacy" of the word "prostitute," which was nevertheless permitted to stand because the entire pamphlet by that time was mostly of historical value.
106. *Ibid.*, p. 44.
107. Gandhi, *Hind Swaraj*, in *CWMG*, X, 45.
108. Quoted in *CWMG*, X, 207.
109. Gandhi, *Hind Swaraj*, in *CWMG*, X, 38.
110. *Kesari*, X: 39 (September 30, 1890), 2. Quoted in Wolpert, p. 51.
111. Wolpert, p. 118.
112. Gandhi, *Hind Swaraj*, in *CWMG*, X, 51, 52.
113. *Ibid.*, pp. 57, 58.
114. *Ibid.*, p. 58.
115. *Ibid.*, pp. 20, 28, 50.
116. *Ibid.*, p. 49.
117. *Ibid.*, p. 62.

## PART THREE: THE EVENT

1. Gandhi, *Autobiography*, pp. 206 ff.
2. *Ibid.*, p. 205.
3. D. G. Tendulkar, *Mahatma, Life of Mohandas Karamchand Gandhi* (8 vols.), Second edition, Delhi: Government of India, Ministry of Information and Broadcasting, The Publications Division, 1960, I, 72.
4. Gandhi, *Autobiography*, p. 205.

5. Gandhi, *Satyagraha in South Africa*, pp. 244–246.
6. Louis Fischer, *The Life of Mahatma Gandhi*, p. 207.
7. Letter to Lakshmidas Gandhi dated May 27, 1906. Reprinted in *CWMG*, V, 334–335.
8. Gandhi, *Satyagraha in South Africa*, p. 33.
9. Undated letter written from Madras sometime after April 17, 1915. Reprinted in *CWMG*, XIII, 49.
10. *The Bombay Chronicle*, Jan. 15, 1915. Reprinted in *CWMG*, XIII, 3.
11. Reported in *The Bombay Chronicle*, Jan. 13, 1915. Reprinted in *CWMG*, XIII, 5.
12. See *CWMG*, XIII, 10–12.
13. What I have learned of Ahmedabad has been supported and immeasurably enriched by Kenneth L. Gillion's notes on the city's history, recently published as *Ahmedabad: A Study in Indian Urban History*, Berkeley: University of California Press, 1968.
14. *Census of India, 1921, Cities of the Bombay Presidency*, Vol. IX, Part I (Report), Poona: Govt. Printing, 1922, p. 64.
15. Cited in Pyarelal, *Mahatma Gandhi, The Early Phase*, p. 62.
16. Jawaharlal Nehru, *The Discovery of India*, Second edition, London: Meridian Books, 1947, p. 304.
17. See Erikson, *Identity: Youth and Crisis*, p. 22.
18. Jawaharlal Nehru, *Glimpses of World History*, New York: John Day, 1942, p. 428.
19. Quoted by Nehru in a letter to his daughter dated Dec. 1, 1932, *ibid.*, p. 417.
20. *Ibid.*, p. 419.
21. Pyarelal, *Mahatma Gandhi, The Early Phase*, p. 34.
22. Nehru, *Glimpses of World History*, p. 419.
23. *Ibid.*, p. 420.
24. *Ibid.*, p. 431.
25. Pyarelal, *Mahatma Gandhi, The Early Phase*, p. 37.
26. *Idem.*
27. See, for example, Philip Woodruff's accounts in *The Men Who Ruled India*, especially Vol. II, *The Guardians*, London: Jonathan Cape, 1954.
28. Sir William Sleeman, *A Journey Through The Kingdom of Oude, 1849–50* (1858 edition), II, pp. 68–69. Quoted in Pyarelal, *Mahatma Gandhi, The Early Phase*, p. 39.
29. *East India Papers*, London (1820), II, 118. Quoted in Pyarelal, *Mahatma Gandhi, The Early Phase*, p. 40.
30. Pyarelal, *Mahatma Gandhi, The Early Phase*, p. 39.
31. Quoted in *ibid.*, p. 40.
32. Forrest's *Selections from The Minutes and Other Official Writings of the Hon. Mountstuart Elphinstone* (1884), p. 102. Quoted *ibid.*, p. 44.
33. Thomas B. Macaulay, "Minute on Indian Education" in *Prose and Poetry*, Cambridge, Mass.: Harvard University Press, 1952, pp. 722, 729.
34. Earl of Ronaldshay, *The Heart of Aryavarta*, p. 45. Quoted in Pyarelal, *Mahatma Gandhi, The Early Phase*, p. 47.
35. Nehru, *Glimpses of World History*, p. 434.
36. *CWMG*, XIII, 59, 60.
37. *Ibid.*, p. 45.
38. *Ibid.*, pp. 144, 145.
39. *Ibid.*, pp. 198, 199.
40. *Ibid.*, pp. 313–315.
41. *CWMG*, XIV, 48.

42. *Ibid.*, p. 72.
43. *CWMG*, XIII, 211–214.
44. *Ibid.*, p. 214.
45. *Ibid.*, pp. 214, 215.
46. *Ibid.*, p. 216.
47. Gandhi, *Autobiography*, p. 277.
48. *Ibid.*, p. 282.
49. *CWMG*, XIII, 191, 192.
50. *Ibid.*, p. 321.
51. *Ibid.*, pp. 419, 420.
52. *Ibid.*, pp. 301, 303.
53. *Ibid.*, p. 302.
54. *Ibid.*, p. 485.
55. Gandhi, *Autobiography*, p. 291.
56. *Ibid.*, pp. 303, 304.
57. *Ibid.*, pp. 301, 302.
58. *CWMG*, XIII, 375.
59. *Idem.*
60. Gandhi, *Autobiography*, p. 303.
61. *CWMG*, XIII, 361.
62. *Ibid.*, p. 365.
63. *Ibid.*, p. 371.
64. *Ibid.*, p. 450.
65. Letter dated December 21, 1917. Reprinted in *CWMG*, XIV, 115.
66. This is a rough translation from Shankerlal's notes for his autobiography, *Gujerati*, which has now appeared in Gujarati. See Prologue, note 3.
67. Letter to Shankerlal on "Ideas About Satyagraha," September 2, 1917. Reprinted in *CWMG*, XIII, 517–520.
68. The following account is based on Narahari Parikh, *Mahadev Desai's Early Life*, translated from Gujarati by Gopalrao Kulkarni, Ahmedabad: Navajivan, 1953.
69. *Ibid.*, p. 46.
70. Mahadev Desai's letter dated 2-9-1917 to Narahari Parikh. Reprinted in full in *ibid.*, pp. 52–54; and excerpted in *CWMG*, XIII, 510–512.
71. This explains why Mahadev did not stay in Champaran (as Kasturba did) to teach in the school program so dear to Gandhi, but rather accompanied him to Bombay and Ahmedabad—there to become a witness to the Event.
72. Parikh, p. 57.
73. *Ibid.*, p. 58.
74. *CWMG*, XIV, 217.
75. Reprinted in *CWMG*, XIV, 245.
76. *CWMG*, XIV, 146.
77. See *ibid.*, p. ix.
78. Reprinted in *CWMG*, XIV, 157.
79. *Ibid.*, p. 158.
80. Reprinted in *CWMG*, XIV, 178, 179.
81. Reprinted in *CWMG*, XIV, 188.
82. Letter dated February 11, 1918. Reprinted in *CWMG*, XIV, 190.
83. *CWMG*, XIV, 195.
84. *Ibid.*, pp. 197, 198.
85. The following statistics are taken from *Praja Bandhu* and from the *Reports* of the Municipality of Ahmedabad for the period indicated.
86. Reprinted in Mahadev Desai, *A Righteous Struggle*, p. 5.
87. Desai, *A Righteous Struggle*, p. 83.

88. *CWMG*, XIV, 211.
89. *The Bombay Chronicle*, February 14, 1918, p. 5.
90. *Ibid.*, February 18, 1918, p. 6.
91. Desai, *A Righteous Struggle*, pp. 9, 10.
92. *CWMG*, XIV, 215.
93. *Ibid.*, p. 217.
94. *Ibid.*, p. 218.
95. *Ibid.*, p. 219.
96. *Idem.*
97. For my conception of ritualization, see Erik H. Erikson, "Ontogeny of ritualization in man," *Philosophical Transactions of the Royal Society of London*, Series B, vol. 251 (1966), pp. 337–349.
98. *CWMG*, XIV, 219, 220.
99. *Ibid.*, p. 222.
100. *Ibid.*, p. 223.
101. Letter to Ramdas dated February 27, 1918. Reprinted *ibid.*, p. 221.
102. *CWMG*, XIV, 225.
103. Reprinted *ibid.*, pp. 225, 226.
104. *CWMG*, XIV, 227.
105. *Ibid.*, pp. 229, 230.
106. *Ibid.*, p. 231.
107. *Ibid.*, pp. 232, 233.
108. *Ibid.*, p. 233.
109. Desai, *A Righteous Struggle*, p. 18.
110. *The Bombay Chronicle*, March 5, 1918, p. 8.
111. *CWMG*, XIV, 236.
112. *Ibid.*, pp. 237, 238.
113. *Ibid.*, p. 239.
114. Leaflet No. 9. Reprinted in *idem.*
115. Letter to Millie Graham Polak dated March 6, 1918. Reprinted in *CWMG*, XIV, 240.
116. *CWMG*, XIV, 242, 243.
117. *Ibid.*, p. 246.
118. *Ibid.*, p. 248.
119. *Ibid.*, p. 250.
120. *Ibid.*, p. 249. Here I prefer Mahadev's translation to that of the *Collected Works*.
121. Desai, *A Righteous Struggle*, pp. 24, 25.
122. *CWMG*, XIV, 254.
123. *Ibid.*, pp. 256, 257.
124. *Ibid.*, pp. 258, 259.
125. Prayer Discourse in the Ashram in *ibid.*, pp. 260–263.
126. *Ibid.*, p. 263.
127. *CWMG*, XIV, 264.
128. *Ibid.*, p. 548.
129. *Ibid.*, p. 266.
130. *Ibid.*, pp. 266, 267.
131. *Ibid.*, p. 267.
132. *Ibid.*, p. 270.
133. *Ibid.*, p. 268.
134. *Idem.*
135. A second speech to the Ahmedabad mill hands on March 18. Reprinted *ibid.*, p. 268.
136. *CWMG*, XIV, 285.

137. *Ibid.*, p. 286.
138. Gandhi, *Autobiography*, p. 324.
139. In a leaflet to the "Sisters and Brothers of the Kheda District," June 22, 1918. Reprinted in *CWMG*, XIV, 440.
140. Letter to the Viceroy, dated April 29, 1918. Reprinted in *CWMG*, XIV, 377, 378.
141. *Ibid.*, p. 379.
142. Letter to the secretary to the Viceroy, dated April 30, 1918. In *CWMG*, XIV, 380.
143. *Ibid.*, p. 381.
144. *CWMG*, XIV, 382.
145. *Ibid.*, p. 385. Italics mine.
146. *Ibid.*, p. 424.
147. *Ibid.*, p. 470.
148. *Ibid.*, 443.
149. *CWMG*, XV, 17.
150. *CWMG*, XIV, 499.
151. *Ibid.*, p. 475.
152. *Ibid.*, p. 512.
153. *Ibid.*, p. 506.
154. *Ibid.*, p. 437.
155. Letter dated June 30, 1918, *ibid.*, pp. 462, 463.
156. Letter dated July 25, 1918 in *CWMG*, XIV, 505.
157. Letter dated July 29, 1918 in *CWMG*, XIV, 509.
158. *Ibid.*, pp. 509, 510.
159. *CWMG*, XIV, pp. 515, 516.
160. *Ibid.*, p. 520.
161. *CWMG*, XV, 18.
162. Letter to Anandshankar Dhruva, dated August 17, 1918. Reprinted *ibid.*, p. 24.
163. *CWMG*, XV, 3, 4.
164. Gandhi, *Autobiography*, p. 332.
165. *CWMG*, XV, 70.
166. *Ibid.*, p. 60.
167. *Ibid.*, pp. 65, 66.
168. *Ibid.*, pp. 43, 44.
169. *Ibid.*, p. 71.
170. *Ibid.*, p. 78.
171. Gandhi, *Autobiography*, p. 337.
172. Gandhi, *Autobiography*, p. 339.
173. *Idem.*
174. *CWMG*, XV, 101, 102.
175. These extracts, in fact, made up Satyagraha Leaflet No. 1 and are reprinted in Appendix II to volume XV of *CWMG*. The source cited is Home Department, Political Files, Series B:373, National Archives, New Delhi.
176. Reprinted in *CWMG*, XV, 183.
177. *CWMG*, XV, 186–188.
178. *Ibid.*, p. 195.
179. *Ibid.*, pp. 209, 210.
180. *Ibid.*, p. 221.
181. *Congress Presidential Addresses from the Silver to the Golden Jubilee*, Second Series (containing full texts of the Presidential Addresses from 1911 to 1934), Madras: Natesan, 1934, p. 401.
182. *Ibid.*, p. 431.

183. See Lloyd and Susanne Rudolph, *The Modernity of Tradition—Political Development in India*, Chicago: The University of Chicago Press, 1967, p. 159.


## PART FOUR: THE LEVERAGE OF TRUTH

1. For an elaboration of this distinction, see Erik H. Erikson, *Insight and Responsibility*, "Psychological Reality and Historical Actuality," New York: Norton, 1964, pp. 159-216.
2. For an approach to the problem of psychological immortality, see Robert Lifton's work, *Revolutionary Immortality—Mao Tse-tung and the Chinese Cultural Revolution*, New York: Random House, 1968.
3. This is uniquely and impressively developed by Joan Bondurant, *Conquest of Violence—The Gandhian Philosophy of Conflict* (revised edition), Berkeley: University of California Press, 1965.
4. A German biographic-psychiatric dictionary spends one of a total of eight lines devoted to the Mahatma on the intelligence that Gandhi "slept with his women servants in one bed"—not specifying the time and duration of such a habit. Similarly, Arthur Koestler in *The Lotus and The Robot*, London: Hutchinson, 1966, relates in a footnote that the aged Gandhi had been found by the British police in bed with a naked young girl, but that they wisely abstained from publishing their discovery. This gossip ignores the fact that the British police at the time of the alleged incident no longer visited Gandhi by surprise at nighttime, that there were neither beds nor doors in the sleeping arrangements, that nakedness is a relative matter in the tropics, and that the whole matter never was a secret.
5. Nirmal Kumar Bose, *My Days With Gandhi*, Calcutta: Nishana, 1953, esp. pp. 131-137, 154-160.
6. Manubehn Gandhi, *Bapu—My Mother*, Ahmedabad: Navajivan, 1949.
7. L. and M. Milne, *The Ages of Life*, New York: Harcourt, Brace & World, 1968, p. 265.
8. Bose, p. 183.
9. As detailed for some in Part Three, III.
10. *CWMG*, XV, 4.
11. Bondurant, p. 25.
12. Erikson, *Insight and Responsibility*, pp. 219-243.
13. Bondurant, p. 111.
14. Pyarelal, "The Right and Wrong Uses of Fasting: How Gandhiji's Standards Apply Today," *The Statesman*, January 3, 1967, p. 6.
15. *The Statesman*, February 15, 1967, p. 7.
16. Quoted in Fischer, *The Life of Mahatma Gandhi*, p. 238.
17. *Ibid.*, pp. 282, 283.
18. Sigmund Freud, "Why War?" Freud's letter to Einstein dated September 1932, in *Collected Papers* (James Strachey, ed.), London: Hogarth Press, 1950, V, 274.
19. Konrad Lorenz, *On Aggression*, M. K. Wilson, trans., New York: Harcourt, Brace & World, 1966.
20. See, for example, Konrad Lorenz' vivid description in *King Solomon's Ring*, New York: Thomas Crowell Co., 1952.
21. See my "Psychoanalysis and Ongoing History: Problems of Identity, Hatred and Non-violence," *American Journal of Psychiatry*, CXXII (September, 1965), 241-250; "Ontogeny of Ritualization in Man," *op. cit.;* and "Concluding Remarks," Discussion on Ritualization of Behavior in

Animals and Man, in *Philosophical Transactions of the Royal Society of London*, Series B, vol. 251 (1966), pp. 523, 524.

22. Erik H. Erikson, "Insight and Freedom," *op. cit.*

23. See Erik H. Erikson, *Young Man Luther, A Study in Psychoanalysis and History*, New York: Norton, 1958.

24. For an extensive bibliography on the history and recent use of Gandhi's methods, see *Nonviolent Direct Action*, A. Paul Hare and Herbert H. Blumberg, eds., Washington and Cleveland: Corpus Books, 1968.

25. See my review of *Thomas Woodrow Wilson* by Sigmund Freud and William C. Bullitt in *The New York Review of Books*, vol. VIII, no. 2, 1967.

26. *CWMG*, XV, 142.

27. Nikita S. Khrushchev, *The Crimes of the Stalin Era*, New York: The New Leader, 1962.

## EPILOGUE: MARCH TO THE SEA

1. Quoted in Louis Fischer, *The Life of Mahatma Gandhi*, p. 266.

2. M. K. Gandhi, *Satyagraha*, Ahmedabad: Navajivan, 1951, p. 233.

3. *Ibid.*, p. 234.

4. *Young India*, March 20, 1930. Quoted *ibid.*, pp. 236, 237.

5. Fischer, p. 273.

6. *Ibid.*, p. 274.

7. For a review of the statesman's period in Gandhi's life I suggest, in addition to the biographies cited, Penderel Moon, *Gandhi and Modern India*, New York: Norton, 1969.

# INDEX

# Index

Freud, Sigmund.  *Inhibitions, Symptoms and Anxiety.*

Freud, Sigmund.  *Introductory Lectures on Psychoanalysis.*

Freud, Sigmund.  *Jokes and Their Relation to the Unconscious.*

Freud, Sigmund.  *Leonardo da Vinci and a Memory of His Childhood.*

Freud, Sigmund.  *New Introductory Lectures on Psychoanalysis.*

Freud, Sigmund.  *On Dreams.*

Freud, Sigmund.  *On the History of the Psycho-Analytic Movement.*

Freud, Sigmund.  *An Outline of Psycho-Analysis* (Rev. Ed.).

Freud, Sigmund.  *The Psychopathology of Everyday Life.*

Freud, Sigmund.  *The Question of Lay Analysis.*

Freud, Sigmund.  *Totem and Taboo.*

Frieze, Irene H., Jacquelynne E. Parsons, Paula B. Johnson, Diane N. Ruble and Gail L. Zellmann.  *Women and Sex Roles: A Social Psychological Perspective.*

Haley, Jay.  *Uncommon Therapy: The Psychiatric Techniques of Milton B. Erickson, M.D.*

Hendin, David.  *Death as a Fact of Life.*

Hendin, Herbert.  *Suicide in America.*

Horney, Karen (Ed.).  *Are You Considering Psychoanalysis?*

Horney, Karen.  *Feminine Psychology.*

Horney, Karen.  *Neurosis and Human Growth.*

Horney, Karen.  *The Neurotic Personality of Our Time.*

Horney, Karen.  *New Ways in Psychoanalysis.*

Horney, Karen.  *Our Inner Conflicts.*

Horney, Karen.  *Self-Analysis.*

Inhelder, Bärbel, and Jean Piaget.  *The Early Growth of Logic in the Child.*

James, William.  *Talks to Teachers.*

Jones, Ernest.  *Hamlet and Oedipus.*

Kagan, Jerome.  *The Growth of the Child: Reflections on Human Development.*

Kagan, Jerome, and Robet Coles (Eds.).  *Twelve to Sixteen: Early Adolescence.*

Katchadourian, Herant.  *Human Sexuality: Sense and Nonsense.*

Kelly, George A.  *A Theory of Personality.*

Klein, Melanie, and Joan Riviere.  *Love, Hate and Reparation.*

Komarovsky, Mirra.  *Dilemmas of Masculinity: A Study of College Youth.*

Kosslyn, Stephen Michael.  *Ghosts in the Mind's Machine: How We Create Pictures in our Brains.*

Lacan, Jacques.  *Ecrits.*

Lacan, Jacques.  *The Four Fundamental Concepts of Psycho-Analysis.*

Lederer, William J.  *Creating a Good Relationship.*

Levy, David M.  *Maternal Overprotection.*

Lifton, Robert Jay.  *Thought Reform and the Psychology of Totalism.*

Light, Donald.  *Becoming Psychiatrists: The Professional Transformation of Self.*

Lunde, Donald T.  *Murder and Madness.*

Mandler, George.  *Mind and Body: Psychology of Emotion and Stress.*

May, Rollo.  *Psychology and the Human Dilemma.*

Meehl, Paul E.  *Psychodiagnosis: Selected Papers.*

Piaget, Jean.  *The Child's Conception of Number.*

Piaget, Jean.  *Genetic Epistemology.*

Piaget, Jean.  *Play, Dreams and Imitation in Childhood.*

Piaget, Jean, and Bärbel Inhelder.  *The Child's Conception of Space.*

Piaget, Jean, and Bärbel Inhelder.  *The Origin of the Idea of Chance in Children.*

Piaget, Jean, Bärbel Inhelder, and Alina Szeminska.  *The Child's Conception of Geometry.*

Piers, Gerhart, and Milton B. Singer.  *Shame and Guilt.*

Piers, Maria W. (Ed.).  *Play and Development.*

Premack, David and Ann James Premack.  *The Mind of an Ape.*

Rank, Otto.  *Truth and Reality.*

Rank, Otto.  *Will Therapy.*

Ruesch, Jurgen, and Gregory Bateson.  *Communication: The Social Matrix of Psychiatry.*

Schwartz, Barry (Ed.).  *Psychology of Learning: Readings in Behavior Theory.*

Schwartz, Barry and Hugh Lacey.  *Behaviorism, Science, and Human Nature: An Introduction to Conditioning.*

Sullivan, Harry Stack.  *Clinical Studies in Psychiatry.*

Sullivan, Harry Stack.  *Conceptions of Modern Psychiatry.*

Sullivan, Harry Stack.  *The Interpersonal Theory of Psychiatry.*

Sullivan, Harry Stack.  *The Psychiatric Interview.*

Sullivan, Harry Stack.  *Schizophrenia as a Human Process.*

van den Berg, J.H.  *The Changing Nature of Man.*

Walter, W. Grey.  *The Living Brain.*

Watson, John B.  *Behaviorism.*

Wheelis, Allen.  *The Quest for Identity.*

Williams, Juanita H.  *Psychology of Women: Behavior in a Biosocial Context (2d Ed.).*

Williams, Juanita H. (Ed.).  *Psychology of Women: Selected Readings.*

Zilboorg, Gregory.  *A History of Medical Psychology.*

*Selected Liveright Paperbacks*

# PSYCHIATRY AND PSYCHOLOGY

Jones, Ernest.  *On the Nightmare.*

Köhler, Wolfgang.  *Dynamics in Psychology.*

Köhler, Wolfgang.  *Gestalt Psychology.*

Köhler, Wolfgang.  *The Mentality of Apes.*

Köhler, Wolfgang.  *The Place of Value in a World of Fact.*

Köhler, Wolfgang.  *The Selected Papers of Wolfgang Köhler.*

Luria, Alexander R.  *The Nature of Human Conflicts.*

Stekel, Wilhelm.  *Impotence in the Male.*

Stekel, Wilhelm.  *Sexual Aberrations: The Phenomena of Fetishism in Relation to Sex.*